Learning Vulkan

Discover how to build impressive 3D graphics with the next-generation graphics API—Vulkan

Parminder Singh

Packt>

BIRMINGHAM - MUMBAI

Learning Vulkan

Copyright © 2016 Packt Publishing

All rights reserved. No part of this book may be reproduced, stored in a retrieval system, or transmitted in any form or by any means, without the prior written permission of the publisher, except in the case of brief quotations embedded in critical articles or reviews.

Every effort has been made in the preparation of this book to ensure the accuracy of the information presented. However, the information contained in this book is sold without warranty, either express or implied. Neither the author, nor Packt Publishing, and its dealers and distributors will be held liable for any damages caused or alleged to be caused directly or indirectly by this book.

Packt Publishing has endeavored to provide trademark information about all of the companies and products mentioned in this book by the appropriate use of capitals. However, Packt Publishing cannot guarantee the accuracy of this information.

First published: December 2016

Production reference: 1121216

Published by Packt Publishing Ltd.
Livery Place
35 Livery Street
Birmingham
B3 2PB, UK.

ISBN 978-1-78646-980-9

www.packtpub.com

Credits

Author

Parminder Singh

Reviewer

Chris Forbes

Commissioning Editor

Ashwin Nair

Acquisition Editors

Smeet Thakkar
Aaron Lazar

Content Development Editor

Sachin Karnani

Technical Editor

Murtaza Tinwala

Copy Editor

Gladson Monteiro

Project Coordinator

Ritika Manoj

Proofreader

Safis Editing

Indexer

Rekha Nair

Production Coordinator

Aparna Bhagat

Graphics

Abhinash Sahu

About the Author

Parminder Singh is a computation graphics engineer with Blackmagic Design, Singapore. He has been working and developing graphic applications in the fields of network simulations, geo-modeling, navigation, automotive, infotainment systems, image processing, and post-production for the past decade. His research interests include GPU programming for scalable graphics and compute applications, porting, and performance optimization techniques.

He is a Vulkan, Metal and OpenGL ES trainer and has also authored *OpenGL ES 3.0 Cookbook*, Packt. His hobbies include traveling, light cooking, and spending quality time with his baby girl.

Feel free to connect Parminder at `https://www.linkedin.com/in/parmindersingh18` or you can reach him at `http://openglescookbook.com`.

Acknowledgments

I dedicate this to my sweet baby girl, Raskeerat, who was born at the same time as we started this project. With a little baby onboard, it's challenging to write a book; I am grateful to my beloved wife Gurpreet Kaur and my family for helping me deliver this project to the community.

I extend my gratitude to Mr. Ulrich Kabatek and the entire graphics team of Continental Automotive; every member of the team had something to offer me to scale my vision of graphics. I am grateful to Blackmagic Design, who helped me extend my horizon to take GPU programming to a whole new level. I express my regards to Mohit Sindhwani and the whole of Quantum Invention's team. It was a great pleasure to work for them and also was a wonderful learning experience.

I am highly indebted to Chris Forbes from Google; his expertise in the graphics domain has raised the bar of this title. I am highly impressed with his reviews and the quality of work he delivered. Chris reviewed this title inch-by-inch and helped us not only to improve the contents but also our understanding of the concepts with his detailed explanation.

Last but not the least, I am thankful to the entire division of Packt, especially Sachin Karnani, who constantly remained involved during the production of this title. Murtaza Tinwala, who brilliantly exhibited his content management and technical skills during the final stages. I'm really happy to have them work with me on this book.

About the Reviewer

Chris Forbes works as a software developer for Google, working on Vulkan validation support and other ecosystem components. Previously he has been involved in implementing OpenGL 3 and 4 support in open source graphics drivers for Linux (www.mesa3d.org), as well as rebuilding classic strategy games to run on modern systems (www.openra.net).

www.PacktPub.com

For support files and downloads related to your book, please visit `www.PacktPub.com`.

Did you know that Packt offers eBook versions of every book published, with PDF and ePub files available? You can upgrade to the eBook version at `www.PacktPub.com` and as a print book customer, you are entitled to a discount on the eBook copy. Get in touch with us at `service@packtpub.com` for more details.

At `www.PacktPub.com`, you can also read a collection of free technical articles, sign up for a range of free newsletters and receive exclusive discounts and offers on Packt books and eBooks.

Mapt

`https://www.packtpub.com/mapt`

Get the most in-demand software skills with Mapt. Mapt gives you full access to all Packt books and video courses, as well as industry-leading tools to help you plan your personal development and advance your career.

Why subscribe?

- Fully searchable across every book published by Packt
- Copy and paste, print, and bookmark content
- On demand and accessible via a web browser

Table of Contents

Preface	1
Chapter 1: Getting Started with the NextGen 3D Graphics API	9
Vulkan and its evolution	9
Vulkan versus OpenGL	11
Important jargons before we get started	13
Learning the fundamentals of Vulkan	14
Vulkan's execution model	14
Vulkan's queues	16
The object model	17
Object lifetime and command syntax	17
Error checking and validation	18
Understanding the Vulkan application	18
Driver	19
Application	19
WSI	19
SPIR-V	19
LunarG SDK	20
Getting started with the Vulkan programming model	20
Hardware initialization	21
Window presentation surfaces	22
Resource setup	23
Pipeline setup	26
Descriptor sets and descriptor pools	26
Shaders with SPIR-V	27
Pipeline management	27
Recording commands	28
Queue submission	30
Summary	31
Chapter 2: Your First Vulkan Pseudo Program	33
Installing Vulkan	33
The Hello World!!! pseudocode	34
Initialization – a handshake with the device	35
Swapchain initialization – querying the WSI extension	39
Command buffer initialization – allocating command buffers	42
Resource objects – managing images and buffers	42

Creating a presentation surface – creating a swapchain	44
Creating a depth image	46
Resource allocation – allocating and binding device memory	48
Supplying shaders – shader compilation into SPIR-V	49
Building layouts – descriptor and pipeline layouts	50
Creating a Render Pass – defining a pass attribute	52
Framebuffer – connect drawing images to the Render Pass	52
Populating geometry – storing a vertex into GPU memory	53
Pipeline state management – creating pipelines	57
Defining states	57
Creating a graphics pipeline	59
Executing the Render Pass – drawing Hello World!!!	60
Acquiring the drawing surface	60
Preparing the Render Pass control structure	61
Render Pass execution	61
Queue submission and synchronization – sending jobs	63
Displaying with presentation layer – rendering a triangle	64
Fitting it all together	**65**
Summary	**66**
Chapter 3: Shaking Hands with the Device	**69**
Getting started with the LunarG SDK	**70**
Setting up our first project with CMake	**71**
How to build the CMake file	76
Introduction to extensions	**77**
Querying layers and extensions	78
Creating a Vulkan instance	**83**
Enabling layers and extensions	87
Testing the enabled layers and extensions	89
Understanding physical and logical devices	**91**
Physical devices	91
Enumerating physical devices	93
Querying physical device extensions	94
Getting the properties of a physical device	95
Interrogating memory properties from the physical device	96
Logical device	96
Creating a logical device	97
Waiting on the host	98
Losing the device	99
Understanding queues and queue families	**99**
Querying queue families	100
Storing the graphics queue handle	102
Creating a queue	103

Implementing devices and queues all together	105
Summary	108
Chapter 4: Debugging in Vulkan	**109**
Peeking into Vulkan debugging	110
Understanding LunarG validation layers and their features	111
Implementing debugging in Vulkan	112
Summary	121
Chapter 5: Command Buffer and Memory Management in Vulkan	**123**
Getting started with command buffers	123
Explicit synchronization	125
Types of command in command buffers	126
Command buffers and queues	126
The order of execution	126
Understanding command pool and buffer APIs	127
Creating a command pool	128
Resetting a command pool	129
Destroying a command pool	130
Command buffer allocation	130
Resetting command buffers	132
Freeing command buffers	132
Recording command buffers	133
Queue submission	134
Queue waiting	136
Implementing the wrapper class for a command buffer	136
Implementing the command buffer allocation process	137
Recording the command buffer allocation process	138
How to use command buffer recording functions	139
Submitting the command to the queue	140
Managing memory in Vulkan	141
Host memory	141
Device memory	143
Allocating device memory	146
Freeing up device memory	147
Accessing device memory from the host	148
Lazily allocated memory	149
Summary	150
Chapter 6: Allocating Image Resources and Building a Swapchain with WSI	**151**
Getting started with image resources	151

Image creation overview ... 153
Understanding image resources ... 155
    Creating images ... 155
        Destroying the created images ... 160
    Understanding image layouts ... 160
    Creating an image view ... 161
        Destroying the image view ... 163
Memory allocation and binding image resources ... 163
    Gathering memory allocation requirements ... 164
    Allocating physical memory on the device ... 165
    Binding the allocated memory to an image object ... 165
Introducing swapchains ... 166
    Understanding the swapchain implementation flow ... 166
    The swapchain implementation's class block diagram ... 169
    Renderer – a window management custom class ... 170
        Creating the presentation window ... 172
        Initializing the renderer ... 173
        Creating the command pool ... 174
        Building swapchain and depth images ... 174
        Rendering the presentation window ... 175
    VulkanSwapChain – the swapchain manager ... 175
        Querying swapchain extensions ... 177
    Creating the surface with WSI and associating it with the created window ... 180
    The graphics queue with present support ... 182
    Querying swapchain image formats ... 184
    Creating the swapchain ... 185
        Swapchain surface capabilities and the presentation mode ... 185
        Managing presentation mode information ... 187
        Retrieving the swapchain's color images ... 189
        Creating color image views ... 193
Creating a depth image ... 195
    Introduction to tiling ... 195
    Creating a depth buffer image object ... 197
    Getting the depth image's memory requirements ... 199
    Determining the type of memory ... 199
    Allocating and binding physical memory to a depth image ... 200
    Image layout transition ... 201
    Image layout transition with memory barriers ... 201
    Creating the image view ... 207
Summarizing the application flow ... 208

Initialization	208
Rendering – displaying the output window	209
Summary	210

Chapter 7: Buffer Resource, Render Pass, Framebuffer, and Shaders with SPIR-V — 211

Understanding the Vulkan buffer resource type	212
Creating the buffer resource object	212
Destroying the buffer	214
Creating a buffer view	214
Destroying the buffer view	215
Creating geometry with a buffer resource	216
Preparing geometry data	216
Creating a vertex buffer	217
Buffer creation overview	218
Implementing a buffer resource – creating the vertex buffer for the geometry	219
Understanding the code flow	223
Understanding a Render Pass	225
Attachments	225
Subpasses	226
Vulkan APIs for the Render Pass	227
Implementing the Render Pass	232
Using the Render Pass and creating the framebuffer	236
Implementing the framebuffer	237
Clearing the background color	239
Setting the background color in the Render Pass instance	241
Rendering the colored background	243
Working with a shader in Vulkan	245
Introduction to SPIR-V	246
Compiling a GLSL shader into SPIR-V	248
Offline compilation with the glslangValidator executable	248
Online compilation with SPIR-V tool libraries	249
Implementing a shader	250
Summary	259

Chapter 8: Pipelines and Pipeline State Management — 261

Getting started with pipelines	262
VulkanPipeline – the pipeline implementation class	265
Caching pipeline objects with a PCO	266
Creating a pipeline cache object	267

[v]

Merging pipeline caches	268
Retrieving data from pipeline caches	269
Implementing the PCO	271
Creating a graphics pipeline	**271**
Implementing a graphics pipeline	275
Destroying pipelines	277
Understanding compute pipelines	**277**
Pipeline State Objects (PSO) in Vulkan	**280**
Dynamic states	282
Implementing dynamic states	283
Vertex input states	284
Implementing vertex input states	285
Input assembly states	286
Implementing input assembly states	287
Primitive restart	287
Primitive topologies	289
Primitives topologies with no adjacency	290
Primitives topologies with adjacency	291
Rasterization	294
Rasterization states	294
Implementing rasterization states	296
Blending	296
Color blend states	297
Implementing color blend states	299
Viewport management	300
The viewport state	300
Implementing the viewport state	302
Depth and stencil tests	302
Depth and stencil states	303
Implementing depth stencil states	304
Multisample states	305
Implementing multisample states	307
Implementing the pipeline	**308**
Summary	**311**
Chapter 9: Drawing Objects	**313**
Overview of the drawing process in Vulkan	**314**
Walking through the header declaration	315
Preparing the drawing object	**316**
Recording Render Pass commands	316
Beginning Render Pass instance recording	316
Transitioning to the next subpass	319
Finishing Render Pass instance recording	320

Implementation	320
Binding pipeline object	321
Implementation	322
Specifying drawing object geometry information	323
Implementation	324
Defining a dynamic viewport	324
Implementation	325
Scissoring	326
Implementation	327
Draw command	328
vkCmdDraw command	328
Implementing drawing object preparation	330
Rendering the drawing object	332
Acquiring the swapchain image	333
Executing the drawing command buffer object	335
Displaying the output with the presentation engine	335
Implementing drawing object rendering	338
Rendering an indexed geometry	342
Understanding synchronization primitives in Vulkan	345
Fences	346
Semaphores	349
Events	351
Resizing the display window	355
Summary	358
Chapter 10: Descriptors and Push Constant	**361**
Understanding the concept of descriptors	361
VulkanDescriptor – a user-defined descriptor class	362
Descriptor set layout	363
Implementing the descriptor set layout	366
Destroying the descriptor set layout	368
Understanding pipeline layouts	369
Creating a pipeline layout	369
Implementing the pipeline layout creation	370
Destroying the pipeline layout	371
Implementing the pipeline layout destruction process	372
Descriptor pool	372
Creating a descriptor pool	372
Implementing the creation of the descriptor pool	373
Destroying the descriptor pool	375
Implementing the destruction of the descriptor pool	375
Creating the descriptor set resources	375
Creating the descriptor sets	380

Allocating the descriptor set object from the descriptor pool	381
Destroying the allocated descriptor set objects	381
Associating the resources with the descriptor sets	382
Implementing descriptor set creation	384

How to implement Uniforms in Vulkan? 386
Prerequisites 387
Execution model overview 388
Initialization 389
Shader implementation 389
Creating descriptors 390
Rendering 391
Binding the descriptor set 392
Update 393
Updating the transformation 394
Push constant updates 396
Defining the push constant resource in the shader 397
Updating the pipeline layout with the push constant 397
Updating the resource data 399
Summary 402

Chapter 11: Drawing Textures 403
Image resource – a quick recap 404
Prerequisites for texture drawing 405
Specifying the texture coordinates 405
Updating the shader program 406
Loading the image files 407
Using the GLI library 408
Local image data structure 408
Implementing the image resource with linear tiling 409
Loading the image file 410
Creating the image object 410
Memory allocation and binding 414
Populating the allocated device memory 415
Creating the command buffer object 416
Setting the image layout 416
Submitting the command buffer 416
Creating an image sampler 417
Filtering 420
Wrapping modes 421
Creating the image view 424
Implementing the image resource with optimal tiling 425

Loading the image file	426
Buffer object memory allocation and binding	426
Populating the allocated device memory	427
Creating the image object	428
Image object memory allocation and binding	428
Creating a command buffer object	429
Setting the image layout	429
Buffer to image copy	430
Setting the optimal image layout	431
Submitting the command buffer	431
Creating an image sampler	432
Creating the image view	433
Copying data content between images and buffers	**434**
Updating the descriptor set	**435**
Summary	**438**
Index	**439**

Preface

This book is all about learning Vulkan from scratch. Vulkan is a next-generation cross-platform graphics and compute API. Despite being a successor of OpenGL API, it is a completely fresh approach to redesigning an API from the base that meets the competitive demand of consumers and works very close with the underlying GPU hardware. Vulkan is a software interface that is capable of controlling GPU hardware settings to harness the power of paralleling computing. The driver layer in Vulkan is really thin and puts more responsibilities on the shoulders of an application programmer to manage the application, its resources, memory management, synchronization, and more; this explicit nature of Vulkan makes it verbose. This book allows the beginner to learn such topics in baby steps, covering each chapter with an easy-to-follow companion example. The chapters are laid out in an incremental fashion; each chapter is built on top of the previous one, exposing the modular difference to our readers.

The Vulkan API certainly requires some level of computer graphics or computing knowledge prior to starting programming on it, as many of the concepts or terminologies are very general and directly used throughout this book.

This book is very practically oriented and prepared with an objective to allow its readers to learn Vulkan theory, concepts, and API specification, and see them in action through companion examples. There are plenty of references throughout the book that help readers to refer to the related concept, helping them to recap the fundamentals as they proceed through.

What this book covers

Chapter 1, *Getting Started with the NextGen 3D Graphics API*, will begin with the fundamentals of the Vulkan API and provides an overview of all its distinct features compared to its predecessor OpenGL API. This chapter will cover the basics, concepts, application model, and technical jargon used in Vulkan programming that is extremely helpful for first-time learners. You will also walk through the Vulkan programming model and see an outline of each module and its role.

Preface

Chapter 2, *Your First Vulkan Pseudo Program*, will help you program a simple Hello World program using a pseudocode approach. This will help the beginners to get a flavor of Vulkan programming and learn the step-by-step process to build their first Vulkan application. You will also learn how to install necessary software and the SDK.

Chapter 3, *Shaking Hands with the Device*, will help you to set up the programming environment to start with building your very first Vulkan example. You will create the Vulkan instance and initialize the program. You will connect with the physical hardware device, explore different types of queues exposed by it, and query various available layers and extensions. This chapter will provide a detailed understanding of the device queue and queue family concept and its relation with logical devices.

Chapter 4, *Debugging in Vulkan*, will describe how to perform debugging in a Vulkan application. Vulkan allows debugging through validation layers. In this chapter, we will discuss the role of each validation layer and program a simple example to understand the debugging in action. In addition, we will also query the layer extensions to add extra features that may not be a part of the Vulkan specifications.

Chapter 5, *Command Buffer and Memory Management in Vulkan*, will thoroughly discuss and implement command buffers in Vulkan. You will understand the role of the command pool and will learn how to record command buffers in Vulkan. The second half of the chapter will cover memory management in Vulkan; you will dig through device memory, and learn methods to allocate or deallocate GPU memory and understand the mapping of CPU and GPU memory.

Chapter 6, *Allocating Image Resources and Building a Swapchain with WSI*, will shed light on image resources and discuss memory management concepts, such as image creation, allocation, binding and mapping. Using this, we will create a depth image for depth testing. This chapter will also introduce the WSI swapchain, which is used for presentation and renders the drawing output onscreen. We will acquire the swapchain color images and create image views that will be used for drawing primitives.

Chapter 7, *Buffer Resource, Render Pass, Frame Buffer, and Shaders with SPIR-V*, will discuss the buffer resource and its usage for implementing the vertex buffer containing a drawing object's geometry information. This chapter will give a detailed introduction to using the Render Pass to define a single unit of work specifying drawing operations using various attachments and subpasses. We will use Render Pass and implement frame buffers in Vulkan and demonstrate simple example to clear the background. As the chapter closes, we will implement our first shader in Vulkan using SPIR-V; we learn about SDK tools that convert GLSL into SPIR-V intermediate representation.

Chapter 8, *Pipelines and Pipeline State Management*, will introduce Vulkan's compute and graphics pipeline. This chapter will provide an overview of the graphic pipeline flow and cover the role of various modules from start to end. We will discuss pipeline state objects, pipeline cache objects, and pipeline layouts. This chapter will cover all the pipeline states thoroughly, also covering dynamics states, input assembly with drawing primitives, rasterization, blending, viewport, depth/stencil testing, and multisampling. We will use these states' objects and implement the graphics pipeline.

Chapter 9, *Drawing Objects*, will thoroughly cover the process of drawing objects in Vulkan. We will record and execute the drawing object command buffers. The recording associates the Render Pass, framebuffer, and pipeline together along with the viewport and geometry data. The command buffer execution involves the submission of the command buffer to the device queue and presenting the drawn swapchain image to the presentation engine. We will also discuss the Vulkan synchronization mechanisms and understand fences, semaphore, and memory barriers. In addition, we will also cover drawing APIs and demonstrate it through some easy-to-follow examples.

Chapter 10, *Descriptors and Push Constant*, will describe how to update shader resources from a Vulkan application using descriptors and push constants. In descriptors, we will discuss and create descriptor pools and descriptor set layout. You will learn how to use the pipeline layouts and use the descriptors to update the buffer resource residing on the device memory and render the updated geometry on screen. Unlike descriptors, push constant do not use the command buffer and provides an optimized path to update the resources. You will implement a small example to understand push constants in action.

Chapter 11, *Drawing Textures*, will bring realism to our rendered 3D drawing object by adding textures. You will learn how to create the image resource and apply samplers to it. You will also learn how to apply textures using linear and optimal tiling. In optimal tiling implementation, you will learn to transfer buffer and image memory through staging.

What you need for this book

Please follow through the hardware and software requirements provided with this book. The reader must have a decent knowledge of C/C++ programming. Coding experience is required.

Who this book is for

This book caters to those who have an interest in or desire to create cross-platform, high-performance graphics, and compute applications across desktop and embedded domains. The programmer may require some knowledge and experience of graphics and compute domain to better co-relate the Vulkan concepts.

Conventions

In this book, you will find a number of text styles that distinguish between different kinds of information. Here are some examples of these styles and an explanation of their meaning.

Code words in text, database table names, folder names, filenames, file extensions, pathnames, dummy URLs, user input, and Twitter handles are shown as follows: "Enumerate the number of physical devices or GPUs on the existing system and get the `vkEnumeratePhysicalDevices()` API."

A block of code is set as follows:

```
foreach layerProperty{
    VkExtensionProperties *instanceExtensions;
    res = vkEnumerateInstanceExtensionProperties(layer_name,
                &instanceExtensionCount, instanceExtensions);
}
```

When we wish to draw your attention to a particular part of a code block, the relevant lines or items are set in bold:

```
// Specify extensions that needs to be enabled on instance.
    instanceInfo.ppEnabledExtensionNames = {
                VK_KHR_SURFACE_EXTENSION_NAME,
                VK_KHR_WIN32_SURFACE_EXTENSION_NAME};

// Create the Instance object
    vkCreateInstance(&instanceInfo, NULL, &instance);
```

New terms and **important words** are shown in bold. Words that you see on the screen, for example, in menus or dialog boxes, appear in the text like this: "This can be done by simply placing a tick against the **Add Python <version> to PATH** checkbox."

> Warnings or important notes appear in a box like this.

> Tips and tricks appear like this.

Reader feedback

Feedback from our readers is always welcome. Let us know what you think about this book—what you liked or disliked. Reader feedback is important for us as it helps us develop titles that you will really get the most out of.

To send us general feedback, simply e-mail `feedback@packtpub.com`, and mention the book's title in the subject of your message.

If there is a topic that you have expertise in and you are interested in either writing or contributing to a book, see our author guide at `www.packtpub.com/authors`.

Customer support

Now that you are the proud owner of a Packt book, we have a number of things to help you to get the most from your purchase.

Downloading the example code

You can download the example code files for this book from your account at `http://www.packtpub.com`. If you purchased this book elsewhere, you can visit `http://www.packtpub.com/support` and register to have the files e-mailed directly to you.

Preface

You can download the code files by following these steps:

1. Log in or register to our website using your e-mail address and password.
2. Hover the mouse pointer on the **SUPPORT** tab at the top.
3. Click on **Code Downloads & Errata**.
4. Enter the name of the book in the **Search** box.
5. Select the book for which you're looking to download the code files.
6. Choose from the drop-down menu where you purchased this book from.
7. Click on **Code Download**.

You can also download the code files by clicking on the **Code Files** button on the book's webpage at the Packt Publishing website. This page can be accessed by entering the book's name in the **Search** box. Please note that you need to be logged in to your Packt account.

Once the file is downloaded, please make sure that you unzip or extract the folder using the latest version of:

- WinRAR / 7-Zip for Windows
- Zipeg / iZip / UnRarX for Mac
- 7-Zip / PeaZip for Linux

The code bundle for the book is also hosted on GitHub at `https://github.com/PacktPublishing/Learning-Vulkan`. We also have other code bundles from our rich catalog of books and videos available at `https://github.com/PacktPublishing/`. Check them out!

Downloading the color images of this book

We also provide you with a PDF file that has color images of the screenshots/diagrams used in this book. The color images will help you better understand the changes in the output. You can download this file from `https://www.packtpub.com/sites/default/files/downloads/LearningVulkan_ColorImages.pdf`.

Errata

Although we have taken every care to ensure the accuracy of our content, mistakes do happen. If you find a mistake in one of our books—maybe a mistake in the text or the code—we would be grateful if you could report this to us. By doing so, you can save other readers from frustration and help us improve subsequent versions of this book. If you find any errata, please report them by visiting http://www.packtpub.com/submit-errata, selecting your book, clicking on the **Errata Submission Form** link, and entering the details of your errata. Once your errata are verified, your submission will be accepted and the errata will be uploaded to our website or added to any list of existing errata under the Errata section of that title.

To view the previously submitted errata, go to https://www.packtpub.com/books/content/support and enter the name of the book in the search field. The required information will appear under the **Errata** section.

Piracy

Piracy of copyrighted material on the Internet is an ongoing problem across all media. At Packt, we take the protection of our copyright and licenses very seriously. If you come across any illegal copies of our works in any form on the Internet, please provide us with the location address or website name immediately so that we can pursue a remedy.

Please contact us at copyright@packtpub.com with a link to the suspected pirated material.

We appreciate your help in protecting our authors and our ability to bring you valuable content.

Questions

If you have a problem with any aspect of this book, you can contact us at questions@packtpub.com, and we will do our best to address the problem.

1
Getting Started with the NextGen 3D Graphics API

Vulkan is a revolutionary high-performance 3D graphics and computing API for modern GPU pipeline architectures to meet the demanding requirements of the community. This API provides a brand-new approach to overcome the complexities and gaps in existing traditional APIs. Vulkan is an explicit API that promises predictable behavior and allows you to have smooth rendering frame rates without causing lags or hitches. This chapter will present an overview of the Vulkan API and its distinct features compared to its predecessor: the OpenGL API. We will take a look at Vulkan's ecosystem and understand its graphics system.

So we will cover the following topics:

- Vulkan and its evolution
- Vulkan versus OpenGL
- Important jargons before we get started
- Learning the fundamentals of Vulkan
- Understanding the Vulkan application
- Getting started with the Vulkan programming model

Vulkan and its evolution

It's almost a quarter-century since the famous OpenGL API came into existence, and it is still evolving. Internally, it is a pure state machine that contains several switches working in a binary state (on/off). These states are used to build dependency mapping in the driver to manage resources and control them in an optimal way to yield maximum performance.

Getting Started with the NextGen 3D Graphics API

This state machine automates resource management implicitly, but it is not intelligent enough to capture application logic, which is the driving force behind resource management. As a result, there might be unexpected situations, such as the implementation going off, resulting in recompilation of the shaders even when the application has not requested it. In addition, the OpenGL API might be subject to other factors, such as unpredictable behavior, multithreading scalability, rendering glitches, and so on. Later in this chapter, we will compare OpenGL with the Vulkan API to understand the difference between the two.

Launched by Khronos in 2016, the Vulkan API has a revolutionary architecture that takes full advantage of modern graphics processor units to produce high-performance graphics and compute applications. If you are not aware of Khronos, it's an association of members and organizations that focus on producing open standards for royalty-free APIs. For more information, refer to `https://www.khronos.org`.

The original concept of Vulkan was designed and developed by AMD, based on their proprietary Mantle API. This API showcased cutting-edge capabilities through several games, thereby proving its revolutionary approach and fulfilling all the competitive demands of the industry. AMD made their Mantle API open source and donated it to Khronos. The Khronos consortium, with the help of many other hardware and software vendors, made collaborative efforts to release Vulkan.

Vulkan is not the only next-gen 3D graphics API; there are competitors, such as Microsoft's Direct-X 12 and Apple's Metal. However, Direct-X is limited to its Windows variants and Metal to Mac (OS X and iOS). Vulkan stands out in that respect. Its cross-platform nature supports almost all the available OS platforms; this list includes Windows (XP, Vista, 7, 8, and 10), Linux, Tizen, SteamOS, and Android.

Vulkan versus OpenGL

Here are the features/improvements in Vulkan that give it an edge over OpenGL:

- **Reduced driver overhead and CPU usage**: Vulkan is designed to be closer to the underlying graphics hardware. Therefore, it provides an application programmer with direct control over computing resources on the host in order to allow the GPU to render as fast as possible. This also allows the software to directly access the graphics processor, allowing better performance.
- **Multithread scalability**: Multithread scaling is really poor in OpenGL, and it is very difficult to take advantage of the threading features to better utilize the CPU. However, Vulkan is specially designed to allow end users to fully exploit its multithreading capability in a very transparent manner with no implicit global states. Jobs under different threads remain separated from the moment they are created and submitted for execution.
- **An explicit API**: OpenGL is an implicit API, where resource management is the driver's responsibility. The driver takes application hints and tracks resources, which is an unnecessary overhead.
  - Vulkan is an explicit API; here, the driver is not responsible for tracking resources and their relationships. This task is assigned to the application. This clean approach is more predictable; the driver is not doing gymnastics behind the scenes to manage resources (as in OpenGL). As a result, job processing is streamlined and straightforward, resulting in optimal performance and predictable behavior.
- **Precompiled intermediate shading language**: Unlike OpenGL, which requires shaders to be provided as **OpenGL Shading Language** (**GLSL**) source code, the **Standard Portable Intermediate Language** (**SPIR-V**) is a standard intermediate language used by Vulkan for parallel computing and graphics.

> Compilers for source languages, such as GLSL, HLSL, or LLVM, must target the SPIR-V specification and provide utilities to provide SPIR-V input. Vulkan takes this ready-to-execute binary-intermediate input and uses it at the shader stage.

- **Driver and Application layer**: In OpenGL, the application layer is thinner as compared to the driver layer, as the driver's automation takes into account resource management and state tracking. Vulkan is the opposite of this. It ensures the driver is closer to the hardware with less overhead. It's an application's responsibility to manage logic, resources, and states. The following diagram shows the thickness of the driver and application code base of both the APIs:

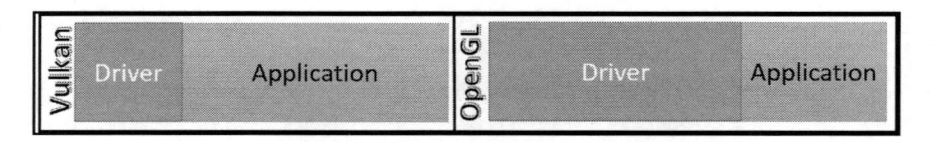

| Vulkan | Driver | Application | OpenGL | Driver | Application |

- **Memory controls**: Vulkan is capable of exposing various memory types on the system and requires the application developer to choose the appropriate memory type for the intended use of each resource. In contrast, OpenGL drivers decide on the placement of resources according to internal heuristics, which vary between vendors, and it may produce suboptimal placement or unexpected hitches if the driver moves the resource later.
- **Predictable**: Vulkan is highly predictable as compared to OpenGL; it does not cause any lags or hitches while rendering. The jobs are submitted upfront as soon as they are given to the driver, whereas the OpenGL job submission process is not upfront and is at the mercy of the driver's scheduler.
- **A single API**: OpenGL has separate versions for a desktop-based API (OpenGL) and embedded API (OpenGL ES). Vulkan is clean and consists of only a single API for any number of platforms. Vulkan supports mobile platforms as a first-class citizen, which is not the case in OpenGL. Usually, the OpenGL implementation first appears on desktop-based versions and is later made available to the OpenGL ES APIs.
- **Direct access to the GPU**: Vulkan gives a lot of control to the application user by advertising its capabilities and hardware facilities. It exposes various types of available physical devices, memory types, command buffer queues, and extensions. This behavior ensures the software layer is much closer to the real hardware.

- **Error checking and validation**: When using OpenGL, well-behaved applications pay a price when it comes to checking for errors, which they will never trigger at the time of execution. In contrast, Vulkan offers these checks and validation as an add-on service, which can be enabled and disabled as and when required. These checks are optional and can be injected into a runtime by enabling error checking and other validation layers. As a result, it causes less CPU overhead by avoiding unnecessary checks. Ideally, these error and validation layers must be turned on during the development phase for the debugging process and turned off during the release process.
- **Supports various GPU hardware**: Vulkan supports mobile and desktop rasterizers as an integrated part of the implementation. It supports tile-based or deferred rasterizers for embedded platforms along with native tiling-based feed forward rasterizers.

Important jargons before we get started

Let's check out some of the important technical jargons used in Vulkan before we dive deep into the fundamental details. This book will cover more of these technical terms as we proceed further.

- **Physical device and device**: A system may contain more than one physical Vulkan-capable hardware device. A *physical device* represents a unique device, whereas a *device* refers to a logical representation of the physical device in an application.
- **Queues**: A queue represents an interface between the execution engine and the application. A physical device always contains one or more queues (graphics, compute, DMA/transfer, and so on). A queue's responsibility is to gather the jobs (command buffers) and dispatch them to the physical device for processing.
- **Memory type**: Vulkan exposes various memory types. At a broader level, there are two types of memory: host and device. As we proceed through this chapter, we will cover these.

- **Command**: A command is an instruction to do some act. A command can be broadly divided into *action*, *set state*, or *synchronization*.
  - **Action commands**: These can be used to draw primitives, clear a surface, copy a buffer, query/timestamp operations, and begin/end subpass operations. These commands are capable of altering framebuffer attachments, reading or writing into the memory (buffer or image), and writing query pools.
  - **Set state commands**: These help bind the pipelines, descriptor sets, and buffers; they also help set a dynamic state and render a pass/subpass state.
  - **Synchronization commands**: Synchronization helps in satisfying the requirements of two or more action commands, which may compete for resources or have some memory dependencies. This includes setting or waiting for events, inserting the pipeline barrier, and rendering pass/subpass dependencies.
- **Command buffer**: A command buffer is a collection of commands; it records the commands and submits them to the queues.

In the next section, we will take an overview of Vulkan to help us understand its working model and fundamental basics. We will also understand the command syntax rules get an idea of API commands by simply looking at them.

Learning the fundamentals of Vulkan

This section will cover the basics of Vulkan. Here we will discuss the following:

- Vulkan's execution model
- Vulkan's queue
- The object model
- Object life-time and command syntax
- Error checking and validation

Vulkan's execution model

A Vulkan-capable system is able to query the system and expose the number of physical devices available on it. Each of the physical devices advertises one or more queues. These queues are categorized into different families, where each family has very specific functionalities. For example, these functionalities could include graphics, compute, data transfer, and sparse memory management. Each member of the queue family may contain one or more similar queues, making them compatible with each other. For example, a given implementation may support data transfer and graphics operations on the same queue.

Vulkan allows you to explicitly manage memory control via the application. It exposes the various types of heap available on the device, where each heap belongs to a different memory region. Vulkan's execution model is fairly simple and straightforward. Here, command buffers are submitted into queues, which are then consumed by the physical device in order to be processed.

A Vulkan application is responsible for controlling a set of Vulkan-capable devices by recording a number of commands into command buffers and submitting them into a queue. This queue is read by the driver that executes the jobs upfront in the submitted order. The command buffer construction is expensive; therefore, once constructed, it can be cached and submitted to the queue for execution as many times as required. Further, several command buffers can be built simultaneously in parallel using multiple threads in an application.

The following diagram shows a simplified pictorial representation of the execution model:

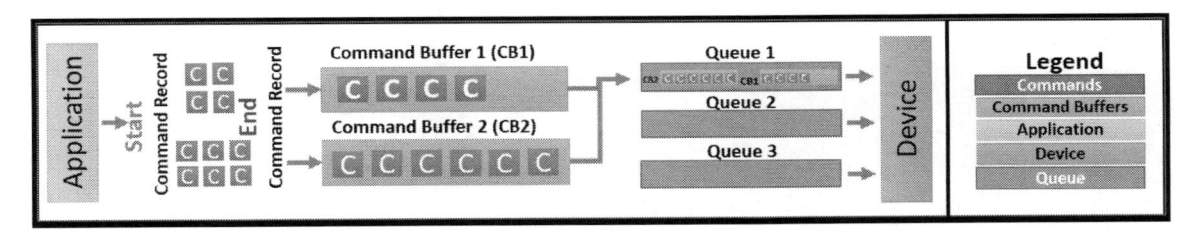

In this, the application records two command buffers containing several commands. These commands are then given to one or more queues depending upon the job nature. The queues submit these command buffer jobs to the device for processing. Finally, the device processes the results and either displays them on the output display or returns them to the application for further processing.

In Vulkan, the application is responsible for the following:

- Producing all the necessary prerequisites for the successful execution of commands:
    - This may include preparing resources, precompiling a shader, and attaching the resources to the shader; specifying the render states; building a pipeline; and drawing calls
- Memory management
- Synchronization

- Between the host and device
- Between the different queues available on the device
- Hazard management

Vulkan's queues

Queues are the medium in Vulkan through which command buffers are fed into the device. The command buffers record one or more commands and submit them to the required queue. The device may expose multiple queues; therefore, it is the application's responsibility to submit the command buffer to the correct queue.

The command buffers can be submitted to the following:

- **Single queue**:
    - The order of the submission of the command buffer and execution or playback are maintained
    - Command buffers are executed in a serial fashion
- **Multiple queues**:
    - Allows the execution of the command buffer in parallel in two or more queues.
    - The order of the submission and execution of command buffers are not guaranteed unless specified explicitly. It is the application's responsibility to synchronize this; in its absence, the execution may be completely out of order with respect.

Vulkan provides various synchronization primitives to allow you to have relative control of the work execution within a single queue or across queues. These are as follows:

- **Semaphore**: This synchronizes work across multiple queues or a coarse-grained command buffer submission in a single queue.
- **Events**: Events controls fine-grained synchronization and are applied on a single queue, allowing us to synchronize work within a single command buffer or sequence of command buffers submitted to a single queue. The host can also participate in event-based synchronization.
- **Fences**: These allow synchronization between the host and device.
- **Pipeline barriers**: A pipeline barrier is an inserted instruction that ensures that commands prior to it must be executed before commands specified after it in the command buffer.

The object model

At the application level, all the entities, including devices, queues, command buffers, framebuffers, pipelines, and so on, are called **Vulkan objects**. Internally, at the API level, these Vulkan objects are recognized with handles. These handles can be of two types: *dispatchable* and *non-dispatchable*.

- **A dispatchable handle**: This is a pointer that refers to an opaque-shaped entity inside. Opaque types do not allow you to have direct access to the structure's field. The fields can only be accessed using API routines. Each dispatchable handle has an associated dispatchable type that is used to pass as a parameter in the API command. Here's an example of this:

| VkInstance | VkCommandBuffer | VkPhysicalDevice | VkDevice | VkQueue |

- **Non-dispatchable handles**: These are 64-bit integer-type handles that may contain the object information itself, rather than a pointer to the structure. Here's an example of this:

VkSemaphore	VkFence	VkQueryPool	VkBufferView
VkDeviceMemory	VkBuffer	VkImage	VkPipeline
VkShaderModule	VkSampler	VkRenderPass	VkDescriptorPool
VkDescriptorSetLayout	VkFramebuffer	VkPipelineCache	VkCommandPool
VkDescriptorSet	VkEvent	VkPipelineLayout	VkImageView

Object lifetime and command syntax

In Vulkan, objects are created and destroyed explicitly as per application logic, and it is the responsibility of an application to manage this.

Objects in Vulkan are created using Create and destroyed using the Destroy command:

- **Create syntax**: Objects are created using the vkCreate* command; this accepts a Vk*CreateInfo structure as a parameter input
- **Destroy syntax**: The objects produced using the Create command are destroyed using vkDestroy*

Objects created as part of the existing object pool or heap are created using the `Allocate` command and released from the pool or heap with `Free`.

- **Allocate syntax**: Objects that are created as part of an object pool use `vkAllocate*` along with `Vk*AllocateInfo` as an argument input.
- **Freeing syntax**: Objects are released back to the pool or memory using the `vkFree*` command.

Any given implementation information can be easily accessed using the `vkGet*` command. The API implementation of the form `vkCmd*` is used to record commands in the command buffer.

Error checking and validation

Vulkan is specially designed to offer maximum performance by keeping error checks and validations optional. At runtime, the error checks and validations are really minimal, making the building of a command buffer and submission highly efficient. These optional capabilities can be enabled using Vulkan's layered architecture, which allows the dynamic injection of various layers (debugging and validation) into the running system.

Understanding the Vulkan application

This section will provide you with an overview of the various components that contribute to, and are helpful in building a Vulkan application.

The following block diagram shows the different component blocks and respective interconnections within the system:

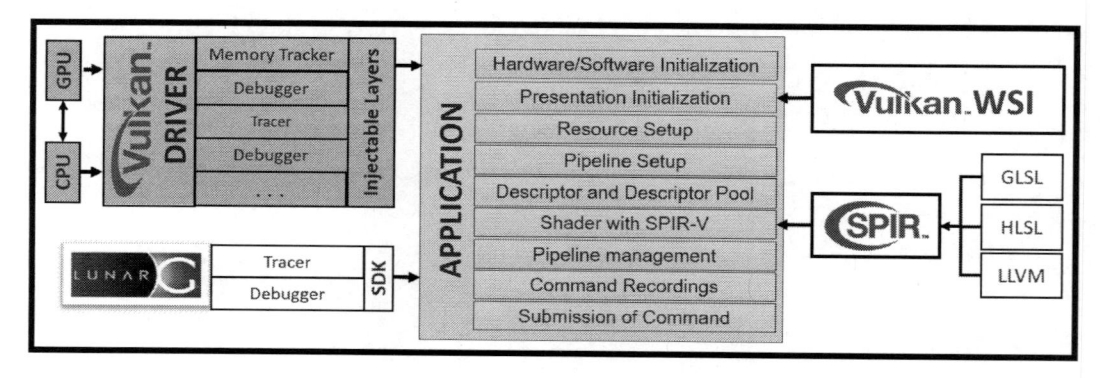

Driver

A Vulkan-capable system comprises a minimum of one CPU and GPU. IHV's vendor supplies the driver of a given Vulkan specification implementation for their dedicated GPU architecture. The driver acts as an interface between the application and the device itself. It provides high-level facilities to the application so it can communicate with the device. For example, it advertises the number of devices available on the system, their queues and queue capabilities, available heaps and their related properties, and so on.

Application

An application refers to a user-written program that is intended to make use of Vulkan APIs to perform graphics or compute jobs. The application starts with the initialization of the hardware and software; it detects the driver and loads all the Vulkan APIs. The presentation layer is initialized with Vulkan's **Window System Integration** (**WSI**) APIs; WSI will be helpful in rendering the drawing image on the display surface. The application creates resources and binds them to the shader stage using **descriptors**. The descriptor set layout helps bind the created resources to the underlying pipeline object that is created (of the graphics or compute type). Finally, command buffers are recorded and submitted to the queue for processing.

WSI

Windows System Integration is a set of extensions from Khronos for the unification of the presentation layer across different platforms, such as Linux, Windows, and Android.

SPIR-V

SPIR-V provides a precompiled binary format for specifying shaders to Vulkan. Compilers are available for various shader source languages, including variants of GLSL and HLSL, which produce SPIR-V.

LunarG SDK

The Vulkan SDK from LunarG comprises a variety of tools and resources to aid Vulkan application development. These tools and resources include the Vulkan loader, validation layers, trace and replay tools, SPIR-V tools, Vulkan runtime installer, documentation, samples, and demos, see `Chapter 3`, *Shaking Hands with the Device* to see detailed description to get started with LunarG SDK. You can read more about it at `http://lunarg.com/vulkan-sdk`.

Getting started with the Vulkan programming model

Let's discuss the Vulkan programming model in detail. Here, the end user, considering he or she is a total beginner, will be able to understand the following concepts:

- The Vulkan programming model
- The rendering execution model, which will be described using a pseudo step-by-step approach
- How Vulkan works

The following diagram shows a top-down approach of the Vulkan application programming model; we will understand this process in detail and also delve into the sublevel components and their functionalities:

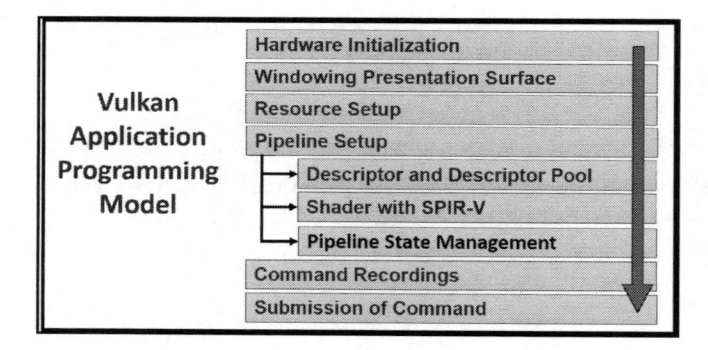

Hardware initialization

When a Vulkan application starts, its very first job is the initialization of the hardware. Here, the application activates the Vulkan drivers by communicating with the loader. The following diagram represents a block diagram of a **Loader** with its subcomponents:

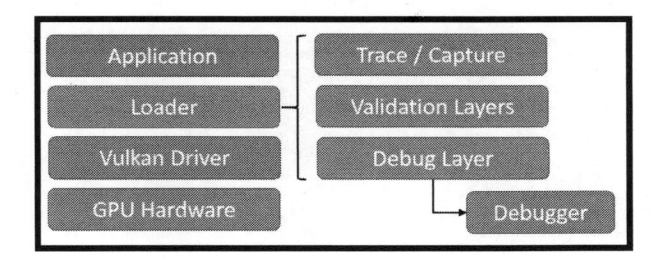

Loader: A loader is a piece of code used in the application start-up to locate the Vulkan drivers in a system in a unified way across platforms. The following are the responsibilities of a loader:

- **Locating drivers**: As its primary job, a loader knows where to search for drivers in the given system. It finds the correct driver and loads it.
- **Platform-independent**: Initializing Vulkan is consistent across all platforms. Unlike OpenGL, where creating a context requires working with a different window system API for each environment, EGL, GLX, and WGL. Platform differences in Vulkan are expressed as extensions.
- **Injectable layers**: A loader supports a layered architecture and provides the capability to inject various layers at runtime. The big improvement is that the driver need not do any of the work (or retain any of the states it would need to do the work) in determining whether the application's use of the API is valid. Therefore, it's advisable to turn on the selected injectable layers, as per application requirements, during the development stage and turn them off at the deployment stage. For example, injectable layers can offer the following:
    - Tracing the Vulkan API commands
    - Capturing rendered scenes and executing them later
    - Error and validation for debugging purposes

The Vulkan application first performs a handshake with the loader library and initializes the Vulkan implementation driver. The loader library loads Vulkan APIs dynamically. The loader also offers a mechanism that allows the automatic loading of specific layers into all Vulkan applications; this is called an **Implicit-Enabled layer**.

Once the loader locates the drivers and successfully links with the APIs, the application is responsible for the following:

- Creating a Vulkan instance
- Querying the physical device for the available queues
- Querying extensions and storing them as function pointers, such as WSI or special feature APIs
- Enabling an injectable layer for error checking, debugging, or the validation process

Window presentation surfaces

Once the Vulkan implementation driver is located by the loader, we are good to draw something using the Vulkan APIs. For this, we need an image to perform the drawing task and put it on the presentation window to display it:

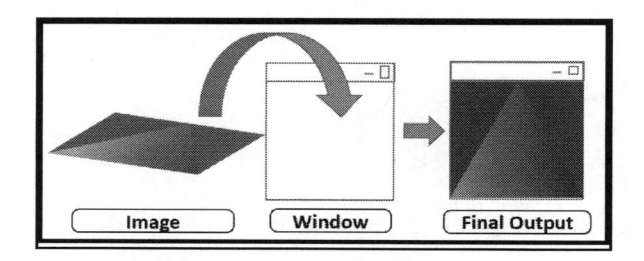

Building a presentation image and creating windows are very platform-specific jobs. In OpenGL, windowing is intimately linked; the window system framebuffer is created along with context/device. The big difference from GL here is that context/device creation in Vulkan needn't involve the window system at all; it is managed through **Window System Integration (WSI)**.

WSI contains a set of cross-platform windowing management extensions:

- A unique cross-platform implementation for the majority of platforms, such as Windows, Linux, Android, and other OSes
- A consistent API standard to easily create surfaces and display them without getting into the details

WSI supports multiple windowing systems, such as Wayland, X, and Windows, and it also manages the ownership of images via a swapchain.

WSI provides a swapchain mechanism; this allows the use of multiple images in such a way that, while the window system is displaying one image, the application can prepare the next.

The following screenshot shows the double-buffering swap image process. It contains two images named **First Image** and **Second Image**. These images are swapped between **Application** and **Display** with the help of **WSI**:

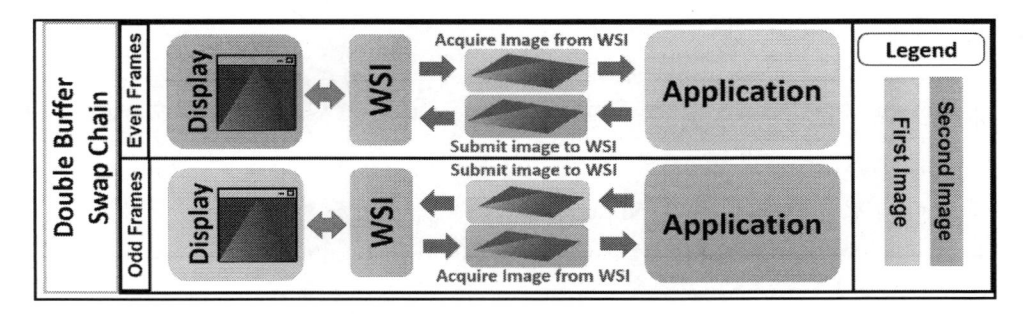

WSI works as an interface between **Display** and **Application**. It makes sure that both images are acquired by **Display** and **Application** in a mutually exclusive way. Therefore, when an **Application** works on **First Image**, **WSI** hands over **Second Image** to **Display** in order to render its contents. Once the **Application** finishes the painting **First image**, it submits it to the **WSI** and in return acquires **Second Image** to work with and vice-versa.

At this point, perform the following tasks:

- Create a native window (like the `CreateWindow` method in the Windows OS)
- Create a WSI surface attached to the window
- Create the swapchain to present to the surface
- Request the drawing images from the created swapchain

Resource setup

Setting up resources means storing data into memory regions. It could be any type of data, for example, vertex attributes, such as position, color, or image type/name. Certainly, the data has resided somewhere in the memory for Vulkan to access it.

Unlike OpenGL, which manages the memory behind the scenes using hints, Vulkan provides full low-level access and control of the memory. Vulkan advertises the various types of available memory on the physical device, providing the application with a fine opportunity to manage these different types of memory explicitly.

Getting Started with the NextGen 3D Graphics API

Memory heaps can be categorized into two types, based upon their performance:

- **Host local**: This is a slower type of memory
- **Device local**: This is a type of memory with high bandwidth; it is faster

Memory heaps can be further divided based upon their memory type configurations:

- **Device local**: This type of memory is physically attached to the physical device:
    - Visible to the device
    - Not visible to the host
- **Device local, host visible**: This type of memory is also physically attached to the device:
    - Visible to the device
    - Visible to the host
- **Host local, host visible**: This refers to the local memory of the host, but it is slower than the local device:
    - Visible to the device
    - Visible to the host

In Vulkan, resources are explicitly taken care of by the application with exclusive control of memory management. The following is the process of resource management:

- **Resource objects**: For resource setup, an application is responsible for allocating memory for resources; these resources could be either images or buffer objects.
- **Allocation and suballocations**: When resource objects are created, only logical addresses are associated with them; there is no physical backing available. The application allocates physical memory and binds these logical addresses to it. As allocation is an expensive process, suballocation is an efficient way to manage the memory; it allocates a big chunk of physical memory at once and puts different resource objects into it. Suballocation is the responsibility of an application. The following diagram shows the suballocated object from the big allocated piece of physical memory:

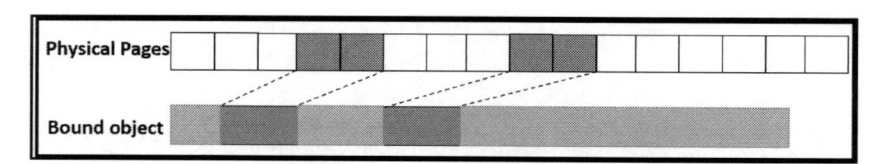

- **Sparse memory**: For very large image objects, Vulkan fully supports sparse memory with all its features. Sparse memory is a special feature that allows you to store large image resources; which are much larger than the actual memory capacity, in the memory. This technique breaks the image into tiles and loads only those tiles that fit the application logic.
- **Staging buffers**: The population of the object and image buffers is done using staging, where two different memory regions are used for the physical allocation. The ideal memory placement for a resource may not be visible to the host. In this case, the application must first populate the resource in a staging buffer that is host-visible and then transfer it to the ideal location.
- **Asynchronous transfer**: The data is transferred asynchronously using asynchronous commands with any of the graphics or DMA/transfer queues.

> Physical memory allocation is expensive; therefore, a good practice is to allocate a large physical memory and then suballocate objects.
>
> In contrast, OpenGL resource management does not offer granular control over the memory. There is no conception of host and device memory; the driver secretly does all of the allocation in the background. Also, these allocation and suballocation processes are not fully transparent and might change from one driver to another. This lack of consistency and hidden memory management cause unpredictable behavior. Vulkan, on the other hand, allocates the object right there in the chosen memory, making it highly predictable.

Therefore, during the resource setup stage, you need to perform the following tasks:

1. Create a resource object.
2. Query the appropriate memory instance and create a memory object like buffer and images.
3. Get the memory requirements for the allocation.
4. Allocate space and store data in it.
5. Bind the memory with the resource object that we created.

Pipeline setup

A pipeline is a set of events that occur in a fixed sequence defined by the application logic. These events consist of the following: supplying the shaders, binding them to the resource, and managing the state:

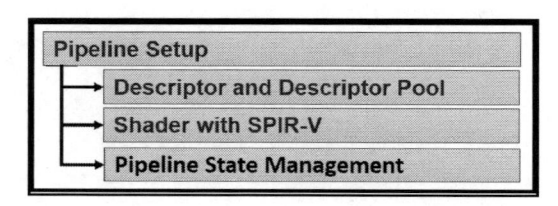

```
Pipeline Setup
  → Descriptor and Descriptor Pool
  → Shader with SPIR-V
  → Pipeline State Management
```

Descriptor sets and descriptor pools

A descriptor set is an interface between resources and shaders. It is a simple structure that binds the shader to the resource information, such as images or buffers. It associates or binds a resource memory that the shader is going to use. The following are the characteristics associated with descriptor sets:

- **Frequent change**: By nature, a descriptor set changes frequently; generally, it contains attributes such as material, texture, and so on.
- **Descriptor pool**: Considering the nature of descriptor sets, they are allocated from a descriptor pool without introducing global synchronization
- **Multithread scalability**: This allows multiple threads to update the descriptor set simultaneously

> **TIP**: Updating or changing a descriptor set is one of the most performance-critical paths in rendering Vulkan. Therefore, the design of a descriptor set is an important aspect in achieving maximum performance. Vulkan supports logical partitioning of multiple descriptor sets at the scene (low frequency updates), model (medium frequency updates), and draw level (high frequency updates). This ensures that the high frequency update descriptor does not affect low frequency descriptor resources.

Shaders with SPIR-V

The only way to specify shaders or compute kernels in Vulkan is through SPIR-V. The following are some characteristics associated with it:

- **Multiple inputs**: SPIR-V producing compilers exist for various source languages, including GLSL and HLSL. These can be used to convert a human-readable shader into a SPIR-V intermediate representation.
- **Offline compilation**: Shaders/kernels are compiled offline and injected upfront.
- **glslangValidator**: LunarG SDK provides the glslangValidator compiler, which can be used to create SPIR-V shaders from equivalent GLSL shaders.
- **Multiple entry points**: The shader object provides multiple entry points. This is very beneficial for reducing the shipment size (and the loaded size) of the SPIR-V shaders. Variants of a shader can be packaged into a single module.

Pipeline management

A physical device contains a range of hardware settings that determine how the submitted input data of a given geometry needs to be interpreted and drawn. These settings are collectively called **pipeline states**. These include the rasterizer state, blend state, and depth stencil state; they also include the primitive topology type (point/line/triangle) of the submitted geometry and the shaders that will be used for rendering. There are two types of states: dynamic and static. The pipeline states are used to create the pipeline object (graphics or compute), which is a performance-critical path. Therefore, we don't want to create them again and again; we want to create them once and reuse them.

Vulkan allows you to control states using pipeline objects in conjunction with **Pipeline Cache Object (PCO)** and the **pipeline layout**:

- **Pipeline objects**: Pipeline creation is expensive. It includes shader recompilation, resource binding, Render Pass, framebuffer management, and other related operations. Pipeline objects could be numbered in hundreds and thousands; therefore, each different state combination is stored as a separate pipeline object.
- **PCO**: The creation of pipelines is expensive; therefore once created, a pipeline can be cached. When a new pipeline is requested, the driver can look for a closer match and create the new pipeline using the base pipeline.

Pipeline caches are opaque, and the details of their use by the driver are unspecified. The application is responsible for persisting the cache if it wishes to reuse it across runs and for providing a suitable cache at the time of pipeline creation if it wishes to reap potential benefits.

- **Pipeline layout**: Pipeline layouts describe the descriptor sets that will be used with the pipeline, indicating what kind of resource is attached to each binding slot in the shader. Different pipeline objects can use the same pipeline layout.

In the pipeline management stage, this is what happens:

- The application compiles the shader into SPIR-V form and specifies it in the pipeline shader state.
- The descriptor helps us connect these resources to the shader itself. The application allocates the descriptor set from the descriptor pool and connects the incoming or outgoing resources to the binding slots in the shader.
- The application creates pipeline objects, which contain the static and dynamic state configuration to control the hardware settings. The pipeline should be created from a pipeline cache pool for better performance.

Recording commands

Recording commands is the process of command buffer formation. Command buffers are allocated from the command pool memory. Command pools can also be used for multiple allocations. A command buffer is recorded by supplying commands within a given start and end scope defined by the application. The following diagram illustrates the recording of a drawing command buffer, and as you can see, it comprises many commands recorded in the top-down order responsible for object painting.

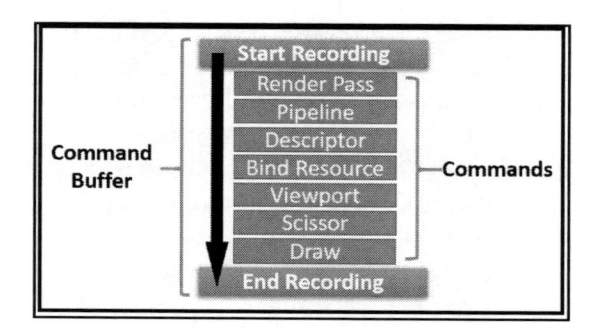

> Note that the commands in the command buffer may vary with the job requirement. This diagram is just an illustration that covers the most common steps performed while drawing primitives.

The major parts of drawing the are covered here:

- **Scope**: The scope defines the start and end of the command buffer recording.
- **Render Pass**: This defines the execution process of a job that might affect the framebuffer cache. It may comprise attachments, subpasses, and dependencies between those subpasses. The attachment refers to images on which the drawing is performed. In a subpass, an attachment-like image can be subpassed for multisampling resolve. Render Pass also controls how the framebuffer will be treated at the beginning of the pass: it will either retain the last information on it or clear it with the given color. Similarly, at the end of the Render Pass, the results are going to be either discarded or stored.
- **Pipeline**: This contains the states' (static/dynamic) information represented by a pipeline object.
- **Descriptor**: This binds the resource information to the pipeline.
- **Bind resource**: This specifies the vertex buffer, image, or other geometry-related information.
- **Viewport**: This determines the portion of the drawing surface on which the rendering of the primitives will be performed.
- **Scissor**: This defines a rectangular space region beyond which nothing will be drawn.
- **Drawing**: The draw command specifies geometry buffer attributes, such as the start index, total count, and so on.

> The creation of a command buffer is an expensive job; it considers the most performance-critical path. It can be reused numerous times if the same work needs to happen on many frames. It can be resubmitted without needing to re-record it. Also, multiple command buffers can be produced simultaneously using multiple threads. Vulkan is specially designed to exploit multithreaded scalability. Command pools ensure there is no lock contention if used in a multithreaded environment.

The following diagram shows a scalable command buffer creation model with a multicore and multithreading approach. This model provides true parallelism with multicore processors.

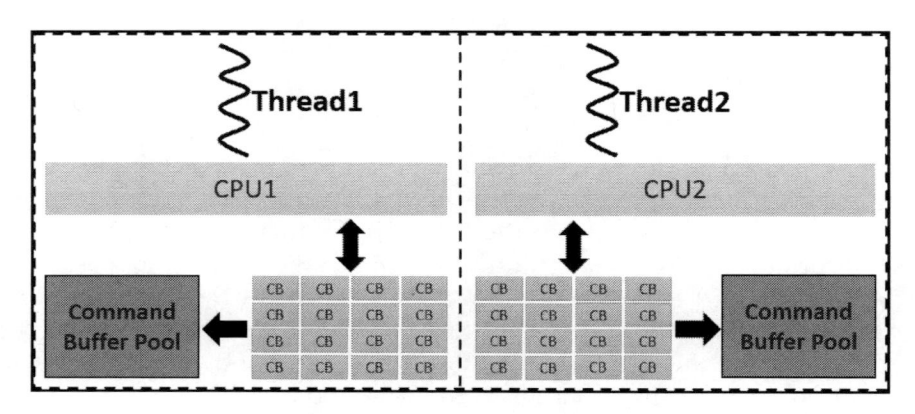

Here, each thread is made to utilize a separate command buffer pool, which allocates either single or multiple command buffers, allowing no fights on resource locks.

Queue submission

Once command buffers are built, they can be submitted to a queue for processing. Vulkan exposes different types of queue to the application, such as the graphics, DMA/transfer, or compute queues. Queue selection for submission is very much dependent upon the nature of the job. For example, graphics-related tasks must be submitted to the graphics queue. Similarly, for compute operations, the compute queue will be the best choice. The submitted jobs are executed in an asynchronous fashion. Command buffers can be pushed into separate compatible queues allowing parallel execution. The application is responsible for any kind of synchronization within command buffers or between queues, even between the host and device themselves.

Queue submission performs the following jobs:

- Acquiring the images from the swapchain on which the next frame will be drawn
- Deploying any synchronization mechanism, such as semaphore and fence, required
- Gathering the command buffer and submitting it to the required device queue for processing
- Requesting the presentation of the completed painted images on the output device

Summary

This introductory chapter has boiled down Vulkan to a level where understanding it will be really easy for beginners. In this chapter, we learned about the evolution of Vulkan and understood the history and people behind it. Then, we distinguished this API from OpenGL and understood the reasons for its existence in the modern computing age. We also looked at simple and easy definitions of the important technical jargon associated with this API. The fundamentals of the Vulkan API provide a precise and enriched overview of its working model. We also saw the basic building blocks of the Vulkan ecosystem and got to know their roles and responsibilities with interconnections. Finally, at the end of the chapter, we understood how Vulkan works with an easy-to-understand step-by-step pseudo programming model approach.

After you finish this chapter, you will be expected to have a basic understanding of the Vulkan API and its detailed working model along with a reasonable familiarity acquaintance with its technical jargon, to take your first steps in Vulkan programming.

In the next chapter, we will start with Vulkan programming using a pseudocode approach. We will create a simple example without going into much details yet still covering important core aspects, the fundamentals of Vulkan API, and data structures to understand the complete process of graphics pipeline programming in Vulkan.

2
Your First Vulkan Pseudo Program

In the last chapter, we provided a very basic introduction to visualize the new Vulkan API. We hovered through the high-level ecosystem design of this API and also understood the internal module's functionality to learn its execution model.

In this chapter, we will learn about the installation process to get ready to work with Vulkan pseudocode programming. The explicit nature of Vulkan makes the programming verbose. In Vulkan, a simple Hello World!!! program may end up with around 1,500 lines of code. This means trying even a simple example will be a challenge for beginners. But let's not hit the panic button; we will go through the entire Hello World!!! program with a simple pseudocode programming model.

Beginners will also learn about a step-by-step approach to building their first Vulkan application in a user-friendly way. In the following chapters of this book, we will delve into the real coding process and get our hands dirty with Vulkan programming. So the learning process is divided into several modules and split across multiple chapters.

This chapter lays the foundation for the remaining chapters. Here, we will build a very simple Hello World!!! pseudocode program, where we will understand the process of building a simple tricolored triangle using Vulkan. We will cover the following topics:

- Installing Vulkan
- The Hello World!!! pseudocode program
- Fitting it all together

Installing Vulkan

Enough discussing about Vulkan. Now we will delve into the installation process and learn all we need to make Vulkan work.

> **TIP**: Before you go ahead with the installation, please go through the software-hardware requirements, which you will find in the code files provided with this book. If your system complies with the requirements mentioned, you are good to go with the installation process.

Please follow these instructions to install Vulkan:

1. **The Vulkan driver**: Most vendors now have their Vulkan support included in the normal driver package. First, install the Vulkan driver. You can choose the installation location; otherwise, the default location will do. For instance, if you are installing NVIDIA drivers, the installer first checks the system configuration to scan any compatibility issues with the installing driver. It will upgrade any preinstalled driver on the system.
2. **Install Python**: Install Python and make sure you add it to the path. This can be done by simply placing a tick against the **Add Python <version> to PATH** checkbox.
3. **Install CMake**: Next, install CMake. Ensure you select **Add CMake to the system PATH for all users**. You can use the default location for installation.
4. **Install the SDK**: Install the LunarG SDK. The default location should be fine.

> The LunarG SDK contains the Vulkan specification, manual, and the necessary libraries that will be helpful in building the project. It also contains demo samples that can be quickly launched to check the status of the installation. If you are able to run the sample executable successfully, it means the Vulkan driver and SDK are installed properly. You can find these samples under `<Lunar-G SDK Path>/Bin` or `<Lunar-G SDK Path>/Bin32` for 32 bits systems.

The Hello World!!! pseudocode

In this section, we will build our first Hello World!!! Vulkan application. The application is built using the pseudocode program model, which offers the following benefits:

- Learning through a step-by-step process how to build a Vulkan application.

- Vulkan coding is lengthy and beginners might get lost in the detail. The pseudocode highlights only the necessary details that are easy to understand.
- A compact form of the program, which is easier for first-time users to memorize.
- Each pseudocode uses the real Vulkan API and explains the control flow.
- By the end of this chapter, if you are a complete beginner, you'll able to understand Vulkan programming and all the necessary clues to build applications from scratch. In addition, you will learn about the high-level concepts of Vulkan APIs with their responsibilities and functionalities.
- For a detailed understanding of the API, use the Vulkan specification available with the LunarG SDK. Or refer to https://www.khronos.org/registry/vulkan/specs/1.0/apispec.html.

> Given the scope of this chapter, it is not possible to provide a line-by-line description of each data structure field and API argument. The pseudocode is only limited to providing a high-level definition, an overview and related functionalities in a maximum of one to two lines for most of the important data structures or APIs. All the Vulkan APIs and related data structures will be thoroughly covered as we proceed through the upcoming chapters in this book.

Initialization – a handshake with the device

Vulkan initialization includes the initialization of validation layer properties and instance object (VkInstance) creation. Once the instance is created, check the available physical devices (VkPhysicalDevice) on the existing system. Choose the intended physical device and create a corresponding logical device (VkDevice) with the help of the instance object. In Vulkan programming, logical devices are used in most of the APIs that represent a logical representation of the physical device.

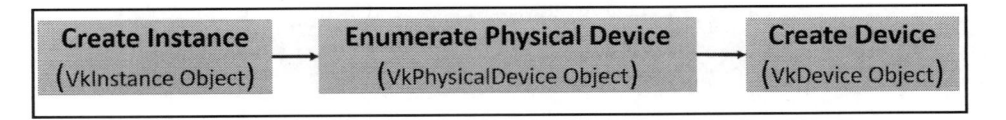

Create Instance (VkInstance Object) → **Enumerate Physical Device** (VkPhysicalDevice Object) → **Create Device** (VkDevice Object)

Vulkan provides debugging capabilities by means of error and validation layers. There are two types of extension:

- **Instance-specific**: This provides global-level extensions
- **Device-specific**: This provides physical-device-specific extensions

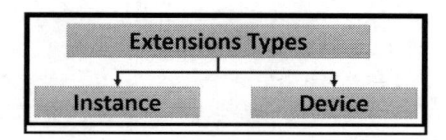

At the beginning, the system is enumerated for global layers and device-specific extensions; these are exposed by the Vulkan driver. The global layers and extensions can be injected into the instance object to be enabled at the global level. However, enabling the extensions only at the device level will enable them only at that specific device.

The initialization is responsible for creating instance and device objects. In addition, global layers/extensions are queried and enabled at either the global or instance level. Similarly, the extensions are enabled on the specific device. The following is the pseudocode for the initialization process:

1. **Enumerating Instance Layer properties**: Vulkan first communicates with the loader and locates the driver. The driver exposes a number of extensions and layers, which may vary with each new installation or from one GPU vendor to another. `vkEnumerateInstanceLayerProperties` retrieves the number of layers and their properties. Each layer may contain multiple extensions that can be queried using `vkEnumerateInstanceExtensionProperties`:

    ```
    /*** 1. Enumerate Instance Layer properties ***/
    // Get number of instance layers
    uint32_t instanceLayerCount;

    // Use second parameter as NULL to return the layer count
    vkEnumerateInstanceLayerProperties(&instanceLayerCount, NULL);

    VkLayerProperties *layerProperty = NULL;
    vkEnumerateInstanceLayerProperties(&instanceLayerCount,
                                       layerProperty);

    // Get the extensions for each available instance layer
    foreach  layerProperty{
       VkExtensionProperties *instanceExtensions;
       res = vkEnumerateInstanceExtensionProperties(layer_name,
                  &instanceExtensionCount, instanceExtensions);
    ```

}

2. **Instance creation**: The instance object (VkInstance) is created using the vkCreateInstance() API with parameters specifying the name of the layer and extensions that are to be enabled for validation or debugging purposes. These names are specified in the VkInstanceCreateInfo structure:

```
/*** 2. Instance Creation ***/
// Vulkan instance object
VkInstance instance;
VkInstanceCreateInfo instanceInfo    = {};

// Specify layer names that needs to be enabled on instance.
instanceInfo.ppEnabledLayerNames    = {
            "VK_LAYER_LUNARG_standard_validation",
            "VK_LAYER_LUNARG_object_tracker" };

// Specify extensions that needs to be enabled on instance.
instanceInfo.ppEnabledExtensionNames = {
            VK_KHR_SURFACE_EXTENSION_NAME,
            VK_KHR_WIN32_SURFACE_EXTENSION_NAME};

// Create the Instance object
vkCreateInstance(&instanceInfo, NULL, &instance);
```

3. **Device creation**: Enumerate the number of physical devices or GPUs on the existing system and get the vkEnumeratePhysicalDevices() API:

```
/*** 3. Enumerate physical devices ***/

VkPhysicalDevice        gpu;         // Physical device
uint32_t           gpuCount;         // Pysical device count
vector<VkPhysicalDevice>gpuList;     // List of physical devices

// Get number of GPU count
vkEnumeratePhysicalDevices(instance, &gpuCount, NULL);

// Get GPU information
vkEnumeratePhysicalDevices(instance, &gpuCount, gpuList);
```

For each physical device, enumerate device-specific extensions in the same way we did during instance creation.

Your First Vulkan Pseudo Program

> For an instance-based enumeration, use the vkEnumerate**Instance**-LayerProperties and vkEnumerate**Instance**ExtensionProperties APIs. However, device-based layer enumeration is deprecated; therefore, the extensions can be enumerated using vkEnumerate-**Device**ExtensionProperties.

With the physical device list in hand, query the following information:

- **Queue and queue types**: Query the available physical device queues and queue properties using the vkGetPhysicalDeviceQueueFamilyProperties API. Among the queried queues, search for the graphics-capable queue and store its queue family index in the application for later use. The graphics queue is chosen because we are only interested in drawing operations.
- **Memory information**: The vkGetPhysicalDeviceMemoryProperties() API retrieves the available memory types on the intended physical device.
- **Physical device properties**: Optionally, you can store physical device properties to retrieve some specific information while programming. This can be done using the vkGetPhysicalDeviceProperties() API.

The device object is created using the vkCreateDevice() API. It's the logical representation of the physical device in the application space. From now onward, the program will use the device object in various places:

```
/*** 4. Create Device ***/

// Get Queue and Queue Type
vkGetPhysicalDeviceQueueFamilyProperties(gpu,
                    &queueCount, queueProperties);

// Get the memory properties from the physical device or GPU
vkGetPhysicalDeviceMemoryProperties(gpu, &memoryProperties);

// Get the physical device or GPU properties
vkGetPhysicalDeviceProperties(gpu, &gpuProps);

// Create the logical device object from physical device
VkDeviceCreateInfo deviceInfo = {};
vkCreateDevice(gpuList[0],&deviceInfo, NULL, &device);
```

The following diagram summarizes the approach to creating a Vulkan instance and device in a cheat sheet fashion; you can refer to it as a quick recap of the process:

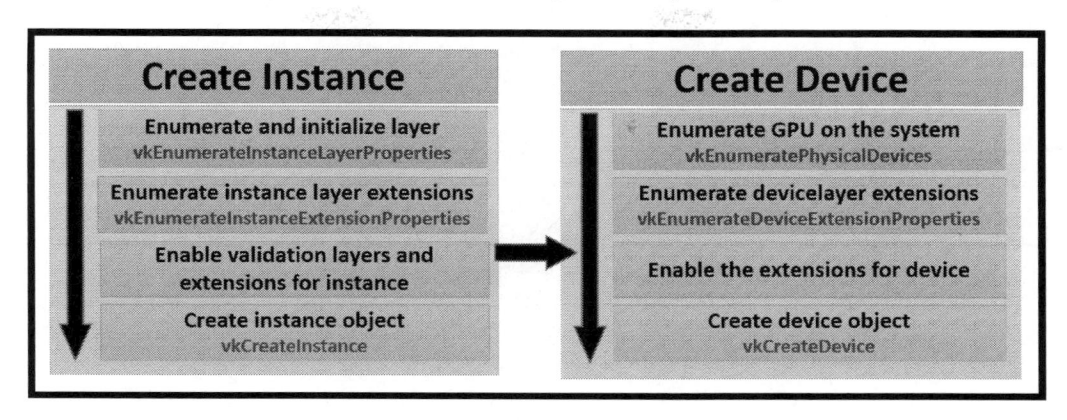

Create Instance
- Enumerate and initialize layer
  vkEnumerateInstanceLayerProperties
- Enumerate instance layer extensions
  vkEnumerateInstanceExtensionProperties
- Enable validation layers and extensions for instance
- Create instance object
  vkCreateInstance

Create Device
- Enumerate GPU on the system
  vkEnumeratePhysicalDevices
- Enumerate devicelayer extensions
  vkEnumerateDeviceExtensionProperties
- Enable the extensions for device
- Create device object
  vkCreateDevice

Swapchain initialization – querying the WSI extension

The presentation is responsible for displaying the rendered content on the output window. For this, we need an empty window to which we can paste our drawing images. Create an empty window using the `CreateWindowEx` (Windows) or `xcb_create_window` (Linux) APIs.

The presentation needs to be initialized first using instance- and device-based WSI extension APIs. These APIs allow you to create the presentation surface using various surface properties.

> These APIs must be dynamically linked and stored as function pointers in the application. Use the `vkGetInstanceProcAddr()` API to query these APIs, as shown in the following tabular form.

For instance-based extension APIs, refer to the following:

vkGetPhysicalDeviceSurfaceSupportKHR	vkGetPhysicalDeviceSurfaceCapabilitiesKHR
vkGetPhysicalDeviceSurfaceFormatsKHR	vkGetPhysicalDeviceSurfacePresentModesKHR
vkDestroySurfaceKHR	

Your First Vulkan Pseudo Program

Similarly, for device-based extension APIs, refer to the following:

vkCreateSwapchainKHR	vkDestroySwapchainKHR	vkGetSwapchainImagesKHR
vkAcquireNextImageKHR	vkQueuePresentKHR	

It's really great to get these APIs to do all the presentation-related fun. Let's see what else is required:

- **Create an abstract surface object**: The very first thing in surface creation is the creation of the VkSurfaceKHR object. This object abstracts the native platform's (Windows, Linux, Wayland, Android, and more) windowing/surface mechanisms. This object is created using the vkCreate<Win32/Wayland/Android>SurfaceKHR() API.
- **Using a graphics queue with the presentation**: Use the created abstract surface object and search for a graphics queue that is capable of supporting the presentation using the vkGetPhysicalDeviceSurfaceSupportKHR() API.

> Store the handle or index of this searched queue. Later, it will be used to query its surface properties and create a logical object of this queue (the next step).

- **Get a compatible queue**: Before you start any type of command buffer recording, the queue must be acquired for command buffer submission. Use the vkGetDeviceQueue() API and specify the handle or index of the compatible queue that we have already queried in the last step.
- **Query the surface formats**: Retrieve all the advertised surface formats that are supported by the physical device using the vkGetPhysicalDeviceSurfaceFormatsKHR API:

```
/*** 5. Presentation Initialization ***/

// Create an empty Window
CreateWindowEx(...);        /*Windows*/
xcb_create_window(...);     /*Linux*/

// Query WSI extensions,store it as function pointers. For example:
// vkCreateSwapchainKHR, vkCreateSwapchainKHR .....
// Create an abstract surface object
VkWin32SurfaceCreateInfoKHR createInfo = {};
vkCreateWin32SurfaceKHR(instance, &createInfo, NULL, &surface);

// Among all queues, select a queue that supports presentation
```

```
foreach Queue in All Queues{
   vkGetPhysicalDeviceSurfaceSupportKHR
            (gpu, queueIndex, surface, &isPresentationSupported);
   // Store this queue's index
   if (isPresentationSupported) {
         graphicsQueueFamilyIndex = Queue.index;
         break;
   }
}

// Acquire compatible queue supporting presentation
// and is also a graphics queue
vkGetDeviceQueue(device, graphicsQueueFamilyIndex, 0, &queue);


// Allocate memory for total surface format count
uint32_t formatCount;
vkGetPhysicalDeviceSurfaceFormatsKHR
               (gpu, surface, &formatCount, NULL);

VkSurfaceFormatKHR *surfaceFormats = allocate memory
               (formatCount * VkSurfaceFormatKHR);

// Grab the surface format into VkSurfaceFormatKHR objects
vkGetPhysicalDeviceSurfaceFormatsKHR
               (gpu, surface, &formatCount, surfaceFormats);
```

The following diagram presents a quick overview of the presentation initialization:

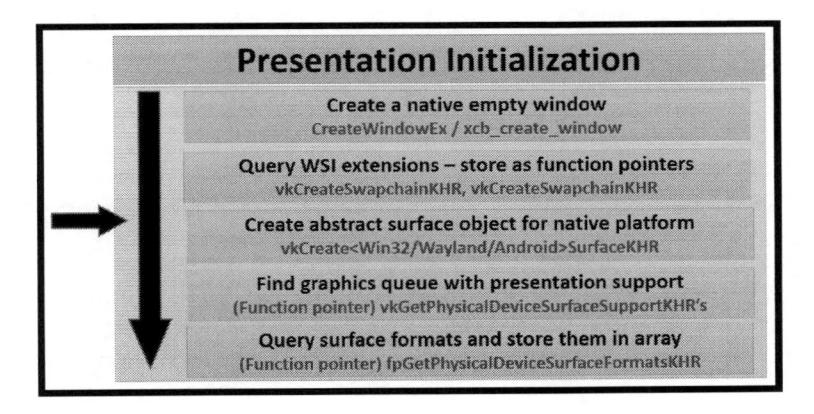

Command buffer initialization – allocating command buffers

Before we start creating a presentation surface, we need command buffers. Command buffers record the commands and submit them to a compatible queue for processing.

Command buffer initialization includes the following:

- **Command pool creation**: Remember, we saved the handle of the compatible graphics queue that supports the presentation. Now we will use that index or handle to create a command pool with the `vkCreateCommandPool()` API, which is compatible with this queue family.
- **Allocate a command buffer**: Command buffers can simply be allocated from the created command pool using the `vkAllocateCommandBuffers()` API.

> There is no need to allocate command buffers from the command pool for each frame if repeatedly used. If the existing command buffers are no longer required, they can be reused efficiently.

The command buffer pool is used to assign memory regions to create a command buffer without introducing global synchronization:

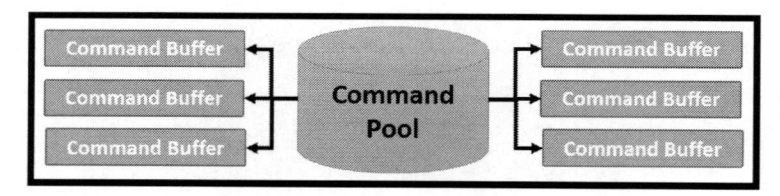

Resource objects – managing images and buffers

It is very important to understand the concept of resource types under Vulkan. From now on, we will deal with resource management quite often. Resource management includes the creation, allocation, and binding of resources. For example, the presentation surface itself treats the drawing surface just like any other generic Vulkan resource type.

Vulkan divides resources into two types, **Buffer** and **Image**, as shown in the following diagram:

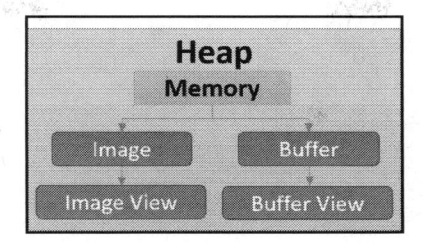

These resources are further divided into views; let's understand these:

- **Buffer**: The buffer object represents resources with linear array types. The buffer object is of the type `VkBuffer` and is created with the `vkCreateBuffer()` API. This API takes a `VkBufferCreateInfo` structure as parameter input, which specifies the various properties that can be used during object creation. For example, you can specify the tiling of an image, usage of an image, size, queue compatibility, and so on. Now let's look at what constitutes a buffer view:
    - **Buffer view**: A buffer view (`VkBufferView`) represents the data buffer itself. It is used to accommodate the data in a contiguous fashion, in a specific data interpretation format. It can be created with the help of the `vkCreateBufferView()` API. It accepts the `VkBufferViewCreateInfo` structure where various buffer-specific properties can be specified, such as its buffer object (`VkBuffer`), format, the range of the buffer view, and more.
- **Image**: This is programmatically represented by `VkImage`. This object stores one- to three-dimensional buffer arrays. The object is created using the `vkCreateImage()` API. Similar to buffer object, this API uses the `VkImageCreateInfo` structure to specify various properties during object creation. Now let's look at what an image view is:
    - **Image view**: Similar to buffer view, an image view object is of the type `VkImageView`. Use the `vkCreateImageView()` API along with the `VkImageViewCreateInfo` structure to create the image view object.

> The application does not consume the buffer (`VkBuffer`) and image (`VkImage`) object directly; instead, it relies on their respective views: `VkBufferView` and `VkImageView`.

[43]

Creating a presentation surface – creating a swapchain

Let's do a quick recap. So far, we have created a Vulkan instance, a logical device to represent our physical device, and we have queried queue properties and also stored the queue family index that supports the presentation. We have created function pointers for WSI extensions and understood Vulkan resource types. We have also initialized and created our command buffers from the command pool.

That covers all we require to kick off our command buffer recording process.

> **What should be recorded into command buffers?**
> a) Building the drawing image and depth image for swapchain and depth/stencil testing.
> b) Creating the shader module to associate with the shader program.
> c) Binding resources to the shaders with a descriptor set and pipeline layout.
> d) Creating and managing the Render Pass and framebuffer object.
> e) Drawing operations.

Start command buffer recording with the `vkBeginCommandBuffer()` API. This defines the starting scope of the command buffer; after this, any command specified will be recorded in the command buffer.

Now, we will learn how to create a swapchain. Here we will acquire the drawing images from the swapchain for rendering purposes:

1. **Getting surface capabilities**: Query the surface capabilities, such as current size, minimum/maximum size possible, possible transformation capabilities, and more, with the `vkGetPhysicalDeviceSurfaceCapabilitiesKHR()` API.

2. **Getting surface presentation modes**: The presentation mode tells how the drawing surface is going to be updated, for example, whether it is going to be updated in an immediate mode or vertical blank dependent and so on. The presentation modes can be retrieved using the `vkGetPhysicalDevice-SurfacePresentModesKHR()` API.

3. **Creating the swapchain**: Use the surface capabilities in conjunction with the presentation modes to create the swapchain object. These capabilities, along with many other parameters such as size, surface format, and more, are specified in the `VkSwapChainCreateInfo` structure that is passed to `vkCreateSwap-chainKHR()` to create the object.

4. **Retrieving the swapchain images**: Query the number of image surfaces advertised by the swapchain and retrieve the respective image objects (VkImage) using the vkGetSwapchainImagesKHR() API. For example, if the swapchain supports double buffering, then it should return a count of two and also two images for drawing.

> For a swapchain image, there is no memory allocation needed on behalf of the application. Internally, the swapchain has already taken care of memory allocation and returned the baked object. The application only needs to specify how to use this image through image views. An image view describes the use of an image.

5. **Setting the image layout**: For each image, set the implementation-compatible layout and add a pipeline barrier. According to the Vulkan specification, a pipeline barrier inserts an execution dependency and a set of memory dependencies between a set of commands; first it inserts the command buffer and then the set of commands in the command buffer. This can be done using the vkCmdPipelineBarrier() API. By inserting the barrier, it is guaranteed that the image view will be available in the specified layout before it is used by the application.

6. **Creating an image view**: As the application uses only the VkImageView objects, create a VkImageView object using vkCreateImageView(). Save the view objects for application use:

```
/*** 6. Creating Swapchain ***/

//Start recording commands into command buffer
vkBeginCommandBuffer(cmd, &cmdBufInfo);

// Getting surface capabilities
vkGetPhysicalDeviceSurfaceCapabilitiesKHR
            (gpu, surface, &surfCapabilities);

// Retrieve the surface presentation modes
vkGetPhysicalDeviceSurfacePresentModesKHR
            (gpu, surface, &presentModeCount, NULL);
VkPresentModeKHR presentModes[presentModeCount];
vkGetPhysicalDeviceSurfacePresentModesKHR
            (gpu, surface, &presentModeCount, presentModes);

// Creating the Swapchain
VkSwapchainCreateInfoKHR swapChainInfo = {};
fpCreateSwapchainKHR(device, &swapChainInfo, NULL, &swapChain);
```

```
// Create the image view of the retrieved swapchain images
vkGetSwapchainImagesKHR
                (device, swapChain, &swapchainImageCount, NULL);
VkImage swapchainImages[swapchainImageCount];
vkGetSwapchainImagesKHR
                (device, swapChain, &swapchainImageCount,
                 swapchainImages);

// Retrieve the Swapchain images
foreach swapchainImages{

    // Set the implementation compatible layout
    SetImageLayout( . . .)

    // Insert pipeline barrier
    VkImageMemoryBarrier imgMemoryBarrier = { ... };
    vkCmdPipelineBarrier(cmd,srcStages,destStages,0,0,
                    NULL,0,NULL,1,&imgMemoryBarrier);

    // Insert pipeline barrier
    vkCreateImageView(device, &colorImageView, NULL,
                    &scBuffer.view);

    // Save the image view for application use
    buffers.push_back(scBuffer);
}
```

The following diagram shows how swapbuffer image objects (`VkImage`) are used in the form of image view objects (`VkImageView`):

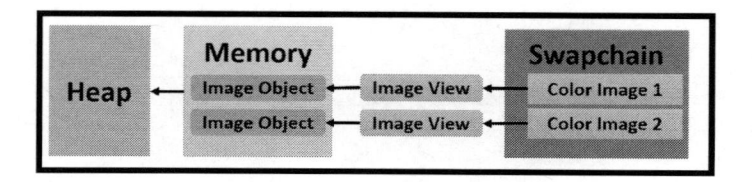

Creating a depth image

The application needs a depth image if it intends to use depth testing. For 2D drawing logic, only the swapchain image is enough. The process of depth image creation is the same as the swapchain image. But there is a difference: unlike swapchain images, which are ready-made (returned by `vkGetPhysicalDeviceSurfaceFormatsKHR()`), the depth image object (`VkImage`) is allocated and created by the application manually.

Chapter 2

The following is the depth image creation process:

1. First, query the physical device format properties for the depth image using the `vkGetPhysicalDeviceFormatProperties()` API.
2. Create an image object using the `vkCreateImage()` API and get the resource memory requirements with the `vkGetImageMemoryRequirements()` API.
3. Next, allocate the memory with the `vkAllocateMemory()` API using the retrieved memory requirement properties. Bind the allocated memory to the created image object by calling the `vkBindImageMemory()` API.
4. Similar to the swapchain drawing images, set the proper image layout and create an image view for application usage. For more details on device memory allocation, refer to the next section, *Resource allocation – allocating and binding device memory*.

Refer to the following diagram; the newly allocated depth image is created (`VkImage`) and connected to its view types (`VKImageView`) whose object resides in the memory:

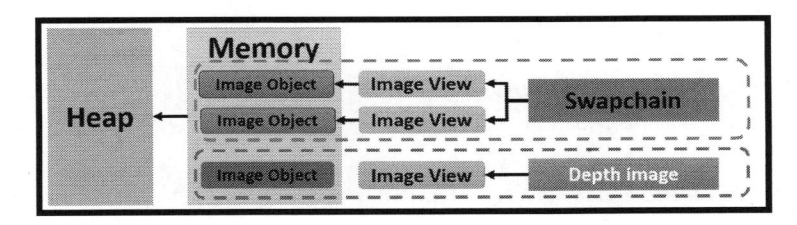

The following pseudocode illustrates the creation of the depth image object, this depth image will be used for depth testing purposes:

```
/*** 7. Creating Depth image ***/
// Query supported format features of the physical device
vkGetPhysicalDeviceFormatProperties(gpus, depthFormat, &properties);

// Create an image object
vkCreateImage(device, &imageInfo, NULL, &imageObject);

// Get the memory requirements for an image resource
vkGetImageMemoryRequirements(device, image, &memRequirements);

// Allocate memory
vkAllocateMemory(device, &memAlloc, NULL, &memorys);

// Bind memory
vkBindImageMemory(device, imageObject, mem, 0);
```

[47]

Your First Vulkan Pseudo Program

```
// Set the implementation compatible layout
SetImageLayout(. . .)

// Insert a pipeline barrier to ensure that specified image
// layout are created before it being used further
vkCmdPipelineBarrier(cmd, srcStages, destStages, 0, 0, NULL,
                    0, NULL, 1, &imgPipelineBarrier);

// Create an Image View
vkCreateImageView(device, &imgViewInfo, NULL, &view);
```

Resource allocation – allocating and binding device memory

When first created, Vulkan resources (for buffer, `VkBuffer`, and for image, `VkImage`) do not have any backing memory associated with them. Before using a resource, we need to allocate memory to it and bind the resource to the memory.

In order to allocate the Vulkan resource objects, first the application needs to query the available memory on the physical device using `vkGetPhysicalDeviceMemoryProperties()`. This API advertises one or more heaps and further exposes one or more memory types from these heaps. The exposed properties are stored in a memory control structure (`VkPhysicalDeviceMemoryProperties`). For a typical PC user, it will expose two heaps: the system RAM and GPU RAM. Further, each of these heaps will be categorized based on their memory types.

> The properties of memory-specific queries, such as heap types, can be queried during application initialization and cached at the application level for later use.

Now, each of these memory types can have various properties that need to be queried from the physical device. For example, some memory types could be either CPU-visible or not; they could be coherent between CPU and GPU access, cached or uncached, and so on. Such queries allow the application to choose the right kind of memory that fits their needs, following is the typical process in Vulkan that a general application uses for resource allocation:

- **Memory requirements**: The resource objects (`VkBuffer` and `VkImage`) are created based upon their object properties, such as tiling mode, usage flags, and more. Now, each of these objects may have different memory requirements that need to be queried by calling `vkGetBufferMemoryRequirements()` or `vkGetImageMemoryRequirements()`. This is helpful in computing the allocation size; for example, the returned size will take care of the padding alignment and so on. It will take account of the specified bitmask of the memory types that are compatible with the resource.

- **Allocation**: The memory is allocated using the `vkAllocateMemory()` API. It accepts the device object (`VkDevice`) and a memory control structure (`VkPhysicalDeviceMemoryProperties`).
- **Binding**: We got the memory requirements that helped us get the right type of memory; using this, we allocate memory. Now we can bind the resource object to this allocated memory using the `vkBindBufferMemory()` or `vkBindImageMemory()` API.
- **Memory mapping**: Memory mapping is how the content of physical device memory is updated. First, map the device memory to the host memory using `vkMapMemory()`. Update the content on this mapped memory region (on host the side) and call the `vkUnmapMemory()` API. This API updates the content of device memory with the updated mapped memory content.

Supplying shaders – shader compilation into SPIR-V

Compile the shader files using `glslangValidator.exe` (a LunarG SDK tool) to convert them from a readable text format to the SPIR-V format, which is a binary-intermediate form that Vulkan understands:

```
// VERTEX SHADER
#version 450

layout (location = 0) in vec4 pos;
layout (location = 1) in vec4 inColor;
layout (location = 0) out vec4 outColor;

out gl_PerVertex {
   vec4 gl_Position;
};

void main() {
   outColor      = inColor;
   gl_Position   = pos;
   gl_Position.y = -gl_Position.y;
   gl_Position.z = (gl_Position.z + gl_Position.w) / 2.0;
```

```
}

// FRAGMENT SHADER
#version 450

layout (location = 0) in vec4 color;
layout (location = 0) out vec4 outColor;

void main() {
   outColor = color;
};
```

The following pseudocode shows the process of creating shader modules within an application. A shader module for a given shader (vertex, fragment, geometry, tessellation, and more) is created by calling the `vkCreateShaderModule()` API. This needs to be provided with the SPIR-V format intermediate binary shader code that is specified in the `VkShaderModuleCreateInfo` control structure:

```
/*** 8. Building shader module ***/

VkPipelineShaderStageCreateInfo vtxShdrStages    = {....};
VkShaderModuleCreateInfo moduleCreateInfo    = { ... };

// spvVertexShaderData contains binary form of vertex shader
moduleCreateInfo.pCode = spvVertexShaderData;

// Create Shader module on the device
vkCreateShaderModule
        (device, &moduleCreateInfo, NULL, &vtxShdrStages.module);
```

Building layouts – descriptor and pipeline layouts

A descriptor connects the resources with the shader through layout binding slots. It is very commonly used to connect uniform and sampler resource types to the shaders.

More than one descriptor layout binding can be present in a single descriptor set; they will be present in the form of blocks or arrays, as shown in the following pseudocode. These blocks are then bundled into a single control structure, `VkDescriptorSetLayoutCreateInfo`, and used to create a descriptor layout object by calling the `vkCreateDescriptorSetLayout()` API. A descriptor set layout represents the type of information a descriptor set contains.

Descriptor layouts are created but are not presently accessible by the underlying pipeline. In order to provide access, we need to create a pipeline layout. A pipeline layout is the means by which the pipeline can access the descriptor set information. It is created by calling the `vkCreatePipelineLayout()` API, which consumes a `VkPipelineLayoutCreateInfo` control structure object containing the preceding descriptor layout:

```
/*** 9. Creating descriptor layout and pipeline layout ***/

// Descriptor layout specifies info type associated with shaders
VkDescriptorSetLayoutBinding layoutBind[2];

layoutBind[0].descriptorType = VK_DESCRIPTOR_TYPE_UNIFORM_BUFFER;
layoutBind[0].binding        = 0;
layoutBind[0].stageFlags     = VK_SHADER_STAGE_VERTEX_BIT;

layoutBind[1].descriptorType =
 VK_DESCRIPTOR_TYPE_COMBINED_IMAGE_SAMPLER;
layoutBind[1].binding        = 0;
layoutBind[1].stageFlags     = VK_SHADER_STAGE_FRAGMENT_BIT;

// Use layout bindings and create a descriptor set layout
VkDescriptorSetLayoutCreateInfo descriptorLayout = {};
descriptorLayout.pBindings   = layoutBind;

VkDescriptorSetLayout descLayout[2];
vkCreateDescriptorSetLayout
        (device, &descriptorLayout, NULL, descLayout.data());

// Now use the descriptor layout to create a pipeline layout
VkPipelineLayoutCreateInfo pipelineLayoutCI = { ... };
pipelineLayoutCI.pSetLayouts = descLayout.data();
vkCreatePipelineLayout
        (device, &pipelineLayoutCI, NULL, &pipelineLayout);
```

> The present example in this chapter makes use of the attributes only (vertex position and color). It does not use any uniform or sampler. Therefore, at this point in the chapter, we do not need to define the descriptor. We will understand more about descriptor sets in detail later, specifically in `Chapter 10`, *Descriptors and Push Constant*.

Creating a Render Pass – defining a pass attribute

Next, create a Render Pass object. A Render Pass contains subpasses and attachments. It describes the structure of the drawing work to the driver, how data will flow between the various attachments or what the ordering requirements are; and runtime behavior, such as how these attachments will be treated at each load or whether it needs to be clear or preserve information. The Render Pass object is created by calling the `vkCreateRenderPass()` API. It accepts the subpass and the attachment control structures as arguments. See the following pseudocode for more information:

```
/*** 10. Render Pass ***/

// Define two attachment for color and depth buffer
VkAttachmentDescription attachments[2];
attachments[0].format = colorImageformat;
attachments[0].loadOp = clear ? VK_ATTACHMENT_LOAD_OP_CLEAR
                      : VK_ATTACHMENT_LOAD_OP_DONT_CARE;
attachments[1].format = depthImageformat;
attachments[1].loadOp = VK_ATTACHMENT_LOAD_OP_CLEAR;

VkAttachmentReference colorReference, depthReference = {...};

// Describe the subpass, use color image and depth image
VkSubpassDescription subpass       = {};
subpass.pColorAttachments          = &colorReference;
subpass.pDepthStencilAttachment    = &depthReference;

// Define RenderPass control structure
VkRenderPassCreateInfo rpInfo      = { &attachments,&subpass ...};

VkRenderPass renderPass; // Create Render Pass object
vkCreateRenderPass(device, &rpInfo, NULL, &renderPass);
```

Framebuffer – connect drawing images to the Render Pass

A framebuffer is a collection of image views, corresponding to the attachment specified in the Render Pass. The image view represents the drawing image or depth image. The Render Pass object is used to control these attachments through the properties that are specified while creating the Render Pass object.

The `VkFramebufferCreateInfo` control structure accepts the Render Pass object and the attachment and other important parameters in it, such as the dimensions, number of attachments, layers, and so on. This structure is passed to the `VkCreateFramebuffer()` API to create the framebuffer object.

> The attachments used to represent the color and depth buffer must be image views (`VKImageView`), not image objects (`VkImage`).

The following diagram shows the created framebuffer object. It contains the image views of the color buffers images for drawing and the depth view for depth testing:

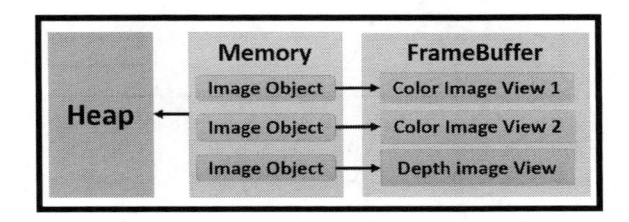

Let's walk through the frame buffer creation process using the following pseudocode:

```
/*** 11. Creating Frame buffers ***/

VkImageView attachments[2]; // [0] for color, [1] for depth
attachments[1] = Depth.view;

VkFramebufferCreateInfo fbInfo   = {};
fbInfo.renderPass     = renderPass;      // Pass render buffer object
fbInfo.pAttachments   = attachments;     // Image view attachments
fbInfo.width          = width;           // Frame buffer width
fbInfo.height         = height;          // Frame buffer height

// Allocate memory for frame buffer objects, for each image
// in the swapchain, there is one frame buffer
VkFramebuffer framebuffers[number of draw imagein swap chain];

foreach (drawing buffer in swapchain) {
    attachments[0] = currentSwapChainDrawImage.view;
    vkCreateFramebuffer(device, &fbInfo, NULL, &framebuffers[i]);
}
```

Populating geometry – storing a vertex into GPU memory

Next, define the geometric shape that will appear on the display output. In this chapter, we used a simple tricolor triangle.

The following screenshot shows the interleaved geometry data associated with this triangle. It contains the vertex position followed by color information for each vertex. This data array needs to be supplied to the physical device via a Vulkan buffer object (VkBuffer).

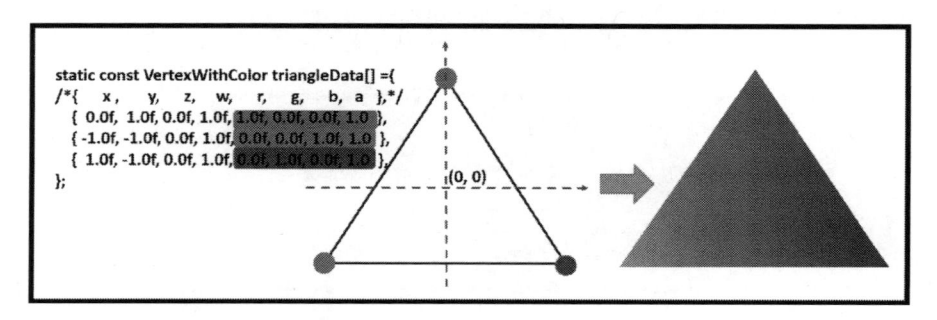

The following pseudocode involves the allocation, mapping, and binding process of the buffer objects:

```
/*** 12. Populate Geometry - storing vertex into GPU memory ***/

static const VertexWithColor triangleData[] ={
/*{   x,      y,     z,    w,     r,    g,    b,    a },*/
   {  0.0f,  1.0f, 0.0f, 1.0f,  1.0f, 0.0f, 0.0f, 1.0 },
   { -1.0f, -1.0f, 0.0f, 1.0f,  0.0f, 0.0f, 1.0f, 1.0 },
   {  1.0f, -1.0f, 0.0f, 1.0f,  0.0f, 1.0f, 0.0f, 1.0 },
};

VkBuffer               buffer;
VkMemoryRequirements   mem_requirement;
VkDeviceMemory         deviceMemory;

// Create buffer object, query required memory and allocate
VkBufferCreateInfo buffer_info = { ... };
vkCreateBuffer(device, &buffer_info, NULL, &buffer);

vkGetBufferMemoryRequirements(device, buffer, &mem_requirement);

VkMemoryAllocateInfo alloc_info = { ... };
```

```
vkAllocateMemory(device, &alloc_info, NULL, &(deviceMemory));

// Copy the triangleData to GPU using mapping and unmapping.
uint8_t *pData;
vkMapMemory(device, deviceMemory, 0, mem_requirement.size,
 0, &pData);
memcpy(pData, triangleData, dataSize); /**** Copying data ****/
vkUnmapMemory(device, deviceMemory);

// Bind the allocated memory
vkBindBufferMemory(device, buffer, deviceMemory, 0);
```

The process of buffer resource creation is very similar to that of image objects. Here, Vulkan provides buffer-based APIs for allocation, mapping, and binding. This is very similar to image object management APIs. The following table shows buffer and image resource management APIs and related data structures:

Buffer object	Image object
VkBuffer	VkImageView
VkBufferCreateInfo	VkImageCreateInfo
vkCreateBuffer	vkCreateImage
vkGetBufferMemoryRequirements	vkGetImageMemoryRequirements
vkBindBufferMemory	vkBindImageMemory
vkCreateBufferView	vkCreateImageView

The buffer is not initially associated with any type of memory. The application must allocate and bind appropriate device memory to the buffer before it can be used. Unlike images, which have to be compulsorily created with the image view in order to use them in the application, the buffer object can be used directly (such as vertex attribute, uniforms, and so on). If the buffer object is required to be accessed in the shader stage, it must be accessed in the form of buffer view objects

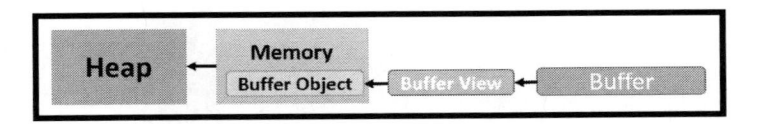

Your First Vulkan Pseudo Program

Once the vertex data is uploaded in the device memory, the pipeline must be informed with the specification of this data. This will be helpful in retrieving and interpreting the data. For example, the preceding geometry vertex data comprises position and color information, stored in an interleaved fashion, and each attribute is 16-bytes wide. This information needs to be communicated to the underlying pipeline with the help of vertex input binding (VkVertexInputBindingDescription) and the vertex input attribute descriptor (VkVertexInputAttributeDescription) control structure.

- The VkVertexInputBindingDescription contains properties that help the pipeline to read the buffer resource data, for example, the stride between each unit of information, considering the rate of information to be read (whether it is vertex-based or based on a number of instances).
- The VkVertexInputAttributeDescription interprets the buffer resource data.

In the following pseudocode, the position and color attributes are read at the 0th and 1st location in the vertex shader. Since the data is in interleaved form, the offset is 0 and 16, respectively:

```
/*** 13. Vertex binding ***/

VkVertexInputBindingDescription viBinding;
viBinding.binding     = 0;
viBinding.inputRate   = VK_VERTEX_INPUT_RATE_VERTEX;
viBinding.stride      = sizeof(triangleData) /*data Stride*/;

VkVertexInputAttributeDescriptionviAttribs[2];
viAttribs[0].binding    = 0;
viAttribs[0].location   = 0;
viAttribs[0].format     = VK_FORMAT_R32G32B32A32_SFLOAT;
viAttribs[0].offset     = 0;
viAttribs[1].binding    = 0;
viAttribs[1].location   = 1;
viAttribs[1].format     = VK_FORMAT_R32G32B32A32_SFLOAT;
viAttribs[1].offset     = 16;
```

> The control structure objects viAttribs and viBinding will be used at the time of pipeline creation. A pipeline object contains several states, among these, the vertex input state consumes the objects that are helpful in reading and interpreting a buffer resource.

Pipeline state management – creating pipelines

A pipeline is a collection of multiple states. Each state contains a set of properties that defines an execution protocol for that state. Collectively, all these states produce a single pipeline. There are two types of pipeline:

- **Graphics pipeline**: This pipeline may comprise multiple shader stages, including vertex, fragment, tessellation, geometry, and so on. It has a pipeline layout and multiple fixed-function pipeline stages.
- **Compute pipeline**: This is used for the compute operation. It consists of a single static compute shader stage and the pipeline layout.

Pipeline state management can be divided into two steps. The first step consists of defining various state objects containing important state control properties. In the second step, a pipeline object is created using these state objects.

Defining states

A pipeline may consume several states, and these are defined here:

- **Dynamic states**: The dynamic state notifies the pipeline about what states are expected to change at runtime. This allows the pipeline to permit a special routine update to the respective state instead of using an initialized value. For example viewport and scissoring are dynamic states. The `VkPipelineDynamicStateCreateInfo` structure specifies all dynamic states and their properties in the application program.
- **Vertex input state**: This state helps the pipeline to understand the reading and interpretation of data. Use the `VkPipelineVertexInputStateCreateInfo` object and specify the object of vertex input binding (`VkVertexInputBindingDescription`) and the vertex input attribute descriptor (`VkVertexInputAttributeDescription`) in it.
- **Rasterization state**: This is the process by which a primitive is converted into a two-dimensional image containing vital information, such as color, depth, and other attributes. It is represented by the `VkPipelineRasterizationStateCreateInfo` structure; this structure can be specified with culling mode, front-face orientation, primitive type, line width, and more.

Your First Vulkan Pseudo Program

- **Color blend attachment state**: Blending is a combination of a source and a destination color; this can be combined in various ways with different attributes and blend equations. This is represented using the `VkPipelineColorBlendStateCreateInfo` structure.
- **Viewport state**: This state is helpful in controlling the viewport transformation. The viewport properties can be specified using `VkPipelineViewportStateCreateInfo`. There could be various viewports. This state helps in determining the vital properties of the selected viewport, such as dimension, start point, depth range, and more. For each viewport, there is a corresponding scissor rectangle defining the scissor test rectangular bounds.
- **Depth stencil state**: The `VkPipelineDepthStencilStateCreateInfo` control structure is used to control the depth bound tests, stencil test, and depth test.
- **Multisample state**: The multisampling state contains important properties that control the behavior of the antialiasing of rasterized Vulkan primitives, such as points, lines, and polygons. The `VkPipelineMultisampleStateCreateInfo` control structure can be used to specify such control properties.
- The following pseudocode defines the various pipeline state objects that will be used in creating the graphics pipeline:

```
/*** 14. Defining states ***/

// Vertex Input state
VkPipelineVertexInputStateCreateInfo vertexInputStateInfo= {...};
vertexInputStateInfo.vertexBindingDescriptionCount = 1;
vertexInputStateInfo.pVertexBindingDescriptions     = &viBinding;
vertexInputStateInfo.vertexAttributeDescriptionCount = 2;
vertexInputStateInfo.pVertexAttributeDescriptions   = viAttribs;

// Dynamic states
VkPipelineDynamicStateCreateInfo dynamicState           = { ... };

// Input assembly state control structure
VkPipelineInputAssemblyStateCreateInfo inputAssemblyInfo= { ... };

// Rasterization state control structure
VkPipelineRasterizationStateCreateInfo rasterStateInfo  = { ... };

// Color blend Attachment state control structure
VkPipelineColorBlendAttachmentState colorBlendSI        = { ... };

// Color blend state control structure
VkPipelineColorBlendStateCreateInfo colorBlendStateInfo = { ... };
```

```
// View port state control structure
VkPipelineViewportStateCreateInfo viewportStateInfo    = { ... };

// Depth stencil state control structure
VkPipelineDepthStencilStateCreateInfo depthStencilStateInfo={..};

// Multisampling state control structure
VkPipelineMultisampleStateCreateInfo multiSampleStateInfo = {..};
```

Creating a graphics pipeline

Pipeline state objects are packed into the `VkGraphicsPipelineCreateInfo` control structure. This structure provides a means to access the pipeline state information inside the graphics pipeline object.

The creation of the pipeline state object could be an expensive operation. It is one of the performance-critical paths. Therefore, pipeline state objects are created from a pipeline cache (`VkPipelineCache`) to offer maximum performance. This allows the driver to create a new pipeline using existing base pipelines.

The graphics pipeline object is created using the `vkCreateGraphicsPipelines()` API. This API accepts the pipeline cache object to allocate the `VkPipeline` object from it and the `VkGraphicsPipelineCreateInfo` object to specify all the states connected with this pipeline:

```
/*** 15. Creating Graphics Pipeline ***/
// Create the pipeline objects
VkPipelineCache pipelineCache;
VkPipelineCacheCreateInfo pipelineCacheInfo;
vkCreatePipelineCache(device, &pipelineCacheInfo, NULL,
                      &pipelineCache);

// Define the control structure of graphics pipeline
VkGraphicsPipelineCreateInfo pipelineInfo;
pipelineInfo.layout                 = pipelineLayout;
pipelineInfo.pVertexInputState      = &vertexInputStateInfo;
pipelineInfo.pInputAssemblyState    = &inputAssemblyInfo;
pipelineInfo.pRasterizationState    = &rasterStateInfo;
pipelineInfo.pColorBlendState       = &colorBlendStateInfo;
pipelineInfo.pMultisampleState      = &multiSampleStateInfo;
pipelineInfo.pDynamicState          = &dynamicState;
pipelineInfo.pViewportState         = &viewportStateInfo;
pipelineInfo.pDepthStencilState     = &depthStencilStateInfo;
pipelineInfo.pStages                = shaderStages;
pipelineInfo.stageCount             = 2;
```

Your First Vulkan Pseudo Program

```
pipelineInfo.renderPass        = renderPass;

// Create graphics pipeline
vkCreateGraphicsPipelines
    (device, pipelineCache, 1, &pipelineInfo, NULL, &pipeline);
```

Executing the Render Pass – drawing Hello World!!!

We are almost there! At this stage, we will render our simple triangle on the drawing surface with the help of the Render Pass stage. The execution of the Render Pass stage requires a drawing surface and a recording of a set of commands that defines a single Render Pass run.

Acquiring the drawing surface

The very first thing we require before we start rendering anything is the drawing framebuffer. We have already created the framebuffer object and associated the swapchain drawing image within it (containing the swapchain image views). Now, we will use the `vkAcquireNextImageKHR()` API to determine the index of the drawing image that is currently available for the drawing operation. Using this acquired index, we refer to the corresponding framebuffer and give it to the Render Pass stage for rendering purposes:

```
/*** 16. Acquiring drawing image ***/

// Define semaphore for synchronizing the acquire of draw image.
// Only acquire draw image when drawing is completed
VkSemaphore imageAcquiredSemaphore;
VkSemaphoreCreateInfo imageAcquiredSemaphoreCI = {...};
imageAcquiredSemaphoreCI.sType=VK_STRUCTURE_TYPE_SEMAPHORE_CREATE_INFO;
vkCreateSemaphore(device, &imageAcquiredSemaphoreCI, NULL,
                &imageAcquiredSemaphore);

// Get the index of the next available swapchain image:
vkAcquireNextImageKHR(device, swapChain, UINT64_MAX,
    imageAcquiredSemaphore, NULL, &swapChainObjCurrentBuffer);
```

A synchronization mechanism is required when two or more swapchain drawing images are being used. A drawing image must only be acquired if it has rendered on the display output and is ready to take the next job; this status is indicated by `vkAcquireNextImageKHR()`. A semaphore object can be used to synchronize the acquiring of the drawing images. A semaphore (`VkSemaphore`) can be created using the vkCreateSemaphore() API; this object will be used in the command buffer submission.

Preparing the Render Pass control structure

Render Pass needs some specific information, such as the frame buffer, Render Pass object, render area dimensions, clear color, depth stencil values, and so on. This information is specified using the VkRenderPassBeginInfo control structure. This structure is later used to define Render Pass execution. The following pseudocode will help you understand the use of this structure in detail:

```
/*** 17. Preparing render pass control structure ***/

// Define clear color value and depth stencil values
const VkClearValue clearValues[2] = {
   [0] = { .color.float32 = { 0.2f, 0.2f, 0.2f, 0.2f } },
   [1] = { .depthStencil = { 1.0f, 0 } },
};

// Render pass execution data structure for a frame buffer
VkRenderPassBeginInfo beginPass;
beginPass.sType = VK_STRUCTURE_TYPE_RENDER_PASS_BEGIN_INFO;
beginPass.pNext= NULL;
beginPass.renderPass        = renderPass;
beginPass.framebuffer       =framebuffers[currentSwapchainImageIndex];
beginPass.renderArea.offset.x       = 0;
beginPass.renderArea.offset.y       = 0;
beginPass.renderArea.extent.width   = width;
beginPass.renderArea.extent.height  = height;
beginPass.clearValueCount           = 2;
beginPass.pClearValues              = clearValues;
```

Render Pass execution

The execution of the Render Pass is defined within a user-defined scope. This scope is interpreted using start and end markers defined by the vkCmdBeginRenderPass() and vkCmdEndRenderPass() APIs respectively. Within this scope, the following commands are specified, automatically linked to the current Render Pass:

1. **Bind the pipeline**: Bind the graphics pipeline with vkCmdBindPipeline().
2. **Bind the geometry buffer**: Supply the vertex data buffer object (of the type VkBuffer) to the Render Pass using the vkCmdBindVertexBuffers() API.

Your First Vulkan Pseudo Program

3. **Viewport and scissor**: Specify the viewport and scissor dimensions by calling the `vkCmdSetViewport()` and `vkCmdSetScissor()` APIs.
4. **Draw object**: Specify the draw command containing information such as how many vertices need to read from the start index, the number of instances, and so on.

Before we finish command buffer recording, set an implementation-compatible image layout and end command buffer recording by calling `vkEndCommandBuffer()`:

```
/**** START RENDER PASS ****/
vkCmdBeginRenderPass(cmd, &beginPass, VK_SUBPASS_CONTENTS_INLINE);

// Bind the pipeline
vkCmdBindPipeline(cmd, VK_PIPELINE_BIND_POINT_GRAPHICS, pipeline);
const VkDeviceSize offsets[1] = { 0 };

// Bind the triangle buffer data
vkCmdBindVertexBuffers(cmd, 0, 1, &buffer, offsets);

// viewport = {0, 0, 500, 500, 0 ,1}
vkCmdSetViewport(cmd, 0, NUM_VIEWPORTS, &viewport);

// scissor  = {0, 0, 500, 500}
vkCmdSetScissor(cmd, 0, NUM_SCISSORS, &scissor);

// Draw command - 3 vertices, 1 instance, 0th first index
vkCmdDraw(cmd, 3, 1, 0, 0);

/**** END RENDER PASS ****/
vkCmdEndRenderPass(cmd);

// Set the swapchain image layout
setImageLayout(VK_IMAGE_LAYOUT_COLOR_ATTACHMENT_OPTIMAL . .);

/**** COMMAND BUFFER RECORDING ENDS HERE ****/
vkEndCommandBuffer(cmd);
```

The following diagram shows the Render Pass execution process. It highlights the operations performed under the Render Pass scope.

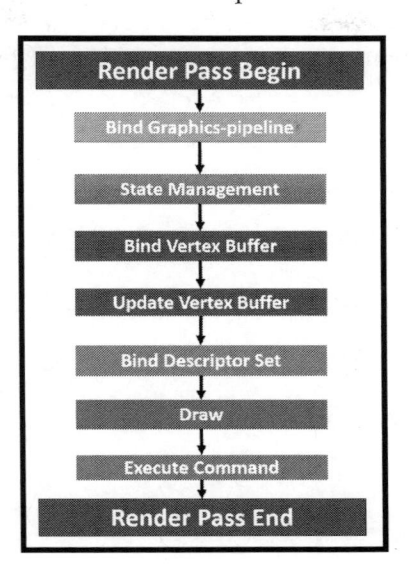

```
Render Pass Begin
        ↓
Bind Graphics-pipeline
        ↓
  State Management
        ↓
  Bind Vertex Buffer
        ↓
 Update Vertex Buffer
        ↓
  Bind Descriptor Set
        ↓
        Draw
        ↓
   Execute Command
        ↓
   Render Pass End
```

Queue submission and synchronization – sending jobs

Finally, we have reached a point where our command buffer is successfully recorded with numerous commands, including the Render Pass information and the graphics pipeline. The command buffer will be processed by submitting it into the queue. The driver will read the command buffer and schedule it.

> Command buffers are generally packed into batches for efficient rendering; therefore, if multiple command buffers exist, then they need to be packed into a single VkCommandBuffer array.

Before a command buffer is submitted, it's important to know the status of the previously submitted batch. If it is processed successfully, then it only makes sense to push a new batch into the queue. Vulkan provides fences (VkFence) as a synchronization mechanism to know whether the previously sent jobs have been completed. A fence object (VkFence) is created using the vkCreateFence() API. This API accepts a VkFenceCreateInfo control structure into it.

Your First Vulkan Pseudo Program

Command buffers are specified in a submission object (`VkSubmitInfo`). This object contains the command buffer list along with a `VkSemaphore` object for the synchronization of a framebuffer with swapchain drawing images. This information is fed into the `vkQueueSubmit()` API; it contains a `VkQueue` object to which the command buffer is going to be submitted and a `VkFence` object to ensure there is synchronization between each command buffer submission:

```
VkFenceCreateInfo fenceInfo = { ... };
VkFence drawFence;
// Create fence forensuring completion of cmdBuffer processing
vkCreateFence(device, &fenceInfo, NULL, &drawFence);

// Fill the command buffer submission control sturctures
VkSubmitInfo submitInfo[1] = { ... };
submitInfo[0].pNext              = NULL;
submitInfo[0].sType              = VK_STRUCTURE_TYPE_SUBMIT_INFO;
submitInfo[0].pWaitSemaphores    = &imageAcquiredSemaphore;
submitInfo[0].commandBufferCount = 1;
submitInfo[0].pCommandBuffers    = &cmd;

// Queue the command buffer for execution
vkQueueSubmit(queue, 1, submitInfo, NULL);
```

Displaying with presentation layer – rendering a triangle

Once the command buffer is submitted to the queue, it is processed asynchronously by the physical device. As a result, it will render a tricolor triangle on the drawing surface of the swapchain. Now, this surface is invisible to the user and it needs to be presented on the display window. The drawing surface is presented with the help of the `VkPresentInfoKHR` control structure. This contains the presentation information, for example, the number of swapchains in the application, the index of a drawing image that needs to be retrieved, and so on. This control structures object is used as a parameter in `vkQueuePresentKHR`. This flips the drawing surface image to the display window.

> Once `vkQueueSubmit` is called, the presentation queue can wait upon the `imageAcquiredSemaphore` semaphore signaled by the last submission before it performs the presentation.

```
// Define the presentation control structure
VkPresentInfoKHR present     = { ... };
present.sType                = VK_STRUCTURE_TYPE_PRESENT_INFO_KHR;
```

```
present.pNext              = NULL;
present.swapchainCount     = 1;
present.pSwapchains        = &swapChain;
present.pImageIndices      = &swapChainObjCurrent_buffer;

// Check if all the submitted command buffers are processed
do {
  res=vkWaitForFences(device,1,&drawFence,VK_TRUE,FENCE_TIMEOUT);
} while (res == VK_TIMEOUT);

// Handover the swapchain image to presentation queue
// for presentation purpose
vkQueuePresentKHR(queue, &present);

// Destroy Synchronization objects
vkDestroySemaphore(device, imageAcquiredSemaphore, NULL);
vkDestroyFence(device, drawFence, NULL);
```

Fitting it all together

This section provides a short description of the working of our first Vulkan pseudo application. The following diagram is a snapshot of the working model:

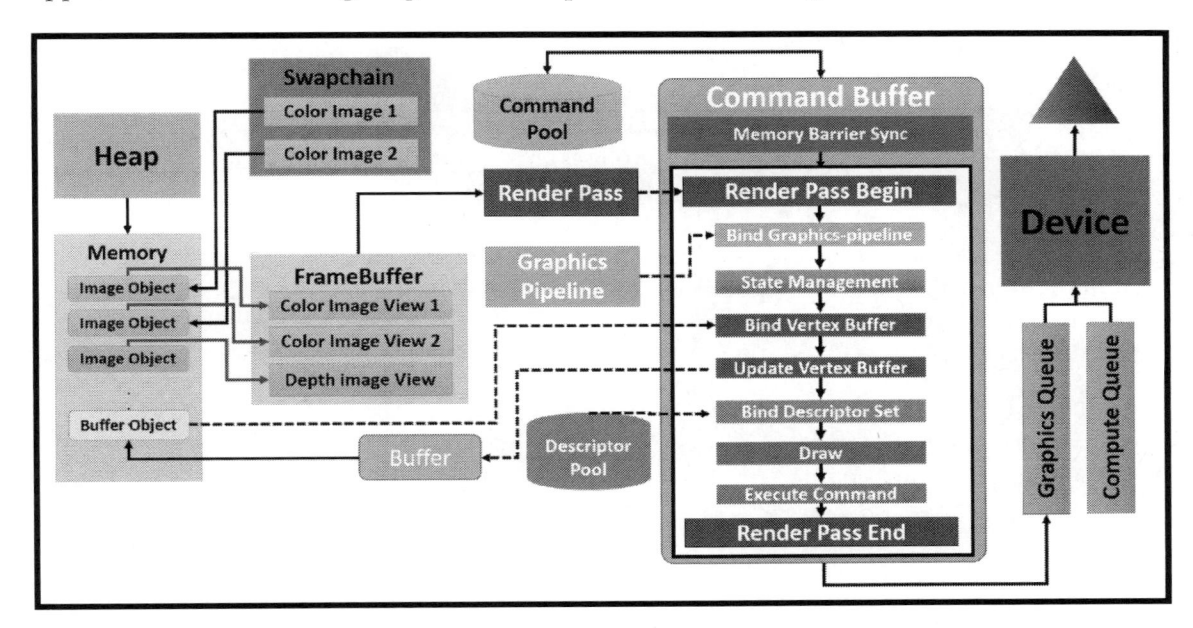

First, the application creates the Vulkan instance and device at the initialization stage with the necessary layers enabled and extensions created. The device exposes various queues (graphics or compute) as shown in the preceding diagram. These queues gather the command buffers and submit them to the physical device for processing.

Using the WSI extension, drawing surfaces are prepared for rendering graphic contents. The swapchain exposes these drawing surface as images, which are used in the form of image views. Similarly, the depth image view is prepared. These image view objects are used by the framebuffer. Render Pass makes use of this framebuffer to define a unit-rendering operation.

The command buffer is allocated from command buffer pools, and it is used to record various commands along with the Render Pass execution process. The Render Pass execution requires some vital Vulkan objects, such as the graphics pipeline, the descriptor set, shader modules, pipeline objects, and geometry data, as shown in the preceding diagram.

Finally, the command buffer is submitted to a presentation-supported (plus graphics) queue. Once submitted, it is processed by the GPU in an asynchronous fashion. Various synchronization mechanisms and memory barriers may be required to make the rendering output hitch-free.

Summary

In this chapter, we explored the step-by-step process of installing Vulkan on your system. Then we pseudo programmed "Hello World!!!" where we rendered a tricolor triangle on the display window.

This introductory chapter has boiled down Vulkan to a level where understanding this graphics API is really easy for beginners. This chapter is a cheat code for Vulkan programming; it can be used as a reference to remember all the programming steps along with all their respective APIs in the correct order.

Aristotle said, *"Well begun is half done!"* With the completion of the first two chapters, we have built a strong foundation to fully understand Vulkan mechanics from scratch; we will do this in the upcoming chapters.

In the next chapter, we will delve into core programming and start building our first Vulkan application. You will learn about layers and extensions and how to enable them implicitly and explicitly. We will also look into the fundamentals of Vulkan instances and the device and queues, which are very helpful to communicate with the GPU. Once we do this, we will query the resources and facilities it exposes. We will also learn how to get queues and their advertised properties.

3
Shaking Hands with the Device

With the knowledge we gained from the last two chapters, we have now reached a level where we can start Vulkan programming from scratch. These two chapters laid the foundation and helped us understand the basic fundamentals of this revolutionary API. Now, at a higher level, we understand the motivation behind this technology, its core blocks, and the associated functionalities and terminologies. In addition, we walked through Vulkan pseudocoding and built a very simple application to understand and visualize the Vulkan programming model.

From this chapter onward, we will dive into the core of Vulkan programming and start transforming our Hello World!!! pseudocode into a real-world executable sample.

> All the chapters in this book are designed and programmed carefully in a structured way; every new chapter is dependent on the previous one. You are advised to follow the sequence of the chapters for an efficient learning experience.

In this chapter, we will cover the following topics:

- Getting started with the LunarG SDK
- Setting up the first project with CMake
- An introduction to layers and extensions
- Creating a Vulkan instance
- Understanding physical and logical devices
- Understanding queues and queue families
- Implementing the device and queues all together

Getting started with the LunarG SDK

All the chapters in this book use the LunarG SDK for Vulkan programming. This SDK can be downloaded from `https://vulkan.lunarg.com`; you'll need a LunarG account to do this.

The SDK's default installation path always locates to `C:\VulkanSDK\` [version]. Upon successful installation, the SDK's `Bin` directory location is added to the `$PATH` environment variable (`C:\VulkanSDK\1.0.26.0\Bin`). In addition, the `VK_SDK_PATH` environment variable is added, pointing to the SDK's path (`C:\VulkanSDK\1.0.26.0`).

The installation will also add the Vulkan loader (`vulkan-1.dll`) to `C:\Windows\System32`. Based on the window target, the loader will be either a 32-bit or 64-bit DLL.

The following are some general terms that will be commonly used throughout the chapter:

Term	Description
ICD	This is the abbreviation for **Installable Client Driver**. It is a Vulkan-compatible display driver. Multiple ICDs–for example, NVIDIA and Intel drivers–can coexist without interfering with each other.
Layers	These are pluggable components that either hook or intercept Vulkan commands. They provide services such as debugging, validation, tracing, and so on.
Loader	A loader's job is to locate the display driver and expose the layer's libraries in a platform-independent way. On Windows, the load library (`vulkan-1.dll`) uses registries to locate ICD and layer configurations.

The following are the folder contencified in the highlighted part of the following code.ts of the LunarG SDK along with the respective descriptions:

Directory	Description
Bin and Bin32	These contain the 32-bit (the `Bin32` folder) and 64-bit (the `Bin` folder) release build of the executable and loader. They also contain the libraries of layers and tools.
Config	This is meant to store different Vulkan configurations. For example, it contains the `vk_layer_settings.txt` file, which is used to set configuration parameters at different validation layers. These configurations can dynamically affect the layers.

Demo	This is the Vulkan demo source for the `cube`, `tri`, and `vulkaninfo` programs.
Doc	This refers to specifications, manuals, release notes, and other important pieces of documentation.
glslang	This contains the source and headers for glslang. It provides a frontend parser for GLSL and a standalone wrapper tool called `glslangValidator` for shader validation.
Include	This contains the necessary header files that help the Vulkan application to be built and compiled.
Runtime installer	The Vulkan runtime installer offers Vulkan runtime libraries that can be included by a Vulkan application or driver. Refer to the `README.txt` file for more information.
Source	This contains the source implementation for loader (`vulkan-1.dll`) and layer libraries.
spir-v tools	This refers to the source code and header files for SPIR-V tools.

> The installation of multiple SDKs does not affect other installations. The `$PATH` variable points to the most recently installed SDK version.

Setting up our first project with CMake

CMake is a build process management tool that works in an operating system in a compiler-independent manner. It makes use of `CMakeLists.txt` to build project solutions. In this section, we will learn the process of building a CMake file for our first Vulkan application. Refer to the following instructions to understand the creation of this configuration file (`CMakeLists.txt`):

1. Create an empty `CMakeLists.txt` file as per the specified folder structure convention, that is, `chapter_3 > Sample Name > CMakeLists.txt`. For the purpose of ensuring compatibility across different CMake versions, you need to specify the minimum supported version. If the current version of CMake happens to be lower than the specified one, then it will stop building the solution. The minimum supported version of CMake is specified with `cmake_minimum_required`. The following is the code from the `CMakeList.txt` file:

```
cmake_minimum_required(VERSION 3.7.1)
```

2. Specify the necessary variables that will be used to locate the path of the Vulkan SDK using the `set` CMake keyword. Also, provide a meaningful name:

```
set (Recipe_Name "3_0_DeviceHandshake")
```

3. In this title we used CMake version 3.7.1 since it comes with a Vulkan module. This module is helpful to auto locate the Vulkan SDK installation, included directories and required libraries to build Vulkan application. In the following CMake code we first try to locate the Vulkan SDK using CMake Vulkan module, if this is unsuccessful then we use manually specify the Vulkan SDK path. Follow the given inline comment in the code for detailed description:

```
# AUTO_LOCATE_VULKAN - accepted value ON or OFF
# ON  - Use CMake to auto locate the Vulkan SDK.
# OFF - Vulkan SDK path can be specified manually.
# This is helpful to test the build on various Vulkan version.
option(AUTO_LOCATE_VULKAN "AUTO_LOCATE_VULKAN" ON )

if(AUTO_LOCATE_VULKAN)

    message(STATUS "Attempting auto locate Vulkan using CMake......")

    # Find Vulkan Path using CMake's Vulkan Module
    # This will return Boolean 'Vulkan_FOUND' indicating
    # the status of find as success(ON) or fail(OFF).
    # Include directory path - 'Vulkan_INCLUDE_DIRS'
    # and 'Vulkan_LIBRARY' with required libraries.
    find_package(Vulkan)

    # Try extracting VulkanSDK path from ${Vulkan_INCLUDE_DIRS}
    if (NOT ${Vulkan_INCLUDE_DIRS} STREQUAL "")
       set(VULKAN_PATH ${Vulkan_INCLUDE_DIRS})
       STRING(REGEX REPLACE "/Include" "" VULKAN_PATH
       ${VULKAN_PATH})
    endif()

    if(NOT Vulkan_FOUND)
    # CMake may fail to locate the libraries but could be able to
    # provide some path in Vulkan SDK include directory variable
    # 'Vulkan_INCLUDE_DIRS', try to extract path from this.

    message(STATUS "Failed to locate Vulkan SDK, retrying again...")

    # Check if Vulkan path is valid, if not switch to manual mode.
       if(EXISTS "${VULKAN_PATH}")
```

```cmake
            message(STATUS "Successfully located the
                    Vulkan SDK: ${VULKAN_PATH}")
        else()
            message("Error: Unable to locate Vulkan SDK. Please
                    turn off auto locate option by
                    specifying 'AUTO_LOCATE_VULKAN' as 'OFF'")
            message("and specify manually path using 'VULKAN_SDK'
                    and 'VULKAN_VERSION' variables
                    in the CMakeLists.txt.")
            return()
        endif()

    endif()

else()

    message(STATUS "Attempting to locate Vulkan SDK
                using manual path......")
    set(VULKAN_SDK "C:/VulkanSDK")
    set(VULKAN_VERSION "1.0.33.0")
    set(VULKAN_PATH "${VULKAN_SDK}/${VULKAN_VERSION}")
    message(STATUS "Using manual specified path: ${VULKAN_PATH}")

    # Check if manual set path exists
    if(NOT EXISTS "${VULKAN_PATH}")
     message("Error: Unable to locate this Vulkan SDK path
     VULKAN_PATH:
     ${VULKAN_PATH}, please specify correct path.
     For more information on correct installation process,
     please refer to subsection 'Getting started with
     Lunar-G SDK' and 'Setting up first project with CMake'
     in Chapter 3, 'Shaking hands with the device' in this
     book 'Learning Vulkan', ISBN - 9781786469809.")
        return()
    endif()

endif()
```

4. With `project` keyword you can specify any desire name of your project. On Windows, **Window System Integration (WSI)** needs the `VK_KHR_WIN32_SURFACE_EXTENSION_NAME` extension API. For this, you need to define the `VK_USE_PLATFORM_WIN32_KHR` preprocessor directives (with -D prefixed) in the CMake file using `add_definitions()`. Include the path where Vulkan header files are placed. Also, add the path of the Bin folder to link the necessary Vulkan runtime/static libraries:

   ```
   # Specify a suitable project name
   project(${Recipe_Name})

   # Add preprocessor definitions here
   add_definitions(-DVK_USE_PLATFORM_WIN32_KHR)
   ```

5. Specify all required libraries in the `VULKAN_LIB_LINK_LIST` variable and later linked it to the building project using `target_link_libraries()`. In addition, provide a correct path for including Vulkan header files using CMake's `include_directories()` API. Also, specify the path from where linked libraries are located using `link_directories()` API.

   ```
   # Add 'vulkan-1' library for build Vulkan application.
   set(VULKAN_LINK_LIST "vulkan-1")

   if(${CMAKE_SYSTEM_NAME} MATCHES "Windows")

           # Include Vulkan header files from Vulkan SDK
             include_directories(AFTER ${VULKAN_PATH}/Include)

           # Link directory for vulkan-1
             link_directories(${VULKAN_PATH}/Bin)

   endif()
   ```

6. The following code is used to group the header and source files together in the build source project for better visualization and management of the code structure:

   ```
   # Bunch the header and source files together
   if (WIN32)
       source_group ("include" REGULAR_EXPRESSION "include/*")
       source_group ("source"  REGULAR_EXPRESSION "source/*")
   endif (WIN32)
   ```

7. Specify the sample's header file path. Read all the header files and source files in the sample using `file()` API and store them in the `CPP_Lists` and `HPP_Lists` variables. Use these lists to specify to the build solution all the files that need to be used for compilation. Provide a name to the project build and link it to all the necessary Vulkan libraries:

   ```
   # Define include path
   include_directories (${CMAKE_CURRENT_SOURCE_DIR}/include)

   # Gather list of header and source files for compilation
   file (GLOB_RECURSE CPP_FILES
                   ${CMAKE_CURRENT_SOURCE_DIR}/source/*.cpp)
   file (GLOB_RECURSE HPP_FILES
                   ${CMAKE_CURRENT_SOURCE_DIR}/include/*.*)

   # Build project, provide name and include files to be compiled
   add_executable (${Recipe_Name} ${CPP_FILES} ${HPP_FILES})

   # Link the debug and release libraries to the project
   target_link_libraries (${Recipe_Name}${VULKAN_LIB_LIST})
   ```

8. Define the project properties and the correct C/C++ standard versions to be used in the project compilation. Specify the path of the binary executable:

   ```
   # Define project properties
   set_property(TARGET ${Recipe_Name} PROPERTY RUNTIME_OUTPUT_
        DIRECTORY ${CMAKE_CURRENT_SOURCE_DIR}/binaries)
   set_property(TARGET ${Recipe_Name} PROPERTY RUNTIME_OUTPUT_
        DIRECTORY_DEBUG ${CMAKE_CURRENT_SOURCE_DIR}/binaries)
   set_property(TARGET ${Recipe_Name} PROPERTY RUNTIME_OUTPUT_
        DIRECTORY_RELEASE ${CMAKE_CURRENT_SOURCE_DIR}/binaries)
   set_property(TARGET ${Recipe_Name} PROPERTY RUNTIME_OUTPUT_
        DIRECTORY_MINSIZEREL ${CMAKE_CURRENT_SOURCE_DIR}/binaries)
   set_property(TARGET ${Recipe_Name} PROPERTY RUNTIME_OUTPUT_
        DIRECTORY_RELWITHDEBINFO ${CMAKE_CURRENT_SOURCE_DIR}/binaries)

   # Define C++ version to be used for building the project
   set_property(TARGET ${Recipe_Name} PROPERTY CXX_STANDARD 11)
   set_property(TARGET ${Recipe_Name} PROPERTY
                        CXX_STANDARD_REQUIRED ON)

   # Define C version to be used for building the project
   set_property(TARGET ${Recipe_Name} PROPERTY C_STANDARD 99)
   set_property(TARGET ${Recipe_Name} PROPERTY
                        C_STANDARD_REQUIRED ON)
   ```

Shaking Hands with the Device

How to build the CMake file

Follow these steps to build the CMake file:

1. Open the command-line terminal and go to the sample's `build` directory. If it is not present, create it. This empty `build` folder will contain the Visual Studio project built through the command line. You can also use the CMake GUI instead.

2. Execute the following command to build the project (choose the correct IDE version). The last parameter specifies the platform architecture; therefore, if you are using a 32-bit machine, use Win32:

   ```
   cmake -G "Visual Studio 14 2015 Win64" ..
   ```

This is how the command-line interface looks:

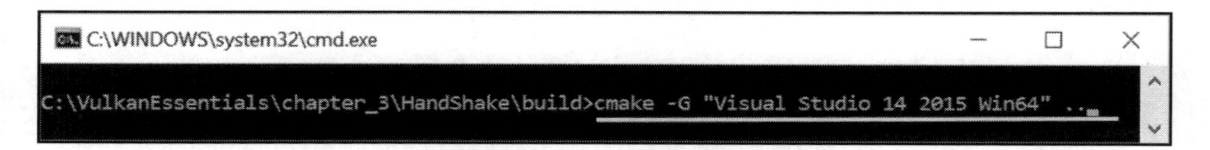

```
C:\WINDOWS\system32\cmd.exe                                           —    □    ×

C:\VulkanEssentials\chapter_3\HandShake\build>cmake -G "Visual Studio 14 2015 Win64" ..
```

The two dots at the end of the command specify the path of `CMakeLists.txt` (one folder level up), which is required by the CMake command to build the project. Upon successful execution, you will find the following project files based on the project name specified:

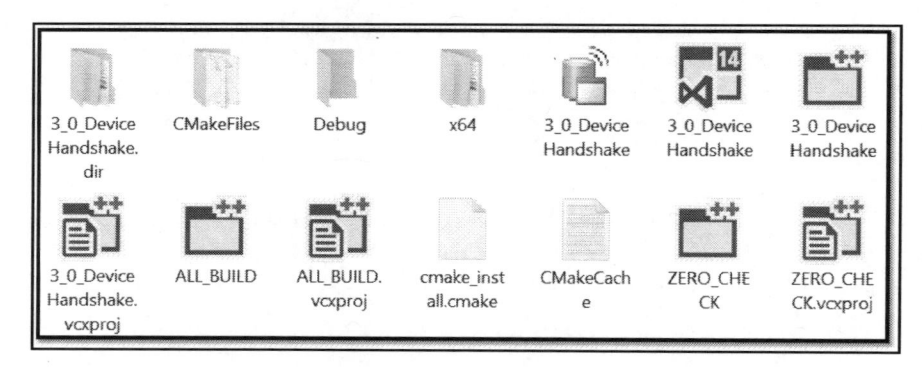

| 3_0_Device Handshake.dir | CMakeFiles | Debug | x64 | 3_0_Device Handshake | 3_0_Device Handshake | 3_0_Device Handshake |
| 3_0_Device Handshake.vcxproj | ALL_BUILD | ALL_BUILD.vcxproj | cmake_install.cmake | CMakeCache | ZERO_CHECK | ZERO_CHECK.vcxproj |

The following diagram shows the folder structure of all the samples that follow in this book:

- **include** — Sample include header files
- **source** — Sample source code files
- **build** — CMake build folder, contains project solution
- **binary** — Place for generated sample executables
- **CMakeList.txt** — CMake config file for building target solutions
- **resource** — Stores resource type like images, icons, meshes
- **external** — Contains third party source code, external libs

(Chapter_<No.> / <Sample Name>)

Introduction to extensions

While implementing a Vulkan application, the very first thing that a developer may need to do, and be interested in, is seeing the extended features, functionalities, and capabilities offered by the API. These allow them to gather vital information that can be used to report errors, debug, and trace commands; they can also be used for validation purposes. Vulkan makes use of *layers* and *extensions* to expose these additional functionalities:

- **Layers**: Layers get hooked up with the existing Vulkan APIs and insert themselves in the chain of Vulkan commands that are associated with the specified layer. It's commonly used for validating the development process. For example, the driver need not check the supplied parameters in the Vulkan API; it's the layer's responsibility to validate whether the incoming parameter is correct or not.
- **Extensions**: Extensions provide extended functionality or features, which may or may not be part of the standard specification. The extension could either be a part of the instance or the device. The extension commands cannot be linked statically; they are queried first and then linked dynamically to the function pointers. These function pointers may already be defined in `vulkan.h` for the registered extension along with the necessary data structures and enumerations.

An extension can be categorized into two types:

- **Instance-based**: This represents global functionalities that are independent of any device and can be accessible without any `VkDevice`
- **Device-based**: Here, the extensions are very specific to a device and require a valid handle of the device to operate on and expose the special functionalities

Shaking Hands with the Device

> It is suggested that layers and extensions should be enabled during the development phase of an application and turned off at the production stage when the product is expected for release. Turning off the extensions and layers at the production stage allows the application to save unnecessary validation overheads, thus offering higher performance.

Before we get started with application programming, let's take a look at which user-defined classes are used by the sample and what their responsibilities are:

- **Main program**: This is an entry point for Hello World!!! It is the application that contains the `main()` function. The program control logic is built within this file (`main.cpp`).
- **Headers.h**: This is the single place where all the headers are included; we will put our Vulkan headers here.
- **VulkanLayerAndExtension**: This class is implemented in `VulkanLayerAndExtension.h/.cpp` and provides layer- and extension-based functionalities for the instance and device. It also offers debugging capabilities.
- **VulkanInstance**: This class creates the Vulkan instance object and is helpful during initialization. It's implemented in `VulkanInstance.h/.cpp`.
- **VulkanDevice**: `VulkanDevice.h/.cpp` is responsible for creating the logical and physical devices. Each physical device is capable of exposing one or more queues. This class also manages a device's queue and its respective properties.

Querying layers and extensions

In this section, we will implement the `main`, `VulkanApplication`, and `VulkanLayerAndExtension` classes. Now we will begin our Vulkan programming. We'll start by querying the advertised Vulkan layers. Refer to the following instructions to implement this:

- The very first thing required for Vulkan programming is to add `<vulkan/vulkan.h>` to the header file `Header.h`. It contains the most commonly used Vulkan APIs and structure declarations.
- Create the `VulkanLayerAndExtension` class and declare the function and variables, as specified in the highlighted part of the following code. Please refer to the inline comments for more details:

```
struct LayerProperties {
   VkLayerProperties                    properties;
   vector<VkExtensionProperties>        extensions;
```

```
};

class VulkanLayerAndExtension{
    // Layers and corresponding extension list
      std::vector<LayerProperties> // Instance/global
      layergetInstanceLayerProperties();

    // Global extensions
      VkResult getExtensionProperties(LayerProperties
               &layerProps, VkPhysicalDevice* gpu = NULL);

    // Device based extensions
      VkResult getDeviceExtensionProperties(VkPhysicalDevice*gpu);
};
```

- Upon application startup, the `getInstanceLayerProperties()` helper function queries either instance or global layers. It gets the total count of the layers and stores all of the layer information in a `VkLayerProperties` vector called `layerProperties`. Both the operations (count and store) are done by calling `vkEnumerateInstanceLayerProperties()` twice. For the first time, calling the API with the second argument as `NULL` returns the layer count in the first argument, `instanceLayerCount`. In the second instance, instead of providing the second argument as `NULL`, pass it as an array/vector of `VkLayerProperties` and fetch detailed property information into it.

> Most enumerated APIs under Vulkan are used to perform more than one functionality, based on the arguments supplied. Just now, we have seen that the `vkEnumerateInstanceLayerProperties` API is not only used to retrieve the layer count (by supplying a `NULL` argument), but also to get the array of layers (by supplying an array of data structures) that contains information.

Here's the syntax of the preceding code:

```
VkResult VulkanLayerAndExtension::getInstanceLayerProperties()
{
    // Stores number of instance layers
    uint32_t instanceLayerCount;
    // Vector to store layer properties
    std::vector<VkLayerProperties>      layerProperties;
    // Check Vulkan API result status
    VkResult result;

    // Query all the layers
```

```cpp
    do {
        result = vkEnumerateInstanceLayerProperties
                (&instanceLayerCount, NULL);

        if (result)
            return result;

        if (instanceLayerCount == 0)
            return VK_INCOMPLETE; // return fail

        layerProperties.resize(instanceLayerCount);
        result = vkEnumerateInstanceLayerProperties
                (&instanceLayerCount, layerProperties.data());
    } while (result == VK_INCOMPLETE);

    // Query all the extensions for each layer and store it.
    std::cout << "\nInstanced Layers" << std::endl;
    std::cout << "===================" << std::endl;
    for (auto globalLayerProp: layerProperties) {

        // Print layer name and its description
        std::cout <<"\n"<< globalLayerProp.description <<
                    "\n\t|\n\t|---[Layer Name]--> " <<
                    globalLayerProp.layerName <<"\n";

        LayerProperties layerProps;
        layerProps.properties = globalLayerProp;

        // Get Instance level extensions for
        // corresponding layer properties
        result = getExtensionProperties(layerProps);

        if (result){
            continue;
        }

        layerPropertyList.push_back(layerProps);

        // Print extension name for each instance layer
        for (auto j : layerProps.extensions){
            std::cout << "\t|\n\t\t|---
            [Layer Extension]--> " << j.extensionName << "\n";
        }

    }
    return result;
}
```

The following is the syntax of `vkEnumerateInstanceLayerProperties()`:

```
VkResult vkEnumerateInstanceLayerProperties (
         uint32_t*             pPropertyCount,
         VkLayerProperties* pProperties);
```

The following table describes the `vkEnumerateInstanceLayerProperties()` API fields:

Parameters	Description
`pPropertyCount`	This variable represents the number of layers at the instance level. This variable works as an input or output variable, depending upon the value passed to `pProperties`.
`pProperties`	This variable can take two values. When specified as `NULL`, the API returns the layer count in `pPropertyCount` with the total number of layers. When used as an array, the API retrieves the information of the layer properties in the same array.

Once we retrieve the layer property information for each layer, we'll use it to iterate through all the layers in order to query the extensions exposed by each layer. We'll do this by calling our user-defined helper function `getExtensionProperties()`.

Upon the successful execution of the layer and their extensions, you'll see the following output on the console:

```
LunarG debug layer
        |---[Layer Name]--> VK_LAYER_LUNARG_api_dump

LunarG Validation Layer
        |---[Layer Name]--> VK_LAYER_LUNARG_core_validation
                |---[Layer Extesion]--> VK_EXT_debug_report

LunarG Standard Validation Layer
        |---[Layer Name]--> VK_LAYER_LUNARG_standard_validation

LunarG Validation Layer
        |---[Layer Name]--> VK_LAYER_LUNARG_device_limits
                |---[Layer Extesion]--> VK_EXT_debug_report
```

Each layer may be capable of supporting one or more extensions. The `getExtensionProperties()` function first enumerates the layers to get the number of extensions exposed. Then, it stores the extension properties information in the `LayerProperties` data structures using the `vkEnumerate-InstanceExtensionProperties()` API. This whole process is very similar to the layer enumeration; refer to `getInstanceLayerProperties()` for more information on the last

Shaking Hands with the Device

step. The `getExtensionProperties()` function queries the extensions for both the instance and device:

```
// This function retrieves extension and its
// properties at instance and device level.
// Pass a valid physical device pointer (gpu) to retrieve
// device level extensions, otherwise use NULL to
// retrieve extension specific to instance level.
VkResult VulkanLayerAndExtension::getExtensionProperties
    (LayerProperties &layerProps, VkPhysicalDevice* gpu)
{
    // Stores number of extension per layer
    uint32_t    extensionCount;
    VkResult    result;
    // Name of the layer
    char*       layerName = layerProps.properties.layerName;

    do {
        // Get the total number of extension in this layer
        if(gpu){
            result = vkEnumerateDeviceExtensionProperties
                        (*gpu, layerName,
                        &extensionCount, NULL);
        }
        else{
            result = vkEnumerateInstanceExtensionProperties
                    (layerName, &extensionCount, NULL);
        }

        if (result || extensionCount == 0)
            continue;

        layerProps.extensions.resize(extensionCount);

        // Gather all extension properties
        if (gpu){
                result = vkEnumerateDeviceExtensionProperties
                        (*gpu, layerName, &extensionCount,
                        layerProps.extensions.data());
        }
        else{
            result = vkEnumerateInstanceExtensionProperties
                        (layerName, &extensionCount,
                        layerProps.extensions.data());
        }

    } while (result == VK_INCOMPLETE);
```

Creating a Vulkan instance

A Vulkan instance is a primary object that is required to build an application; it stores all the application states. It is of the type `VkInstance` and is managed inside the `VulkanInstance` class, which is user-defined (`VulkanInstance.h/cpp`). This class is responsible for the creation and destruction of the Vulkan instance object. The following is the implementation of the header file:

```
class VulkanInstance { // Many lines skipped

    // Vulkan instance object variable
    VkInstance instance;

    // Vulkan instance specific layer and extensions
    VulkanLayerAndExtension        layerExtension;

    // Functions for Creation and Deletion of Vulkan instance
    VkResult createInstance( vector<const char *>& layers,
                    vector<const char *>& extensions,
                    const char* applicationName);

    // Destroy Vulkan instance
    void destroyInstance();
};
```

The creation of a Vulkan instance requires a set of information that is specified using the `VkApplicationInfo` structure object, as represented by `appInfo` in the following code. This structure object provides vital information about the application, such as its name, version, engine, and so on. In addition, it also tells the drivers about the Vulkan API version to be used by the application. If the specified version is not compatible with the underlying driver, the application reports an error (if the validation layer is enabled). For more information, refer to the `apiVersion` field of the `VkApplicationInfo` structure, which is described later in this section:

```
VkResult VulkanInstance::createInstance( vector<const char *>& layers,
    vector<const char *>& extensionNames, char const*const appName) {
    // Set the instance specific layer and extension information
    layerExtension.instanceExtensionNames    = extensionNames;
    layerExtension.instanceLayerNames        = layers;

    // Define the Vulkan application structure
    VkApplicationInfo appInfo = {};
    appInfo.sType            = VK_STRUCTURE_TYPE_APPLICATION_INFO;
    appInfo.pNext            = NULL;
    appInfo.pApplicationName = appName;
    appInfo.applicationVersion = 1;
```

```
    appInfo.pEngineName        = appName;
    appInfo.engineVersion      = 1;
    appInfo.apiVersion         = VK_API_VERSION_1_0;

    // Define the Vulkan instance create info structure
    VkInstanceCreateInfo instInfo = {};
    instInfo.sType       = VK_STRUCTURE_TYPE_INSTANCE_CREATE_INFO;
    instInfo.pNext                    = NULL;
    instInfo.flags                    = 0;
    instInfo.pApplicationInfo         = &appInfo;

    VkResult res = vkCreateInstance(&instInfo, NULL, &instance);
    return res;
}
```

The `VkInstance` object is created using the `vkCreateInstance()` API. This API uses a `VkInstanceCreateInfo` control structure object (`instInfo`). This structure object contains the reference of `appInfo` (`VkApplicationInfo`) to understand application-specific attributes. In addition, the `VkInstanceCreateInfo` object can also be used to enable the instance-specific layer and its corresponding extensions.

> To learn more about layers and enabling them in the Vulkan application, refer to the next section.

The following is the syntax for Vulkan instance creation API:

```
VkResult vkCreateInstance(
        const VkInstanceCreateInfo*      pCreateInfo,
        const VkAllocationCallbacks*     pAllocator,
        VkInstance*                      pInstance);
```

Here are the fields for the `vkCreateInstance` API:

Parameters	Description
pCreateInfo	This refers to the pointer to the `VkInstanceCreateInfo` structure (described later) containing application- (application create info), layer-, and Vulkan-specific information.
pAllocator	This specifies how to control host memory allocation. For more information, refer to the *Host memory* section in Chapter 5, *Command Buffer and Memory Management in Vulkan*.
pInstance	This handles the Vulkan instance object of the type `VkInstance`.

The following is the syntax and structure description for VKInstanceCreateInfo:

```
typedef struct VKInstanceCreateInfo (
        VkStructureType            type;
        const void*                pNextnext;
        VkInstanceCreateFlags      flags;
        const VkApplicationInfo*   pApplicationInfo;
        uint32_t                   enabledLayerCount;
        const char* const*         ppEnabledLayerNames;
        uint32_t                   enabledExtensionCount;
        const char* const*
ppEnabledExtensionNamesenabledExtensionNames;
} VkInstanceCreateInfo;
```

VKInstanceCreateInfo has the following fields:

Parameters	Description
type	This is the type information of this control structure. It must be specified as VK_STRUCTURE_TYPE_INSTANCE_CREATE_INFO.
pNext	This field could either be a valid pointer to an extension-specific structure or Null.
flags	This field is reserved for the future and is not in use at present.
pApplicationInfo	This indicates the object pointer of VkApplicationInfo that contains application-specific information, such as the Vulkan API version, its name and engine version, and so on. For more information, refer to VkApplicationInfo, which is defined in detail later. This field can also be NULL.
enabledLayerCount	This field specifies the count of layers to be enabled at the instance level.
ppEnabledLayerNames	This contains the list of layer names in the form of an array that needs to be enabled at the instance level. Refer to the *Introduction to layer and extensions* section for further information.
enabledExtensionCount	This field specifies the count of extensions to be enabled at the instance level.

Shaking Hands with the Device

`ppEnabledExtensionNames`	This contains a list of extension names in the form of an array that needs to be enabled at the instance level. Refer to the *Introduction to layer and extensions* section for further details.

`VKInstanceCreateInfo` consumes `VkApplicationInfo` as one of its member variables. Let's look at the specs of this structure:

```
typedef struct VkApplicationInfo {
    VkStructureType     type;
    const void*         pNext;
    const char*         pApplicationName;
    uint32_t            applicationVersion;
    const char*         pEngineName;
    uint32_t            pEngineVersion;
    uint32_t            apiVersion;
} VkApplicationInfo;
```

Here are the fields described in the structure:

Parameters	Description
`type`	This is the type information of this control structure. It must be specified as `VK_STRUCTURE_TYPE_APPLICATION_INFO`. The type of this structure.
`pNext`	This field could either be a valid pointer to an extension-specific structure or `Null` as well.
`pApplicatonName`	This field indicates the user-defined application name given to the application, such as Hello World!!!.
`applicationVersion`	Use this field to indicate the versioning of the developer application. This will be helpful in retrieving the application version directly from the application executable itself.
`engineName`	This is the name of the backend engine used by the application.
`engineVersion`	This indicates the backend application's engine versioning if used; if not, the application version will suffice.
`apiVersion`	This field announces the version number of the Vulkan API that is to be used to run the application. The implementation reads this value and validates whether it can be ignored (if specified as 0) or can be used (if specified non-zero), it will report an error (if the API version is not supported). If there is an error, the implementation returns `VK_ERROR_INCOMPATIBLE_DRIVER`.

> The patch version number specified in `apiVersion` is ignored when creating an instance object. Only the major and minor versions of the instance must match those requested in `apiVersion`.

When the application is no longer in use, it can kill the Vulkan instance using the user-defined function `destroyInstance()`:

```
void VulkanInstance::destroyInstance(){
    vkDestroyInstance(instance, NULL); // Destroy the instance
}
```

Inside this function, it calls the `vkDestroyInstance()` API, which accepts the handle of the Vulkan instance that needs to be destroyed. The following is the syntax of this API followed by its description:

```
VkResult vkDestroyInstance(
        VkInstance                      instance,
        const VkAllocationCallbacks*    pAllocator);
```

The following fields are associated with the `vkDestroyInstance` API:

Parameters	Description
instance	The is the handle of the Vulkan instance, which needs to be destroyed.
pAllocator	This specifies the host memory deallocation control.

Enabling layers and extensions

Enabling layers in Vulkan is simple. The application must be aware of the available layers in the current Vulkan implementation. This can be easily done by querying and printing the available instance-based layers; we have already covered this topic under the *Querying layers and extensions* subsection.

Refer to the following steps to enable layers and extensions:

1. Add two vector lists to the `VulkanLayerAndExtension` class. The first list contains the layer names that need to be enabled. The second contains the list of extensions that are used by the application:

```
class VulkanLayerAndExtension{
. . . .
    // List of layer names requested by the application.
        std::vector<const char *> appRequestedLayerNames;
```

Shaking Hands with the Device

```
    // List of extension names requested by the application.
        std::vector<const char *> appRequestedExtensionNames;
    . . .
};
```

2. In this application, we have enabled one layer (`VK_LAYER_LUNARG_api_dump`) and two extensions (`VK_KHR_SURFACE_EXTENSION_NAME` and `VK_KHR_WIN32-_SURFACE_EXTENSION_NAME`) in `main.cpp`. For more information, refer to the next subsection, *Testing the enabled layers and extensions*.

3. The `createInstance()` function contains a list of layers and extensions. If there is no list to specify, assign a `NULL` pointer to `ppEnabledLayerNames` and `ppEnabledExtensionNames`:

```
VkResult VulkanInstance::createInstance(char const*const
    appName, VulkanLayerAndExtension* layerExtension){
    . . . // Many line skipped
    VkInstanceCreateInfo instInfo = {};
    // Specify the list of layer name to be enabled.
    instInfo.enabledLayerCount    = layers.size();
    instInfo.ppEnabledLayerNames  = layers.data();

    // Specify the list of extensions to be enabled.
    instInfo.enabledExtensionCount    = extensionNames.size();
    instInfo.ppEnabledExtensionNames = extensionNames.data();

    VkResult res = vkCreateInstance(&instInfo,NULL,&instance);
}
```

> The LunarG Vulkan SDK supports different types of layers for debugging and validation purposes. In this example, we will enable `VK_LAYER_LUNARG_api_dump`; this layer prints the Vulkan API calls along with their parameters and values. Layers can be injected at runtime for instance-based layers. For more information on the features offered by other layers, refer to the *Understanding layer features* section in the next chapter.

Testing the enabled layers and extensions

Follow these instructions to test the output:

1. Create the `VulkanApplication` class and implement the constructor and a wrapper function (`createVulkanInstance`) to create the instance. Note that this is a singleton class. For more information, refer to the `VulkanApplication.h/.cpp` file:

   ```
   #include "VulkanInstance.h"
   #include "VulkanLED.h"
   class VulkanApplication {
   private:
      VulkanApplication();
   public:
      ~VulkanApplication();
   // Many lines skipped please refer to source
   // code for full implementation.
   public:
      // Create the Vulkan instance object
      VkResult createVulkanInstance
            (vector<const char *>& layers, vector<const char*
            > & extensions, const char* applicationName);

      // Vulkan Instance object
      VulkanInstance         instanceObj;

   };

   // Application constructor responsible for layer enumeration.
   VulkanApplication::VulkanApplication() {
      // At application start up, enumerate instance layers
      instanceObj.layerExtension.getInstanceLayerProperties();
   }
   // Wrapper function to create the Vulkan instance
   VkResult VulkanApplication::createVulkanInstance
            (vector<const char*>& layers, vector<const char *>&
      extensions, const char* appName){

      instanceObj.createInstance(layers, extensions, appName);

      return VK_SUCCESS;
   }
   ```

Shaking Hands with the Device

2. Set the instance-level layers and extensions from the main (`main.cpp`) program, enabling the instance layer `VK_LAYER_LUNARG_api_dump`. Also, add the extensions `VK_KHR_SURFACE_EXTENSION_NAME` and `VK_KHR_WIN32_SURFACE_EXTENSION_NAME`. This layer outputs the API call with their parameters and values:

```
#include "Headers.h"
#include "VulkanApplication.h"

std::vector<const char *> instanceExtensionNames = {
   VK_KHR_SURFACE_EXTENSION_NAME, VK_KHR_WIN32_SURFACE_EXTENSION_NAME
};

std::vector<const char *> layerNames = {
   "VK_LAYER_LUNARG_api_dump"
};


int main(int argc, char **argv){
   VkResult   res;
   // Create singleton object, calls Constructor function
   VulkanApplication* appObj =VulkanApplication::GetInstance();
        appObj->initialize();

}

// Application constructor responsible for layer enumeration.
void VulkanApplication::initialize()
{
   char title[] = "Hello World!!!";

   // Create the Vulkan instance with
   // specified layer and extension names.
   createVulkanInstance(layerNames, instanceExtensionNames,
                                           title);
}
```

3. Compile the project, open the terminal type, and go to the folder containing the executable. Type `[executable name].exe > [redirect file name]`, for example, `3_0_DeviceHandshake.exe > apiDump.txt`:

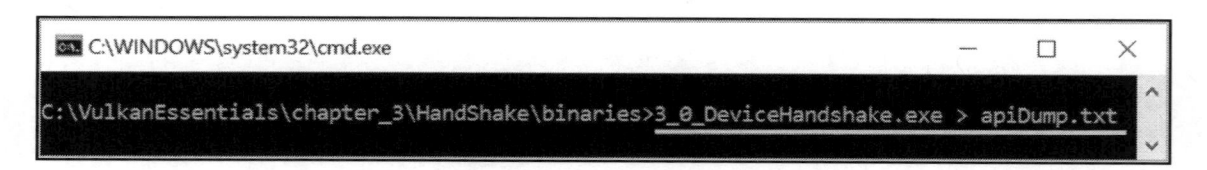

```
C:\WINDOWS\system32\cmd.exe

C:\VulkanEssentials\chapter_3\HandShake\binaries>3_0_DeviceHandshake.exe > apiDump.txt
```

4. This will result in the following output:

```
t{0} vkCreateInstance(pCreateInfo = 000000C697D0F570, pAllocator =
0000000000000000, pInstance = 0000025A40AED010) = VK_SUCCESS
   pCreateInfo (000000C697D0F570)
     sType = VK_STRUCTURE_TYPE_INSTANCE_CREATE_INFO
     pNext = 000000C697D0F548
     flags = 0
     pApplicationInfo = 000000C697D0F6B8
     enabledLayerCount = 1
     ppEnabledLayerNames = 0000025A3F0ED490
     enabledExtensionCount = 2
     ppEnabledExtensionNames = 0000025A3F0ED9E0
      ppEnabledExtensionNames[0] = VK_KHR_surface
      ppEnabledExtensionNames[1] = VK_KHR_win32_surface
      ppEnabledLayerNames[0] = VK_LAYER_LUNARG_api_dump
     pApplicationInfo (000000C697D0F588)
       sType = VK_STRUCTURE_TYPE_APPLICATION_INFO
       pNext = 0000000000000000
       pApplicationName = Draw Cube
       applicationVersion = 1
       pEngineName = Draw Cube
       engineVersion = 1
       apiVersion = 4194304
     pNext (000000C697D0F578)
```

> The layers can also be enabled explicitly, for instance by setting the Windows environment variables to VK_INSTANCE_LAYERS = VK_LAYER_LUNARG_api_dump.

Understanding physical and logical devices

Vulkan divides the representation of a device into two forms known as the logical and physical device:

- **Physical device**: A physical device represents a single workforce that may comprise a single GPU along with other hardware parts that work together to help the system accomplish the submitted jobs. On a very simple system, a physical device can be considered to represent the physical GPU unit.
- **Logical device**: A logical device represents the application view of the actual device.

Physical devices

OpenGL does not expose physical devices; it connects them behind the curtains. Vulkan, on the other hand, exposes the system real computing device or GPU to the application. It allows the application to enumerate the physical devices available on the system.

> In this section, we will add a new user-defined class called `VulkanDevice`; this class is implemented in `VulkanDevice.h/.cpp`. It is responsible for managing the physical (`VkPhysicalDevice`) and logical device (`VkDevice`). In addition, it also manages the physical device's queue families.

The following is the declaration of the `VulkanDevice` class; as we proceed through this chapter, we will uncover most of the functions used in this class. Refer to the accompanying source code for the full implementation of this header file declaration:

```cpp
class VulkanDevice{
public:
  VulkanDevice(VkPhysicalDevice* gpu); ~VulkanDevice();

  // Device related member variables
  VkDevice                 device;       // Logical device
  VkPhysicalDevice*        gpu;          // Physical device
  VkPhysicalDeviceProperties gpuProps;   // Physical device attributes
  VkPhysicalDeviceMemoryProperties memoryProperties;

  // Queue related properties
  // Vulkan Queues object
  VkQueue         queue;
  // Store all queue families exposed by the physical device.
  vector<VkQueueFamilyProperties>queueFamilyProps;

  // Stores graphics queue index
  uint32_t        graphicsQueueFamilyIndex;
  // Number of queue family exposed by device
  uint32_t        queueFamilyCount;
  // Device specific extensions
  VulkanLayerAndExtension    layerExtension;

  // This class exposes the below function to the outer world
  createDevice(),           memoryTypeFromProperties()
  destroyDevice(),          getGrahicsQueueHandle(),
  initializeDeviceQueue(),  getPhysicalDeviceQueuesAndProperties();
};
```

Enumerating physical devices

In order to establish a connection with the available physical devices, an application has to enumerate them. Physical device enumeration is a process by which Vulkan exposes the number of actual devices, which are available on the system, to the application. A list of physical devices can be retrieved using vkEnumeratePhysicalDevices().

The following is the syntax of this API:

```
VkResult  (
          VkInstance              instance,
          uint32_t                pPhysicalDeviceCount,
          VkPhysicalDevice*       pPhysicalDevice);
```

The following are the fields associated with this API:

Parameters	Description
instance	This is the handle of the Vulkan instance.
pPhysicalDeviceCount	This specifies the number of physical devices.
pPhysicalDevice	This is the Vulkan physical device object.

This API is wrapped in the Application class's enumeratePhysicalDevices function. It returns the number of physical device objects on the available system:

```
VkResult VulkanApplication::enumeratePhysicalDevices
            (std::vector<VkPhysicalDevice>& gpuList){
  // Holds the gpu count
  uint32_t gpuDeviceCount;
  // Get the gpu count
  vkEnumeratePhysicalDevices
  (instanceObj.instance, &gpuDeviceCount, NULL);

  // Make space for retrieval
  gpuList.resize(gpuDeviceCount);
  // Get Physical device object
  return vkEnumeratePhysicalDevices
  (instanceObj.instance, &gpuDeviceCount, gpuList.data());

}
```

The following diagram shows the enumerated physical devices on the system and is associated with the `VkInstance` object while querying:

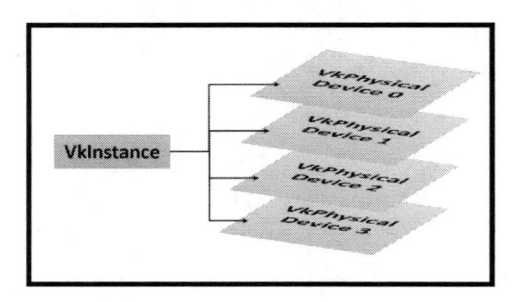

Querying physical device extensions

A physical device exposes extensions similar to Vulkan instances. For each retrieved instance layer property (`VkLayerProperties`), there may exist extension properties for each physical device that can be queried using the `vkEnumerateDeviceExtensionProperties()` API.

The following is the syntax of this API:

```
VkResult vkEnumerateDeviceExtensionProperties (
                VkPhysicalDevice          physicalDevice,
                const char*               pLayerName,
                uint32_t*                 pExtensionCount,
                VkExtensionProperties*    pProperties);
```

Here are the fields associated with this API:

Parameters	Description
`physicalDevice`	This represents the physical device to which the extension properties will be queried.
`pLayerName`	This is the name of the layer for which the extension needs to be queried.
`pExtensionCount`	This refers to the number of extension properties exposed by the current `physicalDevice` for a corresponding `pLayerName`.
`pProperties`	This represents a retrieved array; it contains the extension's property objects that correspond to the `pLayerName`.

The process of querying device-based extension properties is very similar to that of an instance-based one. The following is the implementation of this function:

```
VkResult VulkanLayerAndExtension::getDeviceExtensionProperties
                                    (VkPhysicalDevice* gpu)
{
    // Variable to check Vulkan API result status
    VkResult result;

    // Query all the extensions for each layer and store it.
    std::cout << "\Device extensions" << std::endl;
    std::cout << "====================" << std::endl;
    VulkanApplication* appObj = VulkanApplication::GetInstance();
    std::vector<LayerProperties>* instanceLayerProp =
                        &appObj->GetInstance()->instanceObj.
                        layerExtension.layerPropertyList;

    for (auto globalLayerProp : *instanceLayerProp) {
        LayerProperties layerProps;
        layerProps.properties = globalLayerProp.properties;

        if (result = getExtensionProperties(layerProps, gpu))
            continue;

        layerPropertyList.push_back(layerProps);

        // Many lines skipped..
    }
    return result;
}
```

Getting the properties of a physical device

The properties of a physical device can be retrieved using the `vkGetPhysicalDeviceProperties()` API; the attributes are retrieved in the `VkPhysicalDeviceProperties` control structure. Here's the syntax of this process:

```
void vkGetPhysicalDeviceMemoryProperties (
    VkPhysicalDevice                        physicalDevice,
    VkPhysicalDeviceMemoryProperties*       pMemoryProperties );
```

Shaking Hands with the Device

Here are the fields for `vkGetPhysicalDeviceMemoryProperties`:

Parameters	Description
physicalDevice	This is the GPU handle whose memory properties need to be retrieved.
pMemoryproperties	This is the structure that will retrieve the GPU memory properties.

Interrogating memory properties from the physical device

A single physical device may have different memory types, which are further differentiated based on their properties. It's important for an application to know the characteristics of the memory; this facilitates better allocation of the resources, depending upon the application logic or resource type. The following syntax is to retrieve the physical device memory properties:

```
void vkGetPhysicalDeviceMemoryProperties (
          VkPhysicalDevice                    physicalDevice,
          VkPhysicalDeviceMemoryProperties*   pMemoryProperties );
```

Here are the fields described for `vkGetPhysicalDeviceMemoryProperties`:

Parameters	Description
physicalDevice	This is the GPU handle whose memory properties need to be queried.
pMemoryProperties	This is for retrieving the memory properties.

Logical device

A logical device is the representation of a physical device, but it is used in the application space; it provides a specialized view of the physical device. For example, a physical device may consist of three queues: graphics, compute, and transfers. However, a logical device can be created with a single queue (say, graphics) attached to it; this makes it very easy to submit the command buffers.

Creating a logical device

A logical device is represented using `VkDevice` and can be created using the `vkCreateDevice` API. Here's the syntax of this:

```
VkResult vkCreateDevice(
                VkPhysicalDevice              pPhysicalDevice,
                Const VkDeviceCreateInfo*     pCreateInfo,
                const VkAllocationCallbacks*  pAllocator,
                VkDevice*                     pDevice);
```

For more information on API fields, refer to the following table:

Parameters	Description
`pPhysicalDevice`	This represents the physical device handle whose logical device is to be created.
`pCreateInfo`	This is the `VkDeviceCreateInfo` structure that contains specific information that will be utilized by the `vkCreateDevice()` API to control the creation of a logical device.
`pAllocator`	This specifies how to control host memory allocation. For more information, refer to the *Host memory* section in Chapter 5, *Command Buffer and Memory Management in Vulkan*.
`pDevice`	This refers to the created logical device pointer that contains the newly created `VkDevice` object.

This API uses the `VkDeviceCreateInfo` control structure object (`deviceInfo`), which contains the necessary information required to create a logical device object. For instance, it contains the names of the layers (this feature is deprecated and kept for backward-compatibility) and extensions that need to be enabled on the device. In addition, it also specifies which queue it should be creating and connect to. In our case, we are interested in drawing operations; therefore, we need a queue handle (`graphicsQueueIndex`) that will represent a queue that has the functionality of drawing capabilities. In other words, we need the graphics queue handle.

> The queue information is contained in the `VkDeviceQueueCreateInfo` structure object, `queueInfo`. When a logical device is created, it also creates the associated queues with it, using this structure. For more information on queues, how to find the graphics queue index, and the queue creation process, refer to the next section, *Understanding queues and queue families*.

Shaking Hands with the Device

`VulkanDevice::createDevice` is a user-defined wrapper method that helps to create the logical device object. Here is its implementation:

```
VkResult VulkanDevice::createDevice(vector<const char *>& layers,
                    vector<const char *>& extensions){

VkResult result;
float queuePriorities[1]        = { 0.0 };

// Create the object information
VkDeviceQueueCreateInfo queueInfo     = {};
queueInfo.queueFamilyIndex            = graphicsQueueIndex;
queueInfo.sType = VK_STRUCTURE_TYPE_DEVICE_QUEUE_CREATE_INFO;
queueInfo.pNext                       = NULL;
queueInfo.queueCount                  = 1;
queueInfo.pQueuePriorities            = queuePriorities;

VkDeviceCreateInfo deviceInfo = {};
deviceInfo.sType       = VK_STRUCTURE_TYPE_DEVICE_CREATE_INFO;
deviceInfo.pNext                      = NULL;
deviceInfo.queueCreateInfoCount       = 1;
deviceInfo.pQueueCreateInfos          = &queueInfo;
deviceInfo.enabledLayerCount          = 0;
// Device layers are deprecated
deviceInfo.ppEnabledLayerNames        = NULL;
deviceInfo.enabledExtensionCount      = extensions.size();
deviceInfo.ppEnabledExtensionNames    = extensions.data();
deviceInfo.pEnabledFeatures           = NULL;

result = vkCreateDevice(*gpu, &deviceInfo, NULL, &device);

assert(result == VK_SUCCESS);
return result;
}
```

Waiting on the host

A device is said to be active as long as it has jobs in the queues to process. Once the queues have no more command buffers to process, the device becomes idle. The following `vkDeviceWaitIdle` API waits on the host until all the queues for the logical device become idle. This API accepts the argument that takes the handle of the logical device object for which the idle status is to be checked. Here's the syntax for this:

```
VkResult vkDeviceWaitIdle( VkDevice device);
```

Losing the device

While working with logical (VKDevice) and physical (VKPhysicalDevice) devices for a certain reason–such as hardware malfunction, device error, execution timeouts, power management events, and/or platform-specific events–the devices can be lost. This may result in failing to execute the pending commands buffer.

> **TIP**
> When a physical device is lost, the attempt to create a logical device object (VKDevice) will fail and it will return VK_ERROR_DEVICE_LOST. If the logical device object is lost, certain commands will return VK_ERROR_DEVICE_LOST upon its use. However, the corresponding physical device may remain unaffected. It is not possible to reset the lost state of the logical device, and this loss of state is local to the logical device object (VKDevice) and does not affect any other active logical device objects.

Understanding queues and queue families

Queues are the means by which an application and a physical device communicate. The application provides the jobs in the form of a command buffer that is submitted to the queues. These are read by the physical device and processed asynchronously.

A physical device may support four types of queues, as shown in the following diagram. There could be multiple queues of the same type on a physical device; this allows the application to choose the number of queues and what type of queue it needs. For example, a simple application may require two queues: compute and graphics; here, the former is used for convolution computing and the second renders the computed blur image.

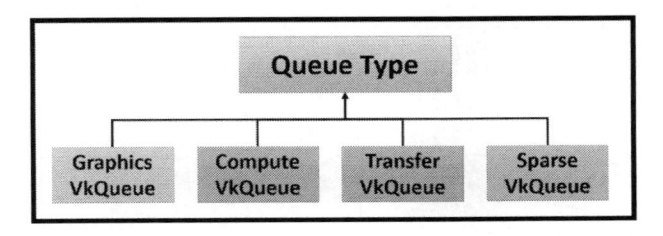

```
                    Queue Type
         ┌─────────┬─────┴─────┬─────────┐
      Graphics   Compute    Transfer    Sparse
      VkQueue    VkQueue    VkQueue    VkQueue
```

Shaking Hands with the Device

A physical device may consist of one or more queue families exposing what types of queue exist inside each queue family. Further, each queue family may have one or more queue count. The following diagram shows three queue families with their respective multiple queues:

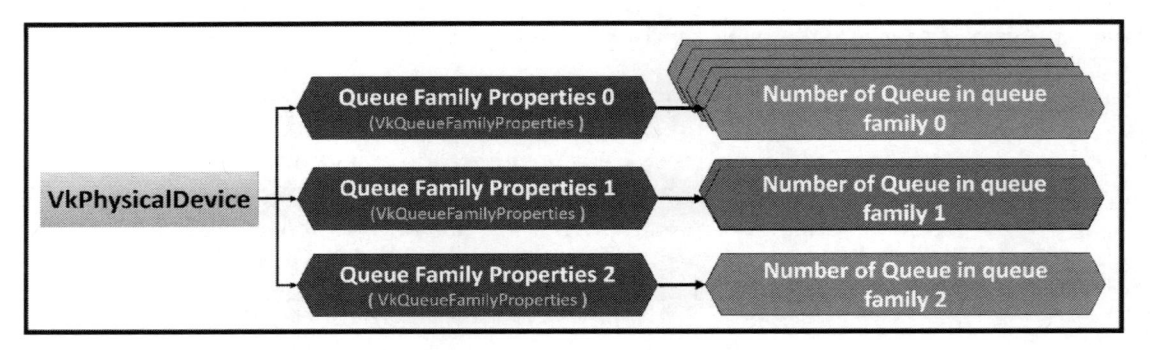

Querying queue families

A physical device is capable of exposing multiple queue families.

The number of queue family properties are exposed by the vkGetPhysicalDeviceQueueFamilyProperties() API, as described here:

```
VkResult vkGetPhysicalDeviceQueueFamilyProperties (
          VkPhysicalDevice          physicalDevice,
          uint32_t*                 pQueueFamilyPropertyCount,
          VkQueueFamilyProperties*  pQueueFamilyProperties);
```

Here are the fields for this API:

Parameters	Description
physicalDevice	This is the physical device handle whose queue properties are to be retrieved.
pQueueFamilyPropertyCount	This refers to the number of queue families exposed by the device.
pQueueFamilyProperties	This field retrieves the queue family properties in an array of size equal to queueFamilyPropertyCount.

Queues are divided into families according to capabilities that are similar in nature. The following code snippet from the `VulkanDevice` class shows how to query the queue families and their properties in the `VkQueueFamilyProperties` control structure object, namely `queueFamilyProps`.

In our implementation, the queue family properties are queried in a wrapper function called `getPhysicalDeviceQueuesAndProperties()`, defined in the `VulkanDevice` class. The following is the implementation:

```
void VulkanDevice::getPhysicalDeviceQueuesAndProperties(){
    // Query queue families count by passing NULL as second parameter
    vkGetPhysicalDeviceQueueFamilyProperties(*gpu, &queueFamilyCount,
    NULL);
    // Allocate space to accomodate Queue properties
    queueFamilyProps.resize(queueFamilyCount);

    // Get queue family properties
    vkGetPhysicalDeviceQueueFamilyProperties
      (*gpu, &queueFamilyCount, queueFamilyProps.data());
}
```

The `queueFlag` field of this structure contains the family information in the form of the following flag bits:

Flag bit	Queue family meaning
VK_QUEUE_GRAPHICS_BIT	This is a graphics queue; it supports graphics-related operations.
VK_QUEUE_COMPUTE_BIT	This is a compute queue; it offers computation capabilities.
VK_QUEUE_TRANSFER_BIT	This is a transfer queue; it supports transfers.
VK_QUEUE_SPARSE_BINDING_BIT	This is a sparse queue; it is capable of sparse memory management.

Each queue family may support one or more queue types, which are indicated by the `queueFlag` field of `VkQueueFamilyProperties`. The `queueCount` specifies the number of queues in the queue family. The third field `timestampVaildBits` is used to time the command execution. The last parameter `minImageTransferGranularity` specifies the minimum granularity image transfer operations in the present queue family support. Here is the syntax for this:

```
typedef struct VkQueueFamilyProperties {
    VkQueueFlags    queueFlags;
    uint32_t        queueCount;
```

Shaking Hands with the Device

```
    uint32_t        timestampValidBits;
    VkExtent3D      minImageTransferGranularity;
} VkQueueFamilyProperties;
```

The following diagram shows how the queue and queue families are related in a physical device. In this particular illustration, a physical device comprises four types of queue family, where each of these contains different capabilities in terms of the queue type (`queueFlags`) it supports and the number of queues (`queueCount`) in each family.

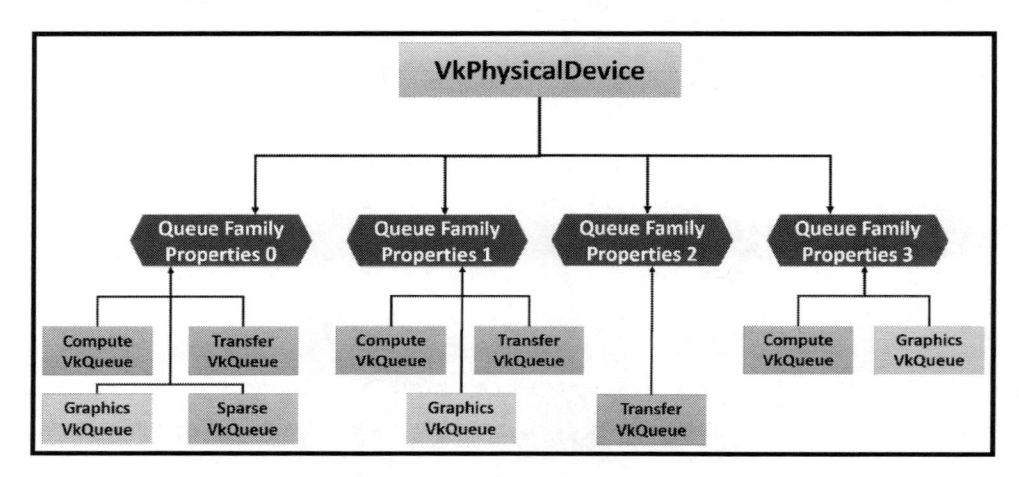

Storing the graphics queue handle

The creation of a logical device object also needs a valid queue handle (in the form of an index) in order to create the associated queue with it. For this, iterate through all the queried queue family properties and check for the
`VkQueueFamilyProperties::queueFlags` bit information to find the appropriate queue. For example, we are interested in the graphics queue handle. The following code stores the handle of the graphics queue in `graphicsQueueIndex`, which is used in the creation of the logical device (`VkDevice`) object:

```
uint32_t VulkanDevice::getGrahicsQueueHandle(){
  bool found = false;
  // 1. Iterate number of Queues supported by the Physical device
  for (unsigned int i = 0; i < queueFamilyCount; i++){
      // 2. Get the Graphics Queue type
    if (queueFamilyProps[i].queueFlags & VK_QUEUE_GRAPHICS_BIT){
        // 3. Get the handle/index ID of graphics queue family.
        found              = true;
        graphicsQueueIndex = i;
```

```
            break;
        }
    }         return 0;
}
```

Creating a queue

Queues are created implicitly when a logical device object is created using the `vkCreateDevice()` API. This API also intakes the queue information in the form of `VkDeviceQueueCreateInfo`. The following is the syntax and associated field's description:

```
typedef struct VkDeviceQueueCreateInfo {
    VkStructureType             type;
    const void*                 pNext;
    VkDeviceQueueCreateFlags    flags;
    uint32_t                    queueFamilyIndex;
    uint32_t                    queueCount;
    const float*                pQueuePriorities;
} VkDeviceQueueCreateInfo;
```

The following table describes each field of this API:

Parameters	Description
`type`	This is the type information of this control structure. It must be specified as `VK_STRUCTURE_TYPE_DEVICE_QUEUE_CREATE_INFO`.
`pNext`	This field could be a valid pointer to an extension-specific structure or `NULL`.
`flags`	These are unused flags, which are reserved for future use.
`queueFamilyIndex`	This queues family information specified in the form of a 32-bit `unsigned int` queue index type. For example, in our case we supplied the `graphicsQueueIndex` variable, which contains the graphics queue index.
`queueCount`	This refers to the number of queue families to be created.
`pQueuePriorities`	This field represents an array of normalized floating-point values that specify the priority of the work submitted to each created queue.

Shaking Hands with the Device

As we already know, queues are automatically created when a logical device object is created. The created queue can then be retrieved by the application using the `vkGetDeviceQueue()` API. The following function (`getDeviceQueue()`) from the `VulkanDevice` class provides a high-level wrapper function to get the device's associated queue:

```
void VulkanDevice::getDeviceQueue(){
   vkGetDeviceQueue(device, graphicsQueueWithPresentIndex, 0, &queue);
}
```

Here is the syntax for this:

```
void vkGetDeviceQueue (
            VkDevice            logicalDevice,
            uint32_t            queueFamilyIndex,
            uint32_t            queueIndex,
            VkQueue*            pQueue);
```

For more information about the API fields, refer to the following table:

Parameters	Description
`logicalDevice`	This refers to the logical device (`VkDevice`) object that owns the queue.
`queueFamilyIndex`	This field indicates the index number of the family to which the queue (`pQueue`) belongs.
`queueIndex`	There could be multiple queues within a queue family, where each queue is identified by a unique index. This field indicates the index of the queue within the queue family (indicated by `queueFamilyIndex`).
`pQueue`	This is the retrieved queue object returned by this API.

> The desired queue object that is intended to be queried from the logical device object will be deferred at this point. This is because we are interested in a queue that is capable of providing presentation capabilities, and for this, we need to wait until Chapter 6, *Allocating Image Resources and Building a Swapchain with WSI*. In this chapter, we will learn how to implement the swapchain for presentation purposes.

Implementing devices and queues all together

In this section, we will revisit all of the knowledge we've gathered in this chapter so far and implement a program to create the device and queues from an application's view. Let's look at a step-by-step process that describes the flow of information.

First, enumerate the physical devices on the system using `enumeratePhysicalDevices()`; the retrieved physical device is stored in the `gpuList` vector. For the sake of simplicity, we are assuming the system has only one GPU (using the first element of `gpuList`). Next, we handshake with the device using the `handShakeWithDevice()` function:

```
/********** VulkanApplication.cpp **********/
// Get the list of physical devices on the system
vector<VkPhysicalDevice> gpuList;

enumeratePhysicalDevices(gpuList);

if (gpuList.size() > 0) {
    appObj->handShakeWithDevice
    (&gpuList[0], layerNames, deviceExtensionNames);
}

void VulkanApplication::initialize()
{
    // Many lines skipped please refer to the source code.

    // Get the list of physical devices on the system
    std::vector<VkPhysicalDevice> gpuList;
    enumeratePhysicalDevices(gpuList);
    // This example use only one device which is available first.
    if (gpuList.size() > 0) {
      handShakeWithDevice(&gpuList[0], layerNames,
                          deviceExtensionNames);
    }
}
```

[105]

Shaking Hands with the Device

The `VulkanApplication::enumeratePhysicalDevices()` function makes use of `vkEnumeratePhysicalDevices` and gathers the number of physical devices (`VKPhysicalDevice`) onboard. The application asserts whether there is a GPU to work with. Next, it allocates the necessary space to store this information in a vector list and provides it to the same API (`vkEnumeratePhysicalDevices`) again, along with the GPU count, to get the physical device objects:

```
/**************** Application.cpp ****************/
VkResult VulkanApplication::enumeratePhysicalDevices
        (vector<VkPhysicalDevice>& gpuList){
   uint32_t gpuDeviceCount;

   VkResult result = vkEnumeratePhysicalDevices
        (instanceObj.instance, &gpuDeviceCount, NULL);
      assert(result == VK_SUCCESS);

            gpuList.resize(gpuDeviceCount); assert(gpuDeviceCount);

   result = vkEnumeratePhysicalDevices
      (instanceObj.instance, &gpuDeviceCount, gpuList.data());
      assert(result == VK_SUCCESS);

   return result;
}
```

`VulkanApplication::handShakeWithDevice()` is responsible for creating the logical device objects and the queues associated with them. It also does some initialization jobs, which are necessary at a later stage of application development, such as getting the physical device properties and memory properties. Here is the syntax for this API:

```
void VulkanApplication::handShakeWithDevice (
VkPhysicalDevice*              gpu,
std::vector<const char*>&      extensions,
int                            queueIndex);
```

Here are the description for the fields:

Parameters	Description
gpu	This is the physical device to which the application performs the handshake.
layers	This is the name of the layer that needs to be enabled at gpu.
extensions	This refers to the extension names that need to be enabled at gpu.

The inside process of the `VulkanApplication::handShakeWithDevice()` function is described as follows:

- Use the `VulkanDevice` object and query the extensions exposed by the associated physical device. The retrieved extensions can be cross-checked against the application-requested extensions to check whether they are supported by the physical device or not.
- Retrieve the physical device properties using `vkGetPhysical-DeviceProperties()` and store them in the local data structure (`gpuProps`) of `VulkanDevice` for later use.
- Get the memory information and its properties offered by the physical device using the `vkGetPhysicalDeviceMemoryProperties()` API.
- Query all the queue families supported by the physical device using the `getPhysicalDeviceQueuesAndProperties()` helper function of `VulkanDevice` class and store their properties for later use.
- Traverse through all the queues and check which queue supports graphics operations. This is done using the `getGraphicsQueueHandle()` function; this function returns the index or handle of the queue, which can be used to perform the graphics operations.
- Finally, `VulkanDevice::createDevice()` is called to create the logical device object associated with the physical device. This function uses the graphics queue handle and also creates the queue associated with the logical device object. In addition, this function also accepts the extensions' name list, which needs to be enabled on the physical device:

```
/**************** Application.cpp ****************/
// High level function for creating device and queues
   VkResult VulkanApplication::handShakeWithDevice(
   VkPhysicalDevice* gpu, std::vector<const char *>& layers,
   std::vector<const char *>& extensions )
   {

   // The user define Vulkan Device object.
   // This will manage the Physical and logical
   // device and their queue and properties
   deviceObj = new VulkanDevice(gpu);
        if (!deviceObj){
           return VK_ERROR_OUT_OF_HOST_MEMORY;
   }
   // Print the devices available layer and their extension
   deviceObj->layerExtension.
                 getDeviceExtensionProperties(gpu);
```

```
    // Get the physical device or GPU properties
    vkGetPhysicalDeviceProperties(*gpu, &deviceObj->gpuProps);

    // Get memory properties from the physical device or GPU.
    vkGetPhysicalDeviceMemoryProperties(*gpu,
                    &deviceObj->memoryProperties);

    // Query the availabe queues on the physical
    // device and their properties.
    deviceObj->getPhysicalDeviceQueuesAndProperties();

    // Retrive the queue which support graphics pipeline.
    deviceObj->getGrahicsQueueHandle();

    // Create Logical Device, ensure that this
    // device is connect to graphics queue
    deviceObj->createDevice(layers, extensions);

    return VK_SUCCESS;
  }
```

Summary

In this chapter, we got our hands dirty with Vulkan programming. We understood the setup and building process of the Vulkan project using CMake and the LunarG SDK. We started with Vulkan basics, with layers and extensions, and learned the step-by-step process to query them. We created a Vulkan instance and demonstrated the instructions to enable and test the layers and extensions at an instance level.

Further, we discussed devices and queues. We explored the differences between physical and logical device objects. We programmed the enumeration of the physical device on a system and learned to enable device-specific extensions. We enumerated the queue families associated with each physical device. Using the queue properties, we chose the graphics queue and created the logical device object.

Finally, we summed up all of our understanding and implemented the process of handshaking with the device, which includes the creation of physical and logical device objects along with their queues.

Debugging provides a better opportunity to learn through mistakes with valid reasons. In the next chapter, we will learn the debugging process in Vulkan, which is extremely important from a developer's perspective. Vulkan is a new graphics API and has a completely different programming paradigm from traditional APIs. The debugging capabilities provide a better way to understand these APIs.

4
Debugging in Vulkan

In the last chapter, we initialized the Vulkan API and about learned the concepts of layers and extensions. We connected with the physical hardware device and understood the different types of queue exposed by it. Since we are gearing up for practical implementations, it's important that we learn the Vulkan debugging in order to avoid unpleasant mistakes.

Vulkan allows you to perform debugging through validation layers. These validation layer checks are optional and can be injected into the system at runtime. Traditional graphics APIs perform validation right up front using some sort of error-checking mechanism, which is a mandatory part of the pipeline. This is indeed useful in the development phase, but actually, it is an overhead during the release stage because the validation bugs might have already been fixed at the development phase itself. Such compulsory checks cause the CPU to spend a significant amount of time in error checking.

On the other hand, Vulkan is designed to offer maximum performance, where the optional validation process and debugging model play a vital role. Vulkan assumes the application has done its homework using the validation and debugging capabilities available at the development stage, and it can be trusted flawlessly at the release stage.

In this chapter, we will learn about the validation and debugging process of a Vulkan application. We will cover the following topics:

- Peeking into Vulkan debugging
- Understanding LunarG validation layers and their features
- Implementing debugging in Vulkan

Peeking into Vulkan debugging

Vulkan debugging validates application implementation. It surfaces not only errors, but also other validations, such as proper API usage. It does so by verifying each parameter passed to it, warning about the potentially incorrect and dangerous API practices in use and reporting any performance-related warnings when the API is not used optimally. By default, debugging is disabled, and it's the application's responsibility to enable it. Debugging works only for those layers that are explicitly enabled at the instance level at the time of instance creation (VkInstance).

When debugging is enabled, it inserts itself into the call chain for the Vulkan commands the layer is interested in. For each command, the debugging visits all the enabled layers and validates them for any potential error, warning, debugging information, and so on.

Debugging in Vulkan is simple. The following is an overview that describes the steps required to enable it in an application:

1. Enable debugging capabilities by adding the VK_EXT_DEBUG_REPORT_EXTENSION_NAME extension at the instance level.
2. Define the set of validation layers intended for debugging. For example, we are interested in the following layers at the instance and device level. For more information about these layer functionalities, refer to the next section:
    - VK_LAYER_GOOGLE_unique_objects
    - VK_LAYER_LUNARG_api_dump
    - VK_LAYER_LUNARG_core_validation
    - VK_LAYER_LUNARG_image
    - VK_LAYER_LUNARG_object_tracker
    - VK_LAYER_LUNARG_parameter_validation
    - VK_LAYER_LUNARG_swapchain
    - VK_LAYER_GOOGLE_threading
3. The Vulkan debugging APIs are not part of the core command, which can be statically loaded by the loader. These are available in the form of extension APIs that can be retrieved at runtime and dynamically linked to the predefined function pointers. So, as the next step, the debug extension APIs vkCreateDebugReportCallbackEXT and vkDestroyDebugReportCallbackEXT are queried and linked dynamically. These are used for the creation and destruction of the debug report.

4. Once the function pointers for the debug report are retrieved successfully, the former API (`vkCreateDebugReportCallbackEXT`) creates the debug report object. Vulkan returns the debug reports in a user-defined callback, which has to be linked to this API.
5. Destroy the debug report object when debugging is no longer required.

Understanding LunarG validation layers and their features

The LunarG Vulkan SDK supports the following layers for debugging and validation purposes. In the following points, we have described some of the layers that will help you understand the offered functionalities:

- `VK_LAYER_GOOGLE_unique_objects`: Non-dispatchable Vulkan objects handles are not required to be unique; a driver may return the same handle for multiple objects that it considers equivalent. This behavior makes tracking the object difficult because it is not clear which object to reference at the time of deletion. This layer packs the Vulkan objects into a unique identifier at the time of creation and unpacks them when the application uses it. This ensures there is proper object lifetime tracking at the time of validation. As per LunarG's recommendation, this layer must be last in the chain of the validation layer, making it closer to the display driver.
- `VK_LAYER_LUNARG_api_dump`: This layer is helpful in knowing the parameter values passed to the Vulkan APIs. It prints all the data structure parameters along with their values.
- `VK_LAYER_LUNARG_core_validation`: This is used for validating and printing important pieces of information from the descriptor set, pipeline state, dynamic state, and so on. This layer tracks and validates the GPU memory, object binding, and command buffers. Also, it validates the graphics and compute pipelines.
- `VK_LAYER_LUNARG_image`: This layer can be used for validating texture formats, rendering target formats, and so on. For example, it verifies whether the requested format is supported on the device. It validates whether the image view creation parameters are reasonable for the image that the view is being created for.
- `VK_LAYER_LUNARG_object_tracker`: This keeps track of object creation along with its use and destruction, which is helpful in avoiding memory leaks. It also validates that the referenced object is properly created and is presently valid.

[111]

Debugging in Vulkan

- `VK_LAYER_LUNARG_parameter_validation`: This validation layer ensures that all the parameters passed to the API are correct as per the specification and are up to the required expectation. It checks whether the value of a parameter is consistent and within the valid usage criteria defined in the Vulkan specification. Also, it checks whether the type field of a Vulkan control structure contains the same value that is expected for a structure of that type.
- `VK_LAYER_LUNARG_swapchain`: This layer validates the use of the WSI swapchain extensions. For example, it checks whether the WSI extension is available before its functions could be used. Also, it validates that an image index is within the number of images in a swapchain.
- `VK_LAYER_GOOGLE_threading`: This is helpful in the context of thread safety. It checks the validity of multithreaded API usage. This layer ensures the simultaneous use of objects using calls running under multiple threads. It reports threading rule violations and enforces a mutex for such calls. Also, it allows an application to continue running without actually crashing, despite the reported threading problem.
- `VK_LAYER_LUNARG_standard_validation`: This enables all the standard layers in the correct order.

> For more information on validation layers, visit LunarG's official website. Check out `https://vulkan.lunarg.com/doc/sdk` and specifically refer to the **Validation Layer Details** section for more details.

Implementing debugging in Vulkan

Since debugging is exposed by validation layers, most of the core implementation of the debugging will be done under the `VulkanLayerAndExtension` class (`VulkanLED.h/.cpp`). In this section, we will learn about the implementation that will help us enable the debugging process in Vulkan:

The Vulkan debug facility is not part of the default core functionalities. Therefore, in order to enable debugging and access the report callback feature, we need to add the necessary extensions and layers:

- **Extension**: Add the `VK_EXT_DEBUG_REPORT_EXTENSION_NAME` extension to the instance level. This will help in exposing the Vulkan debug APIs to the application:

   ```
   vector<const char *> instanceExtensionNames = {
   ```

[112]

```
. . . . // other extensios
VK_EXT_DEBUG_REPORT_EXTENSION_NAME,
};
```

- **Layer**: Define the following layers at the instance level to allow debugging at these layers:

```
vector<const char *> layerNames = {
    "VK_LAYER_GOOGLE_threading",
    "VK_LAYER_LUNARG_parameter_validation",
    "VK_LAYER_LUNARG_device_limits",
    "VK_LAYER_LUNARG_object_tracker",
    "VK_LAYER_LUNARG_image",
    "VK_LAYER_LUNARG_core_validation",
    "VK_LAYER_LUNARG_swapchain",
    "VK_LAYER_GOOGLE_unique_objects"
};
```

> In addition to the enabled validation layers, the LunarG SDK provides a special layer called `VK_LAYER_LUNARG_standard_validation`. This enables basic validation in the correct order as mentioned here. Also, this built-in metadata layer loads a standard set of validation layers in the optimal order. It is a good choice if you are not very specific when it comes to a layer.
> a) `VK_LAYER_GOOGLE_threading`
> b) `VK_LAYER_LUNARG_parameter_validation`
> c) `VK_LAYER_LUNARG_object_tracker`
> d) `VK_LAYER_LUNARG_image`
> e) `VK_LAYER_LUNARG_core_validation`
> f) `VK_LAYER_LUNARG_swapchain`
> g) `VK_LAYER_GOOGLE_unique_objects`

These layers are then supplied to the `vkCreateInstance()` API to enable them:

```
VulkanApplication* appObj = VulkanApplication::GetInstance();
appObj->createVulkanInstance(layerNames,
            instanceExtensionNames, title);

// VulkanInstance::createInstance()
VkResult VulkanInstance::createInstance(vector<const char *>&
    layers, std::vector<const char *>& extensionNames,
    char const*const appName)
{
```

Debugging in Vulkan

```
. . .
    VkInstanceCreateInfo instInfo      = {};

    // Specify the list of layer name to be enabled.
    instInfo.enabledLayerCount   = layers.size();
    instInfo.ppEnabledLayerNames = layers.data();

    // Specify the list of extensions to
    // be used in the application.
    instInfo.enabledExtensionCount    = extensionNames.size();
    instInfo.ppEnabledExtensionNames  = extensionNames.data();
    . . .
    vkCreateInstance(&instInfo, NULL, &instance);
}
```

The validation layer is very specific to the vendor and SDK version. Therefore, it is advisable to first check whether the layers are supported by the underlying implementation before passing them to the `vkCreateInstance()` API. This way, the application remains portable throughout when run against another driver implementation.

The `areLayersSupported()` function is a user-defined utility function that inspects the incoming layer names against system-supported layers. The unsupported layers are notified to the application and removed from the layer names before feeding them into the system:

```
// VulkanLED.cpp

VkBool32 VulkanLayerAndExtension::areLayersSupported
        (vector<const    char *> &layerNames)
{
    uint32_t checkCount = layerNames.size();
    uint32_t layerCount = layerPropertyList.size();
    std::vector<const char*> unsupportLayerNames;
    for (uint32_t i = 0; i < checkCount; i++) {
      VkBool32 isSupported = 0;
      for (uint32_t j = 0; j < layerCount; j++) {
      if (!strcmp(layerNames[i], layerPropertyList[j].
       properties.layerName)) {
            isSupported = 1;
         }
      }

      if (!isSupported) {
          std::cout << "No Layer support found, removed"
            " from layer: "<< layerNames[i] << endl;
          unsupportLayerNames.push_back(layerNames[i]);
      }
```

```
    else {
      cout << "Layer supported: " << layerNames[i] << endl;
    }
  }

  for (auto i : unsupportLayerNames) {
      auto it = std::find(layerNames.begin(),
                  layerNames.end(), i);
      if (it != layerNames.end()) layerNames.erase(it);
  }

  return true;
}
```

The debug report is created using the `vkCreateDebugReportCallbackEXT` API. This API is not a part of Vulkan's core commands; therefore, the loader is unable to link it statically. If you try to access it in the following manner, you will get an undefined symbol reference error:

```
vkCreateDebugReportCallbackEXT(instance, NULL, NULL, NULL);
```

All debug-related APIs need to be queried using the `vkGetInstanceProcAddr()` API and linked dynamically. The retrieved API reference is stored in a corresponding function pointer called `PFN_vkCreateDebugReportCallbackEXT`. The `VulkanLayerAndExtension::createDebugReportCallback()` function retrieves the create and destroy debug APIs, as shown in the following implementation:

```
/********* VulkanLED.h *********/
// Declaration of the create and destroy function pointers
PFN_vkCreateDebugReportCallbackEXT  dbgCreateDebugReportCallback;
PFN_vkDestroyDebugReportCallbackEXT dbgDestroyDebugReportCallback;


/********* VulkanLED.cpp *********/
VulkanLayerAndExtension::createDebugReportCallback(){
    . . .

// Get vkCreateDebugReportCallbackEXT API
dbgCreateDebugReportCallback=(PFN_vkCreateDebugReportCallbackEXT)
vkGetInstanceProcAddr(*instance,"vkCreateDebugReportCallbackEXT");
   if (!dbgCreateDebugReportCallback) {
        std::cout << "Error: GetInstanceProcAddr unable to locate
 vkCreateDebugReportCallbackEXT function.\n";
        return VK_ERROR_INITIALIZATION_FAILED;
   }
   // Get vkDestroyDebugReportCallbackEXT API
   dbgDestroyDebugReportCallback=
```

Debugging in Vulkan

```
    (PFN_vkDestroyDebugReportCallbackEXT)vkGetInstanceProcAddr
    (*instance, "vkDestroyDebugReportCallbackEXT");

    if (!dbgDestroyDebugReportCallback) {
     std::cout << "Error: GetInstanceProcAddr unable to locate
            vkDestroyDebugReportCallbackEXT function.\n";
     return VK_ERROR_INITIALIZATION_FAILED;
    }
    . . .
}
```

The `vkGetInstanceProcAddr()` API obtains instance-level extensions dynamically; these extensions are not exposed statically on a platform and need to be linked through this API dynamically. The following is the signature of this API:

```
PFN_vkVoidFunction vkGetInstanceProcAddr(
                        VkInstance       instance,
                        const char*      name);
```

The following table describes the API fields:

Parameters	Description
instance	This is a `VkInstance` variable. If this variable is `NULL`, then the name must be one of these: `vkEnumerateInstanceExtensionProperties`, `vkEnumerateInstanceLayerProperties`, or `vkCreateInstance`.
name	This is the name of the API that needs to be queried for dynamic linking.

Using the `dbgCreateDebugReportCallback()` function pointer, create the debugging report object and store the handle in `debugReportCallback`. The second parameter of the API accepts a `VkDebugReportCallbackCreateInfoEXT` control structure. This data structure defines the behavior of the debugging, such as what the debug information should include: errors, general warnings, information, performance-related warnings, debug information, and so on. In addition, it also takes the reference of a user-defined function (`debugFunction`); this helps filter and print the debugging information once it is retrieved from the system. Here's the syntax for creating a debugging report:

```
struct VkDebugReportCallbackCreateInfoEXT {
        VkStructureType                  type;
        const void*                      pNext;
        VkDebugReportFlagsEXT            flags;
        PFN_vkDebugReportCallbackEXT     fnCallback;
        void*                            pUserData;
};
```

The following table describes the purpose of the mentioned API fields:

Parameters	Description
type	This is the type information of this control structure. It must be specified as VK_STRUCTURE_TYPE_DEBUG_REPORT_CREATE_INFO_EXT.
flags	This is to define the kind of debugging information to be retrieved when debugging is on; the next table defines these flags.
fnCallback	This field refers to the function that filters and displays debug messages.

The VkDebugReportFlagBitsEXT control structure can exhibit a bitwise combination of the following flag values:

Flag values	Description
VK_DEBUG_REPORT_INFORMATION_BIT_EXT	This is to display user-friendly information describing the background activities in the currently running application, for example, resource details that may be useful when debugging an application.
VK_DEBUG_REPORT_WARNING_BIT_EXT	This is to provide a warning message for potentially incorrect or dangerous use of the API.
VK_DEBUG_REPORT_PERFORMANCE_WARNING_BIT_EXT	This indicates a potentially non-optimal use of Vulkan, which may result in performance loss.
VK_DEBUG_REPORT_ERROR_BIT_EXT	This refers to an error message specifying incorrect API usage, which may cause undefined results–for example, application crash.
VK_DEBUG_REPORT_DEBUG_BIT_EXT	This indicates diagnostic information from the loader and layer.

Debugging in Vulkan

The `createDebugReportCallback` function implements the creation of the debug report. First, it creates the `VulkanLayerAndExtension` control structure object and fills it with relevant information. This primarily includes two things: first, assigning a user-defined function (`pfnCallback`) that will print the debug information received from the system (see the next point), and second, assigning the debugging flag (`flags`) in which the programmer is interested:

```
/********* VulkanLED.h *********/
// Handle of the debug report callback
VkDebugReportCallbackEXT debugReportCallback;
// Debug report callback create information control structure
VkDebugReportCallbackCreateInfoEXT dbgReportCreateInfo = {};


/********* VulkanLED.cpp *********/
VulkanLayerAndExtension::createDebugReportCallback(){
. . .
    // Define the debug report control structure,
    // provide the reference of 'debugFunction',
    // this function prints the debug information on the console.
    dbgReportCreateInfo.sType          = VK_STRUCTURE_TYPE_DEBUG
                                         _REPORT_CREATE_INFO_EXT;
    dbgReportCreateInfo.pfnCallback = debugFunction;
    dbgReportCreateInfo.pUserData   = NULL;
    dbgReportCreateInfo.pNext       = NULL;
    dbgReportCreateInfo.flags       = VK_DEBUG_REPORT_WARNING_BIT_EXT |
                                      VK_DEBUG_REPORT_PERFORMANCE
                                      _WARNING_BIT_EXT |
                                      VK_DEBUG_REPORT_ERROR_BIT_EXT |
                                      VK_DEBUG_REPORT_DEBUG_BIT_EXT;

    // Create the debug report callback and store the handle
    // into 'debugReportCallback'
    result = dbgCreateDebugReportCallback
        (*instance, &dbgReportCreateInfo, NULL, &debugReportCallback);

    if (result == VK_SUCCESS) {
     cout << "Debug report callback object created successfully\n";
    }
    return result;
}
```

Define the `debugFunction()` function that prints the retrieved debug information in a user-friendly way. It describes the type of debug information along with the reported message:

```
VKAPI_ATTR VkBool32 VKAPI_CALL
```

Chapter 4

```
VulkanLayerAndExtension::debugFunction( VkFlags msgFlags,
        VkDebugReportObjectTypeEXT objType, uint64_t srcObject,
        size_t location, int32_t msgCode, const char *pLayerPrefix,
        const char *pMsg, void *pUserData) {
    if (msgFlags & VK_DEBUG_REPORT_ERROR_BIT_EXT) {
        std::cout << "[VK_DEBUG_REPORT] ERROR: ["<<layerPrefix<<"]
                            Code" << msgCode << ":" << msg << std::endl;

    }
    else if (msgFlags & VK_DEBUG_REPORT_WARNING_BIT_EXT) {
        std::cout << "[VK_DEBUG_REPORT] WARNING: ["<<layerPrefix<<"]
                            Code" << msgCode << ":" << msg << std::endl;
    }
    else if (msgFlags & VK_DEBUG_REPORT_INFORMATION_BIT_EXT) {
        std::cout<<"[VK_DEBUG_REPORT] INFORMATION:[" <<layerPrefix<<"]
                            Code" << msgCode << ":" << msg << std::endl;

    }
    else if(msgFlags& VK_DEBUG_REPORT_PERFORMANCE_WARNING_BIT_EXT){
        cout <<"[VK_DEBUG_REPORT] PERFORMANCE: ["<<layerPrefix<<"]
                            Code" << msgCode << ":" << msg << std::endl;
    }
    else if (msgFlags & VK_DEBUG_REPORT_DEBUG_BIT_EXT) {
        cout << "[VK_DEBUG_REPORT] DEBUG: ["<<layerPrefix<<"]
                            Code" << msgCode << ":" << msg <<   std::endl;
    }
     else {
     return VK_FALSE;
     }

    return VK_SUCCESS;
}
```

The following table describes the various fields from the `debugFunction()` callback:

Parameters	Description
msgFlags	This specifies the type of debugging event that has triggered the call, for example, an error, warning, performance warning, and so on.
objType	This is the type object that is manipulated by the triggering call.
srcObject	This is the handle of the object that's being created or manipulated by the triggered call.
location	This refers to the location of the code describing the event.
msgCode	This refers to the message code.

Debugging in Vulkan

`layerPrefix`	This is the layer responsible for triggering the debug event.
`msg`	This field contains the debug message text.
`userData`	Any application-specific user data is specified to the callback using this field.

The `debugFunction` callback has a `Boolean` return value. The `true` return value indicates the continuation of the command chain to subsequent validation layers even after an error has occurred.

However, the `false` value instructs the validation layer to abort the execution when an error occurs. It is advisable to stop the execution at the very first error.

> **TIP**
>
> The presence of an error itself indicates that something has occurred unexpectedly; letting the system run in these circumstances may lead to undefined results or further errors, which could be completely senseless sometimes. In the latter case, where the execution is aborted, it provides a better opportunity for the developer to concentrate and fix the reported error. In contrast, the former approach, where the system throws a bunch of errors, may be cumbersome leaving the developers in a confused state sometimes.

In order to enable debugging at `vkCreateInstance`, provide `dbgReportCreateInfo` to the `pNext` field of `VkInstanceCreateInfo` structure:

```
VkInstanceCreateInfo instInfo    = {};
. . .
instInfo.pNext = &layerExtension.dbgReportCreateInfo;
vkCreateInstance(&instInfo, NULL, &instance);
```

Finally, once the debug is no longer in use, destroy the debug callback object:

```
void VulkanLayerAndExtension::destroyDebugReportCallback(){
    VulkanApplication* appObj = VulkanApplication::GetInstance();
    dbgDestroyDebugReportCallback(instance,debugReportCallback,NULL);
}
```

The following is the output from the implemented debug report. Your output may differ from this based on the GPU vendor and SDK provider. Also, the explanations of the errors or warnings reported are very specific to the SDK itself. But at a higher level, the specification will hold; this means you can expect to see a debug report with a warning, information, debugging help, and so on, based on the debugging flag you have turned on.

Summary

This chapter was short, precise, and full of practical implementations. Working on Vulkan without debugging capabilities is like shooting in the dark. We know very well that Vulkan demands an appreciable amount of programming and developers make mistakes for obvious reasons; they are humans after all. We learn from our mistakes, and debugging allows us to find and correct these errors. It also provides insightful information to build quality products.

Let's do a quick recap. We learned the Vulkan debugging process. We looked at the various LunarG validation layers and understood the roles and responsibilities offered by each one of them. Next, we added a few selected validation layers that we were interested in debugginig. We also added the debug extension that exposes the debugging capabilities; without this, the API's definition could not be dynamically linked to the application. Then, we implemented the Vulkan create user define debug report function and linked it to our debug reporting callback; this callback decorates the captured debug report in a user-friendly and presentable fashion. Finally, we implemented the API to destroy the debugging report callback object.

In the next chapter, we will understand command buffers, explore their role in the Vulkan pipeline, and learn to use them to record and execute API calls. We will also take an in-depth look at the Vulkan memory management for host and device memory; we will learn about various APIs to control them.

5
Command Buffer and Memory Management in Vulkan

A command buffer is a collection of commands, and it is submitted to an appropriate hardware queue for GPU processing. The driver then fetches the command buffers and validates and compiles them before the real GPU processing starts.

This chapter will shed light on command buffer concepts. We will learn about command pool creation, allocation/deallocation of command buffers, and recording commands. We will implement the command buffers and use them in the next chapter to drive a swapchain. A swapchain abstracts the mechanism to interface with platform surfaces and provides an array of images that can be used to perform rendering. Once rendering is done, the image is presented to the native windowing system.

In the second half of the chapter, we will understand memory management in Vulkan. We will discuss the concepts of host and device memory. We will look into memory allocators to manage host memory allocations. At the end of this chapter, we will delve into device memory and learn the methods to allocate/deallocate and use it through mapping.

This chapter will cover the following topics on command buffers and memory allocation:

- Getting started with command buffers
- Understanding the command pool and command buffer APIs
- Recording command buffers
- Implementing the command buffer wrapper class
- Managing memory in Vulkan

Getting started with command buffers

As the name suggests, a command buffer is a buffer or collection of commands in a single unit. A command buffer records various Vulkan API commands that an application is expected to execute. Command buffers once baked can be reused again and again. They record the commands in the sequence that is specified by the application. These commands are meant for carrying out different type jobs; this includes binding vertex buffer, pipeline binding, recording Render Pass commands, setting viewport and scissor, specifying drawing commands, controlling copy operations on image and buffer contents, and more.

There are two types of command buffers: primary and secondary command buffers:

- **Primary command buffers**: These are the owners of the secondary command buffers and responsible for executing them; they are directly submitted to the queues
- **Secondary command buffers**: These are executed through primary command buffers and cannot be directly submitted to queues

The number of command buffers in an application can vary from a few hundred to thousands. The Vulkan API is designed to offer maximum performance; therefore, the command buffers are allocated from the command pools in order to amortize the cost (when used in a multithreaded environment–refer to the *Explicit synchronization* section in this chapter) of resource creation across multiple command buffers. A command buffer cannot be created directly; instead, it is allocated from the command pool:

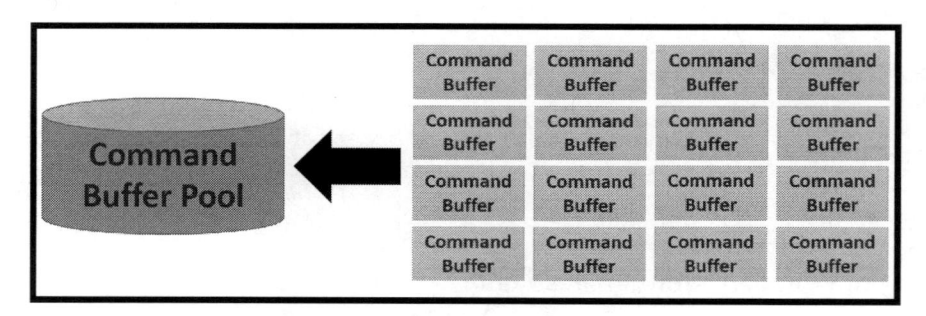

Command buffers are persistent; they are created once and can be reused continuously. Further, if a command buffer is no longer useful, it can be renewed with a simple reset command and made ready for another recording. This is an efficient way as compared to destroying and then creating a new buffer for the same purpose.

Explicit synchronization

When multiple command buffers are created in a multithreaded environment, then it's advisable to separate the synchronization domains by introducing separate command pools for each thread. This makes the cost of command buffer allocations efficient since the application does not need explicit synchronization in a different thread.

However, it is the application's responsibility to manage the synchronization between the command buffers that are shared across multiple threads.

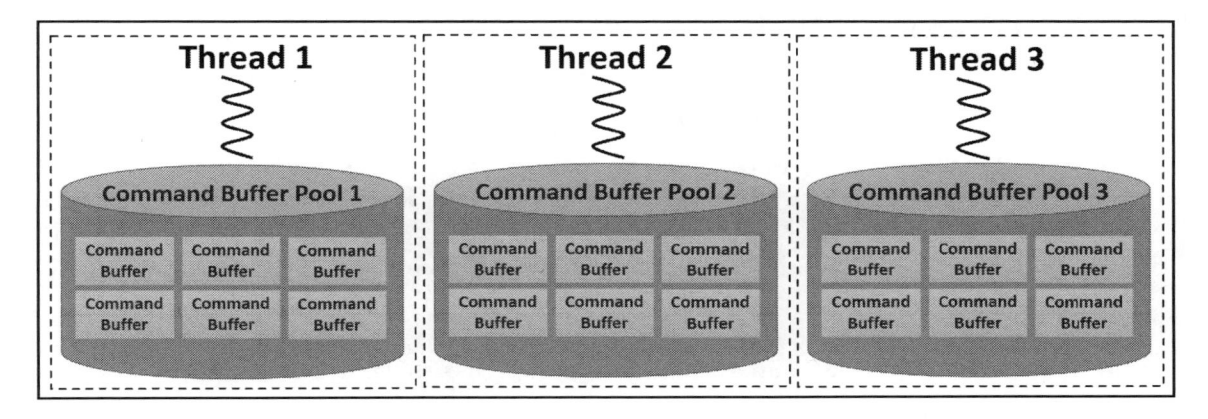

In contrast, OpenGL is an implicit synchronization model. In OpenGL, a lot of things are done automatically, which comes at the cost of a lot of resource tracking, cache flushing, and dependency chain construction. All of this is done behind the curtains, which indeed is an overhead of the CPU. Vulkan is fairly simple in this context; the explicit synchronization guarantees that there is no hidden mechanism nor an element of surprise.

An application is better aware of its resources, and hence, their usage and dependencies. A driver is less likely to pinpoint the dependencies with accuracy. As a result, the OpenGL implementation ends up with unexpected shader recompilations, cache flushes, and so on. Vulkan's explicit synchronization makes it free from these limitations, thereby making the hardware more productive.

Command Buffer and Memory Management in Vulkan

Another differentiation is the submission of the command buffers in OpenGL: command buffers are pushed behind the scenes and are not in control of the application. An application that submits the commands has no guarantee when those jobs will be executed. This is because OpenGL executes command buffers in batches. It waits for the commands to build the batch and then it dispatches them together. On the other hand, Vulkan gives explicit control to the command buffer to allow the processing up front by submitting it to the desired queue.

Types of command in command buffers

A command buffer consists of one or more commands. These commands can be categorized into three types:

- **Action**: This command performs operations such as draw, dispatch, clear, copy, query/timestamp operations, and begin/end a subpass
- **State management**: This includes descriptor sets, bind pipelines, and buffers, and it is used to set the dynamic state, push constants, and the Render Pass/subpass state
- **Synchronization**: These commands are used for synchronization: pipeline barriers, set events, wait events, and Render Pass/subpass dependencies

Command buffers and queues

Command buffers are submitted to a hardware queue where they are processed asynchronously. Submission to queues can be made efficient by batching command buffers and executing them once. Vulkan has a deferred command model where a collection of draw calls in the command buffer and submissions are done separately and considered two different operations. This is helpful from an application perspective. This is because it will have prior knowledge of a large portion of the scene and this can be used as an opportunity to add appropriate optimizations to the submission, which would've been difficult to achieve in OpenGL.

Vulkan provides a logical view of the hardware queue, where each logical view is tightly connected to a hardware queue. A single Vulkan hardware queue can be represented by multiple logical queues, where each queue is being created based on the queue properties. For example, the presentation of rendered swapchain images may require the command buffer to submit them to a graphics queue, which is capable of presentation as well

The order of execution
Command buffers can be submitted to either a single queue or multiple queues:

- **Single queue submission**: Multiple command buffers submitted to a single queue may be executed or overlapped. In single queue submission, a command buffer must obey the order of the execution of operations as per the command order and the API order specification. This book only covers the submission commands used for `vkQueueSubmit`; it does not cover sparse memory binding command buffers (through `vkQueueBindSparse`).
- **Multiple queue submission**: The command buffers submitted to multiple queues may be executed in any order unless explicit ordering constraints are applied through the synchronization mechanism via semaphores and fences.

Understanding command pool and buffer APIs

This section will explain the different APIs that can be used to manage the command pool and command buffers. Here, we will understand the process of creating a command buffer pool that will be used for command buffer allocation. We will also look at the process of resetting and destroying APIs.

The next section of this chapter will be based on implementing these APIs in a ready-to-use wrapper class. The wrapper implementation will be highly useful in the remaining chapters of this book, where we will extensively make use of the command buffer.

> **TIP**
> As a prerequisite for the upcoming chapters, the *Implementing the command pool and command buffers*, *Recording command buffers*, and *Managing memory in Vulkan* sections are important.

Creating a command pool

A command pool is created using the `vkCreateCommandPool()` API. It accepts a `VkCommandPoolCreateInfo` control structure, which guides the implementation about the nature of command buffers that are going to be allocated from this pool. It also indicates which queue family it should belong to. This information, which is provided in advance, is useful to allocate compatible command pools; these pools can be used to optimize the command buffer allocation process for a typical queue submission. Here's the syntax of this:

```
typedef struct VkCommandPoolCreateInfo {
    VkStructureType          sType;
    const void*              next;
    VkCommandPoolCreateFlags flags;
    uint32_t                 queueFamilyIndex;
} VkCommandPoolCreateInfo;
```

The following table describes the various fields of `VkCommandPoolCreateInfo`:

Parameters	Description
`type`	This is the type information of this control structure. It must be specified as `VK_STRUCTURE_TYPE_COMMAND_POOL_CREATE_INFO`.
`next`	This could be a valid pointer to an extension-specific structure or `NULL`.
`flag`	This represents a bitwise enum flag that indicates the behavior of the command pool usage and the command buffer being allocated from it. This enum flag is of the type `VkCommandPoolFlag`, and it can take `VK_COMMAND_POOL_CREATE_TRANSIENT_BIT` and `VK_COMMAND_POOL_CREATE_RESET_COMMAND_BUFFER_BIT` as possible input values. For more information on these flag values, refer to the following tip.
`queueFamilyIndex`	This indicates the queue family to which the command buffer is intended to be submitted.

> **TIP**
> The `VK_COMMAND_POOL_CREATE_TRANSIENT_BIT` enum flag indicates that the command buffers allocated from this pool will be changed frequently and have a shorter lifespan. This means that the buffers will be reset or freed in a relatively short timeframe. This flag notifies the implementation about the nature of the command buffer, and this can be used to control the memory allocation behavior within the pool.
>
> When the `VK_COMMAND_POOL_CREATE_RESET_COMMAND_BUFFER_BIT` flag is set, it indicates that a command buffer allocated from the pool can

Chapter 5

> **TIP**
> be individually reset in two ways: either explicitly by calling `vkResetCommandBuffer` or implicitly by calling `vkBeginCommandBuffer`. If this flag is not set, then these two APIs must not be called on the executable command buffers allocated from the pool. This indicates that they can only be reset in bulk by calling `vkResetCommandPool`.

The command pool in Vulkan is represented by the `VkCommandPool` object. It is created using the `vkCreateCommandPool()` API. The following is the syntax and description of the API:

```
VkResult vkCreateCommandPool(
    VkDevice                          device,
    const VkCommandPoolCreateInfo*    pCreateInfo,
    const VkAllocationCallbacks*      pAllocator,
    VkCommandPool*                    pCommandPool);
```

The following table describes the various fields of this API:

Parameters	Description
`device`	This is the handle of the device that will create the command pool.
`pCreateInfo`	This refers to the `VkCommandPoolCreateInfo` object that indicates the nature of the command buffer in the command pool.
`pAllocator`	This controls host memory allocation.
`pCommandPool`	This represents the `VkCommandPool` object returned by the API.

> For more information on how to control host memory allocation using `VkAllocationCallbacks* allocator`, refer to the *Host memory* topic in the last section of this chapter, namely *Managing memory in Vulkan*.

Resetting a command pool

The command pool (`VkCommandPool`) can be reset using the `vkResetCommandPool()` API. Here is the syntax of this API:

```
VkResult vkResetCommandPool (
    VkDevice                  device,
    VkCommandPool             commandPool,
    VkCommandPoolResetFlags   flags);
```

[129]

The following are the parameters of this API:

Parameters	Description
device	This is the handle of the device that owns the command pool.
commandPool	This refers to the VkCommandPool handle that needs to be reset.
flags	This flag controls the behavior of resetting the pool.

Destroying a command pool

A command pool can be destroyed using the vkDestroyCommandPool() API. Here's the syntax of this:

```
VkResult vkDestroyCommandPool(
    VkDevice                        device,
    VkCommandPool                   commandPool,
    const VkAllocationCallbacks*    allocator);
```

The following are the parameters of this API:

Parameters	Description
device	This is the handle of the device that destroys the command pool.
commandPool	This refers to the VkCommandPool handle that needs to be destroyed.
allocator	This controls host memory allocation. For more information, refer to the *Host memory* section in Chapter 5, *Command Buffer and Memory Management in Vulkan*.

Command buffer allocation

Command buffers are allocated from the command buffer pool (VkCommandPool) using the vkAllocateCommandBuffers() API. This API needs the VkCommandBufferAllocateInfo control structure object, which specifies the various parameters that will be helpful in the allocation process. Upon successful execution of the API, it returns the VkCommandBuffer object. The following is the syntax of this API:

```
VkResult vkAllocateCommandBuffers(
    VkDevice                                device,
    const VkCommandBufferAllocateInfo*      pAllocateInfo,
    VkCommandBuffer*                        pCommandBuffers);
```

Let's take a look at the API fields:

Parameters	Description
`device`	This is the handle of the logical device object that owns the command pool.
`pAllocateInfo`	This is a pointer to a `VkCommandBufferAllocateInfo` structure describing the parameters of the allocation; refer to the next table for more information.
`pCommandBuffers`	This refers to the allocated command buffer object array.

The `VkCommandBufferAllocateInfo` structure has the following fields.

Parameters	Description
`sType`	This refers to the type information telling Vulkan that it is a `VkCommandBufferAllocate` structure, this must be a type of `VK_STRUCTURE_TYPE_COMMAND_BUFFER_ALLOCATE_INFO`:
`pNext`	This refers to `NULL` or an extension-specific structure.
`commandPool`	This is the command pool handle from which memory needs to be allocated for the requested command buffers.

`level`	This is the bitwise enum flag of the type `VkCommandBufferLevel` indicating whether the command buffer is at the primary or secondary level. The following is the syntax of `VkCommandBufferLevel`:
	`typedef enum VkCommandBufferLevel {`
	  `VK_COMMAND_BUFFER_LEVEL_PRIMARY=0,`
	  `VK_COMMAND_BUFFER_LEVEL_SECONDARY=1,`
	`} VkCommandBufferLevel;`

`commandBufferCount`	This refers to the number of command buffers that need to be allocated.

[131]

Resetting command buffers

The allocated command buffer can be reset using the `vkResetCommandBuffer()` API. This API accepts the `VkCommandBuffer` object as the first parameter that needs to be reset. The second parameter is a bitwise mask, `VkCommandBufferResetFlag`, which controls the behavior of the reset operation. This structure has one enum value, namely `VK_COMMAND_BUFFER_RESET_RELEASE_RESOURCES_BIT`. When this value is set, it means that the memory held by the command buffer will be returned to the parent command pool.

The following is the syntax of the API:

```
VkResult vkResetCommandBuffer(
    VkCommandBuffer             commandBuffer,
    VkCommandBufferResetFlags   flags);
```

Freeing command buffers

One or more command buffers can be released using the `vkFreeCommandBuffer()` API. Here's the syntax of this API:

```
void vkFreeCommandBuffers(
    VkDevice                device,
    VkCommandPool           commandPool,
    uint32_t                commandBufferCount,
    const VkCommandBuffer*  pCommandBuffers);
```

The following are the parameters of the `vkFreeCommandBuffers()` API along with their respective descriptions:

Parameters	Description
device	This refers to the logical device that holds the command pool.
commandPool	This refers to the associated command pool from which the memory has to be released.
commandBufferCount	This refers to the number of command buffers that need to be released.
pCommandBuffers	This is an array of command buffer handles that needs to be released.

Recording command buffers

A command buffer is recorded using the vkBeginCommandBuffer() and vkEndCommandBuffer() APIs. These APIs define the scope under which any specified Vulkan commands are recorded. The following example shows the recording of the Render Pass instance creation between these two APIs, which works as the start and end scopes. For more information on creating a Render Pass, refer to the *Understanding the Render Pass* section in Chapter 7, *Buffer Resource, Render Pass, Framebuffer, and Shaders with SPIR-V*.

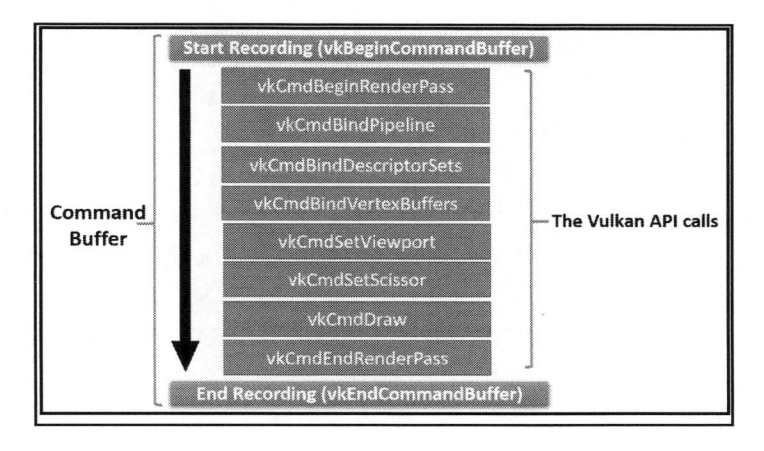

The start of the recording is performed using the vkBeginCommandBuffer() API. This defines the starting scope after which any call specified is considered to be recorded until the end scope is reached (vkEndCommandBuffer()).

The following is the syntax of this API, followed by a description of the necessary parameters:

```
VkResult vkBeginCommandBuffer(
    VkCommandBuffer                 commandBuffer,
    const VkCommandBufferBeginInfo* pBeginInfo);
```

This API accepts two parameters. The first one is the handle of the command buffer in which the calls are to be recorded. The second parameter is a VkCommandBufferBeginInfo structure object that defines additional information telling you how to begin the command buffer recording process.

The following is the API syntax of the VkCommandBufferBeginInfo structure:

```
typedef struct VkCommandBufferBeginInfo {
    VkStructureType                             sType;
    const void*                                 pNext;
    VkCommandBufferUsageFlags                   flags;
    const VkCommandBufferInheritanceInfo*       pInheritanceInfo;
} VkCommandBufferBeginInfo;
```

The accepted parameters in this structure are described as follows:

Parameters	Description
sType	This is the type information of this control structure. It must be specified as VK_STRUCTURE_TYPE_COMMAND_BUFFER_BEGIN_INFO.
pNext	This field could be a valid pointer to an extension-specific structure or NULL.
flags	This is a bitwise mask of the type VkCommandBufferUsageFlagBits indicating the command buffer usage behavior.
pInheritanceInfo	If this field is not NULL, it is used when the command buffer is the secondary command buffer. It contains the VkCommandBufferInheritanceInfo structure.

Command buffer recording is performed using the vkEndCommandBuffer() API. It accepts one parameter, which specifies the command buffer object on which the recording is to be stopped. Here's the syntax for this:

```
VkResult vkEndCommandBuffer(VkCommandBuffer commandBuffer);
```

Queue submission

Once the command buffer (VkCommandBuffer) is recorded, it is ready to be submitted to a queue. The vkQueueSubmit() API helps commit the jobs in an appropriate queue. Let's check out the syntax of this:

```
VkResult vkQueueSubmit(
    VkQueue                 queue,
    uint32_t                submitCount,
    const VkSubmitInfo*     pSubmitInfo,
    VkFence                 fence);
```

The accepted parameters are listed as follows:

Parameters	Description
queue	This is the queue's handle to which the command buffer is submitted.
submitCount	This refers to the number of submitInfo objects.
submitInfo	This refers to the VkSubmitInfo pointer. It contains vital information about each work submission, and the number of work submissions is indicated by submitCount. The next point talks about its API specification.
fence	This is used as a signaling mechanism indicating command buffer completion of the execution. If fence is non-null and submitCount is non-zero, then fence gets signaled when all the command buffers specified in the VkSubmitInfo::pCommandBuffers members of submitInfo are executed. If fence is non-null but submitCount is zero, then the signaled fence indicates that all of the work previously submitted to the queue has been completed.

Let's take a look at VkSubmitInfo. This structure embeds multiple pieces of information into itself. This information is used by the submission process to handle an individual VkSubmitInfo object containing a single command buffer or a bunch of them. The following is the syntax of this:

```
typedef struct VkSubmitInfo {
    VkStructureType              type;
    const void*                  pNext;
    uint32_t                     waitSemaphoreCount;
    const VkSemaphore*           pWaitSemaphores;
    const VkPipelineStageFlags*  pWaitDstStageMask;
    uint32_t                     commandBufferCount;
    const VkCommandBuffer*       pCommandBuffers;
    uint32_t                     signalSemaphoreCount;
    const VkSemaphore*           pSignalSemaphores;
} VkSubmitInfo;
```

The accepted parameters are described as follows:

Parameters	Description
sType	This is the type of the VkSumbitInfo structure, which must be VK_STRUCTURE_TYPE_SUBMIT_INFO.
pNext	This is a pointer to an extension-specific structure or NULL.

`waitSemaphoreCount;`	The refers to the number of semaphores upon which the command buffer is made to wait before it's executed.
`pWaitSemaphores`	This is a pointer to an array of semaphores upon which the command buffers are made to wait before they are executed in a batch.
`pWaitDstStageMask`	This is a pointer to an array of pipeline stages at which each corresponding semaphore wait will occur.
`commandBufferCount`	This refers to the number of command buffers to be executed in a batch.
`pCommandBuffers`	This is a pointer to an array of command buffers to be executed in a batch.
`signalSemaphoreCount`	This refers to the number of semaphores to be signaled once the commands specified in `commandBuffers` completes the execution.
`pSignalSemaphores`	This is a pointer to an array of semaphores that will be signaled when the command buffers for the given batch are executed.

Queue waiting

Once committed to the queue, the application must wait for the queue to finish the submitted jobs and be ready for the next batch. The process of waiting for the queue can be done using the `vkQueueWaitIdle()` API. This API will be blocked until all the command buffers and sparse-binding operations in the queue are not completed. This API accepts one argument, which specifies the handle of the queue upon which the waiting has to be done. The following is the syntax of this API:

```
VkResult vkQueueWaitIdle(VkQueue      queue);
```

Implementing the wrapper class for a command buffer

This section implements the wrapper class for a command buffer called `CommandBufferMgr`. This class contains static functions that can be directly used like utility functions without requiring a class object. The class is implemented in a new file called `wrapper.h/.cpp`; this file will contain multiple utility methods.

Most of the implemented functions in this class are provided with a default implementation. This means that each function provides the user with the flexibility to change the control structure parameters from outside the function call and send them as parametric arguments. The function arguments are inherent defaults, so if you are not specifying anything custom, the function will do all the jobs for you.

The following is the header implementation of the `CommandBufferMgr` class. It declares four static functions that are responsible for allocating memory, recording the command buffer, and submitting the command buffer to the command queue:

```
/*************** Wrapper.h *****************/
class CommandBufferMgr{
public:
    // Allocate memory for command buffers from the command pool
    static void allocCommandBuffer(const VkDevice* device,
        const VkCommandPool cmdPool, VkCommandBuffer* cmdBuf, const
        VkCommandBufferAllocateInfo* commandBufferInfo);
    // Start the command buffer recording
    static void beginCommandBuffer(VkCommandBuffer cmdBuf,
        VkCommandBufferBeginInfo* inCmdBufInfo = NULL);
    // End the command buffer recording
    static void endCommandBuffer(VkCommandBuffer cmdBuf);
    // Submit the command buffer for execution
    static void submitCommandBuffer(const VkQueue& queue, const
        VkCommandBuffer* cmdBufList, const VkSubmitInfo* submit-
        Info = NULL, const VkFence& fence = VK_NULL_HANDLE);
};
```

Implementing the command buffer allocation process

The `allocCommandBuffer()` function allocates a command buffer (`cmdBuf`) from the specified command pool (`cmdPool`). The allocation behavior can be controlled using the `VkCommandBufferAllocateInfo` pointer argument. When the last parameter of this function has its default parameter value (`NULL`), then `VkCommandBufferAllocateInfo` is implemented inside, as shown in the following code, and used for command buffer allocation:

```
void CommandBufferMgr::allocCommandBuffer(const VkDevice* device,
    const VkCommandPool cmdPool, VkCommandBuffer* cmdBuf, const
    VkCommandBufferAllocateInfo* commandBufferInfo){
    VkResult result;
```

```cpp
    // If command information is available use it as it is.
    if (commandBufferInfo) {
        result = vkAllocateCommandBuffers
                    (*device, commandBufferInfo, cmdBuf);
        assert(!result);
        return;
    }

    // Default implementation, create the command buffer
    // allocation info and use the supplied parameter into it
    VkCommandBufferAllocateInfo cmdInfo = {};
    cmdInfo.sType = VK_STRUCTRE_TYPE_COMMAND_BUFFER_ALOCATE_INFO;
    cmdInfo.pNext               = NULL;
    cmdInfo.commandPool         = cmdPool;
    cmdInfo.level               = VK_COMMAND_BUFFER_LEVEL_PRIMARY;
    cmdInfo.commandBufferCount  = (uint32_t) sizeof(cmdBuf)/
                                    sizeof(VkCommandBuffer);
    // Allocate the memory
    result = vkAllocateCommandBuffers(*device, &cmdInfo, cmdBuf);
    assert(!result);
}
```

Recording the command buffer allocation process

API calls can be easily recorded with the simple `beginCommandBuffer()` and `endCommandBuffer()` wrapper functions. Refer to the following code to understand the implementation:

```cpp
void CommandBufferMgr::beginCommandBuffer(VkCommandBuffer cmdBuf,
                VkCommandBufferBeginInfo* inCmdBufInfo){
    VkResult   result;
    // If the user has specified the custom command buffer use it
    if (inCmdBufInfo) {
        result = vkBeginCommandBuffer(cmdBuf, inCmdBufInfo);
        assert(result == VK_SUCCESS);
        return;
    }

    // otherwise, use the default implementation.
    VkCommandBufferInheritanceInfo cmdBufInheritInfo = {};
    cmdBufInheritInfo.sType     = VK_STRUCTURE_TYPE_COMMAND-
                                    _BUFFER_INHERITANCE_INFO;
    cmdBufInheritInfo.pNext     = NULL;
```

```
        cmdBufInheritInfo.renderPass      = VK_NULL_HANDLE;
        cmdBufInheritInfo.subpass = 0;
        cmdBufInheritInfo.framebuffer     = VK_NULL_HANDLE;
        cmdBufInheritInfo.occlusionQueryEnable = VK_FALSE;
        cmdBufInheritInfo.queryFlags           = 0;
        cmdBufInheritInfo.pipelineStatistics   = 0;
        VkCommandBufferBeginInfo cmdBufInfo    = {};
        cmdBufInfo.sType=VK_STRUCTURE_TYPE_COMMAND_BUFFER_BEGIN_INFO;
        cmdBufInfo.pNext = NULL;
        cmdBufInfo.flags = 0;
        cmdBufInfo.pInheritanceInfo       = &cmdBufInheritInfo;

        result = vkBeginCommandBuffer(cmdBuf, &cmdBufInfo);
        assert(result == VK_SUCCESS);
}
```

The following code describes the end of command buffer recording:

```
void CommandBufferMgr::endCommandBuffer(VkCommandBuffer commandBuffer){
    VkResult    result;
    result = vkEndCommandBuffer(commandBuffer);
    assert(result == VK_SUCCESS);
}
```

How to use command buffer recording functions

In this section, we will use the code snippet from Chapter 7, *Buffer Resource, Render Pass, Framebuffer, and Shaders with SPIR-V*, and demonstrate the use of the implemented command buffer management utility functions. These functions grately simplify the code for the command buffer creation and submission processes.

In the following code, the Render Pass instance is created using command buffers. First, the command pool (cmdPool) is created and used to allocate a command buffer (vecCmdDraw) using allocCommandBuffer(). The command buffer recording scope is managed between the beginCommandBuffer() and endCommandBuffer() functions. Under these scope-defining functions, a series of commands is recorded (vkCmdBeginRenderPass, vkCmdBindPipeline, vkCmdDraw, and more). Ignore the working of the commands used for Render Pass instance creation for now; we will understand them in detail in Chapter 7, *Buffer Resource, Render Pass, Framebuffer, and Shaders with SPIR-V*. Here, our purpose is only er recording.

Finally, the command buffer is submitted with `submitCommandBuffer()`; this function is described in detail in the next section:

```
vkCreateCommandPool(device, &cmdPoolInfo, NULL, &cmdPool);
CommandBufferMgr::allocCommandBuffer(&device, cmdPool,vecCmdDraw);

// Start recording the command buffer
CommandBufferMgr::beginCommandBuffer(vecCmdDraw);

// Render pass instance
vkCmdBeginRenderPass( . . . );
vkCmdBindPipeline(. . .);
vkCmdBindDescriptorSets(. . .);
vkCmdBindVertexBuffers(. . .);
vkCmdSetViewport(. . .);
vkCmdSetScissor(. . .);
vkCmdDraw(. . .);
vkCmdEndRenderPass(. . .);

// End recording the command buffer
CommandBufferMgr::endCommandBuffer(vecCmdDraw);
CommandBufferMgr::submitCommandBuffer(queue, &vecCmdDraw);
```

Submitting the command to the queue

Submission of the prepared command buffer is done with the help of the `submitCommandBuffer()` function. It takes four parameters. The first parameter specifies the submission queue (`queue`) to which the second parameter, namely the command buffer (`cmdBuffer`), is to be submitted for execution. The third parameter (`inSubmitInfo`) specifies the behavior involved in controlling the submission process. The last parameter signals the completion of the submitted command buffers (`fence`):

```
void CommandBufferMgr::submitCommandBuffer(const VkQueue& queue,
      const VkCommandBuffer cmdBuffer, const
      VkSubmitInfo* inSubmitInfo, const VkFence& fence){
   VkResult result;
   // If Submit information is available use it as it is.
   // This assumes that the commands are already specified
   // in the structure, hence ignore command buffer
   if (inSubmitInfo){
      vkQueueSubmit(queue, 1, inSubmitInfo, fence);
      result = vkQueueWaitIdle(queue);
      return;
   }
```

```
// Else, create the submit info with specified buffer commands
VkSubmitInfo submitInfo = {};
submitInfo.sType    = VK_STRUCTURE_TYPE_SUBMIT_INFO;
submitInfo.pNext                = NULL;
submitInfo.waitSemaphoreCount   = 0;
submitInfo.pWaitSemaphores      = NULL;
submitInfo.pWaitDstStageMask    = NULL;
submitInfo.commandBufferCount   = (uint32_t)
            sizeof(commandBuffer)/sizeof(VkCommandBuffer);
submitInfo.pCommandBuffers      = commandBuffer;
submitInfo.signalSemaphoreCount = 0;
submitInfo.pSignalSemaphores    = NULL;

result = vkQueueSubmit(queue, 1, &submitInfo, fence);
assert(!result);

result = vkQueueWaitIdle(queue); assert(!result);
}
```

Managing memory in Vulkan

Vulkan divides memory broadly into two types: *host memory* and *device memory*. Further, each type of memory can be uniquely broken down based on the properties and memory type. Vulkan provides a transparent mechanism to view internal memory details and related properties. Such a type of exposure is not possible in OpenGL, and hence the application is unable to explicitly control memory regions and layouts.

Of these memory types, host memory is slower than device memory. However, host memory may be available in abundance. On the other hand, device memory is directly visible to the physical device, making it efficient and faster. In this section, we will learn about host and device memory and a way to access them.

Host memory

Vulkan makes use of host memory to store API internal data structures in the implementation. Vulkan provides allocators, which allow an application to control memory allocation on behalf of host memory. If the application does not use allocators, then the Vulkan implementation uses a default allocation scheme to reserve a memory slot for its data structures.

Host memory is managed by the `VkAllocationCallbacks` control structure, which is passed to Vulkan APIs for custom management of host memory. For example, the command buffer pool creation (`vkCreateCommandPool`) and destroy (`vkDestroyCommandPool`) APIs accept the last argument as the host memory allocator (the `VkAllocationCallbacks` pointer).

The following is the syntax of this control structure:

```
typedef struct VkAllocationCallbacks {
    void*                                   pUserData;
    PFN_vkAllocationFunction                pfnAllocation;
    PFN_vkReallocationFunction              pfnReallocation;
    PFN_vkFreeFunction                      pfnFree;
    PFN_vkInternalAllocationNotification    pfnInternalAlloc;
    PFN_vkInternalFreeNotification          pfnInternalFree;
} VkAllocationCallbacks;
```

The accepted parameters are described as follows:

Parameters	Description
pUserData	This field indicates the user data that can be passed in to manage the memory management callbacks (`alloc`/`realloc`/`free`). The user data may change each time a callback is executed, even with the same object.
pfnAllocation	This is a user-defined function pointer of the signature type `PFN_vkAllocationFunction`. This defines a custom allocation function that can be used to allocate host memory to manage the data structures of the Vulkan API that uses this allocator.
pfnReallocation	This is a user-defined function pointer of the signature type `PFN_vkReallocationFunction`. This defines a custom reallocation function that can be used to reallocate the host memory of Vulkan API data structures.
pfnFree	This refers to the function pointer `PFN_vkfreeFunction`, which points to a custom-defined memory release function.
pfnInternalAlloc	This function pointer is used by the implementation to perform internal allocation. It notifies the application about the allocation that has been made. The function pointer used should match the `PFN_vkInternalAllocationNotification` signatures.

`pfnInternalFree`	When the implementation releases internal allocation, it calls the function pointer `PFN_vkInternalFreeAllocationNotification`, which notifies the application about freeing up allocated memory. This function pointer is used by the implementation to release an internal memory allocation. It notifies the application when the memory is released. The function pointer used should match the `PFN_vkInternalFreeAllocationNotification` signatures.

Given the scope and page limitations of this book, there is only so much that can be covered about memory allocation extension functions, as discussed in the preceding table. For further information, refer to https://www.khronos.org/registry/vulkan/specs/1.0/apispec.html.

Device memory

Device memory is GPU memory that is visible to the physical device. The physical device can read its memory regions directly. Device memory is very close to the physical device, and thus provides faster performance than host memory. Image objects, buffers objects, and uniform buffer objects are all allocated on device memory.

A single physical device may have different types of memory; these are further differentiated based on their heaps and properties. The `vkGetPhysicalDeviceMemoryProperties()` API queries the available memory heaps and memory properties of the physical device. It's important for an application to know its memory characteristics. This allows better allocation of resources, depending upon the application logic or resource type.

The following is the syntax of the `vkGetPhysicalDeviceMemoryProperties()` API:

```
void vkGetPhysicalDeviceMemoryProperties (
VkPhysicalDevice                   physicalDevice,
VkPhysicalDeviceMemoryProperties* pMemoryProperties );
```

The following `vkGetPhysicalDeviceMemoryProperties` fields are available:

Parameters	Description
`physicalDevice`	This refers to the physical device handle whose memory properties need to be queried.
`pMemoryProperties`	The queried memory properties are retrieved in the `VkPhysicalDeviceMemoryProperties` data structure pointer. What follows is a description of this structure.

The `VkPhysicalDeviceMemoryProperties` structure is described as follows:

```
typedef struct VkPhysicalDeviceMemoryProperties {
    uint32_t        memoryTypeCount;
    VkMemoryType    memoryTypes[VK_MAX_MEMORY_TYPES];
    uint32_t        memoryHeapCount;
    VkMemoryHeap    memoryHeaps[VK_MAX_MEMORY_HEAPS];
} VkPhysicalDeviceMemoryProperties;
```

The `vkGetPhysicalDeviceMemoryProperties` structure provides the following information:

- **Memory types**: This contains the number of memory types (`memoryTypeCount`) that can be used to access the available memory type (`VkMemoryType`) on the physical device. A memory type provides vital information by describing a set of memory properties, for example, whether the host memory is cached or not cached. An allocation from a certain memory type is associated with a specific memory heap, which is indicated by another field in this structure called the heap index.
- **Memory heaps**: This field provides the number of memory heaps (`memoryHeapCount`) available on the physical device. This information is used to access the allocated memory space in those heaps. Each heap is represented by `VkMemoryHeap`, which describes a memory resource of a certain size. Each heap may share more than one memory type.

> The correct size of a physical memory resource can be queried accurately with the mechanisms provided by the memory type and memory heap. This allows the memory to be used with a variety of various properties.

The following is the syntax of the `VkMemoryHeap` data structure:

```
typedef struct VkMemoryHeap {
    VkDeviceSize        size;
    VkMemoryHeapFlags   flags;
} VkMemoryHeap;
```

The first field `size` indicates the total size of the memory in the heap; this memory size in bytes is occupied in the heap. The second field `flag` is a bitwise mask of the type `VkMemoryHeapFlagBits`, indicating the heap attributes. Here's the syntax of this:

```
typedef enum VkMemoryHeapFlagBits {
    VK_MEMORY_HEAP_DEVICE_LOCAL_BIT = 0x00000001,
} VkMemoryHeapFlagBits;
```

The flag value with `VK_MEMORY_HEAP_DEVICE_LOCAL_BIT` indicates that the corresponding heap belongs to the device's local memory. This type of memory may have different memory property flags (`VkMemoryPropertyFlagBits`) and performance characteristics as compared to the host local memory.

`VkMemoryType` provides information about the properties of this memory type with bitwise flags (`propertyFlags`) and an index of the heap itself (`heapIndex`). Here's the syntax of this:

```
typedef struct VkMemoryType {
    VkMemoryPropertyFlags   propertyFlags;
    uint32_t                heapIndex;
} VkMemoryType;
```

The following are the possible `VkMemoryPropertyFlagBits` enum flags:

Flags	Description
VK_MEMORY_PROPERTY_DEVICE_LOCAL_BIT	The memory allocation performed with this type is considered to be most efficient for device memory access.
VK_MEMORY_PROPERTY_HOST_VISIBLE_BIT	The memory allocated with this flag type is accessible to the host. The host can make use of mapping functions (`vkMapMemory()`) to access the contents.
VK_MEMORY_PROPERTY_HOST_COHERENT_BIT	This flag indicates that the host cache management commands `vkFlushMappedMemoryRanges` and `vkInvalidateMappedMemoryRanges` are not needed to make host writes visible to device or the device writes visible to the host, respectively.

Command Buffer and Memory Management in Vulkan

`VK_MEMORY_PROPERTY_HOST_CACHED_BIT`	The memory allocated with this memory type is cached on the host. Host memory access to uncached memory is slower than access to cached memory; however, uncached memory is always host-coherent.
`VK_MEMORY_PROPERTY_LAZILY_ALLOCATED_BIT`	The memory is only device-accessible. Make sure that `VK_MEMORY_PROPERTY_HOST_VISIBLE_BIT` and `VK_MEMORY_PROPERTY_HOST_VISIBLE_BIT` are not set with this memory type.

Allocating device memory

Device memory can be allocated in Vulkan using the `vkAllocateMemory()` API. This API returns the `VkDeviceMemory` object if the device memory is successfully allocated. This object is used within the application to access or operate device memory data. The following is the syntax for this:

```
VkResult vkAllocateMemory(
    VkDevice                            device,
    const VkMemoryAllocateInfo*         allocateInfo,
    const VkAllocationCallbacks*        allocator,
    VkDeviceMemory*                     memory);
```

Let's look at the various fields for this API:

Parameters	Description
`device`	This represents the logical device that owns the memory.
`allocateInfo`	This is a pointer to `VkMemoryAllocateInfo`; it describes the parameters for device memory allocation.
`allocator`	This is either `NULL` or is a pointer to the `VkAllocationCallbacks` structure; it controls host memory allocation.
`memory`	This is the handle of the allocated memory of the `VkMemoryHandle` type.

The `VkMemoryAllocateInfo` structure is defined as follows:

```
typedef struct VkMemoryAllocateInfo {
    VkStructureType         type;
    const void*             pNext;
    VkDeviceSize            allocationSize;
    uint32_t                memoryTypeIndex;
} VkMemoryAllocateInfo;
```

[146]

The following table describes each parameter of this structure:

Parameters	Description
`type`	This represents the type information of this structure; it must be `VK_STRUCTURE_TYPE_MEMORY_ALLOCATE_INFO`.
`pNext`	This is a pointer to an extension-specific structure.
`allocationSize`	The refers to the size of the memory that needs to be allocated.
`memoryTypeIndex`	This is the index of the memory type that is used for selecting memory properties and the heap where the memory comes from.

> The implementation supports suballocation very well. For example, if the memory requirement for an image is 512 bytes aligned and for buffer objects is 64 bytes aligned, then `vkAllocateMemory` guarantees that it will meet the specified requirement. It will return 512 bytes of aligned device memory, which can be used to allocate any of the object types. Once memory is allocated, it remains uninitialized. The application should create large `VkDeviceMemory` objects and suballocate ranges out of them for good performance.

The number of allocations performed on the physical device memory is implementation-dependent and can be queried using the `maxMemoryAllocationCount` member of `VkPhysicalDeviceLimits`. When `maxMemoryAllocationCount` is exceeded, `vkAllocateMemory` may return `VK_ERROR_TOO_MANY_OBJECTS`.

Freeing up device memory

The allocated device memory can be freed using the `vkFreeMemory()` API. The following is the syntax for this:

```
void vkFreeMemory(
    VkDevice                    device,
    VkDeviceMemory              memory,
    const VkAllocationCallbacks* allocator);
```

The following table describes each parameter of this structure:

Parameters	Description
`device`	This refers to the logical device that owns the memory.
`memory`	This refers to the `VkDeviceMemory` object that needs to be free.
`allocator`	This controls host memory deallocation.

Accessing device memory from the host

The allocated device memory using the `vkAllocateMemory` API is only visible to the device; it is not visible or accessible to the host. The host can only access those allocated device memory regions that are mappable; the memory allocated with memory property `VK_MEMORY_PROPERTY_HOST_VISIBLE_BIT` is considered mappable.

Using the `vkMapMemory()` API, the mapped device memory can be accessed by the host. This API returns a virtual address pointer that is mapped to the allocated device memory region. The following is the syntax of the API:

```
VkResult vkMapMemory(
    VkDevice              device,
    VkDeviceMemory        memory,
    VkDeviceSize          offset,
    VkDeviceSize          size,
    VkMemoryMapFlags      flags,
    void**                ppData);
```

The accepted parameters are described as follows:

Parameters	Description
`device`	This refers to the logical device that owns the memory.
`Memory`	This refers to the device object memory that needs to be mapped.
`offset`	This refers to the memory offset in bytes right from the start of the memory.
`Size`	This refers to the size of the memory range that needs to be mapped.
`flags`	This is reserved for future use.
`ppData`	This returns the mapped memory address. This is a pointer to the pointer that contains a host-accessible pointer to the beginning of the mapped range.

> The `vkMapMemory` API immediately returns the pointer to the mapped memory. It does not check whether the memory is already mapped. Therefore, it is the application's responsibility to manage the mapped memory. Accessing a type of memory that is already mapped may lead to undefined behavior; the driver may die in a heap.

Once the memory is mapped, it can be used like normal host memory, and the data can be updated on it. Once the memory is updated, it needs to be unmapped so that the device memory can be reflected with the latest changes. The unmapping of the memory is performed using the `vkUnmapMemory()` API. It accepts two parameters. The first is of the type `VkDevice` that indicates the logical device object handle that owns the memory, and the second parameter is the handle to the device memory (`VkDeviceMemory`) that needs to be unmapped. Here is the syntax for this:

```
void vkUnMapMemory(VkDevice device, VkDeviceMemory memory);
```

As we go further in this book, we will learn to use uniforms in the Vulkan API. In `Chapter 10`, *Descriptors and Push Constant*, we will implement device memory allocation and mapping to update the uniform buffer.

Lazily allocated memory

The memory allocated with the `VK_MEMORY_PROPERTY_LAZILY_ALLOCATED_BIT` bit flag is not allocated up front based on the requested size, but it may be allocated in a monotonic fashion, where memory gradually increases in line with application demand. The memory may start from a zero byte size in the beginning and grow with use.

Lazily allocated memory can only be used by image objects of the type `VkImage`. These image objects must contain the memory type as `VK_IMAGE_USAGE_TRANSIENT_ATTACHMENT_BIT`.

At any given moment, the size of the lazily allocated memory presently committed to a specific memory object (`VkDeviceMemory`) can be queried using the `vkGetDeviceMemoryCommitment()` API. The following is the syntax for this:

```
void vkGetDeviceMemoryCommitment(
        VkDevice            device,
        VkDeviceMemory      memory,
        VkDeviceSize*       pCommittedMemoryInBytes);
```

This API accepts three parameters, which are explained in the following table:

Parameters	Description
`device`	This is the logical device that owns the memory.
`memory`	This is the device object memory that needs to be queried for size.
`pCommittedMemoryInBytes`	This returns the currently committed size in device memory.

Summary

In this chapter, we learned about command buffers and memory allocation in the Vulkan API. We understood the concept of command buffers and command pools, and while doing this, we created pools and allocated command buffer objects through them. We got hands-on and built the command buffer wrapper class and implemented the creation, resetting, and destruction of command pools and command buffers. We implemented the recording of command buffers and submitted them to an appropriate queue for processing.

The second part of this chapter was full of memory management concepts for host- and device-based memory. We learned about allocators and their APIs to manage host allocation. We also looked into device memory and understood how Vulkan APIs allocate, map, and free device memory.

Vulkan has two types of resource: buffers and images. In the next chapter, we will learn about Vulkan image resources and use them to create swapchains with the help of command buffers. Buffer resources will be covered in `Chapter 7`, *Buffer Resource, Render Pass, Framebuffer, and Shaders with SPIR-V*.

6
Allocating Image Resources and Building a Swapchain with WSI

In the previous chapter, we covered concepts related to memory management and command buffers. We learned about host and device memory and ways to allocate in the Vulkan API. We also covered command buffers; we implemented command buffer recording API calls and submitted them to queues for processing.

In this chapter, we will make use of our knowledge of command buffers and memory allocation to implement a swapchain and depth image. A swapchain provides the mechanism by which we can render drawing primitives to swapchain color images, which is then passed on to the presentation layer in order to display the primitives in the window. Images are a prerequisite of swap buffer creation; therefore, this chapter will help you gain in-depth knowledge of image resources and their uses in the Vulkan application.

We will cover the following topics:

- Getting started with image resources
- Understanding an image resource
- Memory allocation and binding an image resource
- Introducing swapchains
- Creating a depth image
- Summarizing the application flow

Getting started with image resources

A Vulkan resource is simply a representation of a memory view that contains data. Vulkan primarily has two types of resource: buffers and images. In this chapter, we will only discuss the concept of an image resource; this will be used to implement the swapchain. For more information on the buffer resource type, refer to `Chapter 7`, *Buffer Resource, Render Pass, Framebuffer, and Shaders with SPIR-V*. In order to get an overview of this, you may want to revisit the *Resource objects – managing images and buffers* section in `Chapter 2`, *Your First Vulkan Pseudo Program*.

Vulkan images represent contiguous texture data in 1D/2D/3D form. These images are primarily used as either an attachment or texture:

- **Attachment**: The image is attached to the pipeline for the framebuffer's color or depth attachment and can also be used as an auxiliary surface for multipass processing purposes
- **Texture**: The image is used as a descriptor interface and shared at the shader stage (fragment shader) in the form of samplers

> If you come from an OpenGL background, note that the use of images in Vulkan is entirely different from its counterpart in OpenGL. In Vulkan, the image is created by specifying a number of bitwise fields indicating the kind of image usage, such as color attachment, depth/stencil attachment, a sampled image in a shader, image load/store, and so on. In addition, you need to specify the tiling information (linear or optimal) for the image. This specifies the tiling or swizzling layout for the image data in memory.

The notion of texture in Vulkan is primarily interpreted with *images, image layouts,* and *image views*:

- **Image**: An image represents the texture object in Vulkan. This contains metadata that is utilized for computing memory requirements. The gathered memory requirements are helpful during memory allocation. An image indicates other, and numerous types of information, such as the format, size, and type (sparse map, cube map, and so on). A single image may contain sub-resources, such as multiple images, based on the mipmap level or array layers. Each image or image sub-resource is specified with an image layout.

- **Image layout**: An image layout is an implementation-specific way to store image texture information in a grid coordinate representation in the image memory. The image stored in image memory is very implementation-specific; each image has a specific usage, for example, color attachment, a sampled image in a shader, image load/store, or sparse textures for large images. For these special purposes, the implementation provides image layouts that are specialized in image memory usage to offer optimal performance.

> Each image layout is special. Each may offer only certain features. For example, an image specified with the `VK_IMAGE_LAYOUT_COLOR_ATTACHMENT_OPTIMAL` image layout can be used as a color image attachment for optimal performance; however, it cannot be used for transfer purposes.

- **Image view**: Images cannot be used directly for reading and writing purposes by API calls or pipeline shaders; instead, image views are used. It not only acts like an interface to the image object, but it also provides the metadata that is used to represent a continuous range of image sub-resources.

Image creation overview

In this section, we will provide you with a quick introduction to the image creation process in a step-by-step manner. This will be helpful in getting an overview of the image, image views, and the associated memory allocations. This section is immediately followed by two other sections that will cover images (*Understanding an image resource*) and their memory allocation (*Memory allocation and binding image resources*) along with a detailed description of the corresponding APIs.

The following are step-by-step instructions on how to create an image resource using Vulkan APIs:

1. First, create the image object:
    - Create an image object (`VkImage`) using the `vkCreateImage()` API. This API intakes an array of the `VkImageCreateInfo` structure, which specifies important image characteristics that are helpful in creating one or more image objects. At this time, the image object has no physical allocation on the device; however, it has logical memory information that will be used to allocate memory in the next step. This memory information comes from the `VkImageCreateInfo` object, which contains the format, image size, creation flags, and so on.

2. Then, allocate image memory:
   - **Getting the memory requirements**: Before we allocate the required chunk of image memory, we need to calculate the appropriate size of the memory we want to allocate. This is done using the `vkGetImageMemoryRequirements()` API. It automates the process of calculating the appropriate size of the image based on the image properties. It intakes the `VkCreateImageInfo` object that we described in the previous step.
   - **Determining the memory type**: Next, get the appropriate memory type from the available memory types. Once the type is made available, look for a type that matches the user properties.
   - **Allocating device memory**: Allocate the device memory (`VkDeviceMemory`) with the `vkAllocateMemory()` API.
   - **Binding the allocated memory**: Bind the allocated device memory (`VkDeviceMemory`) to the image object (`VkImage`) using the `vkBindImageMemory()` API.
3. Set the image layout:
   - Set the correct image layout as per application requirements; do this using pipeline image memory barriers with `vkCmdPipelineBarrier()`.
4. Create the image views:
   - Images can only be accessed via image views. This is the final step where we create an image view using `vkCreateImageView()`. The image can now be used by either API calls or pipeline shaders.

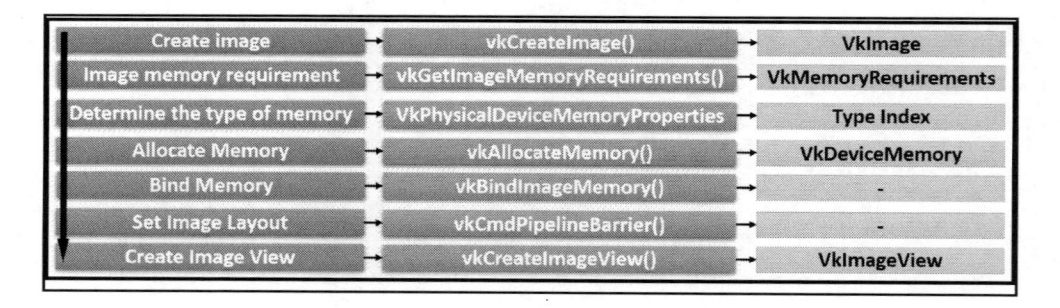

Create image	vkCreateImage()	VkImage
Image memory requirement	vkGetImageMemoryRequirements()	VkMemoryRequirements
Determine the type of memory	VkPhysicalDeviceMemoryProperties	Type Index
Allocate Memory	vkAllocateMemory()	VkDeviceMemory
Bind Memory	vkBindImageMemory()	-
Set Image Layout	vkCmdPipelineBarrier()	-
Create Image View	vkCreateImageView()	VkImageView

Understanding image resources

This section will cover the Vulkan APIs used to create an image resource. Here, we'll look into the concept of a data image, image view, and image layout in detail.

Creating images

An image resource in Vulkan is represented using the `VkImage` object. This object supports a multidimensional image up to three-dimensional data arrays. Images are created using the `vkCreateImage()` API. Here's the syntax to do this:

```
VkResult vkCreateImage(
    VkDevice                     device,
    const VkImageCreateInfo*     pCreateInfo,
    const VkAllocationCallbacks* pAllocator,
    VkImage*                     pImage);
```

The following table describes the various fields of `VkCommandPoolCreateInfo`:

Parameters	Description
device	This refers to the logical device responsible for creating an image.
pCreateInfo	This refers to a `VkImageCreateInfo` pointer.
pAllocator	This controls the host memory allocation process.
pImage	This returns the `VkImage` pointer after it's created.

The `vkCreateImage()` intakes `VkImageCreateInfo` as a second parameter, this control structure is defined here:

```
typedef struct VkImageCreateInfo {
    VkStructureType          sType;
    const void*              pNext;
    VkImageCreateFlags       flags;
    VkImageType              imageType;
    VkFormat                 format;
    VkExtent3D               extent;
    uint32_t                 mipLevels;
    uint32_t                 arrayLayers;
    VkSampleCountFlagBits    samples;
    VkImageTiling            tiling;
    VkImageUsageFlags        usage;
    VkSharingMode            sharingMode;
    uint32_t                 queueFamilyIndexCount;
```

Allocating Image Resources and Building a Swapchain with WSI

```
        const uint32_t*         pQueueFamilyIndices;
        VkImageLayout           initialLayout;
} VkImageCreateInfo;
```

The following table describes the various fields of `VkImageCreateInfo`:

Parameters	Description
sType	This is the type information of this control structure. It must be specified as `VK_STRUCTURE_TYPE_IMAGE_CREATE_INFO`.
pNext	This could be a valid pointer to an extension-specific structure or `NULL`.
flags	This refers to the `VkImageCreateFlagBits` bit field flags. More information on this will be provided later in this section.
imageType	This specifies the 1D/2D/3D dimensionality of the image using the `VkImageType` enum. It must be one of these: `VK_IMAGE_TYPE_1D`, `VK_IMAGE_TYPE_2D`, or `VK_IMAGE_TYPE_3D`.
format	This refers to the image format specified in the `VkFormat` type. It describes the format and type of the data elements that will be contained in the image.
extent	This describes the number of elements in each dimension of the base level.
mipLevels	This refers to the different levels of detail available in the minified sampling image.
arrayLayers	This specifies the number of layers in the image.
samples	This specifies the number of subdata element samples in the image, as defined in `VkSampleCountFlagBits`.
tilings	This specifies the tiling information of the image in the memory. It should be of the type `VkImageTiling` and must be either one of these two enum values: `VK_IMAGE_TILING_OPTIMAL` or `VK_IMAGE_TILING_LINEAR`.
usage	This refers to `VkImageUsageFlagBits` specifying the bit field that describes the intended usage of the image. More information on this will be provided later in this section.

`sharingMode`	This specifies the sharing mode of the image when it will be accessed by multiple queue families. This must be one of these values: `VK_SHARING_MODE_EXCLUSIVE` or `VK_SHARING_MODE_CONCURRENT` from the `VkSharingMode` enum.
`queueFamilyIndexCount`	This represents the number of entries in the `queueFamilyIndices` array.
`queueFamilyIndices`	This is an array of queue families that will access the image. The `sharingMode` must be `VK_SHARING_MODE_CONCURRENT`; otherwise, ignore it.
`initialLayout`	This defines the initial `VkImageLayout` state of all the sub-resources of the images. This must be either `VK_IMAGE_LAYOUT_UNDEFINED` or `VK_IMAGE_LAYOUT_PREINITIALIZED`. For more information on image layouts, refer to the *Understanding the image layouts* section of this chapter.

The image's `usage` flag of the `VkImageCreateInfo` control structure is described using the `VkImageUsageFlagBits` enum flag. The following is the syntax followed by a description of each field type of this enum:

```
typedef enum VkImageUsageFlagBits {
    VK_IMAGE_USAGE_TRANSFER_SRC_BIT = 0x00000001,
    VK_IMAGE_USAGE_TRANSFER_DST_BIT = 0x00000002,
    VK_IMAGE_USAGE_SAMPLED_BIT = 0x00000004,
    VK_IMAGE_USAGE_STORAGE_BIT = 0x00000008,
    VK_IMAGE_USAGE_COLOR_ATTACHMENT_BIT = 0x00000010,
    VK_IMAGE_USAGE_DEPTH_STENCIL_ATTACHMENT_BIT= 0x00000020,
    VK_IMAGE_USAGE_TRANSIENT_ATTACHMENT_BIT = 0x00000040,
    VK_IMAGE_USAGE_INPUT_ATTACHMENT_BIT = 0x00000080,
} VkImageUsageFlagBits;
```

Let's look at these bitwise fields in detail to understand what they mean:

Enum type	Description
`VK_IMAGE_USAGE_TRANSFER_SRC_BIT`	The image is used by the transfer command's (the copy command) source.
`VK_IMAGE_USAGE_TRANSFER_DST_BIT`	The image is used by the transfer command's (the copy command) destination.

`VK_IMAGE_USAGE_SAMPLED_BIT`	This image type is used as a sampler at the shading stage through the image view type, where the associated descriptor set slot (`VkDescriptorSet`) type could be either `VK_DESCRIPTOR_TYPE_SAMPLED_IMAGE` or `VK_DESCRIPTOR_TYPE_COMBINED_IMAGE_SAMPLER`. The sampled image in the shader is used for address calculations, controlling the filtering behavior, and other attributes.
`VK_IMAGE_USAGE_STORAGE_BIT`	Use this image type for load, store, and atomic operations on the image memory. The image view is associated with the descriptor type slot of the type `VK_DESCRIPTOR_TYPE_STORAGE_IMAGE`.
`VK_IMAGE_USAGE_COLOR_ATTACHMENT_BIT`	The image view created from this type of image resource is appropriate for a color attachment or the resolve attachment associated with the frame buffer object (`VkFrameBuffer`).
`VK_IMAGE_USAGE_DEPTH_STENCIL_ATTACHMENT_BIT`	The image view created from this type of image resource is appropriate for a depth/stencil attachment or the resolve attachment associated with the frame buffer object (`VkFrameBuffer`).
`VK_IMAGE_USAGE_TRANSIENT_ATTACHMENT_BIT`	The image type represented by this flag is allocated lazily. The memory type for this must be specified as `VK_MEMORY_PROPERTY_LAZILY_ALLOCATED_BIT`. Note that if this flag is specified, then `VK_IMAGE_USAGE_COLOR_ATTACHMENT_BIT`, `VK_IMAGE_USAGE_DEPTH_STENCIL_ATTACHMENT_BIT`, and `VK_IMAGE_USAGE_INPUT_ATTACHMENT_BIT` must not be used.
`VK_IMAGE_USAGE_INPUT_ATTACHMENT_BIT`	The image view created from this type of image resource is appropriate for an input attachment in the shader stage and in the frame buffer. This image view must be associated with the descriptor set slot (`VkDescriptorSet`) of the type `VK_DESCRIPTOR_TYPE_INPUT_ATTACHMENT`.

> The memory allocated with the `VK_MEMORY_PROPERTY_LAZILY_ALLOCATED_BIT` bit flag is not allocated upfront as per the requested size, but it may be allocated in a monotonic fashion where memory gradually increases with application demand.

The `flag` field in the `VkImageCreateInfo` enum hints the underlying application how it manages various image resources, such as memory, format, and attributes, using the `VkImageCreateFlagBits` enum. The following is the syntax of each type:

```
typedef enum VkImageCreateFlagBits {
    VK_IMAGE_CREATE_SPARSE_BINDING_BIT        = 0x00000001,
    VK_IMAGE_CREATE_SPARSE_RESIDENCY_BIT      = 0x00000002,
    VK_IMAGE_CREATE_SPARSE_ALIASED_BIT        = 0x00000004,
    VK_IMAGE_CREATE_MUTABLE_FORMAT_BIT        = 0x00000008,
    VK_IMAGE_CREATE_CUBE_COMPATIBLE_BIT       = 0x00000010,
    VK_IMAGE_CREATE_FLAG_BITS_MAX_ENUM        = 0x7FFFFFFF
} VkImageCreateFlagBits;
typedef VkFlags VkImageCreateFlags;
```

Now let's understand the flag definitions:

Flags	Description
`VK_IMAGE_CREATE_SPARSE_BINDING_BIT`	The image is fully stored using sparse memory binding.
`VK_IMAGE_CREATE_SPARSE_RESIDENCY_BIT`	Here the images can be stored partially using sparse memory binding. In order to use this field, the image must have the `VK_IMAGE_CREATE_SPARSE_BINDING_BIT` flag.
`VK_IMAGE_CREATE_SPARSE_ALIASED_BIT`	In this type of flag, the image is stored in sparse memory; it can also hold multiple portions of the same image in the same memory regions. The image must be created using the `VK_IMAGE_CREATE_SPARSE_BINDING_BIT` flag.
`VK_IMAGE_CREATE_MUTABLE_FORMAT_BIT`	This format is useful in cases where the image view (`VkImageView`) format is different from the created image object format itself (`VkImage`).
`VK_IMAGE_CREATE_CUBE_COMPATIBLE_BIT`	This format is used for cube mapping. In this case, `VkImageView` must be of the type `VK_IMAGE_VIEW_TYPE_CUBE` or `VK_IMAGE_VIEW_TYPE_CUBE_ARRAY`.

Allocating Image Resources and Building a Swapchain with WSI

Destroying the created images

When the image is no longer required, it can be destroyed using `vkDestroyImage()`. Here's the syntax to do this:

```
void vkDestroyImage(VkDevice         device,
                    VkImage          image,
                    const VkAllocationCallbacks* pAllocator);
```

This API accepts three parameters, which are described in the following table:

Parameters	Description
`device`	This is the logical device that destroys `image`.
`image`	This is the `VkImage` object that needs to be destroyed.
`pAllocator`	This controls the host memory deallocation process. Refer to the *Host memory* section in `Chapter 5`, *Command Buffer and Memory Management in Vulkan*.

Understanding image layouts

Let's take a look at the various image layouts available in the Vulkan specification. They are represented by the `VkImageLayout` enum values, as described in the following list:

- `VK_IMAGE_LAYOUT_UNDEFINED`: This layout does not support device access. This is most suitable for either `intialLayout` or `oldLayout` in an image transition. The transitioning of this layout does not provide any guarantee of preserving the memory data it holds.
- `VK_IMAGE_LAYOUT_GENERAL`: This layout supports all types of device access.
- `VK_IMAGE_LAYOUT_PREINITIALIZED`: This layout also does not support device access and is most suitable for either `intialLayout` or `oldLayout` in an image transition. The contents held by the layout memory are preserved while transitioning. This type of layout is useful in cases where the data is readily available at the initialization time. This way, the data can be directly stored in device memory immediately, without requiring an extra step to execute the layout transition.
- `VK_IMAGE_LAYOUT_COLOR_ATTACHMENT_OPTIMAL`: This layout is very suitable for color images. Therefore, it must only be used with the color and resolved attachment of `VkFrameBuffer`. In order to use this layout, the image must have the usage bit set as `VK_IMAGE_USAGE_COLOR_ATTACHMENT_BIT`.

[160]

> Image sub-resources do not have the usage bits specified individually–they are specified for the whole image only.

- `VK_IMAGE_LAYOUT_DEPTH_STENCIL_ATTACHMENT_OPTIMAL`: This layout must only be used for the depth/stencil attachment of `VkFrameBuffer`. In order to use this layout, the image must have the usage bit set as `VK_IMAGE_USAGE_DEPTH_STENCIL_ATTACHMENT_BIT`.
- `VK_IMAGE_LAYOUT_DEPTH_STENCIL_READ_ONLY_OPTIMAL`: This is similar to `VK_IMAGE_LAYOUT_DEPTH_STENCIL_ATTACHMENT_OPTIMAL`, except that it's used as a read-only `VkFrameBuffer` attachment or a read-only image in a shader, where it must be read as a sampled image, combined image/sampler, and/or input attachment. The image must be created with the usage bit set as `VK_IMAGE_USAGE_DEPTH_STENCIL_ATTACHMENT_BIT`.
- `VK_IMAGE_LAYOUT_SHADER_READ_ONLY_OPTIMAL`: This must be used as a read-only shader image, for example, a sampled image, combined image/sampler, and/or input attachment. The image sub-resource must be created either with the usage bit set as `VK_IMAGE_USAGE_SAMPLED_BIT` or `VK_IMAGE_USAGE_INPUT_ATTACHMENT_BIT`.
- `VK_IMAGE_LAYOUT_TRANSFER_SRC_OPTIMAL`: This must be used as the source image of a transfer command with a transfer pipeline, and its usage is valid only if the image sub-resource has the usage bit set as `VK_IMAGE_USAGE_TRANSFER_SRC_BIT`.
- `VK_IMAGE_LAYOUT_TRANSFER_DST_OPTIMAL`: This must be used as the destination image of a transfer command with a transfer pipeline, and its usage is valid only if the image sub-resource has the usage bit set as `VK_IMAGE_USAGE_TRANSFER_DST_BIT`.

Creating an image view

An image view is created using `vkCreateImageView()`. Here's the syntax of this:

```
VkResult vkCreateImageView(
    VkDevice                        device,
    const VkImageViewCreateInfo*    pCreateInfo,
    const VkAllocationCallbacks*    pAllocator,
    VkImageView*                    pView);
```

Allocating Image Resources and Building a Swapchain with WSI

The following table describes the various fields of `VkCommandPoolCreateInfo`:

Parameters	Description
`device`	This is the handle of the logical device that creates the image view.
`pCreateInfo`	This is the pointer to `VkCreateImageViewInfo`; it controls the creation of `VkImageView`.
`pAllocator`	This controls the host memory allocation process. For more information, refer to the *Host memory* section in Chapter 5, *Command Buffer and Memory Management in Vulkan*.
`pView`	This returns the handle of the created `VkImageView` object.

The `VkCreateImageViewInfo` data structure contains view-specific attributes that are consumed by the `vkCreateImageView()` API to create the image view. The following is the syntax of each field:

```
typedef struct VkImageViewCreateInfo {
    VkStructureType         sType;
    const void*             pNext;
    VkImageViewCreateFlags  flags;
    VkImage                 image;
    VkImageViewType         viewType;
    VkFormat                format;
    VkComponentMapping      components;
    VkImageSubresourceRange subresourceRange;
} VkImageViewCreateInfo;
```

The following table describes the various fields of `VkImageViewCreateInfo`:

Parameters	Description
`sType`	This is the type information of the structure; it must be `VK_STRUCTURE_TYPE_IMAGE_VIEW_CREATE_INFO`.
`pNext`	This is an extension-specific structure. This field could be `NULL` as well.
`flags`	This field is `NULL`; it is reserved for future use.
`image`	This is the handle of `VkImage`.

`viewType`	This indicates the image view type using the enum `VkImageViewType`. It must be either one of these flag values: `VK_IMAGE_VIEW_TYPE_1D`, `VK_IMAGE_VIEW_TYPE_2D`, `VK_IMAGE_VIEW_TYPE_3D`, `VK_IMAGE_VIEW_TYPE_CUBE`, `VK_IMAGE_VIEW_TYPE_1D_ARRAY`, `VK_IMAGE_VIEW_TYPE_2D_ARRAY`, or `VK_IMAGE_VIEW_TYPE_CUBE_ARRAY`.
`format`	This specifies the format (`VkFormat`) of the image.
`components`	This is used for remapping the color/depth/stencil after it has been converted into color components.
`subresourceRange`	This is used for selecting a range of mipmap levels and array layers, which are accessible through the view.

Destroying the image view

An image view is destroyed using the `vkCreateImageView()` API. This API intakes three parameters. The first parameter (`device`) specifies the logical device that is responsible for destroying the image view (`imageView`), which is indicated by the second parameter. The last parameter `pAllocator` controls the host memory allocation process. Here's the syntax of this:

```
void vkDestroyImageView(VkDevice device,
                        VkImageView    imageView,
                        VkAllocationCallbacks* pAllocator);
```

Memory allocation and binding image resources

When an image resource object (`VkImage`) is created, it contains a logical allocation. The image has no physical association with the device memory at that point. The actual memory backing is provided separately at a later stage. The physical allocation is very type-dependent; the images can be categorized into sparse and non-sparse. The sparse resource is specified using sparse creation flags (`VkImageCreateFlagBits` in `VkImageCreateInfo`); however, if the flag is not specified, it is a non-sparse image resource. This chapter will only address non-sparse memory as a reference. For more information on sparse resource allocation, refer to the official Vulkan 1.0 specification.

Allocating Image Resources and Building a Swapchain with WSI

The association of an image with memory is a three-step process: gathering memory allocation requirements for image allocation, allocating the physical chunk on the device memory, and binding the allocated memory to the image resource. Let's take a look at this in detail.

Gathering memory allocation requirements

The non-sparse image resources memory requirement can be queried using the vkGetImageMemoryRequirements() API. Here is the syntax of this:

```
void vkGetImageMemoryRequirements( VkDevice device,
                                   VkImage  image,
                                   VkMemoryRequirements*
                                       pMemoryRequirements);
```

The following are the different fields of the vkGetImageMemoryRequirements() API:

Parameters	Description
device	This refers to the device that owns the image.
image	This refers to the VkImage object.
pMemoryRequirements	This returns the VkMemoryRequirements structure object.

The VkMemoryRequirements structure object contains the memory requirements associated with the image object that we pass to vkGetImageMemoryRequirements(). Here's the syntax of this:

```
typedef struct VkMemoryRequirements {
    VkDeviceSize   size;
    VkDeviceSize   alignment;
    uint32_t       memoryTypeBits;
} VkMemoryRequirements;
```

The parameters of this structure and their respective descriptions are as follows:

Parameters	Description
size	This specifies the size of the image resource required in bytes.
alignment	This refers to the alignment offset in bytes that specifies the offset within the allocation required for the resource.

memoryTypeBits	This is a bitwise flag indicating the supported memory type for the image resource. If the bit i is set, it means it will support the memory type i in the VkPhysicalDeviceMemoryProperties structure of the image resource.

Allocating physical memory on the device

Physical memory is allocated using the vkAllocateMemory() API. This API was discussed in the last chapter. For a detailed description of this API, refer to the *Allocating the device memory* subsection under *Managing memory in Vulkan* in Chapter 5, *Command Buffer and Memory Management in Vulkan*.

Binding the allocated memory to an image object

Once physical memory is allocated to the device, what we need to do is bind this memory to its own image resource object (VkImage). The image resource is bonded with the allocated device memory using the vkBindImageMemory() API. The code for this is as follows:

```
VkResult vkBindBufferMemory(VkDevice          device,
                            VkBuffer          buffer,
                            VkDeviceMemor     memory,
                            VkDeviceSize      memoryOffset);
```

The parameters of this structure are described as follows:

Parameters	Description
device	This is the logical device that owns the memory and image object.
image	This refers to the VkImage object to which we need to bind the memory.
memory	This refers to the allocated VkDeviceMemory.
memoryOffset	This is the offset in bytes that specifies the starting point of the memory to which the image will be bounded.

Introducing swapchains

Swapchains are a mechanism by which the rendering of the drawing primitive is shown on a platform-specific presentation window/surface. A swapchain may contain single or multiple drawing images. These drawing images are called color images. A color image is simply an array of pixel information that resides in a special layout in the memory. The number of draw images in a swapchain is very specific to the implementation. When double images are used, it's called double buffering, and when three surfaces are used, triple buffering.

Among these images, when one image completes the drawing process in the background, it is swapped to the presentation window. In order to fully utilize the GPU, a different image is then treated as a background buffer for the drawing process. This process is repeated back and forth and the swapping of the images takes place continuously. Making use of multiple images improves the frame rate output as the GPU is always constantly busy with the processing part with one of the image, reducing the overall idle time.

The swapping or flipping of the drawing image is dependent upon the presentation mode; this may be updated during the **Vertical Blanking Interval** (**VBI**) or as soon as the drawing is made available. This means that when the monitor is refreshed, the background image is swapped with the front image displaying the new image. A swapchain is available in the form of an API extension, which needs to be enabled with `VK_KHR_SWAPCHAIN_EXTENSION_NAME`. Refer to the *Querying swapchain extensions* section for more information.

Understanding the swapchain implementation flow

The following diagram will provide you with an overview of swapchain implementation from start to finish. This will cover each and every part of the flow in a very brief fashion, allowing you to remain connected throughout the implementation, which will be covered in detail in upcoming sections:

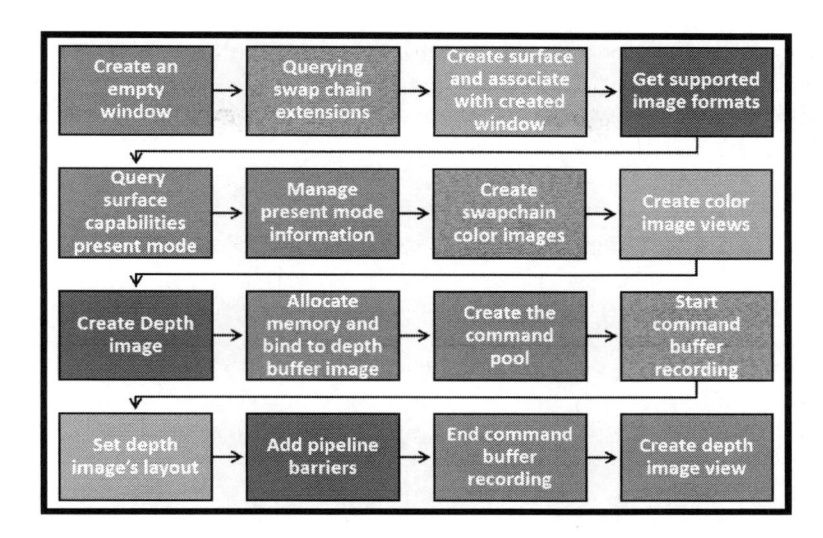

```
┌─────────────────────────────────────────────────────────────────────┐
│  Create an      Querying      Create surface    Get supported       │
│  empty     →    swap chain  → and associate  → image formats        │
│  window         extensions    with created                          │
│                               window                                │
│       ↓                                                             │
│  Query                                                              │
│  surface        Manage         Create           Create color        │
│  capabilities → present mode → swapchain     → image views          │
│  present mode   information    color images                         │
│       ↓                                                             │
│                 Allocate                        Start               │
│  Create Depth   memory and     Create the       command             │
│  image       →  bind to depth→ command       →  buffer              │
│                 buffer image   pool             recording           │
│       ↓                                                             │
│                                End command                          │
│  Set depth      Add pipeline   buffer           Create depth        │
│  image's     →  barriers    →  recording     →  image view          │
│  layout                                                             │
└─────────────────────────────────────────────────────────────────────┘
```

Let's get into the flow and quickly take an overview of each of the specifics:

1. **Create an empty window**: This process provides an empty native platform window that is connected to the swapchain's color images. Each time a frame (image) is written, it is swapped to the presentation layer. The presentation layer relays this information to the attached native window for display purposes.
2. **Querying swap chain extensions**: The swapchain APIs are not part of the standard API specification. They are implementation-specific, and the loader is used to load these APIs in the form of extensions. The loaded extensions are stored in the form of function pointers whose signatures are predefined in the Vulkan specification.
3. **Creating a surface and associate it with the created window**: This process creates a logical platform-specific surface object. At this time, it has no memory backing for the color images. This logical surface object is attached to the empty window, declaring the window as its owner.
4. **Getting supported image formats**: In this step, we query the physical device to check all the image formats it supports.
5. **Querying swapchain image surface capabilities:** This obtains the information on basic surface capabilities, since it is required when we create swapchains images. In addition, it checks the present modes that are available.
6. **Managing the present mode information:** This uses the available present mode information and decide the present mode technique that should be used in the swapchain. A swapchain's present mode decides how the incoming presentation requests will be internally processed and queued.

7. **Creating the swapchain and retrieving the presentation images:** Let's use the above-gathered information and create the swapchain images. The WSI extension returns the color image object; these images are of the type `VkImage`, and are used by the application.

> **TIP:** The WSI images are not owned by the application it belongs to WSI and hence the image layout cannot applied. The image layout can only be applied to images that are owned by the application.

8. **Creating color image views:** Depending upon the system capabilities, the WSI implementation may return 1–3 swapchain images (based on single, double, or triple buffering). For using each image in the application, you will need to create a corresponding image view.
9. **Creating a depth image:** Similar to the color images, you will need a depth image for depth testing; but unlike swapchain images, which are prebaked by the WSI, the depth image needs to be created by the application. First, you will need to create a depth image object (`VkImage`), follow the next steps to allocate the memory, create image layout and finally producing the image view object (`VkImageView`).
10. **Depth image memory allocation:** You will need to allocate the physical device memory and bind it to the depth image object.
11. **Creating the command pool:** We need the command buffer for depth image since this image is owned by us; we will use the command buffer to apply the image layouts.
12. **Creating the command buffer:** You will need to create the command buffer and begin to record the commands responsible for creating the depth image layout using the created depth image object.
13. **Image layout:** This lets you apply a *depth/stencil* compatible image layout on the depth image object.
14. **Add pipeline barriers:** In order to ensure that the image layout is always executed before the creation of the image view, add a pipeline barrier. When a pipeline barrier is inserted, it ensures that the commands prior to it is executed before the commands that follow it in the command buffer.
15. **Ending command buffer recording:** This allows you to stop the command buffer recording.
16. **Creating a depth image view:** After the image object is converted into the compatible image layout, create an image view object (`VkImageView`). The image cannot be directly used in the application; they must be in an image view form.

The created color image view will be submitted to the graphics queue to let the presentation engine render it on the display window. By the end of this chapter, you will be able to display the blank window since nothing is rendered on the swapchain color images so far.

The swapchain implementation's class block diagram

This section will act as a brief introduction to the upcoming section where we will implement the swapchain. This will help us understand the role of these classes as we inch towards a detailed implementation.

> In this chapter, we are introducing three new user-defined custom classes: `VulkanRenderer`, `VulkanSwapChain`, and `VulkanPipeline`. These classes are not associated with any official Vulkan specification API or data structures. These are user-defined and will help us manage the application in an organized way.

The following block diagram shows these module classes and their hierarchical relationship. Besides this, this pictorial representation will also inform you about the responsibility of each and every module. As we proceed to the next chapter, we will introduce a few more classes:

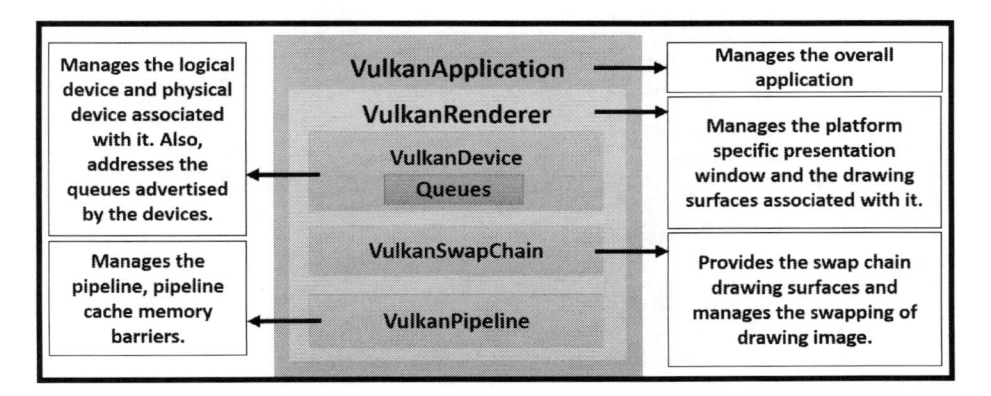

Manages the logical device and physical device associated with it. Also, addresses the queues advertised by the devices.	**VulkanApplication**	Manages the overall application
	VulkanRenderer	Manages the platform specific presentation window and the drawing surfaces associated with it.
	VulkanDevice	
	Queues	
Manages the pipeline, pipeline cache memory barriers.	**VulkanSwapChain**	Provides the swap chain drawing surfaces and manages the swapping of drawing image.
	VulkanPipeline	

Renderer – a window management custom class

The `VulkanRender` class is defined in `VulkanRenderer.h/.cpp`. It manages a unique presentation window and its dependent resources, such as devices, swapchains, pipelines, and so on, in an application. An application can have multiple rendering windows, as described in the following diagram; each renderer takes care of an individual presentation window with all its corresponding resources.

However, since we are at the beginner level, our samples assume only one output presentation window. Therefore, `VulkanApplication` contains a single `VulkanRenderer` class object:

The following is the declaration of the `VulkanRenderer` header file. This class creates the presentation layer's empty window (`createPresentationWindow()`), which will be later filled with the color images of the swapchain. The empty window creation process is very platform-specific; this sample example is only implemented for the Windows platform:

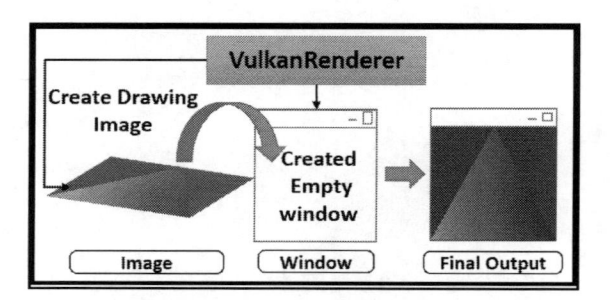

In addition, the `VulkanRenderer` class manages the initialization (`initialize()`) and renders the presentation window, (`render()`). This class also manages the command pool for various command buffers:

```
/************* VulkanRenderer.h *************/
class VulkanRenderer{
// Many line skipped in this header, please refer to
// corresponding source with this chapter.
```

```cpp
public:
    void initialize();      //Simple life cycle

    // Create an empty window
    void createPresentationWindow(int& w, int& height);

    // Windows procedure method for handling events.
    static LRESULT CALLBACK WndProc(HWND hWnd, UINT uMsg, WPARAM
                        wParam, LPARAM lParam);

    void createCommandPool();   // Create command pool
    void createSwapChain();     // Create swapchain Color image
    void createDepthImage();    // Create Depth image

public:
    HINSTANCE   connection;  // hInstance - Windows Instance
    char    name[80];   // name - App name appearing on the window
    HWND    window;     // hWnd - the window handle

    // Data structure used for depth image
    struct{     VkFormat        format;
                VkImage         image;
                VkDeviceMemory  mem;
                VkImageView     view;
    }Depth;

    VkCommandBuffer cmdDepthImage;      // Depth image command buffer
    VkCommandPool   cmdPool;            // Command pool

    int     width, height;              // Window Width and Height

private:
    // Class managers
    VulkanSwapChain*    swapChainObj;
    VulkanApplication*  application;
    // The device object associated with this Presentation layer.
    VulkanDevice*       deviceObj;
};

VulkanRenderer::VulkanRenderer(VulkanApplication * app,
        VulkanDevice* deviceObject){
    // Many lines skipped
    application = app;
    deviceObj   = deviceObject;

    swapChainObj = new VulkanSwapChain(this);
}
```

Creating the presentation window

This section will implement the windowing system that will be used to present the swapchain color images on the display window. This example primarily focuses on Windows and uses the `CreateWindowEx()` API to create an overlapped pop-up or child window with an extended window style. Creating windows is common, and discussing this topic is beyond the scope of this book.

Refer to the online MSDN documentation for more information on the related APIs (https://msdn.microsoft.com/en-us/library/windows/desktop/ms632680(v=vs.85).aspx):

```
void VulkanRenderer::createPresentationWindow(const int&
                    windowWidth, const int& windowHeight){

    width  = windowWidth;
    height = windowHeight;

    WNDCLASSEX  winInfo;
    // Initialize the window class structure:
    memset(&winInfo, 0, sizeof(WNDCLASSEX));
    winInfo.cbSize          = sizeof(WNDCLASSEX);
    winInfo.lpfnWndProc     = WndProc;
    winInfo.hInstance       = connection;
    winInfo.lpszClassName   = name;

    // Register window class
    if (!RegisterClassEx(&winInfo)) { exit(1); }
    // Create window with the registered class
    RECT wr = { 0, 0, width, height };
    AdjustWindowRect(&wr, WS_OVERLAPPEDWINDOW, FALSE);
    window = CreateWindowEx(0, name, name, WS_OVERLAPPEDWINDOW
                |WS_VISIBLE | WS_SYSMENU, 100, 100,
                wr.right - wr.left, wr.bottom - wr.top,
                NULL, NULL, connection, NULL);

    SetWindowLongPtr(window, GWLP_USERDATA, &application);
}
```

On a Microsoft Windows window, we need a windows procedure function to handle event processing. Here we will process the `WM_PAINT`, `WM_SIZE` and `WM_CLOSE` events. The `WM_CLOSE` event is called when a user clicks on the close button on the window. However, the `WM_PAINT` event is used to render the window. We will handle the `WM_PAINT` and `WM_SIZE` message in later chapters:

```
// Windows procedure handlers for MS Windows
LRESULT CALLBACK VulkanRenderer::WndProc(HWND hWnd, UINT uMsg,
WPARAM wParam, LPARAM lParam){
    VulkanApplication* appObj = VulkanApplication::GetInstance();

    switch (uMsg){
        case WM_CLOSE: PostQuitMessage(0); break;

        default: break;
    }

    return (DefWindowProc(hWnd, uMsg, wParam, lParam));
}
```

Initializing the renderer

The initialization creates a presentation window with a given dimension and fulfills various prerequisites for the swapchain implementation. This includes querying the swapchain extension APIs, creating surface objects, finding the best-supported queue for the presentation layer, getting the compatible image format for drawing, and so on. We will discuss each and every part in detail as we proceed through the chapter. The initialization of the `Renderer` class is done using the `initialize()` function, as described in the following code; refer to the comments highlighted in bold to get an overview:

```
void VulkanRenderer::initialize(){
    // Create an empty window with dimension 500x500
    createPresentationWindow(500, 500);
    // Initialize swapchain
    swapChainObj->intializeSwapChain();

    // We need command buffers, so create a command buffer pool
    createCommandPool();
    // Let's create the swapchain color images
    buildSwapChainAndDepthImage();
}
```

Creating the command pool

The `VulkanRenderer` class contains the command pool. This pool will be used for command buffer allocation and for various operations such as the creation of the depth image, pipeline state setup, drawing primitives, and many more. This chapter will demonstrate the first command buffer in action, where we will create the depth image.

In the following code, the command pool is created using the various attributes specified in the `VkCommandPoolCreateInfo` control structure. This control structure contains the index of the graphics queue for which the command buffers need to be allocated. Vulkan specifies such information in the control structures ahead of time, allowing the underlying pipeline to take full advantage of pre-optimizations. For more information on command buffers and command pools, refer to the *Understanding the command pool and buffer APIs* section in Chapter 5, *Command Buffer and Memory Management in Vulkan*:

```
void VulkanRenderer::createCommandPool(){
   VulkanDevice* deviceObj        = application->deviceObj;
   VkCommandPoolCreateInfo cmdPoolInfo = {};
   cmdPoolInfo.sType=VK_STRUCTURE_TYPE_COMMAND_POOL_CREATE_INFO;
   cmdPoolInfo.queueFamilyIndex = deviceObj->
                           graphicsQueueWithPresentIndex;

   vkCreateCommandPool(deviceObj->device, &cmdPoolInfo, NULL,
                           &cmdPool);
}
```

Building swapchain and depth images

The `buildSwapChainAndDepthImage()` function is the entry point for creating swapchain and depth images. We will look at these internal functions in detail as we proceed:

```
void VulkanRenderer::buildSwapChainAndDepthImage(){
    // Get the appropriate queue to submit the command into
    deviceObj->getDeviceQueue();

    // Create swapchain and get the color images
    swapChainObj->createSwapChain(cmdDepthImage);

    // Create the depth image
    createDepthImage();
}
```

Rendering the presentation window

Draw the presentation window on the display and handle Windows messages. When the user presses the close button, exit the presentation window and break the infinite rendering loop:

```
void VulkanRenderer::render(){
    MSG msg;    // message
    while (1) {
        PeekMessage(&msg, NULL, 0, 0, PM_REMOVE);
        if (msg.message == WM_QUIT) {
            break; // If Quit message the exit the render loop
        }
        TranslateMessage(&msg);
        DispatchMessage(&msg);
        RedrawWindow(window, NULL, NULL, RDW_INTERNALPAINT);
    }
}
```

VulkanSwapChain – the swapchain manager

A swapchain is implemented in the `VulkanSwapChain` class inside `VulkanSwapChain.h/.cpp`. This class manages the entire swapchain life cycle from its initialization and creation to its destruction (public functions). The life cycle comprises several smaller intermediate stages, such as querying the API extensions, getting the appropriate image format, getting surface capabilities and the presentation mode, and so on (private functions).

The following is the header file declaration of the `VulkanSwapChain` class, we will go through all the important functionalities:

```
class VulkanSwapChain{
    // Many line are skipped, please refer to source code
    public:
    void intializeSwapChain();
    void createSwapChain(const VkCommandBuffer& cmd);
    void destroySwapChain();

    private:
    VkResult createSwapChainExtensions();
    void getSupportedFormats();
    VkResult createSurface();
    uint32_t getGraphicsQueueWithPresentationSupport();
    void getSurfaceCapabilitiesAndPresentMode();
    void managePresentMode();
```

Allocating Image Resources and Building a Swapchain with WSI

```
        void createSwapChainColorBufferImages();
        void createColorImageView(const VkCommandBuffer& cmd);

    public:
        // User define structure containing public variables used
        // by the swapchain private and public functions.
        SwapChainPublicVariables scPublicVars;

    private:
        // User define structure containing private variables used
        // by the swapchain private and public functions.
        SwapChainPrivateVariables scPrivateVars;
        VulkanRenderer* rendererObj;
        VulkanApplication* appObj;
};
```

In addition to this, the class has two user-defined structures, namely `SwapChainPrivateVariables` and `SwapChainPublicVariables`. This includes the class's private and public member variables:

```
    struct SwapChainPrivateVariables
    {
        // Store the image surface capabilities
        VkSurfaceCapabilitiesKHR        surfCapabilities;

        // Stores the number of present modes
        uint32_t                        presentModeCount;

        // Arrays for retrived present modes
        std::vector<VkPresentModeKHR>   presentModes;

        // Size of the swapchain color images
        VkExtent2D                      swapChainExtent;

        // Number of color images supported
        uint32_t    desiredNumberOfSwapChainImages;
        VkSurfaceTransformFlagBitsKHR preTransform;

        // Stores present mode bitwise flag for swapchain creation
        VkPresentModeKHR                swapchainPresentMode;

        // The retrived drawing color swapchain images
        std::vector<VkImage>            swapchainImages;

        std::vector<VkSurfaceFormatKHR> surfFormats;
    };

    struct SwapChainPublicVariables
```

```
{
    // The logical platform dependent surface object
    VkSurfaceKHR surface;

    // Number of buffer image used for swapchain
    uint32_t swapchainImageCount;

    // Swapchain object
    VkSwapchainKHR swapChain;

    // List of color swapchain images
    std::vector<SwapChainBuffer> colorBuffer;

    // Current drawing surface index in use
    uint32_t currentColorBuffer;

    // Format of the image
    VkFormat format;
};
```

Querying swapchain extensions

The swapchain implementation needs a set of APIs. These APIs are not part of the Vulkan SDK and are dynamically available. The APIs are very specific to the platform implementation and are available in the form of API extensions, which are queried dynamically and stored in the form of a function pointer. This API extension can be queried successfully by specifying the VK_KHR_SWAPCHAIN_EXTENSION_NAME device extension when the VkDevice object is created:

```
std::vector<const char *> deviceExtensionNames = {
    VK_KHR_SWAPCHAIN_EXTENSION_NAME
};

// Look into VulkanDevice::createDevice() for more info
VkDeviceCreateInfo deviceInfo       = {};
deviceInfo.ppEnabledExtensionNames  = deviceExtensionNames;
vkCreateDevice(*gpu, &deviceInfo, NULL, &device);
```

Allocating Image Resources and Building a Swapchain with WSI

The following code snippet codes a macro, thereby helping us query instance- and device-specific extensions. We use this macro to get the WSI extension API's function pointer. For more information on instance- and device-level extensions, refer to the *Introduction to layer and extensions* section in `Chapter 3`, *Shaking Hands with the Device*:

```
#define INSTANCE_FUNC_PTR(instance, entrypoint){
    fp##entrypoint = (PFN_vk##entrypoint) vkGetInstanceProcAddr
                                (instance, "vk"#entrypoint);
    if (fp##entrypoint == NULL) { exit(-1);
}

#define DEVICE_FUNC_PTR(dev, entrypoint){
    fp##entrypoint = (PFN_vk##entrypoint)vkGetDeviceProcAddr
                                (dev, "vk"#entrypoint);

    if (fp##entrypoint == NULL) { exit(-1);
}
```

The following are the extension names at the instance and device level:

```
std::vector<const char *> instanceExtensionNames = {
    VK_KHR_SURFACE_EXTENSION_NAME,
    VK_KHR_WIN32_SURFACE_EXTENSION_NAME,
    VK_EXT_DEBUG_REPORT_EXTENSION_NAME,
};

std::vector<const char *> deviceExtensionNames = {
    VK_KHR_SWAPCHAIN_EXTENSION_NAME
};
```

This macro uses `vkGetInstanceProcAddr()` and `vkGetDeviceProcAddr()` to get the instance- and device-level extensions. For more information on the `vkGetInstanceProcAddr()` API, refer to the *Implementing debugging in Vulkan* section in `Chapter 4`, *Debugging in Vulkan*.

The following code queries instance- and device-level extensions using the user-defined `createSwapChainExtensions()` function:

```
VkResult VulkanSwapChain::createSwapChainExtensions(){

    // Dependency on createPresentationWindow()
    VkInstance& instance    = appObj->instanceObj.instance;
    VkDevice& device        = appObj->deviceObj->device;

    // Get Instance based swapchain extension function pointer
    INSTANCE_FUNC_PTR(instce,GetPhysicalDeviceSurfaceSupportKHR);
    INSTANCE_FUNC_PTR(instance,
```

```
                    GetPhysicalDeviceSurfaceCapabilitiesKHR);
INSTANCE_FUNC_PTR(instance,
                    GetPhysicalDeviceSurfaceFormatsKHR);
INSTANCE_FUNC_PTR(instance,
                    GetPhysicalDeviceSurfacePresentModesKHR);
INSTANCE_FUNC_PTR(instance, DestroySurfaceKHR);

// Get Device based swapchain extension function pointer
DEVICE_FUNC_PTR(device, CreateSwapchainKHR);
DEVICE_FUNC_PTR(device, DestroySwapchainKHR);
DEVICE_FUNC_PTR(device, GetSwapchainImagesKHR);
DEVICE_FUNC_PTR(device, AcquireNextImageKHR);
DEVICE_FUNC_PTR(device, QueuePresentKHR);
}
```

The following table shows the extension APIs that will be required to implement and manage the swapchain. These extensions are at both the instance and device levels and they must be queried. As we go through the various function implementations, we will discuss their extensions in detail:

Instance	Device
For `vkGetPhysicalDeviceSurfaceSupportKHR`, the function pointer is `fpGetPhysicalDeviceSurfaceSupportKHR`.	For `vkCreateSwapchainKHR` the function pointer is `fpGetPhysical`.
For `vkGetPhysicalDeviceSurfaceCapabilitiesKHR` the function pointer is `fpGetPhysicalDeviceSurfaceCapabilitiesKHR`.	For `vkDestroySwapchainKHR` the function pointer is `fpDestroySwapchainKHR`.
For `vkGetPhysicalDeviceSurfaceFormatsKHR` the function pointer is `fpGetPhysicalDeviceSurfaceFormatsKHR`.	For `vkGetSwapchainImagesKHR` the function pointer is `fpGetSwapchainImagesKHR`.
For `vkGetPhysicalDeviceSurfacePresentModesKHR` the function pointer is `fpGetPhysicalDeviceSurfacePresentModesKHR`.	For `vkAcquireNextImageKHR` the function pointer is `fpAcquireNextImageKHR`.
For `vkDestroySurfaceKHR` the function pointer is `fpDestroySurfaceKHR`.	For `vkQueuePresentKHR` the function pointer is `fpQueuePresentKHR`.

The retrieved API extensions are stored in the user-defined function pointer variable. They are renamed by replacing the prefix `vk` with `fp`. For example, the API extension `vkGetPhysicalDeviceSurfaceCapabilitiesKHR()` is stored as `fpGetPhysicalDeviceSurfaceCapabilitiesKHR()`. This is similar for others API extensions as well.

Creating the surface with WSI and associating it with the created window

The Vulkan API can be implemented seamlessly on every platform. A platform is an abstraction of windowing and OS services. Some examples include MS Windows, Android, and Wayland. **Window System Integration (WSI)** provides a platform-independent way to implement windowing or surface management.

Vulkan represents the logical surface object using `VkSurfaceKHR`. Different platforms have different APIs to create the `VkSurfaceKHR` surface object, such as `vkCreateWin32SurfaceKHR()`, `vkCreateAndroidSurfaceKHR()`, and `vkCreateXcbSurfaceKHR()`:

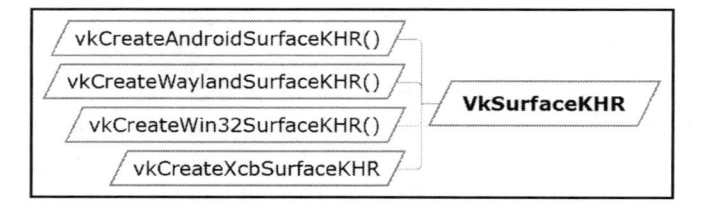

This example will focus on the Windows platform:

```
VkResult vkCreateWin32SurfaceKHR(
    VkInstance                          instance,
    const VkWin32SurfaceCreateInfoKHR*  pCreateInfo,
    const VkAllocationCallbacks*        pAllocator,
    VkSurfaceKHR*                       surface);
```

The following is the description of each and every field:

Parameters	Description
instance	This refers to the `VkInstance` object associated with the surface.
pCreateInfo	This refers to the `VkWin32SurfaceCreateInfoKHR` structure object to control surface management. More information in provided in the following information box.
pAllocator	This is used to control the host-specific memory allocation process.
surface	This returns the pointer of the created surface object.

> The `vkCreate<Platform>SurfaceKHR` structure object is created on the logical surface. It has no backing of the physical memory yet.

The API takes the `VkWin32SurfaceCreateInfo` structure as an input parameter, where various control properties on surface management can be specified. The following is the API syntax:

```
typedef struct VkWin32SurfaceCreateInfoKHR {
    VkStructureType               type;
    const void*                   next;
    VkWin32SurfaceCreateFlagsKHR  flags;
    HINSTANCE                     hinstance;
    HWND                          hwnd;
} VkWin32SurfaceCreateInfoKHR;
```

Let's take a look at all the parameters of the control structure:

Parameters	Description
type	This is the type information of this structure, which must be `VK_STRUCTURE_TYPE_WIN32_SURFACE_CREATE_INFO_KHR`.
next	This refers to `NULL` or an extension-specific pointer.
flag	This field is reserved for future use.
hInstance	This is the instance ID of the created window.
hwnd	This is the handle of the created window; `hwnd` and `hInstance` will be used to associate the surface with the presentation window.

[181]

Allocating Image Resources and Building a Swapchain with WSI

The `VulkanSwapChain` class implements the creation of the logical WSI surface using the `createSurface()` method:

```
// Depends on createPresentationWindow(), need window handle
VkResult VulkanSwapChain::createSurface(){
    VkInstance& instance = appObj->instanceObj.instance;

    // Construct the surface description:
    VkWin32SurfaceCreateInfoKHR createInfo = {};
    createInfo.sType        =
            VK_STRUCTURE_TYPE_WIN32_SURFACE_CREATE_INFO_KHR;
    createInfo.pNext        = NULL;
    createInfo.hinstance    = rendererObj->connection;
    createInfo.hwnd         = rendererObj->window;

    // Create the VkSurfaceKHR object
    return result = vkCreateWin32SurfaceKHR(instance,
            &createInfo, NULL, &scPublicVars.surface);
}
```

The graphics queue with present support

When swapchain color images are painted by the drawing primitives commands, they then submitted to the presentation engine to be displayed on the screen. This request is submitted in the form of a command buffer into the queue which can take up presentation requests and process it. Therefore, we need a graphic queue which is not only capable of accepting drawing command buffers but also supports the presentation. This can be done by querying each graphic queue available on the physical device and checking whether they support the presentation properties or not. The following code help us to achieve the same, we implement a help function `getGraphicsQueueWithPresentationSupport()` where we end up retrieving a single queue supporting graphics and presentation command buffer requests:

```
uint32_t VulkanSwapChain::getGraphicsQueueWithPresentationSupport(){
    VulkanDevice* device    = appObj->deviceObj;
    uint32_t queueCount     = device->queueCount;
    VkPhysicalDevice gpu    = *device->gpu;
    vector<VkQueueFamilyProperties>& queueProps =
                            device->queueProps;

    // Iterate each queue and get presentation status for each.
    VkBool32* supportsPresent = (VkBool32 *)malloc(queueCount *
                            sizeof(VkBool32));
    for (uint32_t i = 0; i < queueCount; i++) {
        fpGetPhysicalDeviceSurfaceSupportKHR(gpu, i,
```

```
                    scPublicVars.surface, &supportsPresent[i]);
    }

    // Search for a graphics queues that supports presentation
    uint32_t graphicsQueueNodeIndex = UINT32_MAX;
    uint32_t presentQueueNodeIndex = UINT32_MAX;
    for (uint32_t i = 0; i < queueCount; i++) {
        if ((queueProps[i].queueFlags &
                    VK_QUEUE_GRAPHICS_BIT) != 0) {

            if (graphicsQueueNodeIndex == UINT32_MAX) {
                graphicsQueueNodeIndex = i;
            }

            if (supportsPresent[i] == VK_TRUE) {
                graphicsQueueNodeIndex = i;
                presentQueueNodeIndex  = i;
                break;
            }
        }
    }
    if (presentQueueNodeIndex == UINT32_MAX) {

        // If didn't find a queue that supports both graphics
        // and present, then find a separate present queue.
        for (uint32_t i = 0; i < queueCount; ++i) {
            if (supportsPresent[i] == VK_TRUE) {
                presentQueueNodeIndex = i;
                break;
            }
        }
    }

    free(supportsPresent);

    // Generate error if could not find queue with present queue
    if (graphicsQueueNodeIndex == UINT32_MAX ||
      presentQueueNodeIndex == UINT32_MAX) {return  UINT32_MAX;}

    return graphicsQueueNodeIndex;
}
```

Querying swapchain image formats

The swapchain needs a supported color-space format for the surface. All the supported formats can be retrieved using the `vkGetPhysicalDeviceSurfaceFormatsKHR()` API. Here's the syntax of this:

```
VkResult vkGetPhysicalDeviceSurfaceFormatsKHR(
    VkPhysicalDevice          physicalDevice,
    VkSurfaceKHR              surface,
    uint32_t*                 pSurfaceFormatCount,
    VkSurfaceFormatKHR*       pSurfaceFormats);
```

The following table describes the various fields of this API:

Parameters	Description
`physicalDevice`	This refers to the logical device associated with the swapchain.
`surface`	This refers to the logical surface created for the swapchain.
`pSurfaceFormatCount`	This is an in and out parameter. When `vkGetPhysicalDeviceSurfaceFormatKHR` is called with `surfaceFormats` as `NULL`, it returns the number of supported surface formats. Otherwise, it is used to retrieve the surfaces based on the number of surface pointers.
`pSurfaceFormats`	This is to retrieve the supported surface formats.

The following implementation gets the number of supported image formats. Using `formatCount`, the surface formats are retrieved into the `VkSurfaceFormatKHR` array. In the event no preferred surface format information is found, we treat the surface format as 32-bit RGBA:

```
void VulkanSwapChain::getSupportedFormats()
{
    VkPhysicalDevice gpu = *rendererObj->getDevice()->gpu;
    VkResult  result;
    // Get the number of VkFormats supported:
    uint32_t formatCount;
    fpGetPhysicalDeviceSurfaceFormatsKHR
            (gpu, scPublicVars.surface, &formatCount, NULL);
    scPrivateVars.surfFormats.clear();
    scPrivateVars.surfFormats.resize(formatCount);

    // Get VkFormats in allocated objects
    result = fpGetPhysicalDeviceSurfaceFormatsKHR(gpu,
    scPublicVars.surface, &formatCount,
    &scPrivateVars.surfFormats[0]);
```

```
        // In case it's a VK_FORMAT_UNDEFINED, then surface has no
        // preferred format. We use RGBA 32 bit format
        if (formatCount == 1 && surfFormats[0].format ==
                                VK_FORMAT_UNDEFINED)
              { scPublicVars.format = VK_FORMAT_B8G8R8A8_UNORM; }
        else
              {scPublicVars.format = surfFormats[0].format;}
}
```

Creating the swapchain

In the following subsection, we will learn the implementation of the swapchain. This consists of querying surface capabilities and presentation modes, retrieving color images, and creating image views.

Swapchain surface capabilities and the presentation mode

The swapchain creation process requires you to know two things in order to create the image surface: surface capabilities and the presentation mode:

1. **Surface capabilities**: This specifies the image surface capabilities offered by the physical device. The `vkGetPhysicalDeviceSurfaceCapabilitiesKHR()` API extension can be used to query these capabilities. The extension is stored in the user-defined function pointer `fpGetPhysicalDeviceSurface-CapabilitiesKHR()`. Its syntax is as follows:

   ```
   VkResult vkGetPhysicalDeviceSurfaceCapabilitiesKHR(
       VkPhysicalDevice              physicalDevice,
       VkSurfaceKHR                  surface,
       VkSurfaceCapabilitiesKHR*     surfaceCapabilities);
   ```

   The advertised capabilities are retrieved in the `VkSurfaceCapabilitiesKHR` object. This includes useful information such as the min/max number of image surfaces supported, image dimension range, the maximum number of image arrays possible, the kinds of transformation features supported by the surface (such as rotation or mirror rotation through 90, 180, and 270 degrees), and so on.

Allocating Image Resources and Building a Swapchain with WSI

2. **The presentation mode**: A swapchain can have various types of presentation mode, and can be retrieved using the `vkGetPhysicalDeviceSurfacePresentModesKHR()` API extension dynamically. The retrieved information is exposed via the `VkPresentModeKHR` enumeration supporting four types of presentation modes (see the next section for more information on the modes). The `presentModelCount` contains the number of presentation modes. The syntax of this API is as follows:

```
VkResult vkGetPhysicalDeviceSurfacePresentModesKHR(

    VkPhysicalDevice      physicalDevice,
    VkSurfaceKHR          surface,
    uint32_t*             presentModeCount,
    VkPresentModeKHR*     presentModes);
```

The following code retrieves the surface capabilities along with the presentation modes and stores the required information in the private class member variables:

```
void VulkanSwapChain::getSurfaceCapabilitiesAndPresentMode(){
    // Some lines are skipped, please refer to the source code
    VkPhysicalDevice gpu = *appObj->deviceObj->gpu;
    fpGetPhysicalDeviceSurfaceCapabilitiesKHR(gpu, scPublicVars.
            surface, &scPrivateVars.surfCapabilities);

    fpGetPhysicalDeviceSurfacePresentModesKHR(gpu, scPublicVars.
            surface, &scPrivateVars.presentModeCount, NULL);

    scPrivateVars.presentModes.clear();
    scPrivateVars.presentModes.resize
            (scPrivateVars.presentModeCount);
    assert(scPrivateVars.presentModes.size()>=1);

    result = fpGetPhysicalDeviceSurfacePresentModesKHR
            (gpu, scPublicVars.surface,
            &scPrivateVars.presentModeCount,
            &scPrivateVars.presentModes[0]);

    fpGetPhysicalDeviceSurfacePresentModesKHR(gpu, scPublicVars.
            surface, &scPrivateVars.presentModeCount,
            scPrivateVars.presentModes);

    if(scPrivateVars.surfCapabilities.currentExtent.width ==
        (uint32_t)-1){
        // If the surface width and height is not defined,
        // then set it equal to image size.
        scPrivateVars.swapChainExtent.width =
                                    rendererObj->width;
```

```
              scPrivateVars.swapChainExtent.height =
                                  rendererObj->height;
}
else{
      // If the surface size is defined, then it must
      // match the swapchain size
        scPrivateVars.swapChainExtent = scPrivateVars.
                   surfCapabilities.currentExtent;
}
}
```

Managing presentation mode information

The color images contained by the swapchain are managed by the presentation engine using the presentation mode schemes. These schemes determine how the incoming presentation requests will be processed and queued internally. The `VkPresentModeKHR()` API supports four types of presentation mode:

Presentation mode	Description
VK_PRESENT_MODE_IMMEDIATE_KHR	This mode immediately renders the presentation requests without waiting for vertical blanking. No internal queue management is required for presentation requests. This mode is highly susceptible to image tearing.
VK_PRESENT_MODE_MAILBOX_KHR	Here, the presentation requests are queued up in a single entry queue, and they wait for the next vertical blanking signal that will allow the presentation engine to update the image. This mode does not cause the tearing effect. When the queue is full, the latest presentation request replaces the prior one. In the event of vertical blanking, a single queue request is popped up and is processed. Any image associated with the prior entry becomes available for reuse by the application.

Allocating Image Resources and Building a Swapchain with WSI

VK_PRESENT_MODE_FIFO_KHR	Here, the presentation requests are queued up in a single entry queue, and they wait for the next vertical blanking to update the current image, where the front image is removed and processed (hence FIFO). Tearing cannot be observed here. A new request is added to the end of the queue and removed from the beginning.
VK_PRESENT_MODE_FIFO_RELAXED_KHR	Here, the presentation engine generally updates the current image during the vertical blanking period. If a vertical blanking period has already passed since the last update of the current image, then the presentation engine does not wait for the subsequent vertical blanking period to push the next presentation image to be processed. The next image is immediately followed for the update. This mode may result in visible tearing. New requests are appended to the end of the queue, and one request is removed from the beginning of the queue and processed during or after each vertical blanking period in which the queue is not empty.

The following code implements the presentation mode scheme. First it checks whether the MAILBOX scheme (non-tearing) is available. In case this mode is not available, then the IMMEDIATE mode is preferred. The default fallback scheme is FIFO:

```
void VulkanSwapChain::managePresentMode()
{
    // MAILBOX - lowest-latency non-tearing mode.If not,try
    // IMMEDIATE, the fastest (but tears). Else, fall back to FIFO.
    scPrivateVars.swapchainPresentMode = VK_PRESENT_MODE_FIFO_KHR;
    for (size_t i = 0; i < scPrivateVars.presentModeCount; i++) {
        if(scPrivateVars.presentModes[i]==VK_PRESENT_MODE_MAILBOX_KHR){
    scPrivateVars.swapchainPresentMode = VK_PRESENT_MODE_MAILBOX_KHR;
    break;
    }
    if(scPrivateVars.swapchainPresentMode!=VK_PRESENT_MODE_MAILBOX_KHR
     &&scPrivateVars.presentModes[i]== VK_PRESENT_MODE_IMMEDIATE_KHR){
    scPrivateVars.swapchainPresentMode=VK_PRESENT_MODE_IMMEDIATE_KHR;
    }
    }
    // Determine the number of VkImage's to use in the swapchain
    scPrivateVars.desiredNumberOfSwapChainImages = scPrivateVars.
      surfCapabilities.minImageCount + 1;
    if ((scPrivateVars.surfCapabilities.maxImageCount > 0) &&
```

```
      (scPrivateVars.desiredNumberOfSwapChainImages >
    scPrivateVars.surfCapabilities.maxImageCount)) {
      // Application must settle for fewer images than desired:
      scPrivateVars.desiredNumberOfSwapChainImages =
          scPrivateVars.surfCapabilities.maxImageCount;
   }
   if(scPrivateVars.surfCapabilities.supportedTransforms &
          VK_SURFACE_TRANSFORM_IDENTITY_BIT_KHR) {
  scPrivateVars.preTransform=VK_SURFACE_TRANSFORM_IDENTITY_BIT_KHR;
   }
   else {
  scPrivateVars.preTransform=
          scPrivateVars.surfCapabilities.currentTransform;
   }
 }
```

> In the real application, it is advisable to prefer `PRESENT_MODE_FIFO_RELAXED_KHR` as the presentation mode as it only tears when the app misses but doesn't tear when the app is fast enough.

Retrieving the swapchain's color images

Swapchain color images are retrieved by creating the `VkSwapchainKHR` swapchain object using the `vkCreateSwapchainKHR()` API extension function pointer. The syntax to do this is as follows:

```
VkResult vkCreateSwapchainKHR(
    VkDevice                          device,
    const VkSwapchainCreateInfoKHR*   createInfo,
    const VkAllocationCallbacks*      allocator,
    VkSwapchainKHR*                   swapchain);
```

This API accepts the `VKSwapChainCreateInforKHR` control structure. This structure contains the necessary information to control the creation of the swapchain object retrieved in the `VkSwapchainKHR` structure. Here's the syntax of this:

```
typedef struct VkSwapchainCreateInfoKHR {
    VkStructureType              type;
    const void*                  next;
    VkSwapchainCreateFlagsKHR    flags;
    VkSurfaceKHR                 surface;
    uint32_t                     minImageCount;
    VkFormat                     imageFormat;
    VkColorSpaceKHR              imageColorSpace;
    VkExtent2D                   imageExtent;
```

Allocating Image Resources and Building a Swapchain with WSI

```
    uint32_t                        imageArrayLayers;
    VkImageUsageFlags               imageUsage;
    VkSharingMode                   imageSharingMode;
    uint32_t                        queueFamilyIndexCount;
    const uint32_t*                 queueFamilyIndices;
    VkSurfaceTransformFlagBitsKHR   preTransform;
    VkCompositeAlphaFlagBitsKHR     compositeAlpha;
    VkPresentModeKHR                presentMode;
    VkBool32                        clipped;
    VkSwapchainKHR                  oldSwapchain;
} VkSwapchainCreateInfoKHR;
```

The `VkSwapchainCreateInfoKHR` structure has the following parameters:

Parameters	Description
type	This specifies the type of the structure. It must be VK_-STRUCTURE_TYPE_SWAPCHAIN_CREATE_INFO_KHR.
next	This refers to NULL or a pointer to an extension-specific structure.
flags	This must be zero. This field is reserved for future use.
surface	This is the surface to which the swapchain images will be presented.
minImageCount	This refers to the minimum number of presentable images needed by the application to implement the swapchain mechanism.
imageFormat	This is the format to be used for swapchain color images.
imageColor-Space	This represents the color space (VkColorSpaceKHR) supported by the swapchain.
imageExtent	This refers to the swapchain's image size or dimensions specified in pixels.
imageArray-Layers	This represents the number of views in a multiview/stereo surface.
imageUsage	This is a VkImageUsageFlagBits bit field indicating how the application will use the swapchain's presentable images.
imageSharingMode	This is the sharing mode used for the images of the swapchain.
queueFamily-IndexCount	The refers to the number of queue families that have access to the images of the swapchain if imageSharingMode is VK_SHARING_MODE_CONCURRENT.

[190]

`queueFamily Indices`	This is an array of queue family indices that have access to the images of the swapchain if `imageSharingMode` is `VK_SHARING_MODE_CONCURRENT`.
`preTransform`	This is a bit field of `VkSurfaceTransformFlag-BitsKHR` that describes the transform relative to the presentation engine's natural orientation, which is applied to the image content prior to the presentation.
`compositeAlpha`	This is the `VkCompositeAlphaFlagBitsKHR` bit field indicating the alpha-compositing mode to use when this surface is composited together with other surfaces on certain windowing systems.
`presentMode`	This is the presentation mode the swapchain will use.
`clipped`	This indicates whether the Vulkan implementation is allowed to discard the rendering operations that affect the regions of the surface that aren't visible.
`oldSwapchain`	This is non-null, and it specifies the swapchain that will be replaced by the new swapchain being created. Upon calling `vkCreateSwapchainKHR` with an old non-null swapchain, any image owned by the presentation engine and not currently being displayed will be freed immediately. Any image that is being displayed will be freed once it is no longer being displayed. This may occur even if the creation of the new swapchain fails. The application must destroy the old swapchain to free all of the memory associated with the old swapchain, including any presentable images the application currently owns. It must wait for the completion of any outstanding rendering before doing so, with the exception of rendering to presentable images that have been successfully submitted to the presentation, as described next, but that are not yet owned by the presentation engine.

In the following code, the `createSwapChainColorBufferImage()` function creates the swapchain using the function pointer of `vkCreateSwapchainKHR` (`fpCreateSwapchainKHR()`). Upon successful creation of the swapchain, the `VkImage` object image surfaces are created behind the scenes. Before acquiring the image surfaces, we allocate sufficient memory space to hold the image buffers. The number of swapchain images and physical surfaces is returned by the `vkGetSwapchainImagesKHR()` API extension's function pointer, namely (`fpGetSwapchainImagesKHR()`).

1. First populate the `VkSwapchainCreateInfoKHR` control structure with the required field values, such as the format of the image, size, presentation mode, color space, and so on. This information is used by the `fpCreateSwapchainKHR()` API function pointer to create the swapchain.

Allocating Image Resources and Building a Swapchain with WSI

2. Once the `VkSwapchainKHR` swapchain object (`swapchainImages`) is created successfully, use it to acquire the image using the `vkGetSwapchainImagesKHR()` API. This API is called twice:
   - When it is called for the first time with the last parameter as `NULL`, it retrieves the number of image (`swapchainImageCount`) present in the swapchain.
   - The `swapchainImageCount` is used to allocate sufficient memory to hold the surface image arrays (`VkImage*`). The same API when called the second time retrieves the image in the allocated `VkImage` array objects called `swapchainImages`, as explained in the following API description:

```
VkResult vkGetSwapchainImagesKHR(
    VkDevice                device,
    VkSwapchainKHR          swapchain,
    uint32_t*               swapchainImageCount,
    VkImage*                swapchainImages);
```

Parameters	Description
`device`	This is the logical device associated with the swapchain.
`swapchain`	This refers to the `VkSwapChainKHR` object.
`swapchainImageCount`	This refers to the number of image the swapchain contains.
`swapchainImages`	This refers to the `VkImage` array object that retrieves the swapchain.

The following code shows the implementation of the swapchain object creation process and the retrieval of the color images. The color images are used to store the color information for each corresponding pixel:

```
void VulkanSwapChain::createSwapChainColorBufferImages()
{
VkSwapchainCreateInfoKHR scInfo = {};
scInfo.sType                =
            VK_STRUCTURE_TYPE_SWAPCHAIN_CREATE_INFO_KHR;
scInfo.pNext                = NULL;
scInfo.surface              = scPublicVars.surface;
scInfo.minImageCount        =
            scPrivateVars.desiredNumberOfSwapChainImages;
scInfo.imageFormat          = scPublicVars.format;
scInfo.imageExtent.width    =
            scPrivateVars.swapChainExtent.width;
scInfo.imageExtent.height   =
```

```
                    scPrivateVars.swapChainExtent.height;
scInfo.preTransform        = scPrivateVars.preTransform;
scInfo.compositeAlpha
                           = VK_COMPOSITE_ALPHA_OPAQUE_BIT_KHR;
scInfo.imageArrayLayers    = 1;
scInfo.presentMode         = scPrivateVars.swapchainPresentMode;
scInfo.oldSwapchain        = VK_NULL_HANDLE;
scInfo.clipped             = true;
scInfo.imageColorSpace     = VK_COLOR_SPACE_SRGB_NONLINEAR_KHR;
scInfo.imageUsage          =
            VK_IMAGE_USAGE_COLOR_ATTACHMENT_BIT |
            VK_IMAGE_USAGE_TRANSFER_DST_BIT;
scInfo.imageSharingMode    = VK_SHARING_MODE_EXCLUSIVE;
scInfo.queueFamilyIndexCount = 0;
scInfo.pQueueFamilyIndices = NULL;

// Create the swapchain object
fpCreateSwapchainKHR(rendererObj->getDevice()->device,
    &swapChainInfo, NULL, &scPublicVars.swapChain);

// Get the number of images the swapchain has
fpGetSwapchainImagesKHR(rendererObj->getDevice()->device,
 scPublicVars.swapChain, &scPublicVars.swapchainImageCount, NULL);

scPrivateVars.swapchainImages.clear();
// Make array of swapchain image to retrieve the images
scPrivateVars.swapchainImages.resize
(scPublicVars.swapchainImageCount);
assert(scPrivateVars.swapchainImages.size() >= 1);

// Retrieve the swapchain image surfaces
fpGetSwapchainImagesKHR(rendererObj->getDevice()->device,
    scPublicVars.swapChain, &scPublicVars.swapchainImageCount,
    scPrivateVars.swapchainImages);
 }
```

Creating color image views

As discussed in the beginning of this chapter, images are not directly used in the form of image objects (VkImage) by the application; instead, image views are used (VkImageView). In this section, we will learn how to create an image view using image objects.

Allocating Image Resources and Building a Swapchain with WSI

Our application implements the image view creation process in the `createColorImageView()` function. The image view is created using the `vkCreateImageView()` API. This API accepts important parameters, such as the image view format, mipmap level, level count, number of array layers, and so on. For more information on image view APIs, refer to the *Creating the image view* subsection under the *Understanding image resources* section in this chapter.

In the following implementation, for each swapchain image object (`VkImage`), we create a corresponding image view by iterating through the list of the image objects available in `scPublicVars.swapchainImageCount`. This count is retrieved using the `fpGetSwapchainImagesKHR()` API, as mentioned in the previous section. The created image views are then pushed back to a vector list, where they will be used later to refer to the correct front and back buffer images:

```
void VulkanSwapChain::createColorImageView(const
   VkCommandBuffer& cmd){
  VkResult   result;
  for(uint32_t i = 0; i < scPublicVars.swapchainImageCount; i++){
    SwapChainBuffer sc_buffer;

    VkImageViewCreateInfo imgViewInfo = {};
    imgViewInfo.sType =
                   VK_STRUCTURE_TYPE_IMAGE_VIEW_CREATE_INFO;
    imgViewInfo.pNext        = NULL;
    imgViewInfo.format          = scPublicVars.format;
    imgViewInfo.components.r    = VK_COMPONENT_SWIZZLE_R;
    imgViewInfo.components.g    = VK_COMPONENT_SWIZZLE_G;
    imgViewInfo.components.b    = VK_COMPONENT_SWIZZLE_B;
    imgViewInfo.components.a    = VK_COMPONENT_SWIZZLE_A;
    imgViewInfo.subresourceRange.aspectMask =
                              VK_IMAGE_ASPECT_COLOR_BIT;
    imgViewInfo.subresourceRange.baseMipLevel   = 0;
    imgViewInfo.subresourceRange.levelCount     = 1;
    imgViewInfo.subresourceRange.baseArrayLayer = 0;
    imgViewInfo.subresourceRange.layerCount    = 1;
    imgViewInfo.viewType     = VK_IMAGE_VIEW_TYPE_2D;
    imgViewInfo.flags        = 0;

    sc_buffer.image = scPrivateVars.swapchainImages[i];
    // Since the swapchain is not owned by us we cannot set
    // the image layout. Upon setting, the implementation
    // may give error, the images layout were
    // created by the WSI implementation not by us.

    imgViewInfo.image = sc_buffer.image;
```

```
result = vkCreateImageView(rendererObj->getDevice()->device,
         &imgViewInfo, NULL, &sc_buffer.view);
    scPublicVars.colorBuffer.push_back(sc_buffer);
}
    scPublicVars.currentColorBuffer = 0;
}
```

Creating a depth image

The depth image surface plays an important role in 3D graphics application. It brings the perception of depth in a rendered scene using depth testing. In depth testing, each fragment's depth is stored in a special buffer called a depth image. Unlike the color image that stores the color information, the depth image stores depth information of the primitive's corresponding fragment from the camera view. The depth image's dimension is usually the same as the color image. Not a hard-and-fast rule, but in general, the depth image stores the depth information as 16-, 24-, or 32-bit float values.

> The creation of a depth image is different from the color image. You must have noticed that we did not use the `vkCreateImage()` API to obtain color image objects while retrieving swapchain images. These images were directly returned from the `fpGetSwapchainImagesKHR()` extension API. In this section, we will go through a step-by-step process to create the depth image.

Introduction to tiling

Image data is stored in a contiguous type of memory and is mapped to the 2D image memory where it is stored in a linear fashion. In the linear arrangement, texels are laid out in contiguous row-by-row memory locations, as shown in the following diagram:

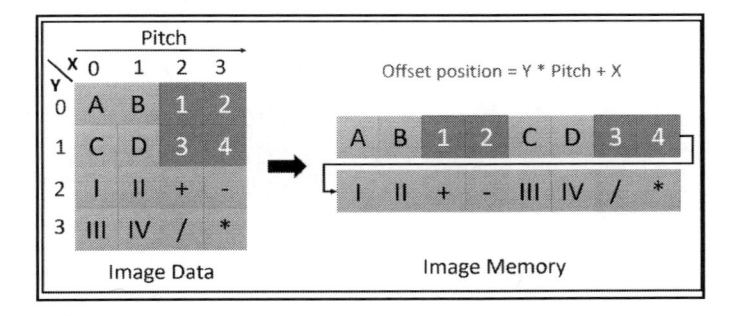

[195]

Allocating Image Resources and Building a Swapchain with WSI

A pitch generally represents the width of an image, which could be more than the padding bytes that are generally added in order to meet alignment requirements. The position offset of a given texel can be calculated using its row and column position along with the given pitch, as shown in the preceding image.

This linear layout is neat as long as texels are accessed in places along the row where no neighboring texel information is required. However, in general, many applications require image information to be fetched along multiple rows. When the image is large in dimension, the pitch length increases and stretches across multiple rows in this linear layout. In a multicache-level system, this leads to a situation where the performance can drop due to slower address translation caused by **translation lookaside buffer** (**TLB**) and cache misses.

On most GPUs, this slower translation of the address is fixed by storing the texels in a swizzle format. This way of storing image texels is called Optimal tiling, where the image texels are stored in a tiled fashion representing multiple columns and rows in a continuous memory chunk. For example, in the following diagram, there are four tiles represented with different colors, where each tile has 2 x 2 rows (pitch) and columns:

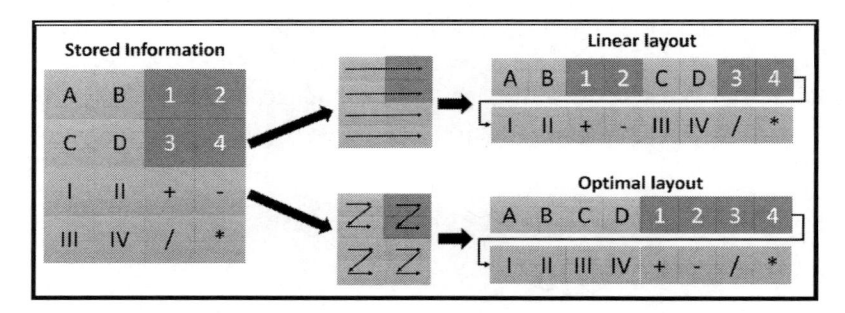

Clearly, in the linear fashion, blocks of the same color are set apart by the other blocks that comes in between; however, in the optimal layout, blocks of the same color are held together, providing a much more efficient way to access the neighboring texels without incurring performance loss. Note that this illustration of optimal tiling just mimics how the principle works; under the hood, there exist highly complex swizzling algorithms that help achieve optimal tiling.

In Vulkan, tiling is defined by `VkImageTiling`, and it represents linear tiling (`VK_IMAGE_TILING_LINEAR`) and optimal tiling (`VK_IMAGE_TILING_OPTIMAL`). The following is the syntax for this:

```
typedef enum VkImageTiling {
    VK_IMAGE_TILING_OPTIMAL    = 0,
    VK_IMAGE_TILING_LINEAR     = 1,
} VkImageTiling;
```

Let's take a look at the tiling types and their respective definitions:

Tiling type	Description
`VK_IMAGE_TILING_OPTIMAL`	These are opaquely tiled and provide optimal access to the underlying memory by laying out the texels in an implementation-dependent arrangement.
`VK_IMAGE_TILING_LINEAR`	As understood by the name, texels here are arranged in a row-major order in a linear fashion. The coherency may cause some padding in each row.

Creating a depth buffer image object

Initialize the depth format with 16-byte float values and query the format properties supported by the physical device specified by `deviceObj->gpu`. The retrieved properties are used to choose the optimal tiling/swizzling (`VK_IMAGE_TILING_OPTIMAL`) layout for the image in the memory.

The depth-related member variables are packed in a user-defined structure called `Depth` in the `Renderer` class. Here's the code that illustrates this:

```
struct{
    VkFormat          format;
    VkImage           image;
    VkDeviceMemory    mem;
    VkImageView       view;
} Depth;
```

Allocating Image Resources and Building a Swapchain with WSI

The various fields of this structure are defined in the following table:

Parameters	Description
format	This refers to the depth image format, namely `VkFormat`.
image	This refers to the `VkImage` depth image object.
mem	This is the allocated memory associated with the depth image object.
view	This is the `VkImageView` object of the depth image object (`VkImage`).

The depth format, tiling information, and other parameters—such as image size and image type—are used to create the `VkImageCreateInfo` control structure. Since we are creating a depth buffer, we need to specify the usage as `VK_IMAGE_USAGE_DEPTH_STENCIL_ATTACHMENT_BIT` in the usage field of the same structure. Use it to create the `VkImage` image object with the `vkCreateImage()` API. For more information on `VkImageCreateInfo` and `vkCreateImage()`, refer to the *Creating images* subsection of the *Understanding image resources* section in this chapter:

```
VkResult result;
VkImageCreateInfo imageInfo = {};

// If the depth format is undefined,
// use fall back as 16-byte value
if (Depth.format == VK_FORMAT_UNDEFINED) {
    Depth.format = VK_FORMAT_D16_UNORM;
}
const VkFormat depthFormat = Depth.format;

VkFormatProperties props;
vkGetPhysicalDeviceFormatProperties(*deviceObj->gpu,
              depthFormat, &props);

if (props.optimalTilingFeatures &
VK_FORMAT_FEATURE_DEPTH_STENCIL_ATTACHMENT_BIT) {
        imageInfo.tiling = VK_IMAGE_TILING_OPTIMAL;
}
    else if (props.linearTilingFeatures &
VK_FORMAT_FEATURE_DEPTH_STENCIL_ATTACHMENT_BIT) {
        imageInfo.tiling = VK_IMAGE_TILING_LINEAR;
}
    else {
        std::cout << "Unsupported Depth Format, try other Depth formats.\n";
        exit(-1);
    }
  imageInfo.sType       = VK_STRUCTURE_TYPE_IMAGE_CREATE_INFO;
```

```
imageInfo.pNext         = NULL;
imageInfo.imageType     = VK_IMAGE_TYPE_2D;
imageInfo.format        = depthFormat;
imageInfo.extent.width  = width;
imageInfo.extent.height = height;
imageInfo.extent.depth  = 1;
imageInfo.mipLevels     = 1;
imageInfo.arrayLayers   = 1;
imageInfo.samples       = NUM_SAMPLES;
imageInfo.queueFamilyIndexCount= 0;
imageInfo.pQueueFamilyIndices   = NULL;
imageInfo.sharingMode   = VK_SHARING_MODE_EXCLUSIVE;
imageInfo.usage         =
        VK_IMAGE_USAGE_DEPTH_STENCIL_ATTACHMENT_BIT;
imageInfo.flags         = 0;

// User create image info and create the image objects
result = vkCreateImage(deviceObj->device, &imageInfo,
                    NULL, &Depth.image);
assert(result == VK_SUCCESS);
```

Getting the depth image's memory requirements

Query the buffer's image memory requirements using the `vkGetImageMemoryRequirements()` API. This will retrieve the total size required for allocating the depth image object's physical memory backing. For more information on API usage, refer to the *Gathering memory allocation requirements* subsection in this chapter:

```
// Get the image memory requirements
VkMemoryRequirements memRqrmnt;
vkGetImageMemoryRequirements
    (deviceObj->device, Depth.image, &memRqrmnt);
```

Determining the type of memory

Use the `memoryTypeBits` field from the queried memory requirements, `memRqrmnt`, and determine the type of memory suitable for allocating the memory of the depth image using `VulkanDevice::memoryTypeFromProperties()`:

```
VkMemoryAllocateInfo memAlloc = {};
memAlloc.sType          = VK_STRUCTURE_TYPE_MEMORY_ALLOCATE_INFO;
memAlloc.pNext          = NULL;
memAlloc.allocationSize = 0;
memAlloc.memoryTypeIndex = 0;
```

Allocating Image Resources and Building a Swapchain with WSI

```
        memAlloc.allocationSize            = memRqrmnt.size;

    bool pass;
    // Determine the type of memory required
    // with memory properties
    pass = deviceObj->memoryTypeFromProperties(memRqrmnt.
              memoryTypeBits, 0, &memAlloc.memoryTypeIndex);
    assert(pass);
```

The `VulkanDevice::memoryTypeFromProperties()` function takes three parameters as inputs. The first one (`typeBits`) represents the type of the memory, the second parameter (`requirementsMask`) specifies the user requirement for the particular memory type, and the last one (`typeIndex`) returns the memory index handles.

This function iterates and checks whether the requested memory type is present. Next, it checks whether the found memory satisfies the user requirements. If successful, it returns `Boolean true` and the index of the memory type; upon failure, it returns `Boolean false`:

```
        bool VulkanDevice::memoryTypeFromProperties(uint32_t typeBits,
            VkFlags requirementsMask, uint32_t *typeIndex)
    {
    // Search memtypes to find first index with those properties
    for (uint32_t i = 0; i < 32; i++) {
        if ((typeBits & 1) == 1) {
        // Type is available, does it match user properties?
                if ((memoryProperties.memoryTypes[i].propertyFlags
                    & requirementsMask) == requirementsMask) {
                    *typeIndex = i;
                    return true;
                }
            }
            typeBits >>= 1;
    }
    // No memory types matched, return failure
    return false;
    }
```

Allocating and binding physical memory to a depth image

The memory requirement guides the application to allocate a specified amount of memory for the depth image. Once the memory is allocated successfully using `vkAllocateMemory()`, it needs to be bound to the depth image (`Depth.image`), making the image the owner of the allocated memory:

```
// Allocate the physical backing for the depth image
result = vkAllocateMemory(deviceObj->device,
          &memAlloc, NULL, &Depth.mem);
assert(result == VK_SUCCESS);

// Bind the allocated memory to the depth image
result = vkBindImageMemory(deviceObj->device,
          Depth.image, Depth.mem, 0);
assert(result == VK_SUCCESS);
```

Image layout transition

GPU hardware that is capable of supporting optimal layouts requires transitioning from the optimal layout to the linear layout and vice versa. Optimal layouts are not directly accessible by the consumer components for read and write purposes. The opaque nature of an optimal layout requires a layout transition, which is the process of converting one type (old type) of layout into another type (new type).

> The CPU may store the image data in a linear layout buffer and then convert it into the optimal layout to allow the GPU to read it in a more efficient manner.

GPU hardware that supports the optimal layout allows you to store the data either in a linear or optimal layout through layout transitioning. The layout transition process can be applied using memory barriers. The memory barriers inspect the specified old and new image layouts and execute the layout transition. It may not be necessary that every layout transition triggers an actual layout conversion operation on the GPU. For instance, when an image object is created for the first time, it may have the initial layout undefined; in such a case, the GPU may only need to access memory in the optimal pattern. For more information on memory barriers, continue with the next section.

Image layout transition with memory barriers

A memory barrier is an instruction that helps synchronize data reads and writes. It guarantees that the operation specified before and after the memory barrier will be synchronized. When this instruction is inserted, it ensures that the memory operation issued before this instruction is completed prior to executing the memory instruction issued after the barrier instruction.

There are three types of memory barrier:

- **Global memory barriers**: This type of memory barrier type is applicable to all kinds of executional memory objects and applies to their respective memory access types. Global memory barriers are represented by the `VkMemoryBarrier` structure's instance.
- **Buffer memory barriers**: This memory barrier type is applicable to a specific range of the specified buffer objects and it applies to their respective memory access types. These memory barriers are represented by the `VkBufferMemoryBarrier` structure's instance.
- **Image memory barriers**: The image memory barrier is represented by the `VkImageMemoryBarrier` instance and is applicable to the different memory access types via a specific image sub-resource range of the specified image object.

The allocated image memory needs to be laid out according to its usage. The image layout helps the memory contents become accessible in an implementation-specific way, given the nature of its usage. There is a general layout available for the image that can be used for anything, but this may not be the appropriate one (`VK_IMAGE_LAYOUT_GENERAL`). In Vulkan, image layouts are represented using `VkImageLayout`. The following are the fields defined for this enumeration:

VkImageLayout fields	Description
`VK_IMAGE_LAYOUT_UNDEFINED`	The image content in this layout and its subrange are pretty much in an undefined state and are assumed to be in this state right after they are created.
`VK_IMAGE_LAYOUT_GENERAL`	This layout permits all operations on the image or its subrange, which is otherwise specified through the usage flags (`VkImageUsageFlag`).
`VK_IMAGE_LAYOUT_COLOR_ATTACHMENT_OPTIMAL`	The image in this layout can only be used with the framebuffer color attachment. It can be accessed via framebuffer color reads and can be written using draw commands.

VK_IMAGE_LAYOUT_DEPTH_STENCIL_ATTACHMENT_OPTIMAL	The image in this layout can only be used with the framebuffer depth/stencil attachment. It can be accessed via framebuffer color reads and can be written using draw commands.
VK_IMAGE_LAYOUT_SHADER_READ_ONLY_OPTIMAL	This layout uses the image as a read-only shader resource. So it can only be accessed by shader reads done via a sampled image descriptor, combined image sampler descriptor, or read-only storage image descriptor (VkDescriptorType).
VK_IMAGE_LAYOUT_TRANSFER_SRC_OPTIMAL	An image (or a subrange of it) in this layout can only be used as the source operand of the commands vkCmdCopyImage, vkCmdBlitImage, vkCmdCopyImageToBuffer, and vkCmdResolveImage.
VK_IMAGE_LAYOUT_TRANSFER_DST_OPTIMAL	An image (or a subrange of it) in this layout can only be used as the destination operand of the commands vkCmdCopyImage, vkCmdBlitImage, vkCmdCopyBufferToImage, vkCmdResolveImage, vkCmdClearColorImage, and vkCmdClearDepthStencilImage.

The layouts in the images applied through special **memory barriers** are called VkImageMemoryBarrier. The memory barriers are inserted with the help of the vkCmdPipelineBarrier() API. The syntax of this API is as follows:

```
void vkCmdPipelineBarrier(
    VkCommandBuffer                 commandBuffer,
    VkPipelineStageFlags            srcStageMask,
    VkPipelineStageFlags            dstStageMask,
    VkDependencyFlags               dependencyFlags,
    uint32_t                        memoryBarrierCount,
    const VkMemoryBarrier*          pMemoryBarriers,
    uint32_t                        bufferMemoryBarrierCount,
    const VkBufferMemoryBarrier*    pBufferMemoryBarriers,
    uint32_t                        imageMemoryBarrierCount,
    const VkImageMemoryBarrier*     pImageMemoryBarriers);
```

Allocating Image Resources and Building a Swapchain with WSI

Let's see the specification of all the fields:

Parameters	Description
`commandBuffer`	This is the command buffer in which the memory barrier is specified.
`srcStageMask`	This is the bitwise mask field specifying the pipeline stages that must complete their execution before the barrier is implemented.
`dstStageMask`	This is the bitwise mask field specifying the pipeline stages that should not start the execution until the barrier is completed.
`dependencyFlags`	This refers to the `VkDependencyFlagBits` values that indicate whether the barrier has screen-space locality.
`memoryBarrierCount`	This refers to the number of memory barriers.
`pMemoryBarriers`	This is the `VkBufferMemoryBarreir` object array with the number of elements equal to `memoryBarrierCount`.
`bufferMemoryBarrierCount`	This refers to the number of buffer memory barriers.
`pBufferMemoryBarrier`	This refers to the `VkMemoryBarreir` object array with the number of elements equal to `bufferMemoryBarrierCount`.
`imageMemoryBarrierCount`	This refers to the number of image type memory barriers.
`pImageMemoryBarriers`	This refers to the `VkImageMemoryBarrier` object array with the number of elements equal to `imageMemoryBarrierCount`.

The following code makes use of an image barrier and sets the appropriate image layout information in the `VkImageMemoryBarrier` control structure (`imgMemoryBarrier`). This control structure is passed to the `vkCmdPipelineBarrier()` API, which sets the execution and applies the memory barriers. The created depth image (`Depth.image`) is set as a framebuffer depth/stencil attachment layout by specifying the `VkImageMemoryBarrier`'s `newLayout` field as `VK_IMAGE_LAYOUT_DEPTH_STENCIL_ATTACHMENT_OPTIMAL`.

Using the created command pool, allocate the `cmdDepthImage` command buffer. This command buffer will be used to record the image layout transition, as mentioned here:

```
/****** void VulkanRenderer::createDepthImage()******/
// Use command buffer to create the depth image. This includes -
// Command buffer allocation, recording with begin/end
// scope and submission.
CommandBufferMgr::allocCommandBuffer(&deviceObj->device,
                    cmdPool, &cmdDepthImage);
CommandBufferMgr::beginCommandBuffer(cmdDepthImage);
{

    // Set the image layout to depth stencil optimal
    setImageLayout(Depth.image,
       VK_IMAGE_ASPECT_DEPTH_BIT,
       VK_IMAGE_LAYOUT_UNDEFINED,
       VK_IMAGE_LAYOUT_DEPTH_STENCIL_ATTACHMENT_OPTIMAL,
      (VkAccessFlagBits)0, cmdDepthImage);
}
 CommandBufferMgr::endCommandBuffer(cmdDepthImage);
 CommandBufferMgr::submitCommandBuffer(deviceObj->queue,
&cmdDepthImage);
```

The image layout is set using the `setImageLayout()` function. This is a helper function that records memory barriers using the `vkCmdPipelineBarrier()` command.

This command is recorded in the `cmdDepthImage` command buffer and guarantees that it will meet the requirement of proper image layouts before it allows the dependent resources to access it.

The `setImageLayout()` helper function transits the existing old image layout format to the specified new layout type. In the present example, the old image layout is specified as `VK_IMAGE_LAYOUT_UNDEFINED` because the image object is created for the first time and has no predefined layout applied. Since we are implementing the image layout for depth/stencil testing, the new intended image layout must be mentioned with the `VK_IMAGE_LAYOUT_DEPTH_STENCIL_ATTACHMENT_OPTIMAL` usage type:

```
void VulkanRenderer::setImageLayout(VkImage image,
         VkImageAspectFlags aspectMask, VkImageLayout oldImageLayout,
         VkImageLayout newImageLayout, VkAccessFlagBits srcAccessMask,
         const VkCommandBuffer& cmd){

// Dependency on cmd
assert(cmd != VK_NULL_HANDLE);
// The deviceObj->queue must be initialized
assert(deviceObj->queue != VK_NULL_HANDLE);
```

```cpp
VkImageMemoryBarrier imgMemoryBarrier = {};
imgMemoryBarrier.sType = VK_STRUCTURE_TYPE_IMAGE_MEMORY_BARRIER;
imgMemoryBarrier.pNext    = NULL;
imgMemoryBarrier.srcAccessMask = srcAccessMask;
imgMemoryBarrier.dstAccessMask = 0;
imgMemoryBarrier.oldLayout     = oldImageLayout;
imgMemoryBarrier.newLayout     = newImageLayout;
imgMemoryBarrier.image         = image;
imgMemoryBarrier.subresourceRange.aspectMask   = aspectMask;
imgMemoryBarrier.subresourceRange.baseMipLevel = 0;
imgMemoryBarrier.subresourceRange.levelCount   = 1;
imgMemoryBarrier.subresourceRange.layerCount   = 1;

if (oldImageLayout == VK_IMAGE_LAYOUT_COLOR_ATTACHMENT_OPTIMAL) {
  imgMemoryBarrier.srcAccessMask = VK_ACCESS_COLOR_ATTACHMENT_WRITE_BIT;
}

switch (newImageLayout)
{
    // Ensure that anything that was copying from this image
    // has completed. An image in this layout can only be
    // used as the destination operand of the commands
    case VK_IMAGE_LAYOUT_TRANSFER_DST_OPTIMAL:
    case VK_IMAGE_LAYOUT_PRESENT_SRC_KHR:
        imgMemoryBarrier.dstAccessMask = VK_ACCESS_TRANSFER_WRITE_BIT;
        break;

    // Ensure any Copy or CPU writes to image are flushed. An image
    // in this layout can only be used as a read-only shader resource
    case VK_IMAGE_LAYOUT_SHADER_READ_ONLY_OPTIMAL:
        imgMemoryBarrier.srcAccessMask = VK_ACCESS_TRANSFER_WRITE_BIT;
        imgMemoryBarrier.dstAccessMask = VK_ACCESS_SHADER_READ_BIT;
        break;

    // An image in this layout can only be used as a
    // framebuffer color attachment
    case VK_IMAGE_LAYOUT_COLOR_ATTACHMENT_OPTIMAL:
        imgMemoryBarrier.dstAccessMask =
                        VK_ACCESS_COLOR_ATTACHMENT_READ_BIT;
        break;

    // An image in this layout can only be used as a
    // framebuffer depth/stencil attachment
    case VK_IMAGE_LAYOUT_DEPTH_STENCIL_ATTACHMENT_OPTIMAL:
        imgMemoryBarrier.dstAccessMask =
                        VK_ACCESS_DEPTH_STENCIL_ATTACHMENT_WRITE_BIT;
        break;
}
```

```
VkPipelineStageFlags srcStages= VK_PIPELINE_STAGE_TOP_OF_PIPE_BIT;
VkPipelineStageFlags destStages = VK_PIPELINE_STAGE_TOP_OF_PIPE_BIT;
vkCmdPipelineBarrier(cmd, srcStages, destStages, 0, 0,
                          NULL, 0, NULL, 1, &imgMemoryBarrier);
}
```

Creating the image view

Finally, we'll let the application use the depth image by means of an image view. We know very well that images cannot be used directly in a Vulkan application. They are used in the form of image views. The following code implements the creation of the image view using the `vkCreateImageView()` API. For more information on the API, refer to the *Creating the image view* subsection under the *Understanding image resources* section in this chapter:

```
/****** void VulkanRenderer::createDepthImage()******/

VkImageViewCreateInfo imgViewInfo = {};
imgViewInfo.sType = VK_STRUCTURE_TYPE_IMAGE_VIEW_CREATE_INFO;
imgViewInfo.pNext = NULL;
imgViewInfo.image = VK_NULL_HANDLE;
imgViewInfo.format = depthFormat;
imgViewInfo.components = { VK_COMPONENT_SWIZZLE_IDENTITY };
imgViewInfo.subresourceRange.aspectMask =
                          VK_IMAGE_ASPECT_DEPTH_BIT;
imgViewInfo.subresourceRange.baseMipLevel    = 0;
imgViewInfo.subresourceRange.levelCount   = 1;
imgViewInfo.subresourceRange.baseArrayLayer = 0;
imgViewInfo.subresourceRange.layerCount   = 1;
imgViewInfo.viewType = VK_IMAGE_VIEW_TYPE_2D;
imgViewInfo.flags                            = 0;

if ( depthFormat == VK_FORMAT_D16_UNORM_S8_UINT ||
     depthFormat == VK_FORMAT_D24_UNORM_S8_UINT ||
     depthFormat == VK_FORMAT_D32_SFLOAT_S8_UINT) {

imgViewInfo.subresourceRange.aspectMask |= VK_IMAGE_ASPECT_STENCIL_BIT;
}

// Create the image view and allow the application to
// use the images.
imgViewInfo.image = Depth.image;
result = vkCreateImageView(deviceObj->device, &imgViewInfo,
            NULL, &Depth.view);
assert(result == VK_SUCCESS);
```

Summarizing the application flow

In this section, we will summarize the flow of swapchain creation and the building of the presentation window. It consists of two parts: *initialization* and *rendering*.

Initialization

The initialization process initializes, creates, and processes the swapchain. The swapchain is not yet connected to the framebuffer render process and the primitives. Therefore, the rendered output will be a blank presentation window for now.

First, `VulkanRenderer` initializes the presentation window and creates a native platform-specific empty window (*500 x 500*). This window renders the swapchain's front buffer drawing image. Next, it initializes the swapchain to meet swapchain prerequisites. The swapchain image view layouts are created using command buffers that are allocated from the preallocated pool of command buffers.

During the initialization of the swapchain, the WSI extensions are queried and stored in the form of function pointers. The logical swapchain surface object is created and associated with the presentation window. Next, a suitable graphics queue is queried from the logical device supporting the presentation; this queue is used to draw operations and present the swapchain images to the display output window. Finally, the device is also checked for all the possible image formats that can used for swapchain images. The creation of the swapchain includes querying the swapchain surface capabilities that specify surface configurations, such as the maximum size of the drawing surface, the available presentation modes, and so on. Using this surface configuration, the swapchain image objects are retrieved. Once the swapchain retrieves the images, it can be used to render the primitives. The swapchain images are retrieved by the WSI; therefore, the application does not own these. These images are finally converted into image views to allow the application to use them in the implementation.

We will also need to create the depth image for depth/stencil testing, and unlike the swapchain image, the depth image is solely the responsibility of the application. The application owns it and therefore can apply the image layout transition on the depth image with an optimal depth layout scheme. The image transition is applied using the memory barrier command, which is packed in the command buffer and submitted to the queue for upfront processing. The memory barrier inserts special instructions that guarantees the transitioning of the layout before it gets consumed.

Rendering – displaying the output window

The following code renders the presentation window:

```
void VulkanRenderer::render(){
    MSG msg;     // message
    while (1) {
        PeekMessage(&msg, NULL, 0, 0, PM_REMOVE);
        if (msg.message == WM_QUIT) {
        break; // If Quit message the exit the render loop
    }
      TranslateMessage(&msg);
      DispatchMessage(&msg);

      // Display the window
      RedrawWindow(window, NULL, NULL, RDW_INTERNALPAINT);
    }
}
```

The following is the output of the preceding code implementation:

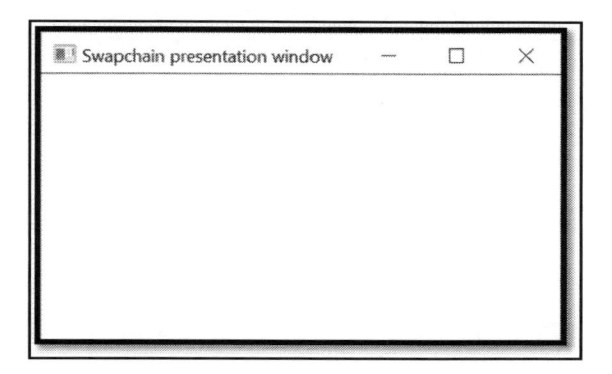

Summary

This chapter was full of image resources. We started with a basic understanding of image resource in Vulkan and learning about image objects, image layouts, and image views. Then we created image objects and allocated device memory to them. We also used WSI extensions to implement the swapchain and retrieved the swapchain images; these images were then associated with the presentation window. Finally, we created image views out of the swapchain images.

Next in this chapter, we implemented the depth buffer image. We also understood the different Vulkan image tilings and the basic difference between them. In addition to this, we also understood image layouts and their implementations using memory barriers.

In the next chapter, we will introduce the framebuffer and render pass. The framebuffer consumes the image views of a swapchain and depth image and associates them with a color and depth attachment. This information is then used by the render pass to define a unit of work. We will also learn about a buffer resource and use it to create the geometry buffer. In addition to this, we will look at SPIR-V to learn shader programming in Vulkan.

7
Buffer Resource, Render Pass, Framebuffer, and Shaders with SPIR-V

In the previous chapter, we learned about Vulkan resource types; we understood what image resources (`VkImage`) are and implemented them in the swapchain image. In this chapter, we will discuss the second type of Vulkan resource called buffer resources (`VkBuffer`) and use them to prepare a simple geometry buffer.

This chapter will also introduce and implement a Render Pass and framebuffer. A Render Pass helps in assembling a single unit of work. It defines the attachments and subpasses associated with it that influence a single render job. A framebuffer consumes the created Render Pass and creates single-frame information for each corresponding swapchain image. Framebuffers associate a set of image views with the set of attachments described in a Render Pass.

Additionally, we will implement our first shader in Vulkan using SPIR-V, which is a binary intermediate language for shaders and kernels.

So, we will cover the following topics:

- Understanding the Vulkan buffer resource type
- Creating geometry with the buffer resource
- Understanding a Render Pass
- Using the Render Pass and creating the framebuffer
- Clearing the background color
- Working with a shader in Vulkan

// Buffer Resource, Render Pass, Framebuffer, and Shaders with SPIR-V

Understanding the Vulkan buffer resource type

A buffer resource represents a contiguous array of data in a linear fashion. Buffer resources are commonly stored attribute data information, such as vertex coordinates, texture coordinates, associated colors, and more. The buffer resource in Vulkan is represented by the `VkBuffer` object, unlike the image resource (`VkImage`), which is represented in the view form (image view, `VkImageView`), the buffer resources can be used directly as the source of vertex data or accessed by shaders through descriptors. They need to be converted explicitly into a buffer view (`VkBufferView`) to allow the shaders to use buffer data contents in the formatted form. In this section, we will make use of the buffer resource directly using the API commands.

First, this section will discuss the buffer resource concepts covering the API specifications to use them in the implementation. Next, we will use these APIs and implement the buffer resources to store the geometry data of a simple triangle. This will be used in the upcoming chapters to render the geometry into the application.

Creating the buffer resource object

The buffer resource (`VkBuffer`) is created using the `vkCreateBuffer` API. The following is the syntax:

```
VkResult vkCreateBuffer(
    VkDevice                       device,
    const VkBufferCreateInfo*      pCreateInfo,
    const VkAllocationCallbacks*   pAllocator,
    VkBuffer*                      buffer);
```

This table describes the various fields of the `vkCreateBuffer()` API:

Parameters	Description
device	This is the logical device responsible for creating the buffer resource.
pCreateInfo	This refers to a `VkBufferCreateInfo` pointer; check the following sections for more information.
pAllocator	This controls the host memory allocation process.
buffer	This returns the `VkBuffer` pointer after it's created.

The `VkBufferCreateInfo` syntax is defined here. The `VkBufferCreateInfo` syntax is defined here:

```
typedef struct VkBufferCreateInfo {
    VkStructureType          type;
    const void*              pNext;
    VkBufferCreateFlags      flags;
    VkDeviceSize             size;
    VkBufferUsageFlags       usage;
    VkSharingMode            sharingMode;
    uint32_t                 queueFamilyIndexCount;
    const uint32_t*          pQueueFamilyIndices;
} VkBufferCreateInfo;
```

The following table describes the various fields of `VkBufferCreateInfo`:

Parameters	Description
`type`	This specifies the type of the structure; this must be of type `VK_STRUCTURE_TYPE_BUFFER_CREATE_INFO`.
`pNext`	This is an extension-specific structure. It can also be `NULL`.
`flags`	These are `VkBufferCreateFlagBits` bit field flags. Refer to `VkBufferCreateFlagBits` in the following sections for more information on flags.
`size`	This refers to the total size of the buffer to be created; the size is specified in bytes.
`usage`	This is `VkBufferUsageFlagBits` specifying the bit field that describes the intended usage of the buffer resource. Refer to the following sections for more information on the usage of `VkBufferUsageFlagBits`.
`sharingMode`	This specifies the sharing mode of the buffer when it will be accessed by multiple queue families. This must be one of these values: `VK_SHARING_MODE_EXCLUSIVE` or `VK_SHARING_MODE_CONCURRENT` from `VkSharingMode`.
`queueFamilyIndexCount`	This represents the number of entries in the `queueFamilyIndices` array.
`pQueueFamilyIndices`	This is an array of queue families that will access the buffer. The `sharingMode` must be `VK_SHARING_MODE_CONCURRENT`; otherwise, just ignore it.

Destroying the buffer

When the buffer is no longer required, it can be destroyed using `vkDestroyBuffer()`:

```
void vkDestroyBuffer(VkDevice          device,
                     VkBuffer          buffer,
                     const VkAllocationCallbacks*   allocator);
```

This API accepts three parameters, which are described in the following table:

Parameters	Description
device	This is the logical device that destroys the buffer object.
buffer	This refers to the `VkBuffer` object that needs to be destroyed.
pAllocator	This controls the host memory deallocation process; refer to the *Host memory* section in `Chapter 5`, *Command Buffer and Memory Management in Vulkan*.

Creating a buffer view

A buffer view is created using `vkCreateBufferView()`. The following is the syntax of this API:

```
VkResult vkCreateBufferView(
    VkDevice                        device,
    const VkBufferViewCreateInfo*   pCreateInfo,
    const VkAllocationCallbacks*    pAllocator,
    VkBufferView*                   pView);
```

This table describes the various fields of `vkCreateBufferView`:

Parameters	Description
device	This is the handle of the logical device that creates the image buffer.
pCreateInfo	This is a pointer to `VkCreateBufferViewInfo`; this controls the creation of `VkBufferView`.
pAllocator	This controls the host memory allocation process; for more information, refer to the *Host memory* section in `Chapter 5`, *Command Buffer and Memory Management in Vulkan*.
pView	This returns the handle of the created `VkBufferView` object.

The buffer view is created using the `vkCreateBufferView()` API. The following is the syntax information:

```
typedef struct VkBufferViewCreateInfo {
    VkStructureType            type;
    const void*                pNext;
    VkBufferViewCreateFlags    flags;
    VkBuffer                   buffer;
    VkFormat                   format;
    VkDeviceSize               offset;
    VkDeviceSize               range;
} VkBufferViewCreateInfo;
```

This table describes the various fields of `VkBufferViewCreateInfo`:

Parameters	Description
`type`	This refers to the type information of the structure; it must be of type `VK_STRUCTURE_TYPE_BUFFER_VIEW_CREATE_INFO`.
`next`	This is an extension-specific structure. This field could be `NULL` as well.
`flags`	This field is reserved for future use.
`buffer`	This is the handle of `VkBuffer`.
`format`	This specifies the format (`VkFormat`) of the buffer data element.
`offset`	This is used for the remapping of color/depth/stencil after they have been converted into color components.
`range`	This is used for selecting a range of mipmap levels and array layers, making them accessible to the view.

Destroying the buffer view

The buffer view could be destroyed using the `vkDestroBufferView()` API. This intakes three parameters. The first specifies the logical device that is responsible for destroying the buffer view indicated by the second parameter. Here is the syntax of this:

```
void vkDestroyBufferView(VkDevice             device,
                         VkBufferView         bufferView,
                         VkAllocationCallbacks* pAllocator);
```

Creating geometry with a buffer resource

In this section, we will create a simple geometrical shape–a triangle. This will be stored in the GPU memory with the help of a buffer resource. Most applications will consume buffers through uniform or storage blocks. The implementation of a buffer resource is very similar to that of an image resource, except the fact that here we would not need to create the buffer view (`VkBufferView`).

Preparing geometry data

Create `MeshData.h` and define the geometry data inside it. Declare the following structures:

```
/*----------------------MeshData.h----------------------*/
// Mesh data structure and Vertex Data
struct VertexWithColor
{
    float x, y, z, w;    // Vertex Position
    float r, g, b, a;    // Color format Red, Green, Blue, Alpha
};

// Interleaved data containing position and color information
static const VertexWithColor triangleData[] =
{
    {  0.0f,  1.0f, 0.0f, 1.0f, 1.0f, 0.0f, 0.0f, 1.0 },
    {  1.0f, -1.0f, 0.0f, 1.0f, 0.0f, 0.0f, 1.0f, 1.0 },
    { -1.0f, -1.0f, 0.0f, 1.0f, 0.0f, 1.0f, 0.0f, 1.0 },
};
```

The geometry is stored in an interleaved fashion, where the three vertices are stored such that they would contain the vertex position information in the Cartesian form, followed by the color information stored in the RGB color space. The position information consists of four components: x, y, z, and w. The color information contains the r, g, b, and a components. The following diagram shows the resultant triangle:

Chapter 7

(0.0f, 1.0f, 0.0f)　　　　　　(1.0f, 0.0f, 0.0f)

(1.0f,-1.0f,0.0f)　　(1.0f,-1.0f,0.0f)　(0.0f, 1.0f, 0.0f)　(0.0f, 0.0f, 1.0f)

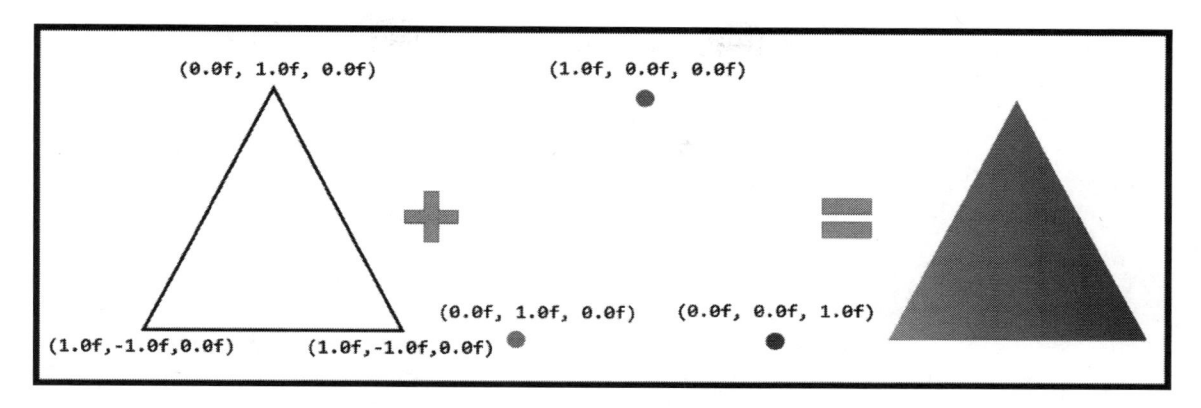

Creating a vertex buffer

Create a new user-defined class called `VulkanDrawable`. This class will be used to draw the intended geometrical shape, which in the present case is a simple triangle. The following is the header file that declares the functions used to create and destroy the buffer resource:

```
class VulkanDrawable
{
    // Many lines skipped, please refer to the source code
public:

    void createVertexBuffer(const void *vertexData, uint32_t
        dataSize, uint32_t dataStride, bool useTexture);
    void destroyVertexBuffer();

    // Structure storing vertex buffer metadata
    struct {
        VkBuffer buffer;
        VkDeviceMemory memory;
        VkDescriptorBufferInfo bufferInfo;
    } VertexBuffer;

    // Stores the vertex input rate
    VkVertexInputBindingDescription      viIpBind;
    // Store metadata helpful in data interpretation
    VkVertexInputAttributeDescription    viIpAttrb[2];
};
```

In addition, the class contains a special user-defined structure to aggregate the vertex buffer resource attributes defined by `VertexBuffer`. This structure contains the `VkBuffer` object. This object will be bound to `VkDeviceMemory` and a buffer descriptor (`VkDescriptorBufferInfo`) containing the necessary metadata for the allocated buffer resource, such as the buffer object, its offset, and the range.

Buffer creation overview

The buffer resource creation process is very similar to that of image resource creation. To get an overview of the image creation process, refer to the *Image creation overview* section in `Chapter 6`, *Allocating Image Resources and Building a Swapchain with WSI*.

Let's take a quick look at buffer creation. The following are step-by-step instructions to create the buffer resource (`VkBuffer`) using Vulkan APIs:

1. **Creating the buffer object**: The buffer object (`VkBuffer`) is created using the `vkCreateBuffer()` API. This API intakes a `VkCreateBufferInfo` structure object that specifies important buffer metadata that is used to create the buffer object. The buffer object's `VkCreateBufferInfo` contains the necessary memory information, such as format, usage, size, creation flags, and so on. This information is used to allocate physical memory from the device. You may consider that the buffer object at this initial stage has no backing memory. The creation of the buffer object does not mean that the physical allocation is done automatically behind the curtains; it has to be done manually, which is described in the next step.

2. **Allocating buffer memory**:
   - **Getting the memory requirements**: Gather the required memory information using the `vkGetBufferMemoryRequirements()` API. This information is helpful in allocating the appropriate size of the memory needed by the buffer resource allocation process. This API intakes the `VkBuffer` created in the first step.
   - **Determining the memory type**: Similar to an image resource, get the proper memory type from what's available and select the one that matches the user properties.
   - **Allocating device memory**: Allocate device memory (`VkDeviceMemory`) with the `vkAllocateMemory()` API.
   - **Staging**: Once physical memory is allocated, it needs to be mapped using `vkMapMemory()` to the localhost so that the geometry data can be uploaded from the host memory to the physical device memory.

[218]

Once the data is copied to the physical device memory, it needs to be unmapped using `vkUnmapMemory()`.
- **Binding the allocated memory**: Bind the device memory (`VkDeviceMemory`) to the buffer object (`VkBuffer`) using the `vkBindBufferMemory()` API.

The following diagram summarizes the complete buffer resource creation workflow:

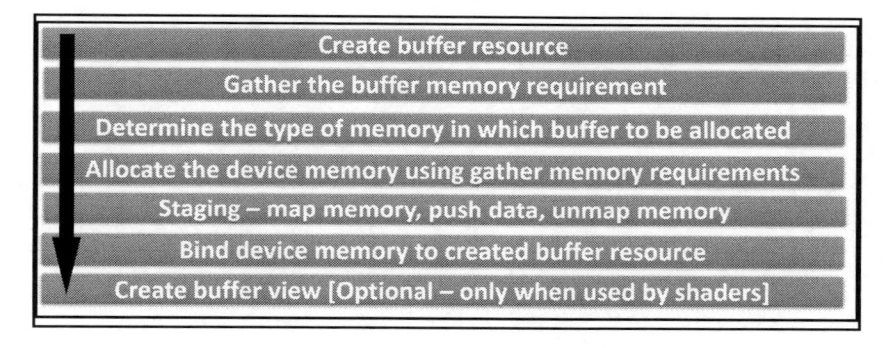

```
Create buffer resource
Gather the buffer memory requirement
Determine the type of memory in which buffer to be allocated
Allocate the device memory using gather memory requirements
Staging – map memory, push data, unmap memory
Bind device memory to created buffer resource
Create buffer view [Optional – only when used by shaders]
```

Implementing a buffer resource – creating the vertex buffer for the geometry

The `VulkanDrawable` class contains the `createVertexBuffer()` function that helps in storing the geometry data in the GPU memory with the help of a buffer resource. The implementation is very similar to creating an image resource, but with a little difference. In this implementation, the buffer view creation process is not required; instead, the buffer object will be used directly.

Some Vulkan implementations may offer the ability to fetch and format vertex attributes, converting vertex input data from buffers as specialized fixed-function hardware rather than performing the fetch as part of the vertex shader. Once the buffer resource is implemented, its binding points are stored in the (`VkVertexInputBindingDescription`) control structure. This structure describes the set of buffers that will be used to fetch the vertex.

Similarly, attributes are stored in the `VkVertexInputAttributeDescription` structure; this describes the format and layout of each attribute to read them from the vertex buffers to a shader variable. Both the pieces of information are consumed at the time of pipeline creation, specifying the vertex input state.

The following is the syntax information of `VkVertexInputBindingDescription`:

```
typedef struct VkVertexInputBindingDescription {
    uint32_t            binding;
    uint32_t            stride;
    VkVertexInputRate   inputRate;
} VkVertexInputBindingDescription;
```

Let's look at the various fields of this structure:

Parameters	Description
`binding`	This field indicates an unsigned 32-bit integer-binding number that describes the control structure.
`stride`	This is specified in bytes; this field indicates the offset between the consecutive elements within the buffer.

`inputRate`	This field indicates whether the buffer attribute is specified at per vertex or instance basis. This field takes the following enum:
	`typedef enum VkVertexInputRate {`
	`   VK_VERTEX_INPUT_RATE_VERTEX = 0,`
	`   VK_VERTEX_INPUT_RATE_INSTANCE = 1,`
	`} VkVertexInputRate;`
	• The `VK_VERTEX_INPUT_RATE_VERTEX` indicates that the vertex attributes will be consumed as per the vertex index basis.
	• The `VK_VERTEX_INPUT_RATE_INSTANCE` indicates that the vertex attributes will be consumed as per the instance index basis.

Similarly, here's the syntax information of `VkVertexInputAttributeDescription`:

```
typedef struct VkVertexInputAttributeDescription {
    uint32_t    location;
    uint32_t    binding;
    VkFormat    format;
    uint32_t    offset;
} VkVertexInputAttributeDescription;
```

The various fields in `VkVertexInputAttributeDescription` are as follows:

Parameters	Description
`location`	This field indicates the shader-binding location of this attribute.
`binding`	This is the binding number from which the data is consumed by the attribute.
`format`	The vertex attribute's data size and type is indicated by this field.
`offset`	This field indicates the offset of this attribute in bytes from the start of an element in vertex input binding.

The vertex buffer is created in the `createVertexBuffer()` function, as shown in the following code snippet. This function accepts the host memory containing the vertex data, its size, and stride information (if any). The last parameter is a boolean flag that indicates whether the geometry data contains the texture coordinates:

```
void VulkanDrawable::createVertexBuffer(const void *vertexData, uint32_t
dataSize, uint32_t dataStride, bool useTexture)
{
    VulkanApplication* appObj = VulkanApplication::GetInstance();
    VulkanDevice* deviceObj   = appObj->deviceObj;

    VkResult   result;
    bool       pass;

    // Create the Buffer resource metadata information
    VkBufferCreateInfo bufInfo = {};
    bufInfo.sType           = VK_STRUCTURE_TYPE_BUFFER_CREATE_INFO;
    bufInfo.pNext           = NULL;
    bufInfo.usage           = VK_BUFFER_USAGE_VERTEX_BUFFER_BIT;
    bufInfo.size            = dataSize;
    bufInfo.queueFamilyIndexCount = 0;
    bufInfo.pQueueFamilyIndices   = NULL;
    bufInfo.sharingMode     = VK_SHARING_MODE_EXCLUSIVE;
    bufInfo.flags           = 0;

    // Create the Buffer resource
    result = vkCreateBuffer(deviceObj->device, &bufInfo,
                NULL, &VertexBuffer.buf);

    // Get the Buffer resource requirements
    VkMemoryRequirements memRqrmnt;
    vkGetBufferMemoryRequirements(deviceObj->device,
            VertexBuffer.buf, &memRqrmnt);

    // Create memory allocation metadata information
```

Buffer Resource, Render Pass, Framebuffer, and Shaders with SPIR-V

```
VkMemoryAllocateInfo alloc_info = {};
alloc_info.sType           = VK_STRUCTURE_TYPE_MEMORY_ALLOCATE_INFO;
alloc_info.pNext           = NULL;
alloc_info.memoryTypeIndex = 0;
alloc_info.allocationSize  = memRqrmnt.size;

// Get the compatible type of memory
pass = deviceObj->memoryTypeFromProperties
            (memRqrmnt.memoryTypeBits,
            VK_MEMORY_PROPERTY_HOST_VISIBLE_BIT |
            VK_MEMORY_PROPERTY_HOST_COHERENT_BIT,
            &alloc_info.memoryTypeIndex);

// Allocate the physical backing for buffer resource
result = vkAllocateMemory(deviceObj->device,
               &alloc_info, NULL, &(VertexBuffer.mem));

VertexBuffer.bufferInfo.range  = memRqrmnt.size;
VertexBuffer.bufferInfo.offset = 0;

// Map the physical device memory region to the host
uint8_t *pData;
result = vkMapMemory(deviceObj->device, VertexBuffer.mem,
               0, memRqrmnt.size, 0, (void **)&pData);

// Copy the data in the mapped memory
memcpy(pData, vertexData, dataSize);

// Unmap the device memory
vkUnmapMemory(deviceObj->device, VertexBuffer.mem);

// Bind the allocated buffer resourece to the device memory
result = vkBindBufferMemory(deviceObj->device,
               VertexBuffer.buf, VertexBuffer.mem, 0);

// The VkVertexInputBinding viIpBind, stores the rate at
// which the information will be injected for vertex input
viIpBind.binding    = 0;
viIpBind.inputRate  = VK_VERTEX_INPUT_RATE_VERTEX;
viIpBind.stride     = dataStride;

// The VkVertexInputAttribute - Description) structure, store
// the information that helps in interpreting the data.
viIpAttrb[0].binding  = 0;
viIpAttrb[0].location = 0;
viIpAttrb[0].format   = VK_FORMAT_R32G32B32A32_SFLOAT;
viIpAttrb[0].offset   = 0;
viIpAttrb[1].binding  = 0;
```

```
    viIpAttrb[1].location   = 1;
    viIpAttrb[1].format     = useTexture ?
        VK_FORMAT_R32G32_SFLOAT : VK_FORMAT_R32G32B32A32_SFLOAT;
    viIpAttrib[1].offset    = 16;
}
```

Understanding the code flow

Let's take a detailed view of the preceding implementation. First, the `VkCreateBufferInfo` structure is created and filled with vertex buffer metadata. This is where we store the buffer usage type; this usage type refers to vertex information (`VK_BUFFER_USAGE_VERTEX_BUFFER_BIT`). The other usage types could be index buffer, uniform buffer, texture buffer, and more. Specify the size of the vertex buffer data in bytes. Since there are no multiple queues involved, we can mark the sharing mode as `VK_SHARING_MODE_EXCLUSIVE`. Pass this structure to the `vkCreateBuffer()` API to create the vertex buffer object (`VertexBuffer::buf`).

Use the created buffer object (`VertexBuffer::buf`) as passed to the `vkGetBufferMemoryRequirements()` API in order to gather the memory requirements (`memRqrmnt`) to allocate the buffer in the API. This information is helpful in allocating the appropriate size of the memory needed by the buffer resource allocation process. This API intakes the `VkCreateBufferInfo` control structure.

Next, get prepared for the allocation process and create `VkMemoryAllocateInfo` (`allocInfo`) with the gathered memory requirement. Specify the allocation size information in bytes and get the compatible memory type for the allocation. The memory is allocated using `vkAllocateMemory`, passing in `allocInfo`, and retrieving the device memory of the type `VkDeviceMemory` in `VertexBuffer.mem`.

Upon the allocation of the physical memory, use `vkMapMemory()` to map the localhost memory so that the geometry data can be copied to the physical device memory. Once the data is copied to the physical device memory, it needs to be unmapped using `vkUnmapMemory()`.

Use the `vkBindBufferMemory()` API and bind the device memory (`VkDeviceMemory`) to the buffer object (`VkBuffer`).

> This example does not need to create the buffer object views. Buffer views (`VkBufferView`) are only created when the buffer data is going to be utilized by the shaders. Use the `vkCreateBufferView()` API to create the buffer view.

Buffer Resource, Render Pass, Framebuffer, and Shaders with SPIR-V

The following is a pictorial representation of the preceding process. It shows three columns, where the first column shows the intended job, the second column defines the Vulkan APIs used to accomplish the job, and the third specifies the returned value types.

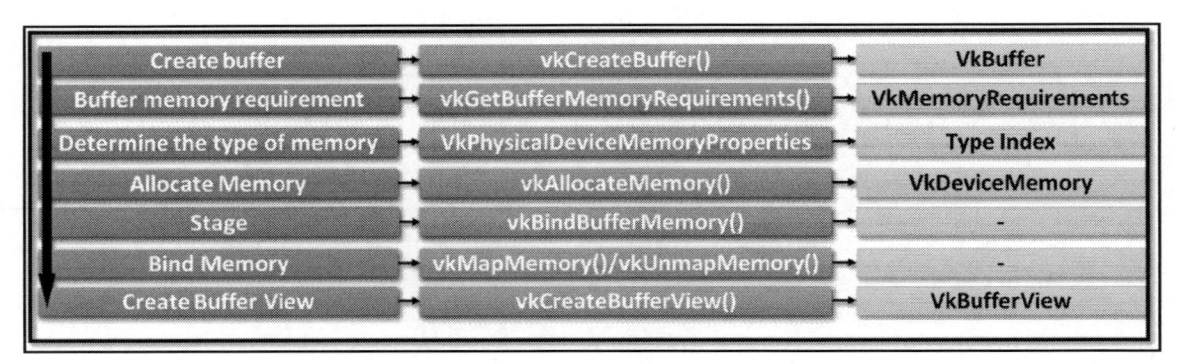

Job	Vulkan API	Return Type
Create buffer	vkCreateBuffer()	VkBuffer
Buffer memory requirement	vkGetBufferMemoryRequirements()	VkMemoryRequirements
Determine the type of memory	VkPhysicalDeviceMemoryProperties	Type Index
Allocate Memory	vkAllocateMemory()	VkDeviceMemory
Stage	vkBindBufferMemory()	-
Bind Memory	vkMapMemory()/vkUnmapMemory()	-
Create Buffer View	vkCreateBufferView()	VkBufferView

As the final step, we need to bind the created buffer resource into the underlying pipeline so that the rate of vertex input information can be defined in `viIpBind` (of the type `VkVertexInputBindingDescription`)—the input rate could be based on a vertex or instance.

The `VkVertexInputAttributeDescription` structure object's `viIpAttrb` stores information related to the position and color attributes and is used to interpret the data. For example, in `viIpAttrb`, we specify the binding point, location in the binding, expected data format, and offset information. In the case of non-interleaved data, it should be 0. Since our data is in the interleaved form, it is 0 and 16 for position and color attributes, respectively; check out the following diagram. The `useTexture` interprets part of vertex data as either texture coordinates or colors. When specified true, it indicates that the vertex data contains texture coordinates (two components, where each component is of 32 bits) instead of color components (four components of 32 bits each).

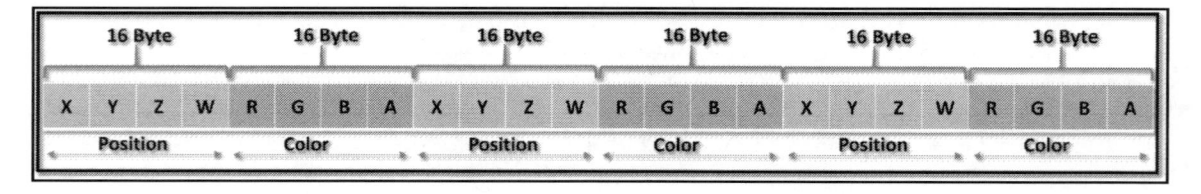

16 Byte	16 Byte	16 Byte	16 Byte	16 Byte	16 Byte
X Y Z W	R G B A	X Y Z W	R G B A	X Y Z W	R G B A
Position	Color	Position	Color	Position	Color

Understanding a Render Pass

A Render Pass tells us about the framebuffer attachments and subpasses that will be used while rendering. Attachments, such as color and depth, indicate how many color and depth images will be there. It specifies what should be the sample bits used to represent each of them and how the contents will be used in the rendering process. It also confirms how the contents would be treated at the beginning and end of each Render Pass instance. A Render Pass used in a command buffer is called a **Render Pass instance**. It manages the dependencies between the subpasses and defines the protocols on how the attachments should be used over the course of the subpasses.

A Render Pass consists of mainly two type of components: *attachments* and *subpasses*. The following are some facts about attachments and subpasses.

Attachments

An attachment refers to a surface region (such as color, depth/stencil, or resolve attachment to perform resolve operations) used at the time of rendering a command. There are five types of attachments described here:

- **Color attachment**: A color attachment represents a drawing target image where render primitives are drawn.
- **Depth attachment**: A depth attachment stores the depth information and uses it for the depth/stencil test operation.
- **Resolve attachment**: A resolve attachment is automatically downsampled from being a multisampled attachment to a corresponding single-sampled attachment at the end of a subpass. Resolve attachments correspond to multisampled color attachments and behave as if there is a `vkCmdResolveImage` at the end of a subpass, from a color attachment to its corresponding resolve attachment. One exception is that the driver may be able to do a better job, such as performing both the *spill and resolve* actions on a tiler at the same time.
- **Input attachment**: This consists of list attachments that will be shared with the shaders. Input attachments are like restricted textures where the only operation a shader may perform is texel fetch (`texture(tex, uv)`)–read from the texel that corresponds to the pixel currently being shaded. Obvious cases of this are one-tap post processing filters (no blurs and so on), the lighting phase of a classic deferred renderer to read from G-buffers, and more.

- **Preserve attachment**: Throughout, in a given subpass, the contents inside the preserve attachment remain unchanged. Preserve attachments aren't expressed in other APIs at all. They express the requirement that the contents of some attachment be kept (as it will be used later) but shouldn't be touched at all by the current subpass. This isn't interesting at all on a desktop GPU, where render target writes go straight into the memory. However, it's very interesting for a tiler: the attachment portion of the on-chip memory can be reused in place of some other attachment during the subpass, without having to spill its contents back to the memory.

In a Vulkan API, the `VkAttachmentDescription` descriptor can be used to specify the various properties of an attachment. This includes its format, sample count, initial layout information, and how its contents are treated at the beginning and end of each Render Pass instance.

Subpasses

In a Render Pass, a subpass reads and writes associated attachments. A current subpass in the Render Pass execution is affected by the rendering commands:

- A subpass can read from the previously written attachment (it must be preserved) and write to the attachment currently associated with it.
- Writing in the color and depth/stencil buffer is also a part of the subpass attachment associated with a Render Pass instance.
- In order to allow a subpass attachment to be used by the subsequent passes, it is the application's responsibility to ensure that the information remains valid until it is not utilized.
- There are also preserve attachments that preserve the contents in the attachments throughout the subpass life cycle. The subpass cannot affect these attachments as they are read/write protected. In other words, they cannot be read/write during a subpass life cycle.

A subpass descriptor is defined by `VkSubpassDescription`. It describes the number of attachments involved in the subpass.

> With advanced information on a subpass, about the subpass's set in Render Pass, the Render Pass provides the underlying implementation an opportunity to optimize the storage and transfer of attachment data between the subpasses. This means multiple passes can be merged together and resolved with a single Render Pass instance.

In our sample example, we are only dealing with a single subpass; therefore, any relevant topic on its dependencies is out of the scope of this book.

Vulkan APIs for the Render Pass

In this section, we will understand the various APIs that are used to implement the Render Pass in Vulkan.

The Render Pass object is created using the `vkCreateRenderPass()` API. This API accepts the `VkCreateRenderPassInfo` control structure that defines the attachments, such as our swapchain color images and depth image. It also contains an important structure (`VkRenderPassCreateInfo`) that defines the protocols on how these attachments will be treated in a single Render Pass.

Let's look at the Render Pass API specification to create the Render Pass object:

```
VkResult vkCreateRenderPass(
    VkDevice                         device,
    const VkRenderPassCreateInfo*    pCreateInfo,
    const VkAllocationCallbacks*     pAllocator,
    VkRenderPass*                    pRenderPass);
```

The following table describes the various fields of this structure:

Parameters	Description
device	This is the logical device handle for which the Render Pass is created.
pCreateInfo	This is a pointer to the `VkRenderPassCreateInfo` structure object.
pAllocator	This controls the host memory deallocation process. Refer to the *Host memory* section in Chapter 5, *Command Buffer and Memory Management in Vulkan*.
pRenderPass	This creates the `VkRenderPass` object pointer.

The `VkRenderPassCreateInfo` structure associates the attachment and subpasses with the Render Pass object. The following is the syntax with the described fields:

```
typedef struct VkRenderPassCreateInfo {
```

```
    VkStructureType                    type;
    const void*                        pNext;
    VkRenderPassCreateFlags            flags;
    uint32_t                           attachmentCount;
    const VkAttachmentDescription*     pAttachments;
    uint32_t                           subpassCount;
    const VkSubpassDescription*        pSubpasses;
    uint32_t                           dependencyCount;
    const VkSubpassDependency*         pDependencies;
} VkRenderPassCreateInfo;
```

The following table describes the fields of this structure:

Parameters	Description
`type`	This is the type of this structure, which must be `VK_STRUCTURE_TYPE_RENDER_PASS_CREATE_INFO`.
`next`	This is either `NULL` or a pointer to an extension-specific structure.
`flags`	This is reserved for future use.
`attachmentCount`	This specifies the number of attachments used by this Render Pass instance. If zero, it means there is no attachment within this Render Pass.
`attachments`	This is an array of `VkAttachmentDescription` structures specifying the properties of the Render Pass attachments. The array size is equal to `attachmentCount`.
`subpassCount`	This specifies the number of subpasses in this Render Pass.
`subpasses`	This is an array of `VkSubpassDescription` structures describing the properties of the subpasses.
`dependencyCount`	This specifies the number of dependencies between the pairs of subpasses. If zero, it means no dependencies exist.
`dependencies`	This is an array that is equal to the `dependencyCount` number of the `VkSubpassDependency` structures, describing the dependencies between pairs of subpasses. This must be `NULL` if `dependencyCount` is zero.

To describe each attachment used in a Render Pass, Vulkan provides the `VkAttachmentDescription` control structure. The following is the syntax of this:

```
    typedef struct VkAttachmentDescription {
        VkAttachmentDescriptionFlags   flags;
        VkFormat                       format;
        VkSampleCountFlagBits          samples;
```

```
    VkAttachmentLoadOp           loadOp;
    VkAttachmentStoreOp          storeOp;
    VkAttachmentLoadOp           stencilLoadOp;
    VkAttachmentStoreOp          stencilStoreOp;
    VkImageLayout                initialLayout;
    VkImageLayout                finalLayout;
} VkAttachmentDescription;
```

This table describes the various fields of this structure:

Parameters	Description
`flags`	This is a bitwise attachment flag of the type `VkAttachmentDescriptionFlags`.
`format`	This is the format of the image used in the attachment.
`sample`	This refers to the number of samples used for the attachment in a Render Pass.
| `loadOp` | This defines the behavior of color and depth attachments, how they will be treated at the beginning of the subpass. For more information, refer to `VkAttachmentStoreOp` in the following section:<br>```
typedef enum VkAttachmentLoadOp {
    VK_ATTACHMENT_LOAD_OP_LOAD      = 0,
    VK_ATTACHMENT_LOAD_OP_CLEAR     = 1,
    VK_ATTACHMENT_LOAD_OP_DONT_CARE = 2,
} VkAttachmentLoadOp;
```<br>These flags are defined as follows:<br>• VK_ATTACHMENT_LOAD_OP_LOAD: The use of this flag preserves the existing contents of the attachment; this means the rendered area's content remains preserved with each Render Pass execution.<br>• VK_ATTACHMENT_LOAD_OP_CLEAR: The rendered area's content is cleared with the specified constant color value defined in the beginning of the Render Pass. With each execution of the Render Pass, the background is first cleared with the specified color and then primitives are drawn on top of it.<br>• VK_ATTACHMENT_LOAD_OP_DONT_CARE: The content inside the render area is undefined and is not preserved. This indicates that upon the completion of the Render Pass instance, the application does not require the contents of the buffer. |
```

`storeOp`	This defines the behavior of the color and depth attachments, how they will be treated at the end of the subpass. For more information, refer to `VkAttachmentStoreOp` in the following section.
	`typedef enum VkAttachmentStoreOp {`
	`    VK_ATTACHMENT_STORE_OP_STORE = 0,`
	`    VK_ATTACHMENT_STORE_OP_DONT_CARE = 1,`
	`} VkAttachmentStoreOp;`
	• `VK_ATTACHMENT_STORE_OP_STORE` means the contents within the render area are written to the memory and will be available for reading after the Render Pass instance is completed, that is, once the writes have been synchronized with `VK_ACCESS_COLOR_ATTACHMENT_WRITE_BIT` (for color attachments) or `VK_ACCESS_DEPTH_STENCIL_ATTACHMENT_WRITE_BIT` (for depth/stencil attachments).
	In other words, the application wants to leave the rendering result in this memory so that it can be utilized in the subsequent subpass or intended to be presented to the display.
	• `VK_ATTACHMENT_STORE_OP_DONT_CARE` means the contents within the render area are not needed after the rendering is done and may be discarded; the contents of the attachment will be undefined inside the render area.

`stencilLoadOp`	This defines the behavior of the stencil aspect of a depth/stencil attachment using `VkAttachmentLoadOp`, how it will be treated at the beginning of the subpass.
`stencilStoreOp`	This defines the behavior of the stencil aspect of a depth/stencil attachment using `VkAttachmentStoreOp`, how it will be treated at the beginning of the subpass.
`initialLayout`	This defines the layout of the attachment image the subresource will be in when a Render Pass instance begins.
`finalLayout`	This defines the layout of the attachment image the subresource will be transitioned to when a Render Pass instance ends. In a given Render Pass instance, an attachment can use a different layout in each subpass, if required.

A subpass can reference to various attachments, such as an input, resolve, color, depth/stencil, and preserve attachment. This is described using a special control structure called `VkSubpassDescription`. Here is the syntax of this structure:

```
typedef struct VkSubpassDescription {
    VkSubpassDescriptionFlags        flags;
```

```
        VkPipelineBindPoint             pipelineBindPoint;
        uint32_t                        inputAttachmentCount;
        const VkAttachmentReference*    pInputAttachments;
        uint32_t                        colorAttachmentCount;
        const VkAttachmentReference*    pColorAttachments;
        const VkAttachmentReference*    pResolveAttachments;
        const VkAttachmentReference*    pDepthStencilAttachment;
        uint32_t                        preserveAttachmentCount;
        const uint32_t*                 pPreserveAttachments;
} VkSubpassDescription;
```

The various fields of this structure are described here:

Parameters	Description
flags	This field is not in use; it is reserved for future use.
pipelineBindPoint	This specifies whether the subpass belongs to the graphics or compute queue. It accepts a VkPipelineBindPoint value.
inputAttachmentCount	This specifies the number of input attachments.
pInputAttachments	This is an array of VkAttachmentReference structures with size equal to inputAttachmentCount. It specifies which attachments can be read at the shading stage and what will be the layout of the attachment images during the subpass.
colorAttachmentCount	This refers to the number of color attachments.
pColorAttachments	This is an array of VkAttachmentReference structures with size equal to colorAttachmentCount, containing the Render Pass's attachments that will be used as color attachments in the subpass. Also, it specifies the layouts the attachment images will be in during the subpass.
pResolveAttachments	This is a pointer to an array of VkAttachmentReference structures. Each of its elements (with the same index in colorAttachments) corresponds to a color attachment.
pDepthStencilAttachment	This specifies which attachment will be used for depth/stencil data and the layout it will be in during the subpass; it is a pointer to VkAttachmentReference.
preserveAttachmentCount	This refers to the number of preserved attachments.

Buffer Resource, Render Pass, Framebuffer, and Shaders with SPIR-V

| pPreserveAttachments | This is an array of the preserveAttachmentCount Render Pass attachment indices describing the attachments that are not used by a subpass; the indices rather describe whose contents must be preserved throughout the subpass. |

Implementing the Render Pass

Let's implement the Render Pass in the existing `VulkanRenderer` class step by step:

1. Include the following Render Pass methods and variables in the `VulkanRender` class in `VulkanRenderer.h`. This includes the creation/destruction of the Render Pass and the command buffer associated with the Render Pass:

   ```
   class VulkanRenderer
   {
   // Many lines skipped, please refer to the source code
   public:
       /***** Member functions *****/

       // Record render pass command buffer
       void createRenderPassCB(bool includeDepth);

       // Render Pass creation
       void createRenderPass(bool includeDepth, bool clear=true);

       // Destroy the render pass object when no more required
       void destroyRenderpass();

       /***** Member variables *****/
       // Render pass created object
       VkRenderPass            renderPass;
   }
   ```

2. At the initialization stage, create the Render Pass using `VulkanRenderer::createRenderPass()`:

   ```
   void VulkanRenderer::initialize()
   {
      const bool includeDepth = true;
      createRenderPass (includeDepth);
   }
   ```

[232]

3. The created color and depth image need to be specified in the attachments. Create an array of the `VkAttachmentDescription` type with the size equal to 2 for both the image types. The information specified in this structure will decide how to treat the image at the beginning and end of the Render Pass. It contains the image format, number of samples, load and store operations, and so on.
4. For both the attachments, set the `loadOp` member to `VK_ATTACHMENT_LOAD_OP_CLEAR`. This tells to clear the buffer at the start of each Render Pass instance. For the color attachment, set the `storeOp` member to `VK_ATTACHMENT_STORE_OP_STORE`, indicating that the rendered output be kept in the buffer that will be used to display it.
5. Next, for both the attachments, specify the binding points in the Render Pass. This allows the Render Pass to know where to look for a specific attachment. The binding points are defined with the help of `VkAttachmentReference`; the other piece of information this control structure intakes is the image layout information that will be used for image layout transitioning. Specify the image layout with `VK_IMAGE_LAYOUT_COLOR_ATTACHMENT_OPTIMAL` and `VK_IMAGE_LAYOUT_DEPTH_STENCIL_ATTACHMENT_OPTIMAL` for color and depth buffer, respectively. The layout informs the underlying engine to store the image in the optimal memory to give the best performance possible.
6. All the attachments are specified in the subpass using `VkSubpassDescription`. Here, specify the color, depth, resolve, and preserve attachments. Finally, all the attachments and subpass-specific information is accumulated in `VkRenderPassCreateInfo` and passed to the `vkCreateRenderPass()` API to create the Render Pass object:

```
void VulkanRenderer::createRenderPass(bool isDepthSupported,
                                      bool clear)
{
    // Dependency on VulkanSwapChain::createSwapChain() to
    // get the color image and VulkanRenderer::
    // createDepthImage() to get the depth image.
    VkResult    result;
    // Attach the color buffer and depth buffer as an
    // attachment to render pass instance
    VkAttachmentDescription attachments[2];
    attachments[0].format = swapChainObj->scPublicVars.format;
    attachments[0].samples= NUM_SAMPLES;
    attachments[0].loadOp = clear ? VK_ATTACHMENT_LOAD_OP_CLEAR
                    : VK_ATTACHMENT_LOAD_OP_DONT_CARE;
    attachments[0].storeOp = VK_ATTACHMENT_STORE_OP_STORE;
    attachments[0].stencilLoadOp =
                    VK_ATTACHMENT_LOAD_OP_DONT_CARE;
    attachments[0].stencilStoreOp =
```

Buffer Resource, Render Pass, Framebuffer, and Shaders with SPIR-V

```
                    VK_ATTACHMENT_STORE_OP_DONT_CARE;
attachments[0].initialLayout =
          VK_IMAGE_LAYOUT_COLOR_ATTACHMENT_OPTIMAL;
attachments[0].finalLayout =
          VK_IMAGE_LAYOUT_COLOR_ATTACHMENT_OPTIMAL;
attachments[0].flags = 0;

// Is the depth buffer present the define attachment
// properties for depth buffer attachment.
if (isDepthSupported)
{
  attachments[1].format    = Depth.format;
  attachments[1].samples   = NUM_SAMPLES;
  attachments[1].loadOp    = clear ?
                VK_ATTACHMENT_LOAD_OP_CLEAR :
                VK_ATTACHMENT_LOAD_OP_DONT_CARE;
  attachments[1].storeOp   =
                VK_ATTACHMENT_STORE_OP_STORE;
  attachments[1].stencilLoadOp =
                VK_ATTACHMENT_LOAD_OP_LOAD;
  attachments[1].stencilStoreOp=
                VK_ATTACHMENT_STORE_OP_STORE;
  attachments[1].initialLayout =
      VK_IMAGE_LAYOUT_DEPTH_STENCIL_ATTACHMENT_OPTIMAL;
  attachments[1].finalLayout   =
      VK_IMAGE_LAYOUT_DEPTH_STENCIL_ATTACHMENT_OPTIMAL;
  attachments[1].flags         = 0;
 }

// Define the color buffer attachment binding point
// and layout information
VkAttachmentReference colorReference    = {};
colorReference.attachment               = 0;
colorReference.layout                   =
          VK_IMAGE_LAYOUT_COLOR_ATTACHMENT_OPTIMAL;

// Define the depth buffer attachment binding point and
// layout information
VkAttachmentReference depthReference    = {};
depthReference.attachment               = 1;
depthReference.layout                   =
      VK_IMAGE_LAYOUT_DEPTH_STENCIL_ATTACHMENT_OPTIMAL;

// Specify the attachments - color, depth,
// resolve, preserve etc.
VkSubpassDescription subpass        = {};
subpass.pipelineBindPoint           =
          VK_PIPELINE_BIND_POINT_GRAPHICS;
```

```
subpass.flags                      = 0;
subpass.inputAttachmentCount       = 0;
subpass.pInputAttachments          = NULL;
subpass.colorAttachmentCount       = 1;
subpass.pColorAttachments          = &colorReference;
subpass.pResolveAttachments        = NULL;
subpass.pDepthStencilAttachment    = isDepthSupported ?
        &depthReference : NULL;
subpass.preserveAttachmentCount    = 0;
subpass.pPreserveAttachments       = NULL;

// Specify the attachment and subpass associate with
// render pass
VkRenderPassCreateInfo rpInfo    = {};
rpInfo.sType        = VK_STRUCTURE_TYPE_RENDER_PASS_CREATE_INFO;
rpInfo.pNext              = NULL;
rpInfo.attachmentCount    = isDepthSupported ? 2 : 1;
rpInfo.pAttachments       = attachments;
rpInfo.subpassCount       = 1;
rpInfo.pSubpasses         = &subpass;
rpInfo.dependencyCount    = 0;
rpInfo.pDependencies      = NULL;

// Create the render pass object
result = vkCreateRenderPass(deviceObj->device, &rpInfo,
            NULL, &renderPass);

assert(result == VK_SUCCESS);
}
```

7. At the deinitialization stage, destroy the Render Pass object using the `vkDestroyRenderPass()` API:

```
void VulkanApplication::deInitialize()
{
    rendererObj->destroyRenderpass();
    . . . .
}

void VulkanRenderer::destroyRenderpass()
{
    vkDestroyRenderPass(deviceObj->device, renderPass, NULL);
}
```

Using the Render Pass and creating the framebuffer

Once the Render Pass is created, it is used to create the framebuffer. Ideally, for each swapchain color image, we need a framebuffer associated with it. For example, if we have a double buffer swapchain image, then we need two framebuffers: one for the front buffer and another for the back buffer image.

The framebuffer in Vulkan is created using the `vkCreateFrameBuffer()` API. Like with other Vulkan APIs, this also has a create info control structure called `VkFrameBufferCreateInfo`. Refer to the following for more information on its syntax and usage:

```
VkResult vkCreateFrameBuffer(
    VkDevice                          device,
    const VkFramebufferCreateInfo*    pCreateInfo,
    const VkAllocationCallbacks*      pAllocator,
    VkFramebuffer*                    pFrameBuffer);
```

The following table describes the various fields of the `vkCreateFrameBuffer()` API:

Parameters	Description
`device`	This is the logical device handle to which the framebuffer is associated.
`pCreateInfo`	This is the pointer to the `VkFrameBufferCreateInfo` structure object.
`pAllocator`	This controls the host memory deallocation process. Refer to the *Host memory* section in Chapter 5, *Command Buffer and Memory Management in Vulkan*.
`pFrameBuffer`	This creates the `VkFrameBuffer` object and returns the pointer.

The `VkFrameBufferCreateInfo` control structure is described in the following syntax:

```
typedef struct VkFramebufferCreateInfo {
    VkStructureType              type;
    const void*                  pNext;
    VkFramebufferCreateFlags     flags;
    VkRenderPass                 renderPass;
    uint32_t                     attachmentCount;
    const VkImageView*           pAttachments;
    uint32_t                     width;
    uint32_t                     height;
    uint32_t                     layers;
} VkFramebufferCreateInfo;
```

The following table describes the various fields of this structure:

Parameters	Description
type	This refers to the type of this structure, which must be VK_STRUCTURE_TYPE_FRAMEBUFFER_CREATE_INFO.
next	This is either NULL or a pointer to an extension-specific structure.
flag	This must be 0; it is reserved for future use.
renderPass	This is the VkRenderPass object that we created in the previous section.
attachment-Count	This refers to the number of attachments associated with the framebuffer.
attachment	This is an array of VkImageView handles for the corresponding image, each of which will be used as the corresponding attachment in the Render Pass instance.
width	This refers to the width of the framebuffer in pixels.
height	This refers to the height of the framebuffer in pixels.
layers	This refers to the layers in the framebuffer.

Implementing the framebuffer

The implementation of a framebuffer is simple; follow these steps:

1. Create the following functions and variables in the VulkanRenderer class. The cmdFrameBuffer declares the command buffer responsible for creating the framebuffer (frameBuffer):

   ```
   class VulkanRenderer
   {
   public:
       // Member functions
       void createFrameBuffer(bool includeDepth,bool clear= true);
       void destroyFrameBuffer ();
       // Number of frame buffer corresponding to each swap chain
       std::vector<VkFramebuffer> framebuffers;
   }
   ```

Buffer Resource, Render Pass, Framebuffer, and Shaders with SPIR-V

2. During the initialization, create the framebuffer using the `createFrameBuffer()` function:

```
void VulkanRenderer::initialize()
{
    const bool includeDepth = true;
    createFrameBuffer(includeDepth);
}
```

3. For each swapchain color image, create its corresponding framebuffer. This is done using the `vkCreateFrameBuffer()` API. This API intakes `VkFrameBufferCreateInfo` in which we specify the depth and color image views as an attachment. Also, pass the created Render Pass object along with the dimensions of the framebuffer in this structure:

```
void VulkanRenderer::createFrameBuffer(bool includeDepth)
{
    // Dependency on createDepthBuffer(), createRenderPass()
    // and recordSwapChain()
    VkResult   result;
    VkImageView attachments[2];
    attachments[1] = Depth.view;

    VkFramebufferCreateInfo fbInfo      = {};
    fbInfo.sType           = VK_STRUCTURE_TYPE_FRAMEBUFFER_CREATE_INFO;
    fbInfo.pNext           = NULL;
    fbInfo.renderPass      = renderPass;
    fbInfo.attachmentCount = includeDepth ? 2 : 1;
    fbInfo.pAttachments    = attachments;
    fbInfo.width           = width;
    fbInfo.height    = height;
    fbInfo.layers    = 1;

    uint32_t i;

    framebuffers.clear();
    framebuffers.resize(swapChainObj->scPublicVars.
                                    swapchainImageCount);

    for (i = 0; i < swapChainObj->scPublicVars
                    .swapchainImageCount; i++) {
     attachments[0] = swapChainObj->scPublicVars.
                    colorBuffer[i].view;

         result = vkCreateFramebuffer(deviceObj->device,
                    &fbInfo, NULL, &framebuffers.at(i));
```

```
                assert(result == VK_SUCCESS);
        }
}
```

4. At the application de-initialization stage, destroy all the framebuffers using the `vkDestroyFrameBuffer()` API:

```
void VulkanApplication::deInitialize()
{
    rendererObj->destroyRenderpass();
    . . . .
}

void VulkanRenderer::destroyFramebuffers()
{
    for (uint32_t i = 0; i < swapChainObj
    ->scPublicVars.swapchainImageCount; i++) {
    vkDestroyFramebuffer(deviceObj->device,
        framebuffers.at(i), NULL);
    }
    framebuffers.clear();
}
```

Clearing the background color

In this section, we use the created Render Pass and framebuffer object and implement the Render Pass instance. This Render Pass instance is very simple and will only clear the background image with a specified color. For each swapchain image, different colors can be specified using the `pClearValues` field of the `VkRenderPassBeginInfo` structure; this structure is then passed to the Render Pass instance.

The Render Pass instance is implemented during the preparation stage in which the command buffers are created. For each swapchain image, a corresponding command buffer object is created. This means, for n swapchain images, we need to create n command buffer objects.

The preparation is done using the `VulkanDrawable::prepare()` function, and the rendering of the swapchain images will be performed using the `VulkanDrawable::render()` function.

The following diagram shows the call stack of the `prepare()` and `render()` function:

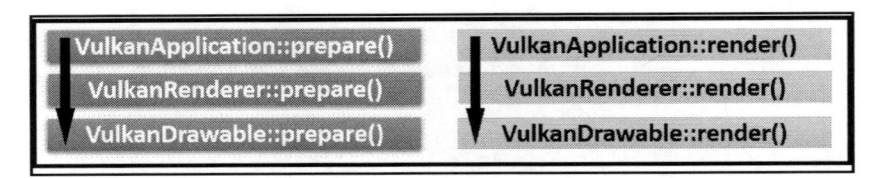

VulkanApplication::prepare()	VulkanApplication::render()
VulkanRenderer::prepare()	VulkanRenderer::render()
VulkanDrawable::prepare()	VulkanDrawable::render()

The following class declaration shows the new member variables and functions added to the `VulkanDrawable` class. The `prepare()` function produces the command buffers in the `vecCmdDraw` vector and records the drawing commands; these are used in the `render()` function where the command buffer executes and renders the swapchain images. The `recordCommandBuffer()` function records the commands in the Render Pass instance.

> For a detailed understanding of the preparation and rendering of a drawing object, refer to the *Preparing the drawing object* and *Rendering the drawing object* sections in `Chapter 9`, *Drawing Objects*.

```
class VulkanDrawable
{
public:
    // Prepares the drawing object before rendering
    // Allocate, create, record command buffer
    void prepare();

    // Renders the drawing object
    void render();

private:
    // Command buffer for drawing
    std::vector<VkCommandBuffer> vecCmdDraw;
    // Prepares render pass instance
    void recordCommandBuffer(int currentImage,
            VkCommandBuffer* cmdDraw);
};
```

Setting the background color in the Render Pass instance

In this section, we will implement the `prepare()` function of `VulkanDrawable`. Inside this, the command buffer wrapper class (`CommandBufferMgr`) is used to manage (allocate, record, and submit) the command buffers (`vecCmdDraw`). The following code implements the `prepare()` function:

```
void VulkanDrawable::prepare()
{
    VulkanDevice* deviceObj = rendererObj->getDevice();
    vecCmdDraw.resize(rendererObj->getSwapChain()->scPublicVars
                                    .colorBuffer.size());

    // For each swapbuffer color image buffer
    // allocate the corresponding command buffer
    for (int i = 0; i < rendererObj->getSwapChain()->scPublicVars.
                                    colorBuffer.size(); i++){
        // Allocate, create and start command buffer recording
        CommandBufferMgr::allocCommandBuffer(&deviceObj->device,
            *rendererObj->getCommandPool(), &vecCmdDraw[i]);
        CommandBufferMgr::beginCommandBuffer(vecCmdDraw[i]);

        // Create the render pass instance
        recordCommandBuffer(i, &vecCmdDraw[i]);

        // Finish the command buffer recording
        CommandBufferMgr::endCommandBuffer(vecCmdDraw[i]);
    }
}
```

The implementation first checks the number of color images supported by the swapchain and creates the same number of command buffer objects, associating each one of them logically with the corresponding swapchain image. The clearing of the swapchain image is always performed on the back image (back buffer), while the front image (front buffer) is used to display the rendered contents. Once the back image is cleared and rendered (if any), it is swapped with the front buffer.

Use the created command buffer (`vecCmdDraw`) and record the commands inside the `recordCommandBuffer()` function. This function specifies the clear color value for each swapchain image using the `pClearValues` field of the `VkRenderPassBeginInfo` data structure that is passed into the `vkCmdBeginRenderPass()` API. The `vkCmdBeginRenderPass()` and `vkCmdEndRenderPass()` APIs define a scope under which the Render Pass instance commands are recorded.

Buffer Resource, Render Pass, Framebuffer, and Shaders with SPIR-V

> For more information on Render Pass commands and its associated APIs, refer to the *Recording the Render Pass commands* section in Chapter 9, *Drawing Objects*.

There are two objects of the clear values (VkClearValue). The first one specifies the clear color value of the associated swapchain image indicated by the currentImage index. The second object specifies the clear color value to be used for the depth image:

```
void VulkanDrawable::recordCommandBuffer(int currentImage, VkCommandBuffer* cmdDraw)
{
    // Specify the clear color value
    VkClearValue clearValues[2];
    switch (currentImage)
    {
        case 0: clearValues[0].color = { 1.0f,0.0f,0.0f,1.0f };break;
        case 1: clearValues[0].color = { 0.0f,1.0f,0.0f,1.0f };break;
        case 2: clearValues[0].color = { 0.0f,0.0f,1.0f,1.0f };break;
        default:clearValues[0].color = { 0.0f,0.0f,0.0f,1.0f };break;
    }

    // Specify the depth/stencil clear value
    clearValues[1].depthStencil.depth   = 1.0f;
    clearValues[1].depthStencil.stencil = 0;

    // Define the VkRenderPassBeginInfo control structure
    VkRenderPassBeginInfo renderPassBegin = {};
    renderPassBegin.sType=VK_STRUCTURE_TYPE_RENDER_PASS_BEGIN_INFO;
    renderPassBegin.renderPass   = rendererObj->renderPass;
    renderPassBegin.framebuffer = rendererObj->
    framebuffers[currentImage];
    renderPassBegin.renderArea.extent.width = rendererObj->width;
    renderPassBegin.renderArea.extent.height= rendererObj->height;
    renderPassBegin.clearValueCount = 2;
    renderPassBegin.pClearValues    = clearValues;
    // Start recording the render pass instance
    vkCmdBeginRenderPass(*cmdDraw, &renderPassBegin,
                         VK_SUBPASS_CONTENTS_INLINE);

    // End of render pass instance recording
    vkCmdEndRenderPass(*cmdDraw);
}
```

Rendering the colored background

The cleared swapchain images are rendered one by one inside the `render()` function, as implemented in the following code snippet. The WSI windowing system extension `vkAcquireNextImageKHR()` is used to query the next available swapchain image index. This index indicates which swapchain image will be available for drawing. Using this index, the corresponding command buffer is selected and submitted to the queue. Once processed on the GPU, the swapchain image is ready for displaying purposes using the presentation engine. The presentation is performed using the WSI extension `fpQueuePresentKHR`. This API intakes the `VkPresentInfoKHR` structure; this contains the swapchain object and the index of the swapchain image that needs to be displayed on the window.

> Rendering the drawing object is a separate topic altogether and is out of the scope of this chapter. For more information on this topic and the associated WSI extensions with their related data structures, refer to the *Rendering the drawing object* section in `Chapter 9`, *Drawing Objects*.

The following code implements the clearing where the background color is cleared every second with red, blue and green background color:

```
void VulkanDrawable::render()
{
    VulkanDevice* deviceObj           = rendererObj->getDevice();
    VulkanSwapChain* swapChainObj     = rendererObj->getSwapChain();

    uint32_t& currentColorImage       = swapChainObj->scPublicVars.
                                        currentColorBuffer;
    VkSwapchainKHR& swapChain         = swapChainObj->scPublicVars.
                                        swapChain;
    // Render each background color for 1 second.
    Sleep(1000);
    // Get the index of the next available swapchain image:
    VkResult result = swapChainObj->fpAcquireNextImageKHR
        (deviceObj->device, swapChain, UINT64_MAX, VK_NULL_HANDLE,
        VK_NULL_HANDLE, &currentColorImage);

    // Queue the command buffer for execution
    CommandBufferMgr::submitCommandBuffer(deviceObj->queue,
    &vecCmdDraw[currentColorImage], NULL);

    // Present the image in the window
    VkPresentInfoKHR present    = {};
    present.sType               = VK_STRUCTURE_TYPE_PRESENT_INFO_KHR;
    present.swapchainCount      = 1;
```

```
    present.pSwapchains            = &swapChain;
    present.pImageIndices          = &currentColorImage;

    // Queue the image for presentation,
    result = swapChainObj->fpQueuePresentKHR
    (deviceObj->queue, &present);
    assert(result == VK_SUCCESS);
}
```

The following is the output of the implemented exercise. The output will display various background colors, and each image will be displayed for one second.

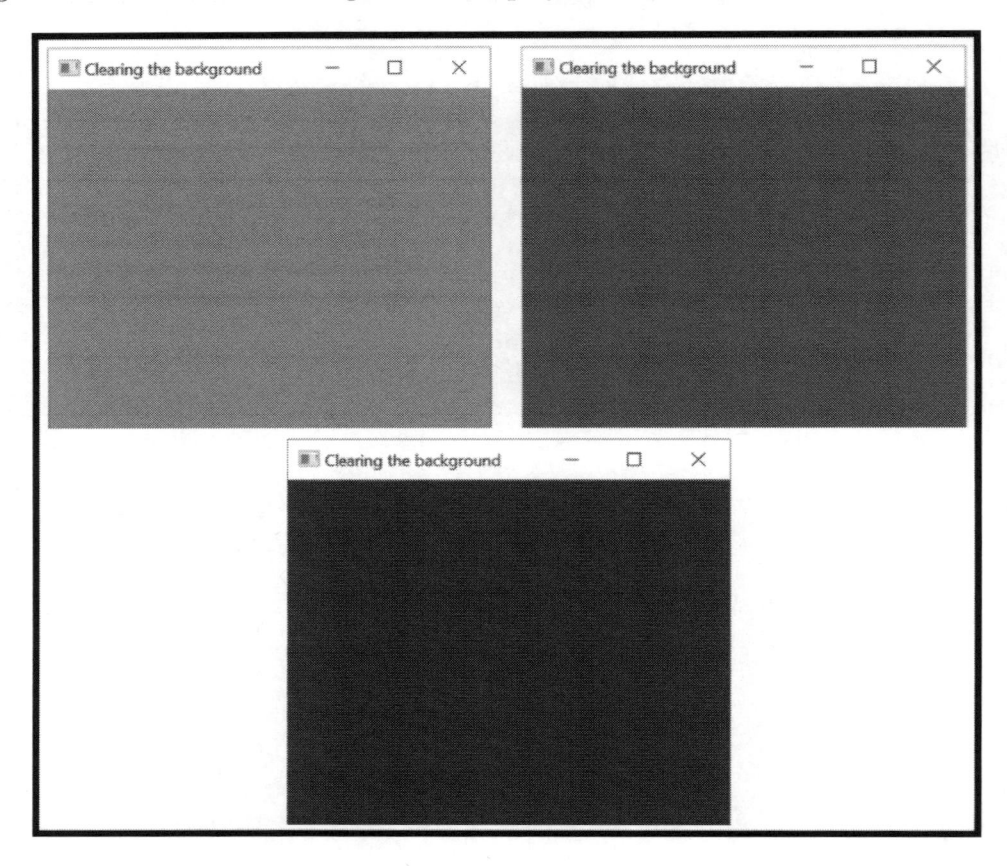

Working with a shader in Vulkan

Shaders are the means by which the programmable stage is controlled in the graphics and compute pipeline.

The graphics pipeline includes vertex, tessellation, geometry, and fragment shaders. Collectively, the first four-vertex, tessellation control, tessellation evaluation, and geometry shaders-are responsible for the vertex-processing stages. These are followed by the fragment shader, which is executed after rasterization.

Here's a bit about the graphics pipeline shaders:

- **Vertex shaders**: The graphics pipeline executes the vertex shader as a result of the primitive assembly. It is used to process geometric vertices. It manipulates the data that may be required by the subsequent shaders (if enabled), such as lighting information by the fragment shader.
- **Tessellation shaders**: This is a vertex-processing stage. When enabled, it subdivides the patches of vertex data into smaller primitives governed by the control and evaluate shaders.
- **Geometry shaders**: This shader when enabled has the capability to produce new geometry at the execution time by using the output from the previous shader stages (tessellation and vertex shaders).
- **Fragment shaders**: The rasterizer (fixed function) produces the fragments using the processed vertices from the previous stages. These fragments are then processed by the fragment shader, which is responsible for coloring them.
- **Compute shaders**: Compute shaders are invoked in the workgroup for computing arbitrary information in a massive parallel computation format. The compute pipeline only consists of the compute shader.

Unlike OpenGL, where GLSL is the official shading language, Vulkan uses SPIR-V, which is a whole new approach to shaders and computing kernels.

Introduction to SPIR-V

Unlike **OpenGL shading language (GLSL)**, which is a human-readable form for a shader, Vulkan totally relies on SPIR-V, which is a low-level binary **intermediate representation (IR)**. As the high-level language is no more a requirement for SPIR-V, it reduces the driver complexity significantly. This allows an application to accept any high-level language (GLSL or HLSL) as long as the GPU vendor provides the compiler to convert it into the SPIR-V form.

SPIR-V is a binary intermediate language used to represent graphical shader stages and compute kernels for multiple APIs. It stores the information in a stream of 32-bit words. It consists of mainly two parts: header and payload. The header consists of the first five slots (5 x 4 bytes = 20 bytes) that are helpful in recognizing the input source as the SPIR-V input stream. However, the payload represents variable length instructions containing the source data.

SPIR-V is a platform-independent intermediate language that can be used for multiple languages that feed multiple drivers under the hood, as shown in the following diagram. Compilers to SPIR-V exist for multiple source languages, such as GLSL or HLSL, or even for reading compute kernels. The shader module provides multiple entry points that can provide good wins in terms of shader code size and disk I/O requirement.

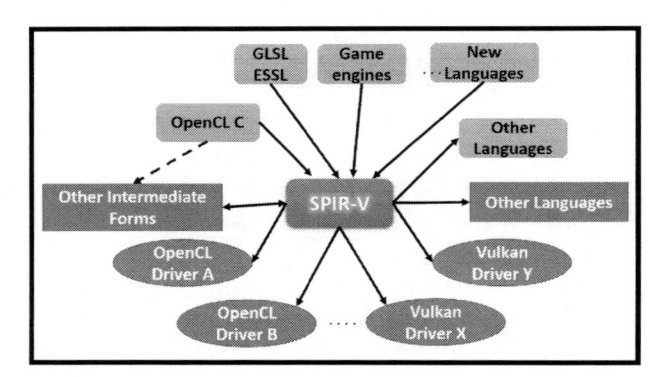

The following diagram used from Khronos's official SPIR-V specification provides an overview of the SPIR-V file format:

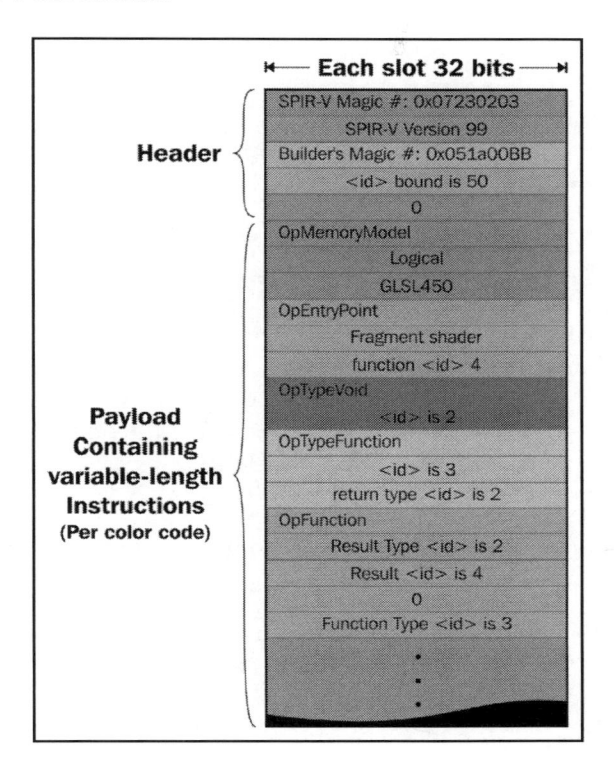

```
                    ←—— Each slot 32 bits ——→
            ┌─── SPIR-V Magic #: 0x07230203
            │    SPIR-V Version 99
   Header  ─┤    Builder's Magic #: 0x051a00BB
            │    <id> bound is 50
            └─── 0
            ┌─── OpMemoryModel
            │    Logical
            │    GLSL450
            │    OpEntryPoint
            │    Fragment shader
            │    function <id> 4
            │    OpTypeVoid
  Payload   │    <id> is 2
 Containing─┤    OpTypeFunction
variable-length  <id> is 3
 Instructions    return type <id> is 2
(Per color code) OpFunction
            │    Result Type <id> is 2
            │    Result <id> is 4
            │    0
            └─── Function Type <id> is 3
                        ·
                        ·
                        ·
```

Although SPIR-V is a high-level language, it is also simple enough to bypass all of the text or string parsing, which is a good thing to achieve higher performance. According to the official specification, SPIR-V first encodes a set of annotations and decorations and then a collection of functions. Each function encodes a **control flow graph** (**CFG**) of basic blocks with additional instructions to preserve source-code-structured control flow. Load/store instructions are used to access declared variables, which include all of the I/O. Intermediate results bypassing load/store use the **static single assignment** (**SSA**) representation. Data objects are represented logically with hierarchical-type information. There is no flattening of aggregates or assignments to physical register banks and so on. Selectable addressing models establish whether general pointers may be used or whether memory access is purely logical.

Compiling a GLSL shader into SPIR-V

In this section, we will implement a very simple vertex and fragment shader in GLSL and convert it into the SPIR-V form in order to utilize it in our Vulkan program. There are two ways in which the GLSL shader can be converted into the SPIR-V binary form-offline and online. The former uses an executable to covert a GLSL source into the SPIR-V native format file; this file is then injected into the running Vulkan program. The latter makes use of a dynamic library to compile the GLSL into the SPIR-V form.

Offline compilation with the glslangValidator executable

The precompiled Lunar-G SDK's binaries include the `glslangValidator` executable, which can be used to convert GLSL into SPIR-V's `.spv` format. This does not require runtime compilation of the data and can be injected upfront. In this approach, the developers cannot change the GLSL program, and seeing the effects that take place upfront, it has to be recompiled again with every change added. This way is suitable for product releases where not to many changes are expected.

For a development cycle, where frequent changes are expected, the online method is suitable. Refer to the next section for more information on this. Also, refer to the following points:

- **Location**: The `glslangValidator` can be located in `<Vulkan SDK Path>\<Vulkan SDK Version>\Bin` on Windows. For a 32-bit platform implementation, refer to the `Bin32` folder instead.

- **Usage**: Its usage is defined as `glslangValidator [option]... [file]...`.

    Here, each file ends in `.<stage>`, where `<stage>` is one of the following:

Stage	Meaning
.conf	To provide an optional configuration file that replaces the default configuration
.vert	For a vertex shader
.tesc	For a tessellation control shader
.tese	For a tessellation evaluation shader
.geom	For a geometry shader
.frag	For a fragment shader

`.comp`	For a compute shader

- **An example**: Refer to the following instruction to compile the GLSL source file into the SPIR-V format (`.spv`):
    - Open the terminal, go to the source folder (let's say the one containing the vertex shader `Tri.vert`), and type the following command; this will result into the `Tri-Vert.spv` SPIR-V format:

    glslangValidator.exe -V Tri.vert -o Tri-Vert.spv

> The `glslangValidator.exe` can also be built using the LunarG SDK glslang source code.

Online compilation with SPIR-V tool libraries

The Lunar SDK also provides on-the-fly compilation using GLslang libraries. We need to compile these libraries from the SDK source code and include them in our source project. This exposes some special APIs that can be used to pass the GLSL shader source code into the project, making it available to the Vulkan shader module in the SPIR-V format behind the curtains.

In order to build the source code and compile them into libraries, you need the following:

- **Location**: Locate the SPIR-V-tool folder using the `<Vulkan SDK Path>\<Vulkan SDK Version>\glslang` path.
- **CMake**: The `GLslang` folder contains `CMakelists.txt`, which can be used to build the platform-specific project. After you build CMake, the following projects will be created: `glslang`, `glslangValidator`, `OGLCompiler`, `OSDependent`, `SPIRV`, and `spirv-remap`. Upon the compilation of the project in the debug and release mode, it will produce the necessary static libraries in the destination build folder.
- **Required libraries**: The following libraries (on Windows) are required in order to support the online compilation of the GLSL files into SPIR-V:
    - `SPIRV.lib`
    - `glslang.lib`
    - `OGLCompiler.lib`
    - `OSDependent.lib`
    - `HLSL.lib`

Implementing a shader

It's time to bring some shader capabilities in our example. This section will help us achieve this step by step. Follow the instructions given here:

Go to the sample application's `CMakeLists.txt` file and make the following changes:

- **A project name**: Give the recipe a proper name and set Vulkan SDK path:

    ```
    set (Recipe_Name "7e_ShadersWithSPIRV")
    ```

- **Header files**: Include the header file specified in the `glslang` directory. This will allow us to include the `SPIRV/GlslangToSpv.h` required in the source program:

- **Static libraries**: From the Vulkan-SDK-compiled projects, we need `SPIRV`, `glslang`, `HLSL OGLCompiler`, and `OSDependent` static libraries.

- **The link library path**: Provide the path to the solution where it can pick the static libraries specified in the preceding point. The variable name, `VULKAN_PATH`, specifies the path for the Lunar SDK:

- The following CMake code adds the required libraries for GLSL to SPIR-V conversion. You can convert a GLSL code into `.spv` form in two ways:
  a) **Offline**: Using Vulkan SDK's `glslangValidator.exe`, this tool does not require additional libraries, the `Vulkan-1.lib` is more than enough. This mode is useful when the project is in the deployment stage where shaders are not undergoing the development cycle's dynamic changes
  b) **Online**: Auto-converting GLSL into `.spv` on runtime using glslang helper functions. At project development stage, the developers do not need to compile the GLSL shader offline for desire shader code changes. The glslang helper functions automatically compiles the GLSL into .spv form. This mode requires a few libraries these are: SPIRV, glslang, OGLCompiler, OSDependent, HLSL.Using CMake's `BUILD_SPV_ON_COMPILE_TIME` variable you can choose either of the desired options to convert the GLSL shader into `.spv` form. For more information, please add the below code in existing `CMakeLists.txt` and follow through the inline comments:

    ```
    # BUILD_SPV_ON_COMPILE_TIME - accepted value ON or OFF
    # ON    - Reads the GLSL shader file and auto convert in SPIR-V form
      (.spv). This requires additional libraries support from VulkanSDK
        like SPIRV glslang OGLCompiler OSDependent HLSL
    # OFF - Only reads .spv files, which need to be compiled offline
        using glslangValidator.exe.
    #For example: glslangValidator.exe <GLSL file name> -V -o <output
    ```

```
             filename in SPIR-V(.spv) form>
    option(BUILD_SPV_ON_COMPILE_TIME "BUILD_SPV_ON_COMPILE_TIME" OFF)

    if(BUILD_SPV_ON_COMPILE_TIME)

        # Preprocessor flag allows the solution to use glslang
          library functions
        add_definitions(-DAUTO_COMPILE_GLSL_TO_SPV)

        # GLSL - use Vulkan SDK's glslang library for compling GLSL to SPV
        # This does not require offline coversion of GLSL shader to
          SPIR-V(.spv) form
        set(GLSLANGDIR "${VULKAN_PATH}/glslang")

        get_filename_component(GLSLANG_PREFIX "${GLSLANGDIR}" ABSOLUTE)

        # Check if glslang directory exists
        if(NOT EXISTS ${GLSLANG_PREFIX})
                message(FATAL_ERROR "Necessary glslang components do not
                exist: "${GLSLANG_PREFIX})
          endif()

        # Include the glslang directory
        include_directories( ${GLSLANG_PREFIX} )

        # If compiling GLSL to SPV using we need the following libraries
        set(GLSLANG_LIBS SPIRV glslang OGLCompiler OSDependent HLSL)

        # Generate the list of files to link, per flavor.
        foreach(x ${GLSLANG_LIBS})
                list(APPEND VULKAN_LIB_LIST debug ${x}d
                optimized ${x})
        endforeach()

        # Note: While configuring CMake for glslang we created the
          binaries in a "build" folder inside ${VULKAN_PATH}/glslang.
        # Therefore, you must edit the below lines for your custom path
          like <Your binary path>/OGLCompilersDLL,
          <Your binary path>/OSDependent/Windows
        link_directories(${VULKAN_PATH}/glslang/build/OGLCompilersDLL )
        link_directories(${VULKAN_PATH}/glslang/build/glslang/
        OSDependent/Windows)
        link_directories(${VULKAN_PATH}/glslang/build/glslang)
        link_directories(${VULKAN_PATH}/glslang/build/SPIRV)
        link_directories(${VULKAN_PATH}/glslang/build/hlsl)
    endif()
```

Implement the user-defined shader custom class called `VulkanShader` in `VulkanShader.h`/`.cpp` to manage all the shader activities. Refer to the implementation here:

```
/************** VulkanShader.h **************/
#pragma once
#include "Headers.h"

// Shader class managing the shader conversion, compilation, linking
class VulkanShader
{
public:
    VulkanShader() {}         // Constructor
    ~VulkanShader() {}        // Destructor

   // Entry point to build the shaders
    void buildShader(const char *vertShaderText,
        const char *fragShaderText);
   // Convert GLSL shader to SPIR-V shader
    bool GLSLtoSPV(const VkShaderStageFlagBits shaderType,
        const char *pshader, std::vector<unsigned int> &spirv);
   // Kill the shader when not required
    void destroyShaders();

   // Type of shader language. This could be - EShLangVertex,
   // Tessellation Control, Tessellation Evaluation, Geometry,
   // Fragment and Compute
    EShLanguage getLanguage
        (const VkShaderStageFlagBits shaderType);

   // Initialize the TBuitInResource
    void initializeResources(TBuiltInResource &Resources);

   // Vk structure storing vertex & fragment shader information

    VkPipelineShaderStageCreateInfo shaderStages[2];
};
```

The user-defined `VulkanShader` class exposes the `buildShader()` function, which allows you to inject the GLSL shaders in order to compile them into the Vulkan project. Behind the curtains, the function makes use of the GLslang SPIR-V library functions to convert them into the native form.

This function builds the shader in four steps:

1. Initialize the GLSL language shader library using `glslang::InitializeProcess()`. Note that this function needs to be called exactly once per process before you use anything else.
2. Convert the GLSL shader code into a SPIR-V shader byte array. This includes the following:
    - Parsing the GLSL source code
    - Adding the parse shader to the program object
    - Linking to the project object
    - Using `glslang::GlslangToSpv()` to covert the compiled binary shader into the SPIR-V format
3. Use the converted SPIR-V shader intermediate binary code to create the shader module using `vkCreateShaderModule()`.
4. Finalize the processing using `glslang::FinalizeProcess()` during the tear down. This function must be called once per process.

This function takes two arguments as parameter input, specifying the vertex and fragment shader. The shaders are used to create the shader module `VkShaderModule` with the help of the `vkCreateShaderModule()` API. This API intakes the `VkPipelineShaderStageCreateInfo` control structure as primary input containing the necessary information of the shader.

For more information, follow the syntax and parameter description given here:

```
VKAPI_ATTR VkResult VKAPI_CALL vkCreateShaderModule(
    VkDevice                          device,
    const VkShaderModuleCreateInfo*   pCreateInfo,
    const VkAllocationCallbacks*      pAllocator,
    VkShaderModule*                   pShaderModule);
```

The following table describes the various fields of this function:

Parameters	Description
device	This is the logical device handle to which the shader module is associated.
pCreateInfo	This is the pointer to the `VkShaderModuleCreateInfo` structure object.
pAllocator	This controls the host memory allocation process. For more information, refer to the *Host memory* section in `Chapter 5`, *Command Buffer and Memory Management in Vulkan*.

Buffer Resource, Render Pass, Framebuffer, and Shaders with SPIR-V

| pShaderModule | This refers to the created `VkShaderModule` object. |

```
typedef struct VkShaderModuleCreateInfo {
            VkStructureType              type;
            const void*                  next;
            VkShaderModuleCreateFlags    flags;
            size_t                       codeSize;
            const uint32_t*              code;
} VkShaderModuleCreateInfo;
```

The following table describes the various fields of this structure:

Parameters	Description
type	This refers to the type of the structure. This must be of the type `VK_STRUCTURE_TYPE_SHADER_MODULE_CREATE_INFO`.
next	This is either `NULL` or a pointer to an extension-specific structure.
flags	This is reserved for future use.
codeSize	This refers to the source code size in bytes. The source is pointed by `code`.
code	This refers to the source code that will be used to create the shader module.

The following code describes the implementation of the shader used in the sample example. The implementation is done in the `buildShader()` function; this helper function presently supports only vertex and fragment shaders, whose source code is passed as parameters into this function in the GLSL form. The following is the implementation:

```
/************** VulkanShader.cpp **************/
// Helper function intaking the GLSL vertex and fragment shader.
// It prepares the shaders to be consumed in the SPIR-V format
// with the help of glslang library helper functions.
void VulkanShader::buildShader(const char *vertShaderText, const char
*fragShaderText)
{
    VulkanDevice* deviceObj = VulkanApplication::GetInstance()
                                                    ->deviceObj;

    VkResult   result;
    bool       retVal;

    // Fill in the control structure to push the necessary
    // details of the shader.
    std::vector<unsigned int> vertexSPV;
    shaderStages[0].sType =  VK_STRUCTURE_TYPE_PIPELINE_
                                    SHADER_STAGE_CREATE_INFO;
    shaderStages[0].pNext = NULL;
```

```
shaderStages[0].pSpecializationInfo = NULL;
shaderStages[0].flags = 0;
shaderStages[0].stage = VK_SHADER_STAGE_VERTEX_BIT;
shaderStages[0].pName = "main";

glslang::InitializeProcess();

retVal = GLSLtoSPV(VK_SHADER_STAGE_VERTEX_BIT,
                    vertShaderText, vertexSPV);
assert(retVal);

VkShaderModuleCreateInfo moduleCreateInfo;
moduleCreateInfo.sType =
                VK_STRUCTURE_TYPE_SHADER_MODULE_CREATE_INFO;
moduleCreateInfo.pNext = NULL;
moduleCreateInfo.flags = 0;
moduleCreateInfo.codeSize = vertexSPV.size() *
                            sizeof(unsigned int);
moduleCreateInfo.pCode = vertexSPV.data();
result = vkCreateShaderModule(deviceObj->device,
        &moduleCreateInfo, NULL, &shaderStages[0].module);
assert(result == VK_SUCCESS);

std::vector<unsigned int> fragSPV;
shaderStages[1].sType = VK_STRUCTURE_TYPE_PIPELINE_
                        SHADER_STAGE_CREATE_INFO;
shaderStages[1].pNext = NULL;
shaderStages[1].pSpecializationInfo = NULL;
shaderStages[1].flags = 0;
shaderStages[1].stage = VK_SHADER_STAGE_FRAGMENT_BIT;
shaderStages[1].pName = "main";

retVal = GLSLtoSPV(VK_SHADER_STAGE_FRAGMENT_BIT,
                    fragShaderText, fragSPV);
assert(retVal);

moduleCreateInfo.sType = VK_STRUCTURE_TYPE_SHADER
                        _MODULE_CREATE_INFO;
moduleCreateInfo.pNext = NULL;
moduleCreateInfo.flags = 0;
moduleCreateInfo.codeSize = fragSPV.size() *
                            sizeof(unsigned int);
moduleCreateInfo.pCode = fragSPV.data();
result = vkCreateShaderModule(deviceObj->device,
        &moduleCreateInfo, NULL, &shaderStages[1].module);
assert(result == VK_SUCCESS);

glslang::FinalizeProcess();
```

}

The `vkCreateShaderModule()` takes the SPIR-V form as an input; therefore, we need the GLslang helper function to convert the GLSL shaders into the native format binary form supported by SPIR-V.

Before you call any glslang function, the library needs to be initialized once per process. This is done by calling `glslang::InitializeProcess()`. Next, the input shader is converted into the stream of SPIR-V bits using the user-defined function `VulkanShader::GLSLtoSPV()`, as mentioned in the following code:

```
bool VulkanShader::GLSLtoSPV(const VkShaderStageFlagBits shader_type, const char *pshader, std::vector<unsigned int> &spirv)
{
    glslang::TProgram& program = *new glslang::TProgram;
    const char *shaderStrings[1];
    TBuiltInResource Resources;
    initializeResources(Resources);

    // Enable SPIR-V and Vulkan rules when parsing GLSL
    EShMessages messages = (EShMessages)(EShMsgSpvRules
                            | EShMsgVulkanRules);

    EShLanguage stage = findLanguage(shader_type);
    glslang::TShader* shader = new glslang::TShader(stage);

    shaderStrings[0] = pshader;
    shader->setStrings(shaderStrings, 1);

    if (!shader->parse(&Resources, 100, false, messages)) {
        puts(shader->getInfoLog());
        puts(shader->getInfoDebugLog());
        return false;
    }

    program.addShader(shader);

    // Link the program and report if errors...
    if (!program.link(messages)) {
        puts(shader->getInfoLog());
        puts(shader->getInfoDebugLog());
        return false;
    }

    glslang::GlslangToSpv(*program.getIntermediate(stage),
            spirv);
```

```
        return true;
}
```

The `GLSLtoSPV` function needs to be compiled for each type of shader to convert its GLSL source code into its SPIR-V form. First it creates an empty shader object and initializes the shader resource structure. Using the shader type passed to the `GLSLtoSPV` function parameter, determine the shader language using the `findLanguage()` helper function (see the following code snippet) and create a `TShader` shader object. Pass the GLSL shader source code to this shader and parse it to check for any potential issues. In case errors are found, report the error to help the user rectify it:

```
EShLanguage VulkanShader::findLanguage(const VkShaderStageFlagBits
shader_type)
{
    switch (shader_type) {
    case VK_SHADER_STAGE_VERTEX_BIT:
        return EShLangVertex;

    case VK_SHADER_STAGE_TESSELLATION_CONTROL_BIT:
        return EShLangTessControl;

    case VK_SHADER_STAGE_TESSELLATION_EVALUATION_BIT:
        return EShLangTessEvaluation;

    case VK_SHADER_STAGE_GEOMETRY_BIT:
        return EShLangGeometry;

    case VK_SHADER_STAGE_FRAGMENT_BIT:
        return EShLangFragment;

    case VK_SHADER_STAGE_COMPUTE_BIT:
        return EShLangCompute;

    default:
        printf("Unknown shader type specified: %d. Exiting!",
                    shaderType);
        exit(1);
    }
}
```

Add the shader object in the program object to compile and link it. Upon the successful linking of the `glslang::GlslangToSpv()` API called, convert the GLSL source program into the intermediate shader (`.spv`) form.

Finally, upon exiting from the application, don't forget to delete the shaders. The shader can be destroyed using the `vkDestroyShaderModule()` API. Refer to the following implementation for more information:

```
void VulkanShader::destroyShaders()
{
    VulkanApplication* appObj = VulkanApplication::GetInstance();
    VulkanDevice* deviceObj = appObj->deviceObj;

    vkDestroyShaderModule(deviceObj->device,
                          shaderStages[0].module, NULL);
    vkDestroyShaderModule(deviceObj->device,
                          shaderStages[1].module, NULL);
}
```

Here is the syntax of the `vkDestroyShaderModule()` API:

```
VKAPI_ATTR void VKAPI_CALL vkDestroyShaderModule(
        VkDevice                      device,
        VkShaderModule                shaderModule,
        const VkAllocationCallbacks*  allocator);
```

The following table describes the various fields of this API:

Parameters	Description
device	This is the logical device to be used to destroy the shader module object.
shaderModule	This is the handle of the shader module that needs to be destroyed.
allocator	This controls the host memory deallocation process. For more information, refer to the *Host memory* section in Chapter 5, *Command Buffer and Memory Management in Vulkan*.

Summary

Following the image resource creation process from the previous chapter, this chapter begins with another type of Vulkan resource called a buffer resource. We not only understood the concept, but also implemented the geometry vertex buffer using it and also looked into the Render Pass and framebuffer to define a unit render job in Vulkan. Finally, we closed the chapter down with the introduction of SPIR-V, which is a new way of specifying the shaders and kernels in the Vulkan. We implemented our first shader in the SPIR-V form, where we input the vertex and fragment shader into GLSL and converted them into the SPIR-V format using the Lunar-G SDK's glslangValidator.

In the next chapter, we will look at the descriptor and descriptor sets. These are the interfaces between the created resources and the shaders. We will use a descriptor to connect our created vertex buffer resource information to the SPIR-V shader implemented in this chapter.

In the next chapter we will cover the pipeline state management in Vulkan. In this we control the hardware setting by means of pipeline states (rasterizer state, blend state, and depth stencil state) and plan the input data for rendering purposes.

8
Pipelines and Pipeline State Management

In the previous chapter, we understood the buffer resource in Vulkan and used it to store geometry data information in the form of a vertex buffer on the physical device memory. We implemented a Render Pass and framebuffer object. Also, we learned about SPIR-V, which is a new way of specifying shaders in Vulkan. In addition, we used the SPIR-V tool library to convert GLSL shaders into the SPIR-V intermediate language at the time of compilation.

We will take this chapter one notch up from what we've learned so far–we'll understand the concept of a pipeline and pipeline state management. In this chapter, we will begin describing the types of pipeline supported by the Vulkan API. There are two types of pipeline–compute and graphics. These pipelines are created using pipeline cache objects, which will be the next topic. As we approach the end of this chapter, we will implement the graphics pipeline and thoroughly understand the various types of pipeline state associated with it.

In this chapter, we will cover the following topics:

- Getting started with pipelines
- Caching the pipeline objects with **pipeline cache object (PCO)**
- Creating the graphics pipeline
- Understanding the compute pipeline
- Pipeline state objects in Vulkan
- Implementing the pipeline

Getting started with pipelines

A pipeline refers to a succession of fixed stages through which a data input flows; each stage processes the incoming data and hands it over to the next stage. The final product will be either a 2D raster drawing image (the graphics pipeline) or updated resources (buffers or images) with computational logic and calculations (the compute pipeline).

Vulkan supports two types of pipeline–*graphics* and *compute*.

- **The graphics pipeline**: This pipeline takes in a set of Vulkan commands through command buffers and draws a 2D raster image of the 2D/3D scene.
- **The compute pipeline**: This pipeline takes in Vulkan commands through command buffers and processes them for computational work.

The following redrawn diagram from the official Vulkan specification (`https://www.khronos.org/registry/vulkan/specs/1.0/xhtml/vkspec.html#pipelines-block-diagram`) shows the Vulkan graphics and compute pipelines:

Chapter 8

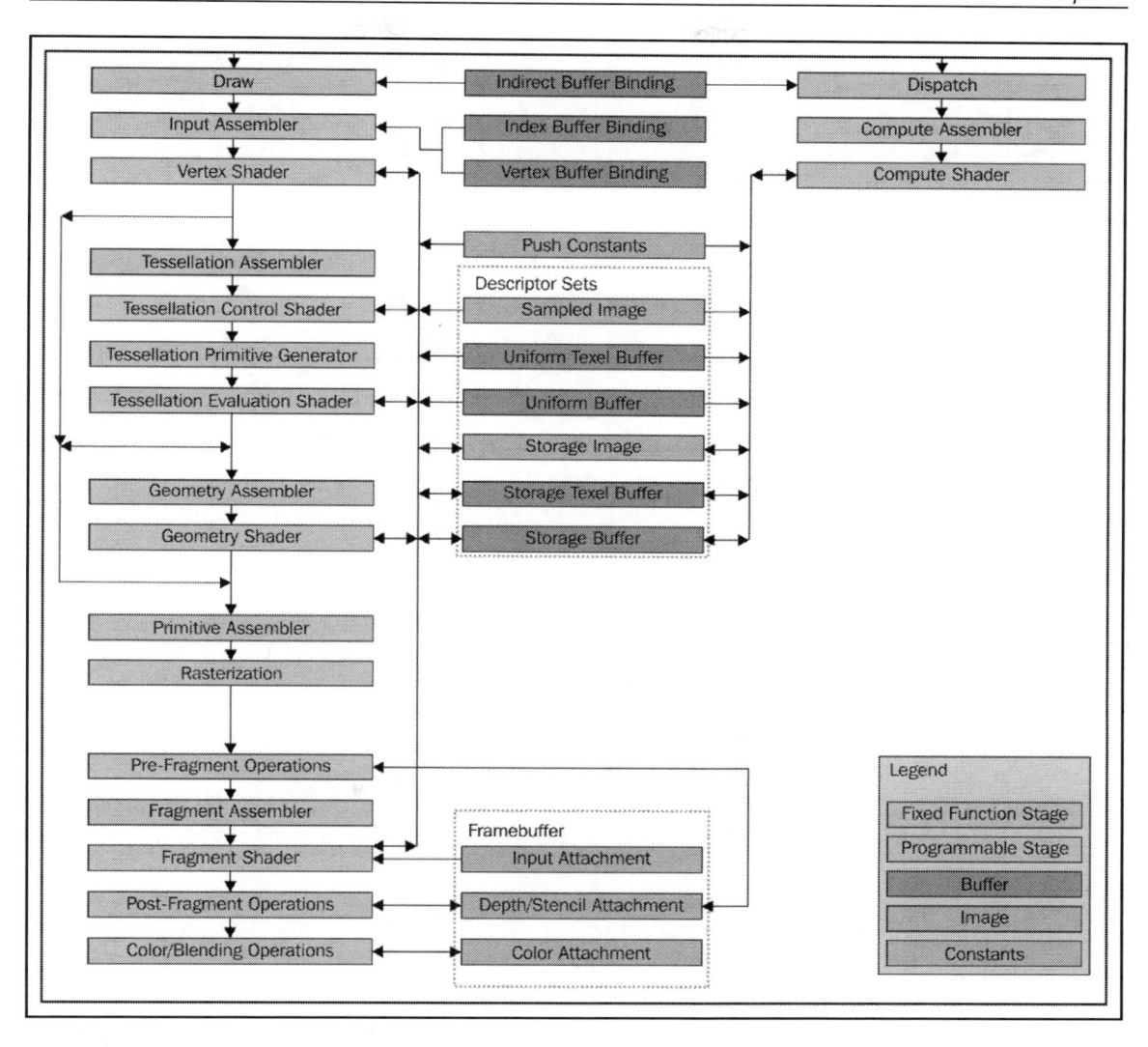

The pipeline journey begins at **Input Assembler**, where the input vertex data is assembled in the form of a point, line, and triangle based on the primitive topology specified. Using the **Vertex Shader** programmable stage, the input vertex data is transformed into a clip space. The geometry is tessellated in the **Tessellation Control Shader** and **Tessellation Evaluation Shader** assembler. **Geometry Shader** has the unique capability of producing multiple primitives out of a single incoming primitive.

Pipelines and Pipeline State Management

Next, **Primitive Assembler** takes all the transformed coordinates from the previous stage and arranges them in line with the specified draw or primitive-type (point, line, and triangle) information provided at the input stage. The primitives are clipped when the associated vertex coordinates fall outside the viewing volume, and when this happens, the clipped fragments (outside the view) are discarded.

Rasterization is the process of converting transformed screen space primitives (point, line, and triangle) into discrete elements called fragments. These fragments are controlled by the next stage, called **Fragment Shader**. Fragment shaders perform computation on a single fragment. These fragments finally become a part of the framebuffer, which is collectively subjected to a number of conditional updates, such as depth testing, stenciling, and fragment blending.

The buffer and image memory types can be processed in a separate pipeline in the form of a 1D/2D/3D workgroup called the compute pipeline. The compute pipeline is extremely powerful in accomplishing jobs in parallel processing; it is primarily used in the field of image processing and physics computation. Both the buffer and image memory can be modified (read/write) by the compute pipeline.

This pipeline broadly consists of three concepts: *pipeline state objects, pipeline cache objects,* and *pipeline layouts*. These can be used to effectively control the underlying pipeline operations:

- **Pipeline state objects (PSO)**: The physical device or the GPU is capable of doing several types of operation directly in the hardware. Such operations may include rasterizers and conditional updates, such as blending the depth test, stenciling, and so on. Vulkan offers the ability to control these hardware settings with the help of PSOs. The other hardware-base-controlled operations may include the assembly of the primitive topology type (point/line/triangle) on a given geometrical shape, viewport control, and more.
- **Pipeline cache objects (PCOs)**: The pipeline cache provides a mechanism for faster retrieval and reuse of stored pipelines. This gives an application a better chance of avoiding the redundancy of creating similar or duplicate pipeline objects.
- **Pipeline layouts**: The buffer and images are indirectly connected to the shader and can be accessed using shader resource variables. The resource variables are connected to the buffer and image views. These resource variables are managed through descriptors and the descriptor set layout. Within the pipeline, the pipeline layouts manage the sequence of descriptor set layouts.

> A descriptor is an interface between the stored resource and the shader stage. The resources are connected to the logical layout bindings defined by the descriptor set layout, and the pipeline layout provides unprecedented access to descriptor sets within the pipeline. Descriptors will be covered in detail in `Chapter 10`, *Descriptors and Push Constant*, where we will learn to use uniforms.

VulkanPipeline – the pipeline implementation class

In this chapter, we are introducing a new user-defined class called `VulkanPipeline`. This class will manage pipeline implementation for Vulkan applications. Pipeline creation is a performance-critical path as it deals with a lot of pipeline state management objects; therefore, the reusability of pipeline objects is highly advisable. The Vulkan pipeline provides a pipeline-caching mechanism through a PCO. This reduces the overhead in creating similar pipelines–the driver looks for a closer match and creates the new pipeline using the base pipeline.

The pipeline implementation must be placed at a level where drawing an object can easily access the PCO in a centralized manner to enhance the chance of pipeline reusability. For this, there are two choices: place the `VulkanPipeline` class inside `VulkanApplication` (at the application level, this may be the primary thread) or `VulkanRenderer` (for each independent renderer thread). Both the options are fine as long as the application manages the pipeline objects correctly with proper handling of memory leaks and thread synchronization. This book follows the latter option, so we place `VulkanPipeline` in `VulkanRenderer` to avoid thread synchronization, making it simpler for beginners.

The following block diagram shows a pictorial view that represents the application system with the integration of the user-defined `VulkanPipeline` class:

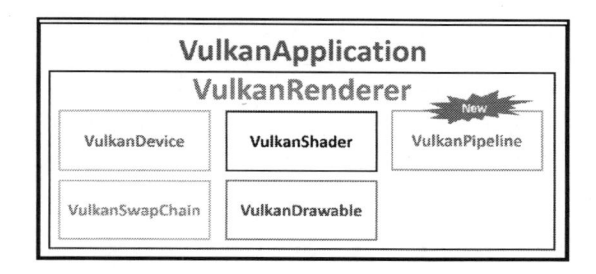

Pipelines and Pipeline State Management

The following is the declaration of the `VulkanPipeline` header file (`VulkanPipeline.h`):

```
/*********** VulkanPipeline.h ************/
class VulkanPipeline
{
public:
    // Creates the pipeline cache object and stores pipeline object
    void createPipelineCache();

    // Returns the created pipeline object, it takes the drawable
    // object which contains the vertex input rate and data
    // interpretation information, shader files, Boolean flag to
    // check depth is supported or not, and a flag to check if the
    // vertex input are available.
    bool createPipeline(VulkanDrawable* drawableObj,
        VkPipeline*     pipeline,     VulkanShader*    shaderObj,
        VkBool32        includeDepth, VkBool32         includeVi = true);

    // Destruct the pipeline cache object
    void destroyPipelineCache();
public:
    // Pipeline cache object
    VkPipelineCache    pipelineCache;

    // References to other user defined class
    VulkanApplication*     appObj;
    VulkanDevice*          deviceObj;
};
```

The header file declaration contains the helper functions that allow you to create the pipeline cache object (`VkPipelineCache`) and produce the pipelines (`VkPipeline`).

Caching pipeline objects with a PCO

A pipeline cache is a pool that stores baked pipelines. It enables an application to reduce the pipeline creation overhead between pipeline runs and also between the subsequent application run. The following is the difference between the two:

- **Between pipelines**: The pipeline construction can be reused when new pipelines are created. The pipeline cache object is passed as a parameter to the pipeline creator API (`vkCreateGraphicsPipelines`). By doing so, the underlying mechanism ensures that it reuses the pipeline if a similar one exists. This is widely useful in the creation of drawing objects that are redundant in nature, for example, paint brush strokes, sprites, mesh geometries, and so on.

- **Between applications**: While creating a pipeline, you deal with a lot of pipeline state objects, which is an expensive path. Reusability across running applications is a wise design and is efficient in terms of execution time and memory space. A pipeline cache inside a Vulkan application can be effectively reused by serializing the pipeline cache objects. The application retrieves the stored pipeline object from the serialized pipeline cache and preinitializes it. In subsequent runs, the same serialized PCOs can be reused across multiple application runs.

For more information on the specification and implementation of a pipeline cache object, refer to the following subsections.

Creating a pipeline cache object

A PCO can be used to create either a graphics (vkCreateGraphicsPipelines) or compute pipeline (vkCreateComputePipelines). Creating these pipelines with a PCO ensures the reusability of the pipeline objects. If the PCO does not contain a similar pipeline, then it creates a new one and adds it to its pool.

A PCO can be created using the vkCreatePipelineCache() API. Upon its successful creation, it returns a VkPipelineCache object. This API accepts four parameters, as described here:

```
VkResult vkCreatePipelineCache(
    VkDevice                                device,
    const VkPipelineCacheCreateInfo*        pCreateInfo,
    const VkAllocationCallbacks*            pAllocator,
    VkPipelineCache*                        pPipelineCache);
```

The following are the various parameters accepted by the vkCreatePipelineCache() API:

Parameters	Description
device	This is an object of the logical device (of the type VkDevice) that is used to create the pipeline cache object (VkPipelineCache).
pCreateInfo	This is the VkPipelineCacheCreateInfo control structure that contains the metadata or state information that will be used to create the PCO object.
pAllocator	This controls host memory allocation. For more information, refer to the *Host memory* section in Chapter 5, *Command Buffer and Memory Management in Vulkan*.

| pPipelineCache | This returns the created VkPipelineCache object pointer. |

The second parameter of the vkCreatePipelineCache() API is of the type VkPipelineCacheCreateInfo; this control structure contains the state/metadata information necessary to create and initialize the pipeline cache object. The following is the syntax of this structure:

```
typedef struct VkPipelineCacheCreateInfo {
    VkStructureType              sType;
    const void*                  pNext;
    VkPipelineCacheCreateFlags   flags;
    size_t                       initialDataSize;
    const void*                  pInitialData;
} VkPipelineCacheCreateInfo;
```

Let's look at this structure's various fields:

Parameters	Description
sType	This is the type information of the control structure. It must be specified as VK_STRUCTURE_TYPE_IMAGE_VIEW_CREATE_INFO.
pNext	This could be a valid pointer to an extension-specific structure or NULL.
flags	This field is reserved for future use.
initialDataSize	This is the length of the data (in bytes) indicated by initialData. If this field value is 0, then it signifies that the pipeline cache will be initially empty. Then pInitialData is ignored.
pInitialData	This field indicates the retrieved datafrom some previously created pipeline cache. This will be used for initializing the contents of the newly created pipeline cache object. The initialization contents of the created pipeline cache object may remain empty if the data of pInitialData is incompatible with the device.

Merging pipeline caches

Two pipeline caches can be merged together into one using the vkMergePipelineCaches() API. This API merges a destination pipeline cache into the source pipeline cache. It intakes four parameters. The first parameter device is the logical device for which the merging will be carried out. The number of source pipeline caches is specified by pSrcCaches with a count equal to srcCacheCount. The final merging cache is stored in the destination pipeline cache called `dstCache`.

The following is the syntax of this API:

```
VkResult vkMergePipelineCaches(
    VkDevice                device,
    VkPipelineCache         dstCache,
    uint32_t                srcCacheCount,
    const VkPipelineCache*  pSrcCaches);
```

Retrieving data from pipeline caches

A pipeline cache object can save its information in the form of streams of bytes. This stored information can be reused in future, when an application reruns or is executed again. The pipeline cache data can be retrieved using the `vkGetPipelineCacheData()` API:

```
VkResult vkGetPipelineCacheData(
    VkDevice         device,
    VkPipelineCache  pipelineCache,
    size_t*          dataSize,
    void*            data);
```

The following table describes each parameter of this API:

Parameters	Description
`device`	This refers to the logical device that is used to create the pipeline cache object.
`pipelineCache`	This is the pipeline cache object from which the data is to be retrieved.
`dataSize`	When data is `NULL`, this field is used to query the size of the pipeline cache data in bytes from the `pipelineCache` object.
`data`	When `dataSize` is non-zero, this API reads the `dataSize` bytes from the `pipelineCache` object and retrieves the data.

The stored PCO information can be reused to preinitialize and populate the pipeline cache objects when the application starts. The compilation results may depend on the vendor and other device details. In order to ensure the application is compatible with the pipeline cache data, the header information can be used.

The retrieved data contains a header and a payload. The header provides the necessary information about the written data to ensure there is compatibility when an application runs the next time. The following diagram shows the format of the stored pipeline cache object:

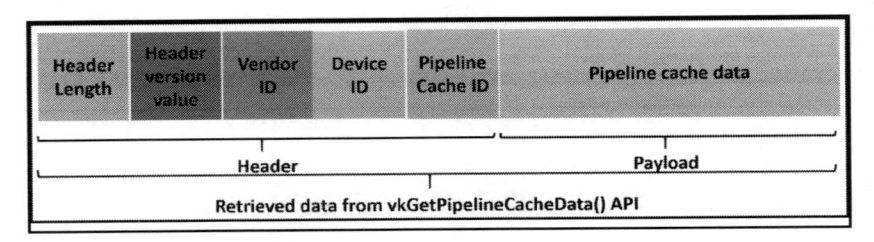

[Diagram: Header (Header Length | Header version value | Vendor ID | Device ID | Pipeline Cache ID) + Payload (Pipeline cache data). Retrieved data from vkGetPipelineCacheData() API]

The header consists of five fields, which may change in line with the specification. The header size is not fixed as per the specification but is read as the first four bytes from the data. This byte information encodes the length of the entire pipeline cache object's retrieved data header (in bytes), including each and every field in the header.

The following table specifies these fields' specification along with their size in bytes:

Offset	Size	Meaning
0	4	This specifies the pipeline cache header's length in bytes. This 4-byte array of information is written with the least significant byte placed first in the sequence.
4	4	This represents the header version (VkPipelineCacheHeaderVersion) of the pipeline cache. This is an array of bytes with the least significant byte placed first.
8	4	This specifies the vendor ID, which is the same as VkPhysicalDeviceProperties::vendorID. This is a 4-byte array with the least significant byte placed first.
12	4	This specifies the device ID, which is the same as VkPhysicalDeviceProperties::deviceID. This is also a 4-byte array with the least significant byte placed first.
16	4	This specifies a unique identifier that represents the pipeline cache object. The ID is equal to VkPhysicalDeviceProperties::pipelineCacheUUID.

Implementing the PCO

The PCO is implemented in `VulkanPipeline.cpp` in the `createPipelinceCache()` function. `VkPipelineCacheCreateInfo` is initialized and passed to the `vkCreatePipelineCache()` API. The `initialDataSize` is 0 and `pInitialData` is NULL, as there is no old, retrievable PCO data to be used in the initialization of the created PCO:

```
void VulkanPipeline::createPipelineCache()
{
    VkResult result;
    VkPipelineCacheCreateInfo pipelineCacheInfo;
    pipelineCacheInfo.sType           = VK_STRUCTURE_TYPE_PIPELINE
                                        _CACHE_CREATE_INFO;
    pipelineCacheInfo.pNext           = NULL;
    pipelineCacheInfo.initialDataSize = 0;
    pipelineCacheInfo.pInitialData    = NULL;
    pipelineCacheInfo.flags           = 0;

    // Create the pipeline cache using VkPipelineCacheCreateInfo
    result = vkCreatePipelineCache(deviceObj->device,
            &pipelineCacheInfo, NULL, &pipelineCache);
    assert(result == VK_SUCCESS);
}
```

Creating a graphics pipeline

A graphics pipeline consists of programmable, fixed-function pipeline stages, Render Passes, subpasses, and pipeline layouts. The programmable stages include multiple shader stages, such as the vertex, fragment, tessellation, geometry, and compute shaders. The fixed-function states consist of multiple **pipeline state objects** (**PSOs**) that represent the dynamic, vertex input, input assembly, rasterization, blending, viewport, multisampling, and depth-stencil states.

A graphics pipeline object (`VkPipeline`) is created using the `vkCreateGraphicsPipelines()` API. This API intakes the programmable stages, fixed-function pipeline stages, and pipeline layouts through a metadata control structure called `VkGraphicsPipelineCreateInfo`. The following is the syntax of the `vkCreateGraphicsPipelines()` API:

```
VkResult vkCreateGraphicsPipelines(
    VkDevice                        device,
    VkPipelineCache                 pipelineCache,
    uint32_t                        createInfoCount,
```

Pipelines and Pipeline State Management

```
        const VkGraphicsPipelineCreateInfo*        pCreateInfos,
        const VkAllocationCallbacks*               pAllocator,
        VkPipeline*                                pPipelines);
```

Let's look at the various fields of the `vkCreateGraphicsPipelines()` API:

Parameters	Description
device	This is the logical device for which the pipeline object is to be created.
pipelineCache	This is a valid pointer to the pipeline cache object. If this value is NULL, then the pipeline cache will not be used to create the pipeline object.
createInfoCount	This represents the number of graphics pipelines (VkGraphicsPipelineCreateInfo) in the pCreateInfos array.
pCreateInfos	This is the VkGraphicsPipelineCreateInfo array.
pAllocator	This field controls host memory allocation. For more information, refer to the *Host memory* section in Chapter 5, *Command Buffer and Memory Management in Vulkan*.
pPipelines	This returns the VkPipeline object array containing the graphics pipeline objects. The number of objects depends on createInfoCount.

Here is the syntax of the metadata control structure `VkGraphicsPipelineCreateInfo`, we discussed earlier:

```
typedef struct VkGraphicsPipelineCreateInfo {
  VkStructureType                              sType;
  const void*                                  pNext;
  VkPipelineCreateFlags                        flags;
  uint32_t                                     stageCount;
  const VkPipelineShaderStageCreateInfo*       pStages;
  const VkPipelineVertexInputStateCreateInfo*  pVertexInputState;
  const VkPipelineInputAssemblyStateCreateInfo* pInputAssemblyState;
  const VkPipelineTessellationStateCreateInfo* pTessellationState;
  const VkPipelineViewportStateCreateInfo*     pViewportState;
  const VkPipelineRasterizationStateCreateInfo* pRasterizationState;
  const VkPipelineMultisampleStateCreateInfo*  pMultisampleState;
  const VkPipelineDepthStencilStateCreateInfo* pDepthStencilState;
  const VkPipelineColorBlendStateCreateInfo*   pColorBlendState;
  const VkPipelineDynamicStateCreateInfo*      pDynamicState;
  VkPipelineLayout                             layout;
  VkRenderPass                                 renderPass;
  uint32_t                                     subpass;
  VkPipeline                                   basePipelineHandle;
  int32_t                                      basePipelineIndex;
} VkGraphicsPipelineCreateInfo;
```

Let's look at the various fields for this structure:

Parameters	Description
sType	This is the type information of this control structure. It must be specified as VK_STRUCTURE_TYPE_GRAPHICS_PIPELINE_CREATE_INFO.
pNext	This could be a valid pointer to an extension-specific structure or NULL.
flags	This field provides hints to help the implementation understand how the pipeline will be generated. These hints are provided using the VkPipelineCreateFlagBits enum. The VkPipelineCreateFlagBits enum has three fields: • **VK_PIPELINE_CREATE_DISABLE_OPTIMIZATION_BIT**: The pipelines created from this flag will not be optimized. Since there is no optimization path, the overall time to create this pipeline may be reduced. • **VK_PIPELINE_CREATE_ALLOW_DERIVATIVES_BIT**: The pipeline created using this flag is permitted to be the parent of the subsequent pipelines that are going to be created using the vkCreateGraphicsPipelines() API. • **VK_PIPELINE_CREATE_DERIVATIVE_BIT**: The pipeline created using this flag becomes the child of the previously created pipeline.
stageCount	This indicates the number of shaders to be used in the current pipeline.
pStages	This field indicates what all shader stages need to be included in the pipeline using an array of VkPipelineShaderStageCreateInfo. The total size of this array is equal to stageCount.
pVertexInputState	This field indicates the vertex input pipeline state through the VkPipelineVertexInputStateCreateInfo pointer object.
pInputAssemblyState	This field determines the behavior of the input assembly state using the VkPipelineInputAssemblyStateCreateInfo pointer object.

Pipelines and Pipeline State Management

`pTessellationState`	This field indicates the tessellation control and evaluation shader stages' states. These states are specified using the `VkPipelineTessellationStateCreateInfo` pointer object. This must be `NULL` if the tessellation control and evaluation shader stages are not included in the pipeline.
`pViewportState`	This field indicates the vertex states through the `VkPipelineViewportStateCreateInfo` pointer object. This field must be `NULL` if the pipeline has rasterization disabled.
`pRasterizationState`	This field indicates the pipeline rasterization state using the `VkPipelineRasterizationStateCreateInfo` structure's pointer object.
`pMultisampleState`	This refers to the `VkPipelineMultisampleStateCreateInfo` object pointer. This field must be `NULL` if the pipeline has rasterization disabled.
`pDepthStencilState`	This field indicates the pipeline's depth/stencil state by using a pointer to the `VkPipelineDepthStencilStateCreateInfo` control structure. This would be `NULL` if rasterization is disabled or the subpass in the Render Pass does not use a depth/stencil attachment.
`pColorBlendState`	This is a pointer to `VkPipelineColorBlendStateCreateInfo` indicating the pipeline color's blend state. This field must be `NULL` if the pipeline has rasterization disabled or if the subpass in the Render Pass does not use any color attachments.
`pDynamicState`	This is a pointer to `VkPipelineDynamicStateCreateInfo`, which indicates the pipeline's dynamic states. This field can be changed independently of other pipeline states. If no dynamic states are specified, then this field can be specified as `NULL`, notifying the pipeline that there is no dynamic states to be considered in this pipeline.
`layout`	This field specifies the binding locations used by the pipeline and the descriptor sets.
`renderPass`	This field specifies the subpasses and attachments that will be used by the pipeline.
`subPass`	This notifies the pipeline about the Render Pass's subpass index under which it will be used.

`basePipelineHandle`	This field specifies the base pipeline from where this pipeline will be derived.
`basePipelineIndex`	This field specifies the index of the `pCreateInfos` parameter in the base pipeline. It will be used to derive this pipeline object.

Implementing a graphics pipeline

Graphics pipelines are implemented in the `createPipeline()` function of `VulkanPipeline`. This function takes four parameters. The first parameter contains the vertex input and data interpretation. The second parameter contains the return value in which the array of pipelines will be created. The third parameter is a Boolean flag indicating depth testing. And the last parameter is used to specify whether to consider the vertex input or not.

The graphics pipeline consists of several pipeline state objects, render passes, shader objects, and subpasses, as shown in the following diagram. The implementation of the pipeline is done by creating a `VkGraphicsPipelineCreateInfo` object (`pipelineInfo`) and specifying all the various state objects, shader objects, and render pass object into it. Finally, the pipeline object is consumed by the `vkCreateGraphicsPipelines()` API to create the pipeline. The following diagram shows the graphics pipeline and all its interface controllers:

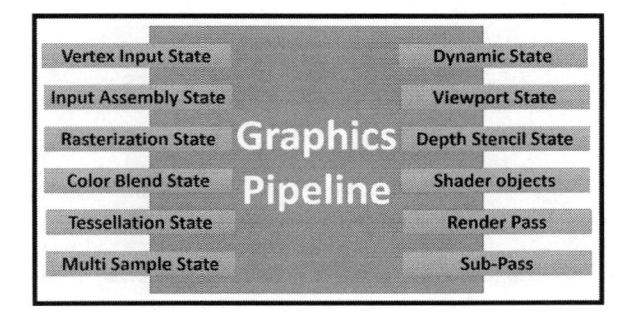

This is the code implementation of the graphics pipeline object:

```cpp
bool VulkanPipeline::createPipeline(VulkanDrawable* drawableObj,
VkPipeline* pipeline, VulkanShader* shaderObj, VkBool32 includeDepth,
VkBool32 includeVi)
{
    // Please refer to Dynamic State for more info
    VkPipelineDynamicStateCreateInfo dynamicState = {};

    // Please refer to Vertex Input States subsection for more info
    VkPipelineVertexInputStateCreateInfo vertexInputStateInfo = {};
    . . .

    // Please refer to Input Assembly States subsection for more info
    VkPipelineInputAssemblyStateCreateInfo inputAssemblyInfo = {};

    // Please refer to Rasterization State subsection for more info
    VkPipelineRasterizationStateCreateInfo rasterStateInfo = {};

    // Please refer to Color Blend Attachment for more info
    VkPipelineColorBlendAttachmentState
            colorBlendAttachmentStateInfo[1] = {};

    // Please refer to Color Blend State subsection for more info
    VkPipelineColorBlendStateCreateInfo colorBlendStateInfo = {};

    // Please refer to Viewport State subsection for more info
    VkPipelineViewportStateCreateInfo viewportStateInfo = {};

    // Please refer to Depth Stencil state subsection for more info
    VkPipelineDepthStencilStateCreateInfo depthStencilStateInfo = {};

    // Please refer to Multi Sample state subsection for more info
    VkPipelineMultisampleStateCreateInfo   multiSampleStateInfo = {};

    // Populate the VkGraphicsPipelineCreateInfo structure to specify
    // programmable stages, fixed-function pipeline stages render
    // pass, sub-passes and pipeline layouts
    VkGraphicsPipelineCreateInfo pipelineInfo = {};
    pipelineInfo.sType                =
         VK_STRUCTURE_TYPE_GRAPHICS_PIPELINE_CREATE_INFO;
    pipelineInfo.pVertexInputState    = &vertexInputStateInfo;
    pipelineInfo.pInputAssemblyState  = &inputAssemblyInfo;
    pipelineInfo.pRasterizationState  = &rasterStateInfo;
    pipelineInfo.pColorBlendState     = &colorBlendStateInfo;
    pipelineInfo.pTessellationState   = NULL;
    pipelineInfo.pMultisampleState    = &multiSampleStateInfo;
    pipelineInfo.pDynamicState        = &dynamicState;
```

```
pipelineInfo.pViewportState        = &viewportStateInfo;
pipelineInfo.pDepthStencilState    = &depthStencilStateInfo;
pipelineInfo.pStages               = shaderObj->shaderStages;
pipelineInfo.stageCount            = 2;
pipelineInfo.renderPass            = appObj->rendererObj->
                                     renderPass;
pipelineInfo.subpass               = 0;

// Create the pipeline using the meta-data store in the
// VkGraphicsPipelineCreateInfo object
if (vkCreateGraphicsPipelines(deviceObj->device, pipelineCache,
      1, &pipelineInfo, NULL, pipeline) == VK_SUCCESS){
   return true;
}
else {
   return false;
}
}
```

Destroying pipelines

A created pipeline can be destroyed using the `vkDestroyPipeline` API. This API accepts three parameters. The first parameter specifies the logical device (`VkDevice`) that will be used to destroy the pipeline. The second parameter is an object of pipeline (`VkPipeline`), which is intended to be destroyed. The third parameter `pAllocator` controls host memory allocation. For more information, refer to the *Host memory* section `Chapter 5`, *Command Buffer and Memory Management in Vulkan*:

```
void vkDestroyPipeline(
    VkDevice                       device,
    VkPipeline                     pipeline,
    const VkAllocationCallbacks*   pAllocator);
```

Understanding compute pipelines

A compute pipeline consists of a single static compute shader stage and the pipeline layout. The compute shader stage is capable of doing massive parallel arbitrary computations. On the other hand, the pipeline layout connects the compute pipeline to the descriptor using the layout bindings. The `vkCreateComputePipeline()` API can be used to create a compute pipeline:

```
VkResult vkCreateComputePipelines(
    VkDevice                               device,
```

```
VkPipelineCache                      pipelineCache,
uint32_t                             createInfoCount,
const VkComputePipelineCreateInfo*   pCreateInfos,
const VkAllocationCallbacks*         pAllocator,
VkPipeline*                          pPipelines);
```

The following table describes the various fields of the `vkCreateGraphicsPipelines()` API:

Parameters	Description
device	This is the logical device (`VkDevice`) from which the compute pipeline object is going to be created.
pipelineCache	This is a valid pointer to the pipeline cache object. If this value is `NULL`, then the pipeline cache will not be used to create the compute pipeline object.
createInfoCount	This represents the number of compute pipelines (`VkComputePipelineCreateInfo`) in the `pCreateInfos` array.
pCreateInfos	This refers to the `VkComputePipelineCreateInfo` structure array's objects.
pAllocator	This field controls host memory allocation. For more information, refer to the *Host memory* section in `Chapter 5`, *Command Buffer and Memory Management in Vulkan*.
pPipelines	This returns the `VkPipeline` object array containing the number of compute pipelines created.

The `VkComputePipelineCreateInfo` structure defines the state information of the compute pipeline that is consumed by the `vkCreateComputePipelines()` API to create the compute pipeline object. The syntax of this API is as follows:

```
typedef struct VkComputePipelineCreateInfo {
    VkStructureType                   type;
    const void*                       next;
    VkPipelineCreateFlags             flags;
    VkPipelineShaderStageCreateInfo   stage;
    VkPipelineLayout                  layout;
    VkPipeline                        basePipelineHandle;
    int32_t                           basePipelineIndex;
} VkComputePipelineCreateInfo;
```

Let's look at the various fields of the `VkComputePipelineCreateInfo` structure:

Parameters	Description
`sType`	This is the type information of the `VkComputePipelineCreateInfo` structure. It must be specified as `VK_STRUCTURE_TYPE_COMPUTE_PIPELINE_CREATE_INFO`.
`pNext`	This could be a valid pointer to an extension-specific structure or `NULL`.
`flags`	This field provides the hints that help the implementation understand how the pipeline will be generated. These hints are provided in the form of the `VkPipelineCreateFlagBits` enum. The `VkPipelineCreateFlagBits` enum has three fields: • **VK_PIPELINE_CREATE_DISABLE_OPTIMIZATION_BIT**: The compute pipeline created from this flag will not be optimized. In the absence of the optimization path, the overall time to create the pipeline is expected to be reduced. • **VK_PIPELINE_CREATE_ALLOW_DERIVATIVES_BIT**: The compute pipeline created using this flag is permitted to be the parent of the subsequent compute pipelines that are going to be created using the `vkCreateGraphicsPipelines()` API. • **VK_PIPELINE_CREATE_ DERIVATIVE_BIT**: The compute pipeline created using this flag becomes the child of the previously created pipeline.
`stage`	This specifies the compute shader using the `VkPipelineShaderStageCreateInfo` structure.
`layout`	This field specifies the binding locations used by the pipeline and the descriptor sets.
`basePipelineHandle`	This field specifies the base pipeline from where this pipeline will be derived.
`basePipelineIndex`	This field specifies the index of the `pCreateInfos` parameter in the base pipeline that will be used to derive this pipeline object.

The `VkPipelineShaderStageCreateInfo` structure used in the compute pipeline specifies vital information about the compute shader that is going to be used in the compute pipeline. It contains the type of shader, which must be `VK_SHADER_STAGE_COMPUTE_BIT`. In addition, it also specifies the shader source in the form of a shader module and the entry point function in the compute shader source:

```
typedef struct VkPipelineShaderStageCreateInfo {
    VkStructureType                     sType;
    const void*                         pNext;
    VkPipelineShaderStageCreateFlags    flags;
    VkShaderStageFlagBits               stage;
    VkShaderModule                      module;
    const char*                         pName;
    const VkSpecializationInfo*         pSpecializationInfo;
} VkPipelineShaderStageCreateInfo;
```

Let's look at the various fields of this structure:

Parameters	Description
sType	This is the type information of this structure. It must be specified as `VK_STRUCTURE_TYPE_PIPELINE_SHADER_STAGE_CREATE_INFO`.
pNext	This could be a valid pointer to an extension-specific structure or `NULL`.
flags	This field is reserved for future use.
stage	This specifies the pipeline stage using the `VkShaderStageFlagBits` structure.
Module	This is the `VkShaderModule` object, which contains the intended compute shader.
pName	This is the name (UTF-8 formatted string) of the entry point in the compute shader.
pSpecializationInfo	This is the `VkSpecializationInfo` pointer object.

Pipeline State Objects (PSO) in Vulkan

Pipeline state objects in a pipeline are the means by which the hardware settings of the physical devices are controlled. There are various types of pipeline state objects specified in the pipeline; which work in a predefined order. The input data and resources in these stages are subjected to changes in line with user-specified behavior. Each stage processes the input and passes it on to the next one. Depending upon application requirements, the pipeline state stage can be bypassed as per the user's choice. This is entirely configurable through `VkComputePipelineCreateInfo`.

Let's have an overview of these pipeline state objects before we cover them in detail:

- **The dynamic state**: This specifies the dynamic states used in this pipeline
- **The vertex input state**: This specifies the data input rate and its interpretation
- **The input assembly state**: This assembles the vertex data into the primitive's topology (line, point, and triangle variants)
- **The rasterization state**: This operation is related to rasterization, such as polygon fill mode, front facing information, culling mode information, and so on
- **The color blend state**: This specifies the blending factor and operation between the source and destination fragments
- **The viewport state**: This defines viewports, scissors, and dimensions
- **The depth/stencil state**: This specifies how to carry out the depth/stencil operation
- **The multisampling state**: This controls the samples to be used in pixel depiction during the rasterization for anti-aliasing purposes

The following diagram specifies each stage in the PSO:

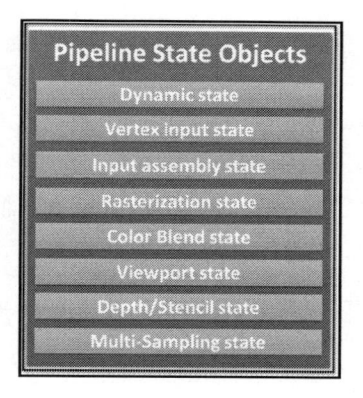

Pipeline State Objects
Dynamic state
Vertex input state
Input assembly state
Rasterization state
Color Blend state
Viewport state
Depth/Stencil state
Multi-Sampling state

In the following subsections, we will discuss each stage in detail. We will cover the concept of pipeline states, their official specification, and sample code implementation.

We will implement all the pipeline state objects in `VulkanPipeline` class inside the `createPipeline()` function. This function first sets up the pipeline state objects, these objects are used to create the graphics pipeline.

Dynamic states

The dynamic state specifies the total number of dynamic states used in the present pipeline and their respective objects in the pipeline. It includes the viewport, stencil, line widths, blending constants, stencil comparison masks, and so on. Each dynamic state in Vulkan is represented using the `VkDynamicState` enum.

> **TIP**: The updates on dynamic states are not expensive; in contrast, the static states must be carefully set to avoid the performance-critical paths.

The following is the syntax of the dynamic state API:

```
typedef struct VkPipelineDynamicStateCreateInfo {
    VkStructureType                      sType;
    const void*                          pNext;
    VkPipelineDynamicStateCreateFlags    flags;
    uint32_t                             dynamicStateCount;
    const VkDynamicState*                pDynamicStates;
} VkPipelineDynamicStateCreateInfo;
```

Let's look at the various fields of this structure:

Parameters	Description
`sType`	This field specifies the type of the current structure. The value of this field must be `VK_STRUCTURE_TYPE_PIPELINE_DYNAMIC_STATE_CREATE_INFO`.
`pNext`	This could be a valid pointer to an extension-specific structure or `NULL`.
`flags`	This is a reserved field for future use.
`dynamicStateCount`	This refers to the count of `VkDynamicState` objects specified in `pDynamicStates`.
`pDynamicStates`	This is an array of `VkDynamicState` enums that represent all the dynamic states that will use the values from the dynamic state command instead of the values from the pipeline state's `CreateInfo` command.

In the next subsection, we will use this API and implement dynamic states.

Implementing dynamic states

The very first pipeline state implemented in the `VulkanPipeline::createPipeline()` function is the dynamic state. First, it creates an empty array of `VkDynamicState` called `dynamicStateEnables` and fills it up with the dynamic states. This array informs the pipeline about those states that can be changed at runtime. For example, the following implementation contains two dynamic states: viewport (`VK_DYNAMIC_STATE_VIEWPORT`) and scissor (`VK_DYNAMIC_STATE_SCISSOR`). This implementation specifies the viewport and scissor parameters and that they can be changed at runtime.

The `dynamicStateEnables` is pushed into the `VkPipelineDynamicStateCreateInfo` control structure object, which will later be consumed by `pipelineInfo` (`VkGraphicsPipelineCreateInfo`) to create the graphics pipeline. The following is the code implementation:

```
/********** VulkanPipeline.cpp /**********/
// Inside VulkanPipeline::createPipeline()
// Initialize the dynamic states, initially it's empty
VkDynamicState dynamicStateEnables[VK_DYNAMIC_STATE_RANGE_SIZE];
memset(dynamicStateEnables, 0, sizeof (dynamicStateEnables));

// Specify the dynamic state information to pipeline through
// VkPipelineDynamicStateCreateInfo control structure.
VkPipelineDynamicStateCreateInfo dynamicState = {};
dynamicState.sType                =
VK_STRUCTURE_TYPE_PIPELINE_DYNAMIC_STATE_CREATE_INFO;
dynamicState.pNext                = NULL;
dynamicState.pDynamicStates       = dynamicStateEnables;
dynamicState.dynamicStateCount    = 0;

// Specify the dynamic state count and VkDynamicState enum
// stating which dynamic state will use the values from dynamic
// state commands rather than from the pipeline state creation info.
dynamicStateEnables[dynamicState.dynamicStateCount++]      =
                    VK_DYNAMIC_STATE_VIEWPORT;
dynamicStateEnables[dynamicState.dynamicStateCount++]      =
                    VK_DYNAMIC_STATE_SCISSOR;
```

Once the dynamic states are constructed, we can go ahead and build the next pipeline state object. The next stage in this process is the vertex input stage, which is described in the following section.

Vertex input states

The vertex input state specifies input binding (`VkVertexInputBindingDescription`) and vertex attribute descriptors (`VkVertexInputAttributeDescription`). Input binding helps the pipeline access the resource through the binding at the rate at which the data is consumed. On the other hand, the vertex attribute descriptor stores important information such as the location, binding, format, and so on. This is used to interpret vertex data. For more information, refer to the *Implementing the buffer resource – creating the vertex buffer for the geometry* section in `Chapter 7`, *Buffer Resource, Render Pass, Framebuffer, and Shaders with SPIR-V*.

The preceding information is wrapped into the `VkPipelineVertexInputStateCreateInfo` structure object, which will be used later to create the graphics pipeline. For a detailed explanation of this structure, refer to the following specification. Here's the syntax of this structure:

```
typedef struct VkPipelineVertexInputStateCreateInfo {
    VkStructureType                             sType;
    const void*                                 pNext;
    VkPipelineVertexInputStateCreateFlags       flags;
    uint32_t                                    vertexBindingDescriptionCount;
    const VkVertexInputBindingDescription*      pVertexBindingDescriptions;
    uint32_t                                    vertexAttributeDescriptionCount;
    const VkVertexInputAttributeDescription*    pVertexAttributeDescriptions;
} VkPipelineVertexInputStateCreateInfo;
```

The following table specifies each field of this control structure:

Parameters	Description
sType	This is the type information of the structure. It must be specified as `VK_STRUCTURE_TYPE_PIPELINE_VERTEX_INPUT_STATE_CREATE_INFO`.
pNext	This could be a valid pointer to an extension-specific structure or `NULL`.
flags	This field is reserved for future implementation.
vertexBindingDescriptionCount	This is the total number of vertex binding instances specified in the `VkVertexInputBindingDescription` object (`pVertexBindingDescriptions`).
pVertexBindingDescriptions	This is a pointer to an array of `VkVertexInputBindingDescription` objects.
vertexAttributeDescriptionCount	This is the total number of vertex attribute descriptions specified in the `VkVertexInputAttributeDescription` object (`pVertexAttributeDescriptions`).

| pVertexAttributeDescriptions | This is a pointer to an array of VkVertexInputAttributeDescription. |

Let's understand the implementation of the vertex input state in the following subsection.

Implementing vertex input states

In the `VulkanPipeline::createPipeline()` function, the vertex input states are implemented as demonstrated in the following code. This state helps the pipeline understand how the data sent will be interpreted using the vertex attribute descriptions specified in the `VkVertexInputAttributeDescription` object. Another piece of information it contains is the rate at which the vertex data will be consumed for processing, which is specified in the input binding description (`VkVertexInputBindingDescription`). There are two ways in which the data can be consumed: per-vertex or per-instance basis. The last `createpipelines` argument `drawableObj` (of the type `VulkanDrawable`) contains the vertex attribute descriptions and vertex input binding description:

```
/********** VulkanPipeline.cpp **********/
// Inside VulkanPipeline::createPipeline(VulkanDrawable*
// drawableObj, VkPipeline* pipeline, VulkanShader*
// shaderObj, VkBool32 includeDepth, VkBool32 includeVi)
VkPipelineVertexInputStateCreateInfo vertexInputStateInfo = {};
vertexInputStateInfo.sType                               =
   VK_STRUCTURE_TYPE_PIPELINE_VERTEX_INPUT_STATE_CREATE_INFO;
vertexInputStateInfo.pNext                               = NULL;
vertexInputStateInfo.flags                               = 0;
vertexInputStateInfo.vertexBindingDescriptionCount       = 1;
vertexInputStateInfo.pVertexBindingDescriptions          =
   &drawableObj->viIpBind;
vertexInputStateInfo.vertexAttributeDescriptionCount     = 2;
vertexInputStateInfo.pVertexAttributeDescriptions        =
                                        drawableObj->viIpAttrb;
```

Following the vertex input state, we have the input assemble state. This stage assembles the incoming data into meaningful shapes with the help of basic primitives, such as a point, line, or triangle.

Input assembly states

When the graphics pipeline receives the vertex data, it is very similar to a bucket filled with unassembled Lego bricks. These vertices are connected in the form of point, line, and triangle variants to give any arbitrary shape as per the user specification. This shape then affects the rasterization stage to produce the corresponding fragments associated with the shape primitives. This whole process is similar to assembling Lego bricks to make a sensible geometrical shape out of them.

These vertices assemble into primitives at a stage called input assembly, which is specified using the `VkPipelineInputAssemblyStateCreateInfo` structure. This contains the necessary primitive topology information to help vertices to connect with each other, based on the rules specified. The input assembly structure specifies the topology in the `VkPrimitiveTopology` structure. Refer to the following syntax and the implementation:

```
typedef struct VkPipelineInputAssemblyStateCreateInfo {
    VkStructureType                            sType;
    const void*                                pNext;
    VkPipelineInputAssemblyStateCreateFlags    flags;
    VkPrimitiveTopology                        topology;
    VkBool32                                   primitiveRestartEnable;
} VkPipelineInputAssemblyStateCreateInfo;
```

Let's look at the various fields of this structure:

Parameters	Description
type	This is the type information of this control structure. It must be specified as VK_STRUCTURE_TYPE_PIPELINE_INPUT_ASSEMBLY_STATE_CREATE_INFO.
next	This could be a valid pointer to an extension-specific structure or NULL.
flag	This field is reserved for future implementation.
topology	This field specifies the type of the primitive topology being used, using the VkPrimitiveTopology enums.
primitiveRestartEnable	This Boolean flag determines whether a special marker or vertex index is used as the primitive restart feature. The special index value should either be 0xFFFFFFFF or 0xFFFF when vkCmdBindIndexBuffer is VK_INDEX_TYPE_UINT32 or VK_INDEX_TYPE_UINT16, respectively. For list-based topologies, primitive restart is not applicable.

Implementing input assembly states

Specify the primitive topology for the drawing object using the `VkPipelineInputAssemblyStateCreateInfo` function in `VulkanPipeline::createPipeline()`. In the following implementation, we used `VK_PRIMITIVE_TOPOLOGY_TRIANGLE_LIST`, which uses a set of three vertices to produce a filled triangle. Next, we specify whether the primitive restart feature is enabled or not:

```
/********** VulkanPipeline.cpp /**********/
// Inside VulkanPipeline::createPipeline()
    VkPipelineInputAssemblyStateCreateInfo inputAssemblyInfo = {};
inputAssemblyInfo.sType = VK_STRUCTURE_TYPE_PIPELINE_INPUT_-
ASSEMBLY_STATE_CREATE_INFO;
    inputAssemblyInfo.pNext     = NULL;
    inputAssemblyInfo.flags     = 0;
    inputAssemblyInfo.primitiveRestartEnable = VK_FALSE;
    inputAssemblyInfo.topology  =VK_PRIMITIVE_TOPOLOGY_TRIANGLE_LIST;
```

Let's understand what primitive restart is in detail.

Primitive restart

Primitive restart are applicable to only index geometries and used with (`vkCmdDrawIndexed` and `vkCmdDrawIndexedIndirect`) drawing APIs.

This feature uses a special marker in a single index array data to recognize disconnected geometries of the same drawing type in a single batch. This is useful in cases where you may have multiple small drawing geometries with a low number of vertices; these multiple geometries can be combined into one index array with each geometry separated using the special reset marker.

The marker used by the primitive restart feature to separate geometries is the highest value of the data type `unsigned short (0xFFFF (65535))` or `unsigned int (0xFFFFFFFF (4294967295))`; with these, the element index array is specified:

- **Applicable topology**: The primitive restart feature is applicable in the following topologies; the key rule to remember is that it is not applicable on list-type primitive topologies. For more information on topologies, refer to the next section, *Primitive topologies*:
    - VK_PRIMITIVE_TOPOLOGY_LINE_STRIP
    - VK_PRIMITIVE_TOPOLOGY_TRIANGLE_STRIP
    - VK_PRIMITIVE_TOPOLOGY_TRIANGLE_FAN
    - VK_PRIMITIVE_TOPOLOGY_LINE_STRIP_WITH_ADJACENCY

Pipelines and Pipeline State Management

- `VK_PRIMITIVE_TOPOLOGY_TRIANGLE_STRIP_WITH_ADJACENCY`
- **Usage**: The primitive restart feature can be used by enabling the `primitiveRestartEnable` field (with `VK_TRUE`) of the `VkPipelineInputAssemblyStateCreateInfo` structure and specifying a valid topology in the `topology` field of the same structure.

Let's see the effect of primitive restart on a triangle strip topology. The following diagram uses a set of 11 continuous indices to draw a long and single geometry shape. These indices do not contain any primitive restart markers:

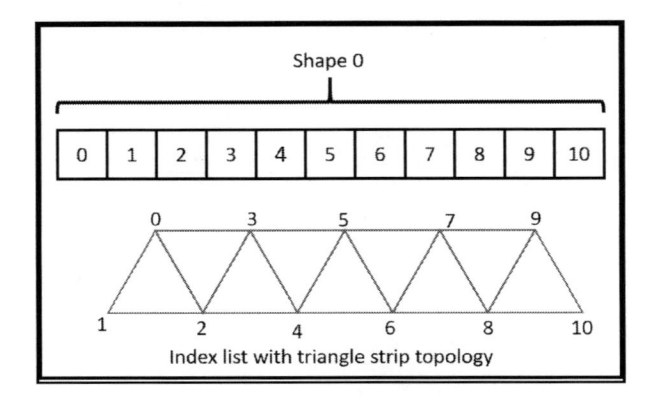

Index list with triangle strip topology

However, interestingly, when the 5th index (**4**) is replaced using the primitive restart marker **0xFFFF**, then it divides this single index list into two. The first half (left of the reset marker) is a new geometry shape that is disconnected from the second half (right of the reset marker), producing another new shape. The Vulkan implementation marches through the start of the index list; when it finds the reset marker, it disconnects the visited indices from the rest of the list and treats them as a separate index list to form a new disconnected shape, as shown in the following image:

Chapter 8

Index list inserted with reset marker on triangle strip topology

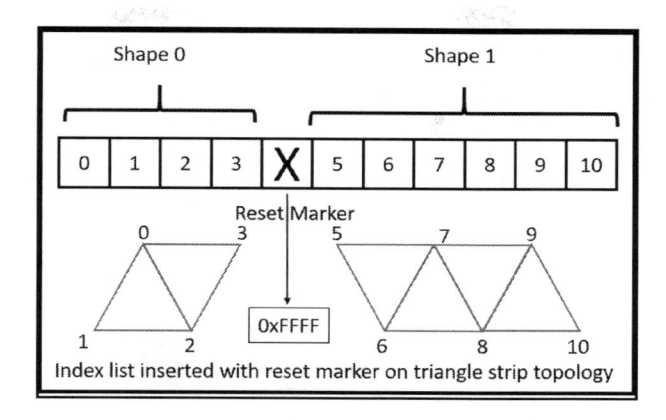

In the next section, we will understand the Vulkan topology and learn about the basic primitives: point, line, and triangle and their related variants.

Primitive topologies

The primitive topology defines the rules that are applied to connect the vertices to produce arbitrary shapes. These shapes comprise a single or several basic primitives: points, lines, and triangles. A primitive topology is specified using VkPrimitiveTopology:

```
typedef enum VkPrimitiveTopology {
    VK_PRIMITIVE_TOPOLOGY_POINT_LIST                    = 0,
    VK_PRIMITIVE_TOPOLOGY_LINE_LIST                     = 1,
    VK_PRIMITIVE_TOPOLOGY_LINE_STRIP                    = 2,
    VK_PRIMITIVE_TOPOLOGY_TRIANGLE_LIST                 = 3,
    VK_PRIMITIVE_TOPOLOGY_TRIANGLE_STRIP                = 4,
    VK_PRIMITIVE_TOPOLOGY_TRIANGLE_FAN                  = 5,
    VK_PRIMITIVE_TOPOLOGY_LINE_LIST_WITH_ADJACENCY      = 6,
    VK_PRIMITIVE_TOPOLOGY_LINE_STRIP_WITH_ADJACENCY     = 7,
    VK_PRIMITIVE_TOPOLOGY_TRIANGLE_LIST_WITH_ADJACENCY  = 8,
    VK_PRIMITIVE_TOPOLOGY_TRIANGLE_STRIP_WITH_ADJACENCY = 9,
    VK_PRIMITIVE_TOPOLOGY_PATCH_LIST                    = 10,
} VkPrimitiveTopology;
```

Primitive topologies can be divided into two types: adjacency and non-adjacency. In the former type, special mathematical rules are used to identify adjacent vertices in a set of vertices that are used for drawing primitives. The adjacent vertices are accessible in the geometric shaders. On the other hand, the latter type does not have the concept of adjacency vertices.

Primitives topologies with no adjacency

Let's take a quick look at each of these primitives in the following table:

Primitive topology types	Description
`VK_PRIMITIVE_TOPOLOGY_POINT_LIST`	Each incoming vertex position represents a point primitive. For this, the provoking vertex index is *i*.
`VK_PRIMITIVE_TOPOLOGY_LINE_LIST`	Each pair of vertices is used to render a line between them. For this, the provoking vertex index is *2i*.
`VK_PRIMITIVE_TOPOLOGY_LINE_STRIP`	Each vertex makes a line between itself and the vertex that precedes it. For this, the provoking vertex index is *i*.
`VK_PRIMITIVE_TOPOLOGY_TRIANGLE_LIST`	A set of three vertices is used to form a filled triangle. For this, the provoking vertex index is *3i*.

`VK_PRIMITIVE_TOPOLOGY_TRIANGLE_STRIP`	Every vertex makes a triangle with the preceding two vertices. For this, the provoking vertex index is *i*. 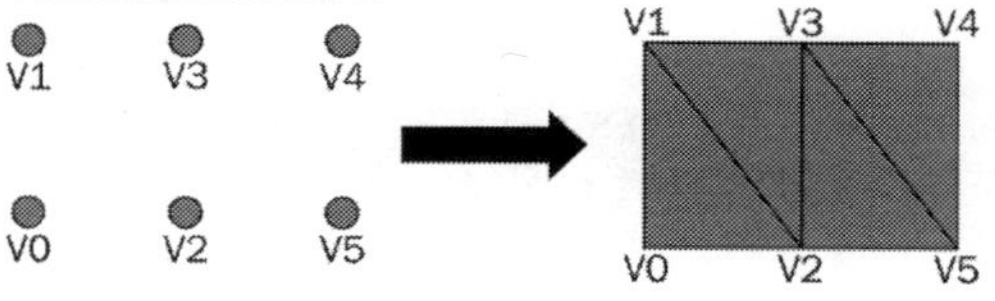
`VK_PRIMITIVE_TOPOLOGY_TRIANGLE_FAN`	Every vertex makes a triangle with the first vertex and the vertex that precedes it. This generates a fan-like pattern. For this, the provoking vertex index is *i+1*. 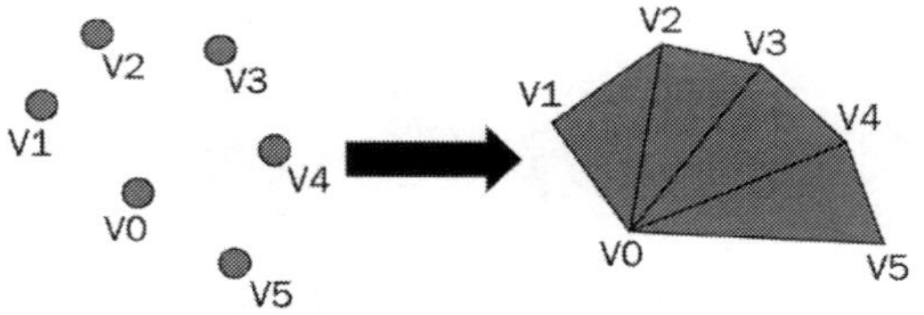

Primitives topologies with adjacency

In this section, we will understand line and triangle primitives with the adjacency rule:

- `VK_PRIMITIVE_TOPOLOGY_LINE_LIST_WITH_ADJACENCY`: This enum type defines a line list with adjacency. Here, for a given N number of vertices, each of the *4i+1*st and *4i+2*nd vertices is used to draw a line segment. The *4i+0*th and *4i+3*rd vertices are considered as adjacency vertices of the *4i+1*st and *4i+2*nd vertices, respectively; here, *i* ranges from 0 to *N-1*. If the geometry shader stage is active, then these adjacency vertices are accessible in the geometry shader; if not, they are ignored:

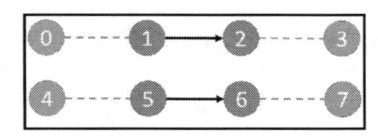

- `VK_PRIMITIVE_TOPOLOGY_LINE_STRIP_WITH_ADJACENCY`: This type of line enum defines a line strip with adjacency. For a given N+3 vertices, each of the $i+1^{st}$ to $i+2^{nd}$ vertices are used to draw a line segment. The number of vertices must be more than four; otherwise, the drawing is ignored. For each line segment i, the $i+0^{th}$ and $i+3^{rd}$ vertices are considered the adjacency vertices of the $i+1^{st}$ and $4i+2^{nd}$ vertices, respectively.

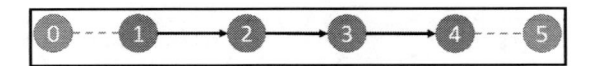

- `VK_PRIMITIVE_TOPOLOGY_TRIANGLE_LIST_WITH_ADJACENCY`: This enum type defines the triangle list with the adjacency. Here, for a given $6n+k$ vertices, the $6i^{th}$, $6i+2^{nd}$, and $6i+4^{th}$ vertices resolve into a triangle (refer to the following diagram: 0, 2 and 4), where i ranges from 0, 1, 2,... to $n-1$, and k could be either 0, 1, 2, 3, 4, or 5. If k is not zero, then the last k vertices are ignored.

    For each determined triangle, the i, $6i+1^{st}$, $6i+3^{rd}$, and $6i+5^{st}$ vertices (refer to the following diagram: 0, 1, 3 and 5) have their adjacent edges produced by the pair of vertices $6i$ and $6i+2^{nd}$, $6i+2^{nd}$ and $6i+4^{th}$, and $6i+4^{th}$ and $6i^{th}$. In the diagram, these adjacent edges are represented by 0 to 2, 2 to 4, and 4 to 6. If the geometry shader stage is active, then the adjacent vertices of each triangle are accessible in a geometry shader; if not, they will be ignored.

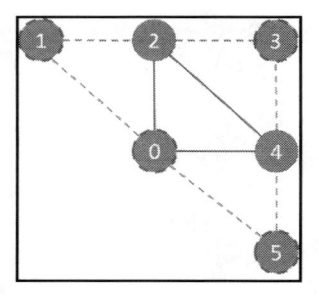

- `VK_PRIMITIVE_TOPOLOGY_TRIANGLE_STRIP_WITH_ADJACENCY`: This is another type of adjacency triangle enum. For a given $2(n+2)+k$ vertices, there are n triangles drawn such that k can take either 0 or 1. The final vertex is ignored if k is equal to 1. If the geometry shader stage is active, then the adjacent vertices of each triangle are accessible in a geometry shader; if not, they are ignored.

The following rule table describes the triangle strip with the adjacency vertices' drawing order for each triangle:

Primitive	Primitive Vertices			Adjacent Vertices		
	1st	2nd	3rd	1/2	2/3	3/2
only (i=0, n=1)	0	2	4	1	5	3
first (i=0)	0	2	4	1	6	3
middle (i odd)	2i+2	2i	2i+4	2i-2	2i+3	2i+6
middle (i even)	2i	2i+2	2i+4	2i-2	2i+6	2i+3
last (i=n-1, i odd)	2i+2	2i	2i+4	2i-2	2i+3	2i+5
last (i=n-1, i even)	2i	2i+2	2i+4	2i-2	2i+5	2i+3

The following diagram shows the rendering of the primitive under the triangle strip with the adjacency rule:

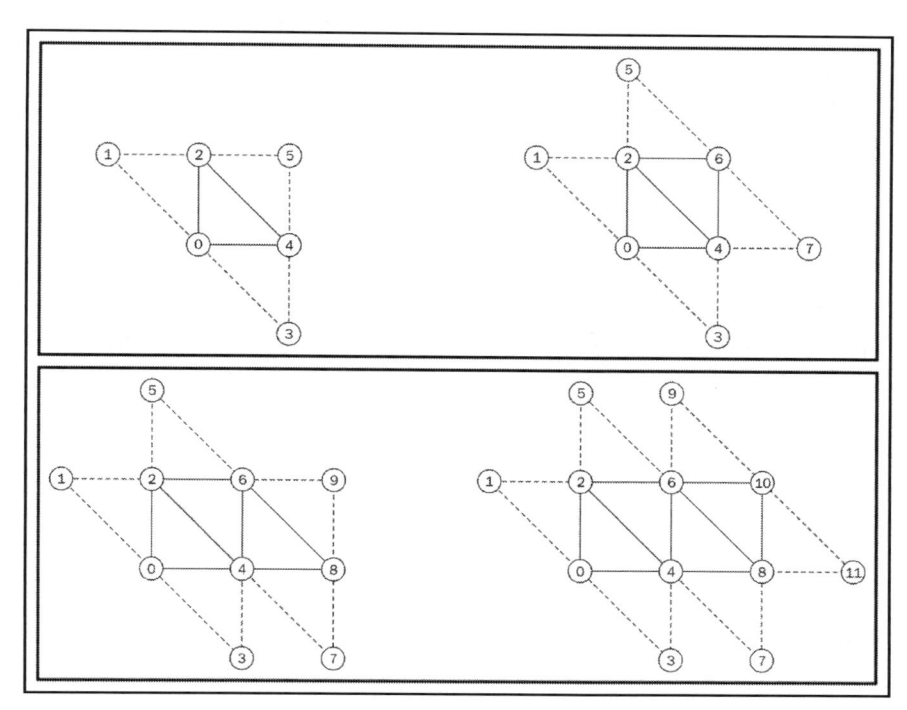

In this next section, we will turn primitives into fragments using rasterization.

Rasterization

Fragments are produced using primitive topologies in the rasterization stage. A rasterized image consists of tiny squares called fragments, arranged in grid fashion. Fragments are a logical combination of the (x, y) position in the framebuffer, corresponding to a depth (z) along with the related data and attributes added by the fragment shaders.

Each primitive goes through the rasterization process and the corresponding fragments are determined according to the topology shape. In this, each primitive's integer position is computed, resulting in the corresponding point or square on the framebuffer grid. Along with the position, one or more depth values with their attributes, which are responsible for determining the final fragment color, are stored in the framebuffer. There can be one or more depth values for each computed point; this indicates that there are multiple overlapped primitives (fully or partially) contending for the same position. These fragments are then resolved based on the depth and associated attributes.

The fragments could be non-square, and this does not affect how the rasterization process works. Rasterization is independent of the aspect ratio of the fragments. The fragments are assumed to be squares since a square simplifies antialiasing and texturing.

The final computed fragment is a pixel that corresponds to the framebuffer. Any fragment that belongs outside the framebuffer dimension is discarded and never considered in the later stages of the pipeline, including any of the early per-fragment tests. The fragment shader processes the surviving fragments and modifies the existing depth value and the associated data with the fragments.

Rasterization states

Rasterization is managed through the rasterization state, which can be programmatically controlled using the `VkPipelineRasterizationStateCreateInfo` structure. This structure provides vital information associated with the rasterization stage—such as the polygon fill mode, front facing, and culling mode—and checks whether the depth is enabled in the rasterization process. It also checks whether the discarded fragments are enabled. Here is the syntax information:

```
typedef struct VkPipelineRasterizationStateCreateInfo {
    VkStructureType                             pType;
    const void*                                 pNext;
    VkPipelineRasterizationStateCreateFlags     flags;
    VkBool32                                    depthClampEnable;
    VkBool32                                    rasterizerDiscardEnable;
    VkPolygonMode                               polygonMode;
    VkCullModeFlags                             cullMode;
```

```
    VkFrontFace                             frontFace;
    VkBool32                                depthBiasEnable;
    float                                   depthBiasConstantFactor;
    float                                   depthBiasClamp;
    float                                   depthBiasSlopeFactor;
    float                                   lineWidth;
} VkPipelineRasterizationStateCreateInfo;
```

The following table describes each of the parameters of this structure:

Parameters	Description
`pType`	This is the type information of this control structure. It must be specified as `VK_STRUCTURE_TYPE_PIPELINE_-RASTERIZATION_STATE_CREATE_INFO`.
`pNext`	This could be a valid pointer to an extension-specific structure or `NULL`.
`flags`	This field is reserved for future implementation.
`depthClamp-Enable`	This Boolean flag controls whether the fragment's depth values are clamped with the z planes of the frustum instead of the clipping primitives.
`rasterizer-DiscardEnable`	Before the rasterization stage is reached, this flag value can be used to control whether the corresponding primitives are to be discarded.
`polygonMode`	The triangle primitive can be rendered in various modes, such as point, filled, or outline. This mode is represented by the `VkPolygonMode` enum, which has the `VK_POLYGON_MODE_FILL`, `VK_POLYGON_MODE_LINE`, and `VK_POLYGON_MODE_POINT` values for fill, line, and point representation, respectively.
`cullMode`	This indicates the culling mode for primitives using `VkCullModeFlagBits`. It has `VK_CULL_MODE_NONE`, `VK_CULL_MODE_FRONT_BIT`, `VK_CULL_MODE_BACK_BIT`, and `VK_CULL_MODE_FRONT_AND_BACK` enum values that specify no culling, front triangle face culling, back triangle face culling, and both front and back face culling, respectively.
`frontFace`	This indicates that the direction of the triangle vertices' orientation is to be considered as front-facing using the `VkFrontFace` enum; this indicates clockwise (`VK_FRONT_FACE_CLOCKWISE`) and counter-clockwise (`VK_FRONT_FACE_COUNTER_CLOCKWISE`) orientation.
`depthBiasEnable`	The bias fragment's depth values can be controlled using this field.
`depthBias-ConstantFactor`	For each fragment's depth value, a constant depth can be added using this scalar factor.
`depthBiasClamp`	This field is a scalar factor that is used to represent the highest or lowest depth bias of a fragment.
`depthBiasSlope-Factor`	This field is a scalar factor that applies to the depth bias calculation on the fragment's slope.
`lineWidth`	This is the scalar value that controls the rasterized line segments width.

Implementing rasterization states

In this section, we will implement the rasterization state inside the `VulkanPipeline::createPipeline()` function. Rasterization produces the fragments associated with the primitives involved in this stage. The following implementation specifies that the primitives need to be render-filled. It culls out the back faces where the front face is determined by the front-facing rule, which considers the vertices to be ordered in a clockwise direction:

```
/********** VulkanPipeline.cpp **********/
// Inside VulkanPipeline::createPipeline()
VkPipelineRasterizationStateCreateInfo rasterStateInfo = {};
rasterStateInfo.sType        =
VK_STRUCTURE_TYPE_PIPELINE_RASTERIZATION_STATE_CREATE_INFO;
rasterStateInfo.pNext                    = NULL;
rasterStateInfo.flags                    = 0;
rasterStateInfo.polygonMode              = VK_POLYGON_MODE_FILL;
rasterStateInfo.cullMode                 = VK_CULL_MODE_BACK_BIT;
rasterStateInfo.frontFace                = VK_FRONT_FACE_CLOCKWISE;
rasterStateInfo.depthClampEnable         = includeDepth;
rasterStateInfo.rasterizerDiscardEnable  = VK_FALSE;
rasterStateInfo.depthBiasEnable          = VK_FALSE;
rasterStateInfo.depthBiasConstantFactor  = 0;
rasterStateInfo.depthBiasClamp           = 0;
rasterStateInfo.depthBiasSlopeFactor     = 0;
rasterStateInfo.lineWidth                = 1.0f;
```

In the next section, we will look at the color-blending state in the Vulkan API and its implementation.

Blending

Blending is a process in which a source fragment is merged into a destination fragment with some special rules that are determined by the blending factors. Both the source and destination fragment consist of four components; among these, three correspond to the color components (R, G, B) and one to the alpha component that controls opacity.

For each given sample location in the framebuffer, the incoming source fragment (Rs, Gs, Bs, As) are merged into the destination fragment (Rd, Gd, Bd, Ad) and stored in the fragment location (x, y) in the framebuffer.

The blending computations are performed with higher precession; they are always carried out on the floating point basis, where the precession is not lower than the destination components. Therefore, any signed and unsigned normalized fixed point is converted into a floating point first to achieve the highest precession possible.

Blending is controlled by the blending operation, blending factor, and blend constants:

- **Blending operations**: These define the basic math equations that are used to combine the source and destination values, for example, addition (VK_BLEND_OP_ADD), subtraction (VK_BLEND_OP_SUBTRACT), and reverse subtraction (VK_BLEND_OP_REVERSE_SUBTRACT).
- **Blending factors**: The weighting of each component is determined by the blending factors. These factors can be used to modify the blending operation used.
- **Blending constants**: This is a constant color component (R, G, B, A) that is used for blending and produces a new set of color components.

Color blend states

Inside the graphics pipeline, the blend state is specified using the VkPipelineColorBlendStateCreateInfo control structure:

```
typedef struct VkPipelineColorBlendStateCreateInfo {
    VkStructureType                               sType;
    const void*                                   pNext;
    VkPipelineColorBlendStateCreateFlags          flags;
    VkBool32                                      logicOpEnable;
    VkLogicOp                                     logicOp;
    uint32_t                                      pAttachmentCount;
    const VkPipelineColorBlendAttachmentState*    attachments;
    float                                         blendConstants[4];
} VkPipelineColorBlendStateCreateInfo;
```

The following table describes the various fields of this structure:

Parameters	Description
sType	This is the type information of this control structure. It must be specified as VK_STRUCTURE_TYPE_PIPELINE_COLOR_BLEND_STATE_CREATE_INFO.
pNext	This could be a valid pointer to an extension-specific structure or NULL.
flags	This field is reserved for future use.

Pipelines and Pipeline State Management

`logicOpEnable`	This is a Boolean flag to determine whether to apply logical operations or not.
`logicOp`	If `logicOpEnable` is enabled, then this field specifies which logical operation to apply.
`attachmentCount`	This indicates the total number of object elements in `pAttachments` of the type `VkPipelineColorBlendAttachmentState`.
`pAttachments`	This is an array of elements (of the type `VkPipelineColorBlend-AttachmentState`).
`blendConstants`	Based on the blend factors used, this indicates the four color values (R, G, B, A) used in the blending.

The `VkPipelineColorBlendStateCreateInfo` control structure takes `VkPipelineColorBlendAttachmentState` as an input. It specifies the blend factor and blend operation for each color attachment in the number of subpasses used in the present pipeline. Here is the syntax of this:

```
typedef struct VkPipelineColorBlendAttachmentState {
    VkBool32                 blendEnable;
    VkBlendFactor            srcColorBlendFactor;
    VkBlendFactor            dstColorBlendFactor;
    VkBlendOp                colorBlendOp;
    VkBlendFactor            srcAlphaBlendFactor;
    VkBlendFactor            dstAlphaBlendFactor;
    VkBlendOp                alphaBlendOp;
    VkColorComponentFlags    colorWriteMask;
} VkPipelineColorBlendAttachmentState;
```

The various fields of `VkPipelineColorBlendAttachmentState` are as follows:

Parameters	Description
`blendEnable`	This indicates whether blending is enabled for the corresponding color attachment. The source fragment's color remains unmodified when blending is disabled.
`srcColorBlendFactor`	This field specifies the blend factor that is applied to calculate the source factors (Sr, Sg, Sb).
`dstColorBlendFactor`	This field specifies the blend factor that is applied to calculate the destination factors (Dr, Dg, Db).
`colorBlendOp`	This indicates which blend factor to apply on the source's and destination's color to calculate and write the final color value (RGB) into the color attachment.

`srcAlphaBlendFactor`	This field specifies the blend factor that is applied to calculate the source's alpha channel, namely Sa.
`dstAlphaBlendFactor`	This field specifies the blend factor that is applied to calculate the destination's alpha channel, namely Da.
`alphaBlendOp`	This field specifies which blend factor is applied on the source's and destination's alpha channel to compute and write the final alpha value (A) into the color attachment.
`colorWriteMask`	This field specifies the color channel's (R, G, B, A) bitmask value that is used to write into the color attachment buffer.

Implementing color blend states

The process of color blending is implemented in the `VulkanPipeline::createPipeline()` function. This function defines the blending attributes for the color attachment with the `VkPipelineColorBlendAttachmentState` structure object (`colorBlendAttachmentStateInfo`). This structure determines whether the color blending is enabled or disabled. If enabled, then various properties, such as alpha and color blending operations, are specified. There are multiple blend operation (`VkBlendOp`) equations that can be used to merge the two, such as adding, subtracting, reverse subtracting, and so on. In addition, for both the source and destination fragments, color and alpha blend factors are initialized here.

Next, create the `VkPipelineColorBlendStateCreateInfo` object's `colorBlendStateInfo` and pass `colorBlendAttachmentStateInfo` into it. This structure specifies the color attachments that will be treated using color blending state information. In addition, the logical blending operation is also initialized using `logicOp` (of the type `VkLogicOp`). The other important piece of information specified is the color blend constant. Refer to the following code implementation:

```
/********** VulkanPipeline.cpp **********/
// Inside VulkanPipeline::createPipeline()
// Create the color blend attachment information
VkPipelineColorBlendAttachmentState
            colorBlendAttachmentStateInfo[1] = {};
colorBlendAttachmentStateInfo[0].colorWriteMask = 0xf;
colorBlendAttachmentStateInfo[0].blendEnable   = VK_FALSE;

// Define color and alpha blending operation.
colorBlendAttachmentStateInfo[0].alphaBlendOp = VK_BLEND_OP_ADD;
colorBlendAttachmentStateInfo[0].colorBlendOp = VK_BLEND_OP_ADD;
```

```cpp
// Set the source and destination color/alpha blend factors
colorBlendAttachmentStateInfo[0].srcColorBlendFactor =
                        VK_BLEND_FACTOR_ZERO;
colorBlendAttachmentStateInfo[0].dstColorBlendFactor =
                        VK_BLEND_FACTOR_ZERO;
colorBlendAttachmentStateInfo[0].srcAlphaBlendFactor =
                        VK_BLEND_FACTOR_ZERO;
colorBlendAttachmentStateInfo[0].dstAlphaBlendFactor =
                        VK_BLEND_FACTOR_ZERO;

VkPipelineColorBlendStateCreateInfo colorBlendStateInfo = {};
colorBlendStateInfo.sType            = VK_STRUCTURE_TYPE-
                _PIPELINE_COLOR_BLEND_STATE_CREATE_INFO;
colorBlendStateInfo.flags            = 0;
colorBlendStateInfo.pNext            = NULL;
colorBlendStateInfo.attachmentCount  = 1;
// Specify the color blend attachment state object
colorBlendStateInfo.pAttachments = colorBlendAttachmentStateInfo;
colorBlendStateInfo.logicOpEnable    = VK_FALSE;
colorBlendStateInfo.blendConstants[0] = 1.0f;
colorBlendStateInfo.blendConstants[1] = 1.0f;
colorBlendStateInfo.blendConstants[2] = 1.0f;
colorBlendStateInfo.blendConstants[3] = 1.0f;
```

Now we move on to pipeline states. We start with discussing viewport management.

Viewport management

A viewport is a portion of the surface region on which the rendering of the primitives will be performed. It defines the physical dimensions in pixels using the `VkViewport` structure, which states a 2D presentation region and the depth range. These two are combined and then used to perform the viewport transformation.

Now for a bit about viewport transformation. During the viewport transformation process, the normalized device coordinates are converted into framebuffer coordinates using the viewport's 2D region and depth range defined in `VkViewport`.

The viewport state

The viewport transformation process is part of the graphics pipeline and is controlled using the `VkPipelineViewportStateCreateInfo` control structure. This structure not only defines the viewports, but the scissors as well.

Using this structure, more than one viewport can be specified; the maximum number of viewports can be determined using `VkPhysicalDeviceLimits::maxViewports` minus one. The following is the syntax for this:

```
typedef struct VkPipelineViewportStateCreateInfo {
    VkStructureType                      sType;
    const void*                          pNext;
    VkPipelineViewportStateCreateFlags   flags;
    uint32_t                             viewportCount;
    const VkViewport*                    pViewports;
    uint32_t                             scissorCount;
    const VkRect2D*                      pScissors;
} VkPipelineViewportStateCreateInfo;
```

Let's look at the various fields of this structure:

Parameters	Description
sType	This is the type information of this control structure. It must be specified as VK_STRUCTURE_TYPE_PIPELINE_VIEWPORT_STATE_CREATE_INFO.
pNext	This could be a valid pointer to an extension-specific structure or NULL.
flags	This field is reserved for future implementation and must be specified as NULL; this field is currently not in use.
viewportCount	This indicates the total number of viewports in the pViewports array used by the pipeline.
pViewports	This is a pointer to an array of viewports (of the type VkViewport) indicating the dimension of each viewport. This value is ignored if the viewport state is dynamic.
scissorCount	This indicates the number of scissors used in the pipeline. This must be equal to the number of viewports specified by viewportCount.
pScissors	This is a pointer to an array of rectangular bounding regions for each corresponding viewport specified by the VkRect2D control structure.

In the following subsection, we will implement the viewport's state object.

Implementing the viewport state

The following is the viewport implementation in the `VulkanPipeline::createPipeline()` function. First, create the `VkPipelineViewportStateCreateInfo` object and assign the number of viewports and scissors used by this pipeline. In the beginning of this section, we declared that the viewport state is a dynamic state. This indicates to the pipeline that the viewport parameters are subject to changes and will be set using `vkSetCmdViewport()` in the `initViewport()` function. Therefore, the `pViewports` and `pScissors` parameters are `NULL` by default:

```
/********** VulkanPipeline.cpp **********/
// Inside VulkanPipeline::createPipeline()

// Define the number of viewport, this must be equal to number
// of scissors should be equal.
#define NUMBER_OF_VIEWPORTS 1
#define NUMBER_OF_SCISSORS NUMBER_OF_VIEWPORTS

// Create the viewport state create info and provide the
// the number of viewport and scissors being used in the
// rendering pipeline.
VkPipelineViewportStateCreateInfo viewportStateInfo = {};
viewportStateInfo.sType             = VK_STRUCTURE_TYPE_-
                                      PIPELINE_VIEWPORT_STATE_
                                      CREATE_INFO;
viewportStateInfo.pNext             = NULL;
viewportStateInfo.flags             = 0;

// Number of viewports must be equal to number of scissors.
viewportStateInfo.viewportCount     = NUMBER_OF_VIEWPORTS;
viewportStateInfo.scissorCount      = NUMBER_OF_SCISSORS;
viewportStateInfo.pScissors         = NULL;
viewportStateInfo.pViewports        = NULL;
```

Depth and stencil tests

A depth test is a stored fragment that may contain different depth values belonging to each of the overlapped primitives on the same framebuffer location. These values are compared and stored in the depth buffer attachment. This is done to conditionally clip out the fragments based on the value stored in the depth buffer attachment; for a given fragment, the value is generally stored at the location (x_f, y_f) in the framebuffer.

A stencil test makes use of the depth/stencil attachment and compares the value stored at the framebuffer location (x_f, y_f) with a given reference value. Depending upon the stencil test state, the stencil value and the stencil write masks are updated in the stencil/depth attachments.

The depth and stencil states are controlled using the `VkPipelineDepthStencilStateCreateInfo` structure. Depth and stencil tests can be enabled or disabled using the member variables `depthBoundsTestEnable` and `stencilTestEnable`.

Depth and stencil states

The following is the syntax and description of `VkPipelineDepthStencilStateCreateInfo`:

```
typedef struct VkPipelineDepthStencilStateCreateInfo {
    VkStructureType                          sType;
    const void*                              pNext;
    VkPipelineDepthStencilStateCreateFlags   flags;
    VkBool32                                 depthTestEnable;
    VkBool32                                 depthWriteEnable;
    VkCompareOp                              depthCompareOp;
    VkBool32                                 depthBoundsTestEnable;
    VkBool32                                 stencilTestEnable;
    VkStencilOpState                         front;
    VkStencilOpState                         back;
    float                                    minDepthBounds;
    float                                    maxDepthBounds;
} VkPipelineDepthStencilStateCreateInfo;
```

Let's look at the various fields of this structure:

Parameters	Description
sType	This is the type information of this control structure. It must be specified as `VK_STRUCTURE_TYPE_PIPELINE_DEPTH_STENCIL_STATE_CREATE_INFO`.
pNext	This could be a valid pointer to an extension-specific structure or `NULL`.
flags	This field is reserved for future implementation and must be specified as `NULL`; this field is currently not in use.
depthTestEnable	This is the Boolean flag to check whether the depth test is enabled.
depthWriteEnable	This field checks whether the depth writes are enabled.
depthCompareOp	This field is the comparison operator that will be used in the depth test.

[303]

Pipelines and Pipeline State Management

`depthBoundsTestEnable`	This is the Boolean flag that checks whether the depth bound test is enabled or disabled.
`stencilTestEnable`	This checks whether the stencil test is enabled or disabled.
`front`	This is the parameter that corresponds to the front control of the stencil test.
`back`	This is the parameter that corresponds to the back control of the stencil test.
`minDepthBounds`	This is the minimum range of values used in the depth bounds test.
`maxDepthBounds`	This is the maximum range of values used in the depth bounds test.

At the beginning of this function (`createPipeline()`), we defined some dynamic states (`VkDynamicState`) that indicate to the pipeline which states will be controlled dynamically in the pipeline. If the depth state (`VK_DYNAMIC_STATE_DEPTH_BOUNDS`) is not defined dynamically, then the depth bounds test is defined by the `minDepthBounds` and `maxDepthBounds` members of `VkPipelineDepthStencilStateCreateInfo`.

On the other hand, if the dynamic depth bound test is enabled, then the depth bound range can be set at runtime using the `vkCmdSetDepthBounds` API. This API takes three parameters. The first parameter is the command buffer, and the next two parameters specify the minimum and maximum depth bounding values. Here's the syntax of this API:

```
void vkCmdSetDepthBounds(
    VkCommandBuffer     commandBuffer,
    float               minDepthBounds,
    float               maxDepthBounds);
```

Implementing depth stencil states

The next state defined in `createPipeline()` is the depth/stencil state. In the following code, `VkPipelineDepthStencilStateCreateInfo` is created, and it determines whether the depth and stencil tests are enabled using the `includeDepth` boolean flag. In the present case, the depth test is enabled; therefore, we should provide more information to the pipeline specify how to carry out the depth and stencil operation. This information may include a depth comparison operation, which tells how the depth buffer values are compared to the incoming depth values to update the depth buffer when the depth write is enabled. Similarly, some of the other fields that are defined are compare masks and the minimum and maximum depth bound ranges. Refer to the implementation in the following code:

```
/********** VulkanPipeline.cpp **********/
// Inside VulkanPipeline::createPipeline()
VkPipelineDepthStencilStateCreateInfo depthStencilStateInfo = {};
depthStencilStateInfo.sType                 = VK_STRUCTURE_TYPE_PIPELINE-
```

```
                _DEPTH_STENCIL_STATE_CREATE_INFO;
            depthStencilStateInfo.pNext                = NULL;
            depthStencilStateInfo.flags                = 0;
            depthStencilStateInfo.depthTestEnable      = includeDepth;
            depthStencilStateInfo.depthWriteEnable     = includeDepth;
            depthStencilStateInfo.depthCompareOp       = VK_COMPARE_OP_LESS
                _OR_EQUAL;
            depthStencilStateInfo.depthBoundsTestEnable    = VK_FALSE;
            depthStencilStateInfo.stencilTestEnable        = VK_FALSE;
            depthStencilStateInfo.back.failOp     = VK_STENCIL_OP_KEEP;
            depthStencilStateInfo.back.passOp     = VK_STENCIL_OP_KEEP;
            depthStencilStateInfo.back.compareOp      = VK_COMPARE_OP_ALWAYS;
            depthStencilStateInfo.back.compareMask    = 0;
            depthStencilStateInfo.back.reference      = 0;
            depthStencilStateInfo.back.depthFailOp    = VK_STENCIL_OP_KEEP;
            depthStencilStateInfo.back.writeMask      = 0;
            depthStencilStateInfo.minDepthBounds      = 0;
            depthStencilStateInfo.maxDepthBounds      = 0;
            depthStencilStateInfo.stencilTestEnable = VK_FALSE;
            depthStencilStateInfo.front           = depthStencilStateInfo.back;
```

In the next section, we will look at the multisampling state, which controls the appearance of rastered images in order to improve the quality of the presentation.

Multisample states

Multisampling is a mechanism that removes the aliasing effects produced during the Vulkan primitive rasterization. The antialiasing takes multiple samples from the geometry for a given pixel to generate a smooth approximation such that it minimizes the stair-step case effect and makes the edges appear smooth.

Antialiasing is a technique in computer graphics that improves the quality of the rendered image or video output displayed on the screen by minimizing jagged lines or the stair-step case effect. The raster framebuffer is composed of hundreds of tiny square pixels arranged in a grid format. During image rasterization, the geometry is sampled for a given pixel using a sampling scheme, which will be discussed later in this section. Basically, the cause of antialiasing is point sampling. These samples are represented by rectangular pixels, which are not sufficient to produce curved shapes. Edges in the image, which are round (not horizontal or vertical), are responsible for this stair-step case effect, as they end up coloring the pixels as in a stair arrangement. The aliasing problem is not much noticeable when an image or scene is still, but as soon as they are in motion, jagged edges are highly visible.

Pipelines and Pipeline State Management

Once the primitives (points, lines, and triangles) are baked into the final presentation pixels, they are treated with the multisampling process. This allows you to make the Vulkan primitive antialiased by making the edges appear smoother, not jagged. This efficient technique saves a tremendous amount of computation cost)among many other antialiasing techniques). It is the number-one choice of GPU hardware vendors. A multisample takes more than one sample in the computation process for a given pixel in a single pass. In multisampling, a given pixel in the primitive is sampled multiple times where each sampling can utilize the color, depth, and/or stencil values independently, which are later resolved into a single combined color.

In line with the Vulkan specification, the rasterization rules for single-sample modes in Vulkan have been defined in such a way that they are equivalent to a multisample mode with a single sample in the center of each pixel.

Multisampling can be organized within the pipeline using the `VkPipeline-MultisampleStateCreateInfo` structure. Refer to the following subsection to understand the API specification and its implementation. First, let's look at the syntax of this structure:

```
typedef struct VkPipelineMultisampleStateCreateInfo {
    VkStructureType                          sType;
    const void*                              pNext;
    VkPipelineMultisampleStateCreateFlags    flags;
    VkSampleCountFlagBits                    rasterizationSamples;
    VkBool32                                 sampleShadingEnable;
    float                                    minSampleShading;
    const VkSampleMask*                      pSampleMask;
    VkBool32                                 alphaToCoverageEnable;
    VkBool32                                 alphaToOneEnable;
} VkPipelineMultisampleStateCreateInfo;
```

Let's look at the various fields of this structure:

Parameters	Description
sType	This is the type information of this control structure. It must be specified as VK_STRUCTURE_TYPE_-PIPELINE_MULTISAMPLE_STATE_CREATE_INFO.
pNext	This could be a valid pointer to an extension-specific structure or NULL.
flags	This field is NULL; it is reserved for future use.
rasterizationSamples	This field indicates the number of samples used per pixel in the rasterization.
sampleShadingEnable	The Boolean flags indicate whether the fragment shading will be executed according to a per-sample or per-fragment basis. If the value is VK_TRUE, it is per-sample, otherwise per-fragment.

`minSampleShading`	This specifies the minimum number of unique samples required to shade for each fragment.
`pSampleMask`	This field is the bitmask that is used for ANDing the static coverage information with the rasterization-generated coverage information.
`alphaToCoverageEnable`	This field controls whether the value of the alpha component of the fragment's first color output can be used to generate a temporary coverage value.
`alphaToOneEnable`	This controls whether the multisampling coverage can replace the alpha component value of the fragment's first color output.

Implementing multisample states

The last state defined in the `VulkanPipeline::createPipeline()` function is the multisampling state. First, define the `VkPipelineMultisampleStateCreateInfo` structure with the correct type information to help the underlying implementation understand the kind of object that is passed in. The `sType` must be specified as `VK_STRUCTURE_TYPE_PIPELINE_MULTISAMPLE_STATE_CREATE_INFO`. Next, indicate the number of samples used as coverage values per pixel in `rasterizationSample`, which is `VK_SAMPLE_COUNT_1_BIT` in the present case.

Various pixel sampling schemes exists. When the `standardSampleLocations` member of `VkPhysicalDeviceFeatures` is `VK_TRUE`, then the sample counts are defined using the samples shown in the following screenshot:

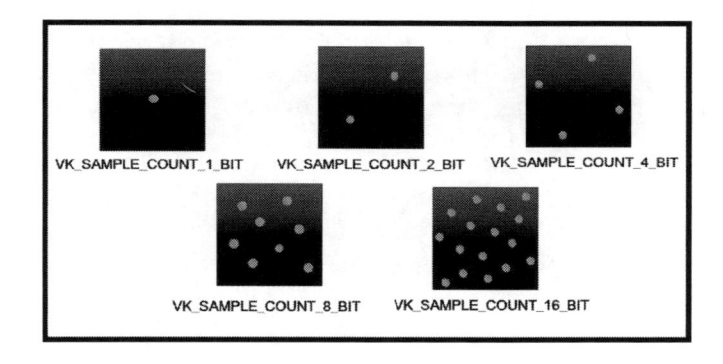

Pipelines and Pipeline State Management

There could be different sample schemes based on the number of samples in a given pixel, which could vary from 1 to 64 samplings. Samplings contain various positions that contribute weights based on a position relative to an origin in the upper left corner of the pixel. When `rasterizationSamples` is `VK_SAMPLE_COUNT_1_BIT`, sampling uses the pixel center:

```
/************ VulkanPipeline.cpp *************/
// Inside VulkanPipeline::createPipeline()
VkPipelineMultisampleStateCreateInfo   multiSampleStateInfo = {};
multiSampleStateInfo.sType       =
    VK_STRUCTURE_TYPE_PIPELINE_MULTISAMPLE_STATE_CREATE_INFO;
multiSampleStateInfo.pNext                      = NULL;
multiSampleStateInfo.flags                      = 0;
multiSampleStateInfo.rasterizationSamples       = NUM_SAMPLES;
```

So far, in the *Creating a graphics pipeline* section and the *Pipeline state objects in Vulkan* section, we learned how to create a graphics pipeline and specify various pipeline state objects into it. In the next section, we will understand the execution model of creating the pipeline in our sample application.

Implementing the pipeline

The graphics pipeline is implemented at the initialization stage of the application in the `VulkanRenderer` class. The `VulkanRenderer::createPipelineStateManagement()` function is responsible for executing the creation of the pipeline. Inside this function, the `cmdPipelineStateMgmt` command buffer object is created into which the pipeline creation process's commands are recorded. These recorded commands are then submitted to the graphics queue, that is, to the underlying implementation.

The following diagram shows the execution process. Here, first the command buffer is allocated for managing the pipeline operation. Under this, the pipeline cache object is created using the `VulkanPipeline::createPipelineCache()` function; once this is done, the pipeline is created in `VulkanPipeline::createPipeline()`. The following diagram shows the calling sequence:

Chapter 8

```
void VulkanRenderer::initialize()
          ↓
void VulkanRenderer::initialize()
          ↓
void VulkanRenderer::createPipelineStateManagement()
          ↓
voidCommandBufferMgr::beginCommandBuffer(cmdPipelineStateMgmt)
          ↓
void VulkanPipeline::createPipelineCache()
          ↓
void VulkanPipeline::createPipeline()
          ↓
void CommandBufferMgr::endCommandBuffer(cmdPipelineStateMgmt)
          ↓
void CommandbufferMgr::submitCommandBuffer(cmdPipelineStateMgmt)
```

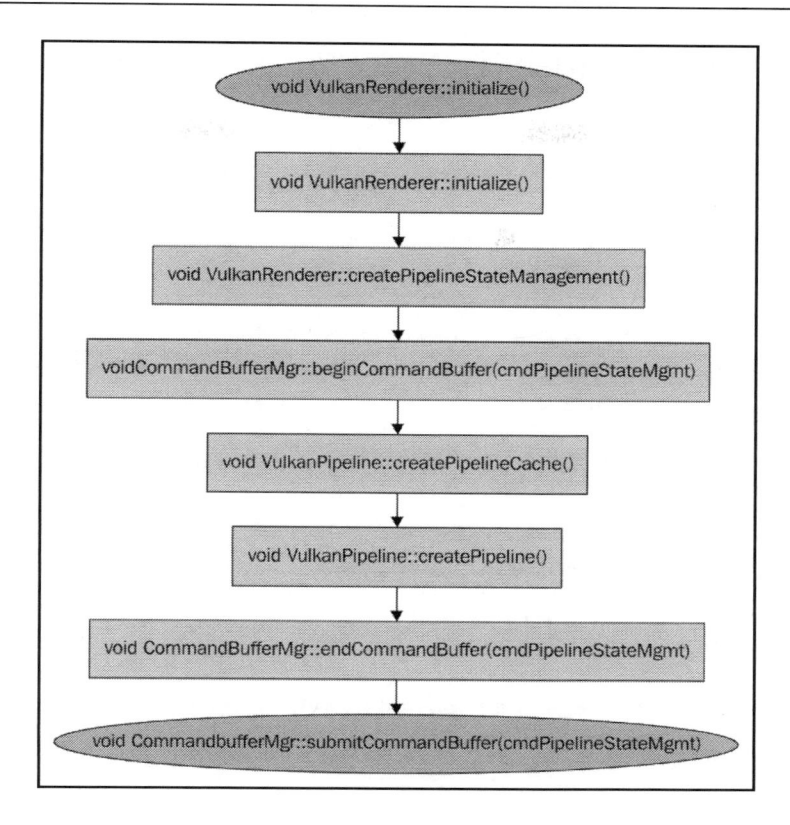

Each drawing object (we will implement drawing objects in the next chapter) is associated with the created pipeline object (`pipeline`). If there are multiple drawing objects, they can reuse the pipeline object instead of creating a new one for each object. Therefore, it is the application's responsibility to control the redundancy of the pipeline object association with each drawing object:

```
// Create the pipeline and manage the pipeline state objects
void VulkanRenderer::createPipelineStateManagement()
{
    // Create the pipeline cache
    pipelineObj.createPipelineCache();

    const bool depthPresent = true;
    // For the each drawing object create the associated pipeline.
    for each (VulkanDrawable* drawableObj in drawableList){
        VkPipeline* pipeline=(VkPipeline*)malloc(sizeof(VkPipeline));
        if (pipelineObj.createPipeline(drawableObj, pipeline,
                                       &shaderObj, depthPresent)){
            pipelineList.push_back(pipeline);
```

[309]

```
                drawableObj->setPipeline(pipeline);
        }
        else
        {
            free(pipeline);
            pipeline = NULL;
        }
      }
}
```

When the pipeline object is no longer required, it can be deleted. In the following sample implementation, when the application closes, it deletes all the pipeline objects along with the associated pipeline cache in the `deInitialization()` function:

```
void VulkanApplication::deInitialize(){
    // Destroy all the pipeline objects
    rendererObj->destroyPipeline();

    // Destroy the associate pipeline cache
    rendererObj->getPipelineObject()->destroyPipelineCache();
    . . . .
}

// Destroy each pipeline object existing in the renderer
void VulkanRenderer::destroyPipeline(){
    for each (VkPipeline* pipeline in pipelineList){
        vkDestroyPipeline(deviceObj->device, *pipeline, NULL);
        free(pipeline);
    }
    pipelineList.clear();
}

// Destroy the pipeline cache object when no more required
void VulkanPipeline::destroyPipelineCache(){
    vkDestroyPipelineCache(deviceObj->device, pipelineCache, NULL);
}
```

Summary

In this chapter, we learned about the various pipelines available in the Vulkan API. We understood the graphics and compute pipelines and implemented one of the former in our sample example. We also learned about the pipeline cache object, which is a pool of pipelines that help in achieving better performance. The pipeline cache object can be stored in binary form and can be later uploaded and reused between application runs.

The graphics pipeline comprises many pipeline state objects. In this chapter, we covered all the states in detail along with their implementation. As part of these pipeline state objects, we discussed the dynamics state, vertex input state, input assembly state, rasterization, blending, viewport management, depth and stencil test, and multisampling state.

Finally, we used the pipeline cache object and pipeline state objects to build a graphics pipeline object.

In the next chapter, we will make use of the created graphics pipeline object and render our first Vulkan drawing object on the display. Drawing the object consists of two major tasks: preparing and rendering the drawing object. The preparation includes defining the Render Pass, binding the graphics pipeline, supplying geometry, viewport/scissoring, and building the drawing commands. While rendering, a swapchain is acquired and the prepared drawing commands are executed; this renders the drawing object on the presentation layer. In addition, we will understand Vulkan synchronization primitives; at this point, we will discuss fences, semaphores, and events.

9
Drawing Objects

In the last two chapters, we implemented the Render Pass instance and displayed swapchain images with specified background colors. In the previous chapter, we put various pipeline states together along with Render Pass in the graphics pipeline. In this chapter, we will put all previous implementations together to build the first Hello World! program in Vulkan and display our first rendering object on the display output.

This chapter thoroughly covers the process of drawing objects in Vulkan; it comprises recording and executing the drawing object's command buffers. The recording associates the Render Pass, framebuffer, and the pipeline together with the viewport and geometry data. Command buffer execution involves submitting the command buffer in the device queue and presenting the drawn swapchain image onto the presentation engine. Toward the end of this chapter, we will discuss various synchronization primitives available in the Vulkan API.

In this chapter, we will cover the following topics:

- Overview of the drawing process in Vulkan
- Preparing the drawing object
- Rendering the drawing object
- Rendering an indexed geometry
- Understanding synchronization primitives in Vulkan
- Resizing the display window

Overview of the drawing process in Vulkan

Implementing a drawing object in Vulkan is simple; it consists of two phases: *preparation*, or building the drawing object, and *rendering* it. The former phase produces the command buffer and records the drawing commands. In the latter phase, the command buffer executes these drawing commands to render the object. Let's take a look at these phases in detail:

1. **Preparing the drawing object**: This phase produces the command buffers required to draw objects:
    - **Command buffer creation**: For each swapchain color image, create a corresponding command buffer object. For example, if the swapchain is a double buffer, then it will contain two color images. As a result, we should be creating two command buffers that correspond to each image.
    - **Command buffer recording**: For the command buffer created, record the Render Pass instance commands single subpass at ; refer to the following steps:
        - Associate the created Render Pass object and framebuffer with the required dimensions of the presentation's render area.
        - Specify the scalar values for clearing the background color and depth image. We implemented this step in `Chapter 7`, *Buffer Resource, Render Pass, Framebuffer, and Shaders with SPIR-V*. For more information, please refer to the *Clearing the background color* section.
        - Bind the graphics pipeline object.
        - Bind the resources used by the pipeline, including vertex buffers and descriptor sets.
        - Define the viewport and scissoring region.
        - Draw the object.
2. **Rendering the drawing object**: Here, the created command buffers in the preparation phase are reused and executed again and again to render the drawing object:
    - Get the swapchain image that is available to perform rendering on it.
    - Submit the command buffer to render the object.
    - Display the rendered drawing image on the presentation engine.

The *preparation* and *rendering* of the drawable object are implemented through the `prepare()` and `render()` functions of the `VulkanDrawable` class.

Walking through the header declaration

In this section, we will take a look at the header file declaration for `VulkanDrawable`. Please follow through the inline comments to understand the functionality and purpose of each function and variable. As we proceed through the chapter, we will implement these functions and discuss them in detail. The following are the new member variables and functions added:

```cpp
class VulkanDrawable
{
  public:
  // Prepares the drawing object before rendering,
  // allocate, create, record command buffer
  void prepare();

  // Renders the drawing object
  void render();

  // Initialize the viewport parameters here
  void initViewports(VkCommandBuffer* cmd);

  // Initialize the scissor parameters here
  void initScissors(VkCommandBuffer* cmd);

  // Destroy the drawing command buffer object
  void destroyCommandBuffer();
  private:
  // Command buffer for drawing
  std::vector<VkCommandBuffer> vecCmdDraw;

  // Prepares render pass instance
  void recordCommandBuffer(int currentImage,
  VkCommandBuffer* cmdDraw);

  // Viewport and Scissor variables
  VkViewport viewport;
  VkRect2D scissor;
  VkSemaphore presentCompleteSemaphore;
  VkSemaphore drawingCompleteSemaphore;
};
```

[315]

Drawing Objects

The `prepare()` function creates the command buffer objects, which are used in the `render()` function to draw the object. The `prepare()` function allocates the memory for the command buffer (`vecCmdDraw`) from the command pool (`VulkanRenderer::cmdPool`) and creates the command buffer object. The command buffer commands are recorded inside the `recordCommandBuffer()` function; this creates the Render Pass instance and other important jobs, such as associating the graphics pipeline with the drawing object and specifying the viewport and scissoring management through `initViewport()` and `initScissor()`.

The `render()` function uses the prepared recorded command buffer and renders the drawing on the available swapchain color image. Once the drawing is finished on the swapchain's color image, then it is given to the presentation engine for display purposes.

Preparing the drawing object

The preparation of the drawing object is implemented in the `prepare()` function; this function has already been covered in Chapter 7, *Buffer Resource, Render Pass, Framebuffer, and Shaders with SPIR-V*. For more information, please refer to the subsection *Setting the background color in Render Pass instance* under *Clearing the background color*.

Recording Render Pass commands

The Render Pass instance records the command's single subpass at a time. A Render Pass may contain one or more subpasses. For each subpass, the commands are recorded using the `vkCmdBeginRenderPass()` and `vkCmdEndRenderPass()` APIs. These two APIs together define a scope under which iterating through different subpasses will record the commands for that particular subpass.

Beginning Render Pass instance recording

The `vkCmdBeginRenderPass()` API begins Render Pass instance command recording for a given subpass. The following is the specification:

```
void vkCmdBeginRenderPass(
    VkCommandBuffer                 commandBuffer,
    const VkRenderPassBeginInfo*    pRenderPassBegin,
    VkSubpassContents               contents);
```

The `vkCmdBeginRenderPass` API accepts three parameters. The first parameter–`commandBuffer` of the `VkCommandBuffer` type–indicates the command buffer into which the commands are recorded. The second parameter–`pRenderPassBegin`–is a `VkRenderPassBeginInfo` type control structure into which Render Pass metadata is passed (more information is provided in the following section). The last parameter is of the `VkSubpassContents` type and indicates where and how the contents will be recorded in the subpass execution.

The following are the two types of `VkSubpassContents`:

- `VK_SUBPASS_CONTENTS_INLINE`: In this type, the primary command buffer directly records the subpass contents and doesn't permit the secondary command buffer to execute within this subpass
- `VK_SUBPASS_CONTENTS_SECONDARY_COMMAND`: Here, the secondary command buffer is invoked through primary command buffers and is responsible for recording the subpass contents

What are primary and secondary command buffers?

The primary command buffer does not have any parent command buffer. However, the secondary command buffers are always executed from the primary command buffers behaving as its parent. The secondary command buffers are not directly submitted into the device queue; these are recorded into the primary command buffer and executed using the `vkCmdExecuteCommands()` API.
```
void vkCmdExecuteCommands(
    VkCommandBuffer         commandBuffer,
    uint32_t                commandBufferCount,
    const VkCommandBuffer*  pCommandBuffers);
```

This API takes three arguments. The first argument–`commandBuffer` (of type `VkCommandBuffer`)–is the primary command buffer object handle. The second parameter–`commandBufferCount`(of type `uint32_t`)–indicates the total number of secondary command buffers that needs to be invoked under the primary command buffer. The last parameter–`pCommandBuffers` (of type `VkCommandBuffer*`)–specifies a complete list of the secondary command buffer objects to be passed in.

How are secondary command buffers useful?

Secondary command buffers are useful in recording common operations into modular units. These modular capsules can be attached to any of your desired primary buffer as required. In the absence of the secondary

[317]

Drawing Objects

> **TIP** command buffer, such common operations will be recorded as part of the primary buffer, making them bulky and resulting in redundancy pollution.

Let's take a look at the `VkRenderPassBeginInfo` structure syntax and its parameters:

```
typedef struct VkRenderPassBeginInfo {
    VkStructureType         sType;
    const void*             pNext;
    VkRenderPass            renderPass;
    VkFramebuffer           framebuffer;
    VkRect2D                renderArea;
    uint32_t                clearValueCount;
    const VkClearValue*     pClearValues;
} VkRenderPassBeginInfo;
```

The following are the various parameters of the `VkRenderPassBeginInfo` structure:

Parameters	Description
sType	This is the type information of this control structure. It must be specified as VK_STRUCTURE_TYPE_RENDER_PASS_BEGIN_INFO.
pNext	This could be a valid pointer to an extension-specific structure or could be NULL.
renderPass	The Render Pass instance consumes the Render Pass object to begin the recording.
framebuffer	The Render Pass is also associated with a VkFramebuffer object that contains color and depth attachments.
renderArea	This field indicates the rectangular region affected as a result of the Render Pass execution.
clearValueCount	This indicates the number of clear values for color or depth.
pClearValues	This field contains the clear values associated with attachments specified in the framebuffer.

While defining the `renderArea` in the Render Pass instance, if the rendering region is smaller than the framebuffer, then it may cause a performance penalty. In such case, it's advisable either to keep the render area equal to the framebuffer region or to qualify the granularity for the Render Pass. Render area granularity can be checked using the `vkGetRenderAreaGranularity()` API.

```
void vkGetRenderAreaGranularity(
    VkDevice            device,
    VkRenderPass        renderPass,
    VkExtent2D*         pGranularity);
```

This API accepts three parameters: the first parameter–`device`–is the `VkDevice` that is associated with `renderPass`; the second parameter is the `renderPass` object; the last parameter retrieves the granularity size in `pGranularity`.

Transitioning to the next subpass

In a given Render Pass instance, when a subpass recording is finished, the application can switch or transit to the next subpass using the `vkCmdNextSubpass()` API.

```
void vkCmdNextSubpass(
    VkCommandBuffer     commandBuffer,
    VkSubpassContents   contents);
```

This API accepts two parameters as shown in the following table:

Parameters	Description
`commandBuffer`	This indicates the command buffer into which the commands are recorded.
`contents`	This indicates where and how the contents will be provided in the next subpass execution. For more information on `VkSubpassContents`, please refer to the previous subsection–*Beginning the Render Pass instance*.

[319]

Drawing Objects

Finishing Render Pass instance recording

The `vkCmdEndRenderPass()` API ends the Render Pass instance command buffer recording for the subpass that is currently being executed. This API takes one parameter specifying the handle of the command buffer on which the recording must be stopped.

```
void vkCmdEndRenderPass(
   VkCommandBuffer commandBuffer);
```

Implementation

The current subpass is specified with a clear black color, which will paint the swapchain image with this value, making the background appear black. In addition, other parameters, such as the Render Pass object, framebuffer, and dimension, are also specified. There are many other commands that get executed in the Render Pass instance; this will be discussed in the next section, the following implementation shows the Render Pass instance recording using the `vkCmdBeginRenderPass()` and `vkCmdEndRenderPass()` APIs:

```
void VulkanDrawable::recordCommandBuffer(int currentImage, VkCommandBuffer*
cmdDraw)
{
VulkanDevice* deviceObj= rendererObj->getDevice();
// Specify the clear color value
VkClearValue clearValues[2];
clearValues[0].color.float32[0]= 0.0f;
clearValues[0].color.float32[1]= 0.0f;
clearValues[0].color.float32[2]= 0.0f;
clearValues[0].color.float32[3]= 0.0f;

// Specify the depth/stencil clear value
clearValues[1].depthStencil.depth   = 1.0f;
clearValues[1].depthStencil.stencil = 0;

// Define the VkRenderPassBeginInfo control structure
VkRenderPassBeginInfo renderPassBegin;
renderPassBegin.sType                    =
    VK_STRUCTURE_TYPE_RENDER_PASS_BEGIN_INFO;
renderPassBegin.pNext                    = NULL;
renderPassBegin.renderPass               = rendererObj->renderPass;
renderPassBegin.framebuffer              = rendererObj->
                                           framebuffers[currentImage];
renderPassBegin.renderArea.offset.x      = 0;
renderPassBegin.renderArea.offset.y      = 0;
renderPassBegin.renderArea.extent.width  = rendererObj->width;
renderPassBegin.renderArea.extent.height = rendererObj->height;
renderPassBegin.clearValueCount          = 2;
```

```
renderPassBegin.pClearValues           = clearValues;

// Start recording the render pass instance
vkCmdBeginRenderPass(*cmdDraw, &renderPassBegin,
   VK_SUBPASS_CONTENTS_INLINE);

// Execute the commands as per requirement
. . . .
// pipeline bind, geometry, viewport, scissoring

// End of render pass instance recording
vkCmdEndRenderPass(*cmdDraw);
. . . .
}
```

Binding pipeline object

In the Render Pass instance, the first thing we will need to do is bind the pipeline using the `vkCmdBindPipeline()` API. This API binds a specific pipeline (either *Graphics* or *Compute*) with the current command buffer that is using this command.

```
void vkCmdBindPipeline(
    VkCommandBuffer        commandBuffer,
    VkPipelineBindPoint    pipelineBindPoint,
    VkPipeline             pipeline);
```

Parameters	Description
`commandBuffer`	This indicates the command buffer object (used in Render Pass recording) that will be bound to the `pipeline` object.

`pipelineBindPoint`	This field indicates the type of the pipeline binding point to which the pipeline object will be bounded. This field is of type `VkPipelineBindPoint` and can take one of the following two given values:
	`typedef enum VkPipelineBindPoint {`
	`VK_PIPELINE_BIND_POINT_GRAPHICS = 0,`
	`VK_PIPELINE_BIND_POINT_COMPUTE = 1,`
	`} VkPipelineBindPoint;`
	The first value indicates the bind point for graphics pipeline and the second for the compute pipeline.

`pipeline`	This indicates the pipeline object to which the command buffer will be bounded.

Drawing Objects

Each pipeline–*graphics* or *compute*–is very specific to the commands that it affect once bounded:

- **Compute pipeline**: When the pipeline is bound to `VK_PIPELINE_BIND_POINT_COMPUTE`, only the `vkCmdDispatch` and `vkCmdDispatchIndirect` commands behavior can be controlled. Any other command under this pipeline state will remain unaffected. For more information on these commands, please refer to the official *Vulkan specification* documentation at `https://www.khronos.org/registry/vulkan/specs/1.0/xhtml/vkspec.html`.
- **Graphics pipeline**: When the pipeline is bound to `VK_PIPELINE_BIND_POINT_GRAPHICS`, the `vkCmdDraw`, `vkCmdDrawIndexed`, `vkCmdDrawIndirect`, and `vkCmdDrawIndexedIndirect` commands can be controlled. Any other command under this pipeline state will remain unaffected.

Implementation

The following code shows the binding of the graphics pipeline with the existing command buffer object `cmdDraw`, The `pipeline` object is connected with the graphics bind point (`VK_PIPELINE_BIND_POINT_GRAPHICS`):

```
void VulkanDrawable::recordCommandBuffer(int currentImage, VkCommandBuffer* cmdDraw){
    . . . .
    // Bound the command buffer with the graphics pipeline
    vkCmdBindPipeline(*cmdDraw, VK_PIPELINE_BIND_POINT_GRAPHICS,
    *pipeline);
    . . . .
}
```

> For more information on pipeline creation and the pipeline object specified in the implementation, please refer to `Chapter 8`, *Pipelines and Pipeline State Management*.

Specifying drawing object geometry information

The geometry information for the drawing object can be specified using the vertex buffer. Remember, we built the buffer resource in Chapter 7, *Buffer Resource, Render Pass, Framebuffer, and Shaders with SPIR-V* and stored the vertex information in the `VertexBuffer.buf` of the `VulkanDrawble` class.

> For more information on , and to recap, vertex buffer building, please refer to the *Understanding the buffer resource* and *Creating geometry with buffer resource* section in Chapter 7, *Buffer Resource, Render Pass, Framebuffer, and Shaders with SPIR-V*.

Vertex data contains vertex position and color information together in an interleaved form. Bind this vertex data to the command buffer under the graphics pipeline state using the `vkCmdBindVertexBuffers()` API. This command bounds a specific vertex buffer to a command buffer on a per-draw basis.

```
void vkCmdBindVertexBuffers(
    VkCommandBuffer             commandBuffer,
    uint32_t                    firstBinding,
    uint32_t                    bindingCount,
    const VkBuffer*             pBuffers,
    const VkDeviceSize*         pOffsets);
```

The following table lists the fields and indicates the description of each parameter:

Parameters	Description
`commandBuffer`	This is the command buffer object into which the `vkCmdBindVertexBuffers` command will be recorded.
`firstBinding`	This field indicates the index of the vertex input binding, which will be updated by the command.
`bindingCount`	This indicates the number of vertex input bindings whose state will be updated by the command.
`pBuffers`	This field is an array of the `VkBuffer` vertex buffer handles that are passed into.
`pOffsets`	This field is an array of vertex buffer offsets.

Drawing Objects

Implementation

Bind the command buffer object with the necessary information to pick the geometry data using the `vkCmdBindVertexBuffer()` API; this API takes the vertex buffer information of the drawing object that we are interested in to draw on the display:

```
void VulkanDrawable::recordCommandBuffer(int currentImage, VkCommandBuffer* cmdDraw){
    . . . .
    // Bound the vertex buffer with the command buffer
    vkCmdBindVertexBuffers(*cmdDraw, 0, 1, &VertexBuffer.buf, offsets);
    . . . .
}
```

Defining a dynamic viewport

A viewport determines the portion of the drawing surface region on which the drawing object primitives will be rendered. In Chapter 8, *Pipelines and Pipeline State Management,* we learned to manage viewport state under the graphics pipeline in the *Viewport management* subsection under *Understanding the Pipeline State Objects (PSO)* and created a pipeline state object. Viewport parameters can be controlled statically or dynamically:

- **Statical control**: If the dynamic state `VK_DYNAMIC_STATE_VIEWPORT` is *disabled*, then the viewport parameters are not supposed to be changed and specified once the viewport pipeline state object is created using the `VkPipelineViewportStateCreateInfo` class' member variable `pViewport`.

- **Dynamical control**: On the other hand, when the dynamic state `VK_DYNAMIC_STATE_VIEWPORT` is *enabled* while creating the pipeline state object, then the viewport transformation parameters are allowed to be changed at runtime. These parameters can be controlled dynamically at runtime using the `vkCmdSetViewport()` API. The following is the syntax and description of this API:

```
void vkCmdSetViewport(
    VkCommandBuffer    commandBuffer,
    uint32_t           firstViewport,
    uint32_t           viewportCount,
    const VkViewport*  pViewports);
```

The fields and a description of each parameter follow:

Parameters	Description
commandBuffer	This field specifies the command buffer object that will be used to record this command.
firstViewport	The firstViewport is an index into the internal viewports array, indicating the first viewport that requires to be updated.
viewportCount	These are the total number of viewports in the pViewport whose parameters will be updated by the command.
pViewports	This is a pointer array of the VkViewport structure specifying the dimensions of the viewport region.

```
typedef struct VkViewport {
    float    x;
    float    y;
    float    width;
    float    height;
    float    minDepth;
    float    maxDepth;
} VkViewport;
```

The fields and a description of each parameter follow:

Parameters	Description
x, y	This is the upper-left corner of the viewport (x, y).
width, height	This indicates the width and height of the viewport.
minDepth, maxDepth	This is the depth range for the viewport. minDepth could be greater than or equal to maxDepth.

Implementation

The viewport is initialized using the initViewport() function by passing the current command buffer object into which the vkCmdSetViewport() command will be recorded. The vkCmdSetViewport() API sets the viewport parameters, which are dynamically set in the viewport region, specifying the upper-left dimension and depth information of the viewable region:

```
void VulkanDrawable::recordCommandBuffer(int currentImage, VkCommandBuffer*
cmdDraw){
    . . . .
```

```
    // Define the dynamic viewport here.
    initViewports(cmdDraw);
    . . . .
}
void VulkanDrawable::initViewports(VkCommandBuffer* cmd)
{
    viewport.height    = (float)rendererObj->height;
    viewport.width     = (float)rendererObj->width;
    viewport.minDepth  = (float) 0.0f;
    viewport.maxDepth  = (float) 1.0f;
    viewport.x         = 0;
    viewport.y         = 0;
    vkCmdSetViewport(*cmd, 0, NUMBER_OF_VIEWPORTS, &viewport);
}
```

Scissoring

A scissor defines a rectangular region; any framebuffer fragment's location (x, y) falling outside this rectangular region is discarded.

If this pipeline state object is not created with the dynamic state `VK_DYNAMIC_STATE_VIEWPORT` enabled, then scissor rectangles are controlled using the `VkPipelineViewportStateCreateInfo` class's member variable `pScissors`. On the other hand, if the pipeline state object is created with the dynamic state `VK_DYNAMIC_STATE_VIEWPORT` enabled, then the scissor rectangle parameter can be specified and controlled dynamically using the `vkCmdSetScissor()` API.

Similar to viewport parameters, scissor parameters can be controlled statically or dynamically:

- **Static control**: When viewport parameters are not expected to change, then it means the viewing dimensions are fixed. This can be indicated to the underlying pipeline using dynamic states by *disabling* the `VK_DYNAMIC_STATE_VIEWPORT`. Such a case informs the pipeline about the static nature of the viewport, which could be beneficial for decision-making and avoiding any kind of housekeeping that the viewports dynamic factors required. For static viewport configuration, the scissor parameters read from the viewport pipeline state object `VkPipelineViewportStateCreateInfo` class's member variable `pScissors`.

- **Dynamical control**: On the other hand, if the dynamic state `VK_DYNAMIC_STATE_VIEWPORT` is *enabled*, scissor parameters can be changed dynamically and specified through a special API called `vkCmdSetViewport()`. The following is the syntax and description of this API:

    ```
    void vkCmdSetScissor(
      VkCommandBuffer  commandBuffer,
      uint32_t         firstScissor,
      uint32_t         scissorCount,
      const VkRect2D*  pScissors);
    ```

The fields and a description of each parameter follow:

Parameters	Description
`commandBuffer`	This field specifies the command buffer object that will be used to record this command.
`firstScissor`	The `firstScissor` is an index to the internal scissors array, indicating the first scissor to be updated.
`scissorCount`	This is the total number of scissors in the `pScissors` array, whose parameters will be updated by the command.
`pScissors`	This is a pointer to an array of the `VkRect2D` structure specifying the 2D dimensions of the scissor area.

Implementation

Scissoring is initialized using the `initScissors()` function specifying the non-clipping region. Anything outside this rectangular region will be discarded. The `vkCmdSetScissor()` API sets the scissoring parameters, which can be dynamically set, indicating the rectangular dimensions used for single or multiple scissoring:

```
void VulkanDrawable::recordCommandBuffer(int currentImage, VkCommandBuffer* cmdDraw){
. . . .
    // Define the scissor here.initScissors(cmdDraw);
. . . .
}
void VulkanDrawable::initScissors(VkCommandBuffer* cmd)
{
    scissor.extent.width    = rendererObj->width;
    scissor.extent.height   = rendererObj->height;
    scissor.offset.x        = 0;
    scissor.offset.y        = 0;
```

```
        vkCmdSetScissor(*cmd, 0, NUMBER_OF_SCISSORS, &scissor);
}
```

Draw command

The draw command helps in assembling the primitives. Vulkan supports index- and nonindex-based draw commands. A draw command can affect the framebuffer by the order in which fragments are ordered. In cases where multiple instances of a draw command are used, the API order is used to process the draw commands. For nonindex-based commands, the rule is to put primitives with lowered number instances earlier in the order. For index-based commands, the primitive with a lower number of vertex index values is placed earlier in the API order.

Vulkan renders drawing objects by recording draw commands in the command buffer. There are four different drawing commands available in Vulkan, which are broadly divided into the following two types of categories:

- The first type (vkCmdDraw and vkCmdDrawIndexed) specifies the drawing parameters in the command buffer object itself
- In contrast, the second type (vkCmdDrawIndirect and vkCmdDrawIndexedIndirect) uses buffer memory to read the parameters from a drawing API, which is suffixed with the Indirect keyword and is of the latter type; otherwise, it's the former one

vkCmdDraw command

The vkCmdDraw() API reads the drawing parameters from the command buffer; the vertex information is accessed in the form of an array in sequential order, starting from the first vertex (firstVertex) to the total number of vertices specified by the vertexCount. The vkCmdDraw API renders primitives specified by the input assembly state under the pipeline state object using vertex array data information.

This API supports instancing, which allows efficient rendering of an object multiple times without calling multiple draw commands. Such drawing features are very helpful in situations such as crowd simulation, tree rendering, clone patterns, and so on. The total number of drawing instances is specified using instanceCount, starting from the first instance index indicated by firstInstance.

```
void vkCmdDraw(
    VkCommandBuffer    commandBuffer,
    uint32_t           vertexCount,
    uint32_t           instanceCount,
    uint32_t           firstVertex,
    uint32_t           firstInstance);
```

The fields and a description of each parameter follow:

Parameters	Description
commandBuffer	This field specifies the command buffer object (VkCommandBuffer) into which the recording is performed.
vertexCount	This is the total count of the vertex intended to draw.
instanceCount	This field indicates the total number of instances to be drawn using this command.
firstVertex	This field specifies the very first vertex index from which the vertices are read in order to draw them.
firstInstance	This field specifies the very first instance ID of the instance to draw.

The present example in this chapter makes use of the following command:

```
vkCmdDraw(*cmdDraw, 3, 1, 0, 0);
```

This command consumes the following triangle data, which represents three vertices in the interleaved form, hence the second parameter is specified as 3; since there is only one instance, the third parameter is 1. The drawing should start from the first vertex, which is indicated by index 0 as the fourth parameter. The last parameter is 0, pointing to the first instance ID:

```
struct VertexWithColor
{
    float x, y, z, w;    // Vertex Position
    float r, g, b, a;    // Color format Red, Green, Blue, Alpha
};

static const VertexWithColor triangleData[] =
{
    { 0.0f,  1.0f, 0.0f, 1.0f, 1.0f, 0.0f, 0.0f, 1.0 },/*Vertex0*/
    { 1.0f, -1.0f, 0.0f, 1.0f, 0.0f, 0.0f, 1.0f, 1.0 },/*Vertex1*/
    {-1.0f, -1.0f, 0.0f, 1.0f, 0.0f, 1.0f, 0.0f, 1.0 },/*Vertex2*/
};
```

Drawing Objects

> Another type of drawing command used in this chapter is the vkCmdDrawIndexed() API. This API renders indexed geometry. For detailed information, please refer to the *Rendering an indexed geometry* section at the end of this chapter. But before jumping to this section, you must work through all the remaining sections to understand the rendering of drawing objects in Vulkan.

Implementing drawing object preparation

The drawing object's preparation process is executed inside the recordCommandBuffer function of the VulkanDrawable class. This function records the commands associated with the drawing object for each swapchain buffer in a separate command buffer object (cmdDraw). The process includes the following steps.

Record the Render Pass instance using the vkCmdBeginRenderPass() API; this accepts the VkRenderPassBeginInfo class's object (renderPassBegin) as an input parameter, which contains the Render Pass and framebuffer objects that indicate the attachments, subpasses, and image views associated with this Render Pass instance. For more information on Render Pass and framebuffer objects, please refer to Chapter 7, *Buffer Resource, Render Pass, Framebuffer, and Shaders with SPIR-V*.

The other information the renderPassBegin carries is the extent of the drawing region on the framebuffer. In addition, the clear values for color, depth, or stencil image are also set inside. This information clears the buffer attachments associated with the specified clear value. For example, the clear value associated with the color buffer attachment works like a background color.

> The last parameter passed into the vkCmdBeginRenderPass is VK_SUBPASS_CONTENTS_INLINE; it indicates that only primary command buffers are supposed to record the subpass contents, and within this subpass, the secondary commands will not be executed.

Use vkCmdBindPipeline() and bind the command buffer with the graphics pipeline object that we created in Chapter 8, *Pipelines and Pipeline State Management*.

For dynamically setting the viewport and scissoring region, use initViewports() and initScissors() and set the vkCmdSetViewport() and vkCmdSetScissor() APIs with the required rectangular region dimensions.

> When the `vkCmdSetViewport()` and `vkCmdSetScissor()` APIs are used during runtime to specify the viewport and scissor dimensions, the dynamic states (`VkDynamicState`) must be enabled with `VK_DYNAMIC_STATE_VIEWPORT`.

Specify the draw command using the non-indexed drawing API `vkCmdDraw()`. The first argument specifies the command buffer object (`VkCommandBuffer`) into which the drawing command will be recorded. The second argument 3 specifies the number of vertices the geometry is intended to draw. The third argument 1 specifies that there needs to draw single instance at a time. The fourth argument specifies the first vertex index (0) to draw; the last argument 0 specifies the first index to be used for instance-based drawing responsible for controlling the rate at which data advances from an instanced array.

Finish the Render Pass instance recording using `vkCmdEndRenderPass()` and passing the current command buffer object into it.

The recording of the command buffer is implemented as follows:

```
void VulkanDrawable::recordCommandBuffer(int currentImage, VkCommandBuffer* cmdDraw)
{
    VulkanDevice* deviceObj                  = rendererObj->getDevice();
    VkClearValue clearValues[2];
    clearValues[0].color.float32[0]          = 0.0f;
    clearValues[0].color.float32[1]          = 0.0f;
    clearValues[0].color.float32[2]          = 0.0f;
    clearValues[0].color.float32[3]          = 0.0f;
    clearValues[1].depthStencil.depth        = 1.0f;
    clearValues[1].depthStencil.stencil      = 0;

    VkRenderPassBeginInfo renderPassBegin;
    renderPassBegin.sType                    = VK_STRUCTURE_TYPE_
                                               RENDER_PASS-_BEGIN_INFO;
    renderPassBegin.pNext                    = NULL;
    renderPassBegin.renderPass               = rendererObj->renderPass;
    renderPassBegin.framebuffer              = rendererObj->
                                               framebuffers[currentImage];
    renderPassBegin.renderArea.offset.x      = 0;
    renderPassBegin.renderArea.offset.y      = 0;
    renderPassBegin.renderArea.extent.width  = rendererObj->width;
    renderPassBegin.renderArea.extent.height = rendererObj->height;
    renderPassBegin.clearValueCount          = 2;
    renderPassBegin.pClearValues             = clearValues;

    // Start recording the render pass instance
    vkCmdBeginRenderPass(*cmdDraw, &renderPassBegin,
```

```
                VK_SUBPASS_CONTENTS_INLINE);

                // Bound the command buffer with the graphics pipeline
                vkCmdBindPipeline(*cmdDraw, VK_PIPELINE_BIND_POINT_GRAPHICS,
                *pipeline);

                // Bound the command buffer with the graphics pipeline
                const VkDeviceSize offsets[1] = { 0 };
                vkCmdBindVertexBuffers(*cmdDraw, 0, 1, &VertexBuffer.buf,
                offsets);

                // Define the dynamic viewport here
                initViewports(cmdDraw);

                // Define the scissoring
                initScissors(cmdDraw);

                // Issue the draw command with 3 vertex, 1 instance starting
                // from first vertex
                vkCmdDraw(*cmdDraw, 3, 1, 0, 0);

                // End of render pass instance recording
                vkCmdEndRenderPass(*cmdDraw);

        }
```

Rendering the drawing object

Once the Render Pass instance is prepared and recorded successfully in the drawing object's command buffer, we can reuse it each time to draw the object.

Drawing an object comprises three steps. First, we will need to *acquire the index to the next available swapchain image* onto which the primitive will be drawn or rasterized. Second, we will need to *submit the command buffer* to the graphics queue to execute the recorded command on the GPU; the GPU executes these commands and paints the available swapchain drawing images with the draw commands. Finally, the *drawn image is handed over to the presentation engine,* which renders the output onto the attached display window. The following subsections will describe each of these three steps in detail.

Acquiring the swapchain image

Before executing the Render Pass instance-recorded commands, we will need to acquire a swapchain image onto which the drawings will be performed. For this, we will need to query the index of the swapchain image that will be available from the system using the WSI extension `vkAcquireNextImageKHR()`; this will return the index of the swapchain image that your application will render to. This extension is available in the form of a function pointer of type `PFN_vkAcquireNextImageKHR`.

Upon the API call, it acquires the presentable image onto which the current command buffer will be used to paint and notifies the application that the target presentable image has changed.

> Multiple factors influence the availability of presentable images when the API is called. This includes presentation engine implementation, how the `VkPresentModeKHR` is being used, the total number of images in the swapchain, the number of images that the application owns at any given time, and of course the application's performance.

```
VkResult vkAcquireNextImageKHR(
    VkDevice            device,
    VkSwapchainKHR      swapchain,
    uint64_t            timeout,
    VkSemaphore         semaphore,
    VkFence             fence,
    uint32_t*           pImageIndex);
```

The fields and a description of each parameter follow:

Parameters	Description
`device`	This indicates the logical `VkDevice`, which is associated with the swapchain object.
`swapchain`	This indicates the swapchain object (`VkSwapchainKHR`) from which the drawing image will be acquired.
`timeout`	This parameter indicates whether the API is blocking or nonblocking. When a time-out (in nanosecond) is specified, it indicates for how long the function waits or blocks, if no image is available. If the time-out is 0, then this API will not block and return the success or failure error. This field guarantees that the `vkAcquireNextImageKHR()` API never blocks the system and returns the ownership after a finite time in case of failure.

Drawing Objects

semaphore	This is the `VkSemaphore` object and must be unsignaled and should not have any uncompleted signal or wait operations pending. It will be signaled when the presentation engine has released ownership of the image and the device can modify its contents. If not used in the API, this can be equal to `VK_NULL_HANDLE`.
fence	This is a `VkFence` object and must be unsignaled and not have any uncompleted signal operations pending. It will become signaled when the presentation engine has released ownership of the image. If not used in the API, this can be equal to `VK_NULL_HANDLE`. This can be used to measure the frame generation work that matches the presentation rate.
pImageIndex	This retrieves the index of the next presentable image. This index belongs to the index into the array of image handles returned by the `vkGetSwapchainImagesKHR()` API. If the API does not return the `VK_SUCCESS` instance, it means the pointed index is not modified.

> `vkAcquireNextImageKHR()` cannot have both semaphore and fence specified as `VK_NULL_HANDLE`; one of them must be a valid input.

The following table specifies the return value from the `vkAcquireNextImageKHR()` API, which depends on the timeout field:

Return value	Description
`VK_SUCCESS`	This means that it has successfully acquired the presentable image.
`VK_ERROR_SURFACE_LOST_KHR`	This appears when the presentable surface is no longer available.
`VK_NOT_READY`	This indicates that no image is available and when `timeout` is 0.
`VK_TIMEOUT`	When `timeout` is a nonzero mean (> 0 and <`UINT64_MAX`), this indicates that no presentable image is available in the allowed duration.
`VK_SUBOPTIMAL_KHR`	In this case, the returned presentable image no longer matches with swapchain surface properties, but it can still be used.

VK_ERROR_OUT_OF_DATE_KHR	Here, the returned presentable image is no longer compatible with the swapchain and thus cannot be further used for presentation with swapchain. In this case, the application must query the compatible surface properties and recreate the swapchain with the required surface properties in order to continue with presentation service.

Executing the drawing command buffer object

The drawing command buffer object is executed by submitting it into the graphics queue using the `CommandBufferMgr::submitCommandBuffer()` function, which internally calls the `vkQueueSubmit()` API to submit the command buffer.

> For more information on the `submitCommandBuffer()` API and its usage, please refer to *Chapter 5*, *Command Buffer and Memory Management in Vulkan*. In this chapter, you can refer to the subsection *Submitting the command to queue* under *Implementing the wrapper class for command buffer*.

Displaying the output with the presentation engine

When the drawing object's command buffer is executed, the target presentation image is painted with the recorded commands. This image is then queued to the presentation engine using the `vkQueuePresentKHR()` API, which renders the output presentation image onto the display output.

```
VkResult vkQueuePresentKHR(
    VkQueue                  queue,
    const VkPresentInfoKHR*  pPresentInfo);
```

The following parameters are used inside the `vkQueuePresentKHR()` API:

Parameters	Description
queue	This is a `VkQueue` object, which is capable of presentation and has graphics queue capabilities. Also, this queue belongs to the same device as the image's swapchain.
pPresentInfo	This is a pointer to a `VkPresentInfoKHR` structure specifying the presentation metadata.

[335]

Drawing Objects

The following is the syntax and description of `VkPresentInfoKHR()`:

```
typedef struct VkPresentInfoKHR {
    VkStructureType         sType;
    const void*             pNext;
    uint32_t                waitSemaphoreCount;
    const VkSemaphore*      pWaitSemaphores;
    uint32_t                swapchainCount;
    const VkSwapchainKHR*   pSwapchains;
    const uint32_t*         pImageIndices;
    VkResult*               pResults;
} VkPresentInfoKHR;
```

The fields and a description of each parameter follow:

Parameters	Description
`sType`	This specifies the type of this structure; this must be `VK_STRUCTURE_TYPE_PRESENT_INFO_KHR`.
`pNext`	This could be a valid pointer to an extension-specific structure or could be `NULL`.
`waitSemaphoreCount`	This field indicates the count of semaphores the presentation engine should wait on before displaying the image.
`pWaitSemaphores`	This specifies the semaphores to wait on before issuing the present request. This is a `Non-NULL VkSemaphore` object array with size equal to `waitSemaphoreCount`.
`swapchainCount`	There can be more than one swapchain presented; this field indicates the number of swapchains that will be presented using this API command.
`pSwapchains`	This indicates an array of the `VkSwapchainKHR` objects with size equal to the `swapchainCount` entries.
`pImageIndices`	This is an array of presentable image indices of each swapchain's presentable images, with total entries specified by `swapchainCount`. Each entry in the index array indicates the presentable image that will be used in the presentation.
`pResults`	This field, if `non-NULL`, returns the status (`VkResult` typed) for each presentable image; the number of entries is equal to `swapchainCount`. If an application does not require the per-swapchain results, the `pResults` can be set as `NULL`.

Chapter 9

> The `vkQueuePresentKHR` is capable of presenting multiple presentable images from corresponding swapchains. It releases the ownership of the images (indicated by `pImageIndices`; refer to the following `VkPresentInfoKHR`) to the presentation engine. These presented images must not be used again until the application regains control of them using the `vkAcquireNextImageKHR()` API (and must wait until the returned semaphore is signaled, or fence is completed).

The presentation images sent to the queue are always processed in order; the transfer of the ownership of a presentation image to the presentation engine happens with the submission in the queue. These presentable images are only performed if the submitted semaphore is signaled, indicating that no prior rendering operation is pending. The presentation time is very implementation-specific; it may be affected by the semantics of the presentation engine and the native platform in use.

The following table specifies the return value from the `vkQueuePresentKHR()` API:

Return value	Description
VK_SUCCESS	This means that it has successfully acquired the presentable image.
VK_ERROR_SURFACE_LOST_KHR	This appears when the presentable surface is no longer available.
VK_SUBOPTIMAL_KHR	In this case, the returned presentable image no longer matches with swapchain surface properties, but it can still be used for paint purposes successfully.
VK_ERROR_OUT_OF_DATE_KHR	Here, the returned presentable image is no longer compatible with the swapchain and thus cannot be further used for presentation with the swapchain. In this case, the application must query the compatible surface properties and recreate the swapchain with the required surface properties in order to continue with the presentation service.

Drawing Objects

When a presentable image is given to the presentation engine, the presentation does not change the contents of this image. If this image is again reacquired using `vkAcquireNextImageKHR()` and the transitioning is taken away from the `VK_IMAGE_LAYOUT_PRESENT_SRC_KHR` layout, even then the contents remain the same as they were before transitioning. In contrast, if some other mechanism modifies the platform window other than Vulkan, then the contents of all the presentable images in the swapchain become undefined.

Implementing drawing object rendering

Let's understand the implemented rendering code. First, acquire the presentable image index using the `vkAcquireNextImageKHR()` API extension; the index is returned in the `currentColorImage` variable. This swapchain extension is stored as a function pointer (`fpAcquireNextImageKHR`) in the `VulkanRender`class.

> For more information on querying swapchain extensions, please refer to the subsection *Querying swapchain extensions* in `Chapter 6`, *Allocating Image Resources and Building a Swapchain with WSI*.

You must provide at least one of the sync objects (semaphore or fence); otherwise, you will have no idea when you can use the image. For example, your image will still be read by the presentation engine when you try to acquire it. The `vkAcquireNextImageKHR()` is permitted to return as soon as it has identified the image that it has to give you next, not when that image is actually usable. For this reason, synchronization is very important at this step. Vulkan provides two ways to synchronize the swapchain image using *semaphore* and *fences*. When semaphore and fences are used, they ensure that when the image is acquired it has no previous pending operation (such as the presentation engine reading it).

In this example, we used a semaphore object (`presentCompleteSemaphore`) for synchronization purposes; this object is passed into the `vkAcquireNextImageKHR()` to be associated with the image, and this semaphore is signaled when the image can be rendered.

Use the retrieved image index (`currentColorImage`) and get the corresponding command buffer from the `vecCmdDraw` vector. Create the `VkSubmitInfo` control structure and specify the create semaphore object (`presentCompleteSemaphore`) in order to submit the command buffer. Upon submission, the commands will only begin execution when a semaphore is signaled; in other words, the image is ready to paint with drawing commands.

As a final approach, the painted image is then queued in the presentation engine for display purposes using the `fpQueuePresentKHR` API (`vkQueuePresentKHR`), transferring the ownership to the presentation engine. It is very important to ensure that when an image is used by the presentation engine it is not being painted or has any pending operations since the last command buffer submission. This can be simply checked using another semaphore object called `drawingCompleteSemaphore`; this object is passed into the `VkSubmitInfo` class `pSignalSemaphores` field before the command buffer is submitted into the queue. This semaphore is signaled when the command buffer is successfully processed, removing any chance to overlap with the presentation engine's ownership. Once the presentable image is displayed, the presentation engine relinquishes the ownership. `vkAcquireNextImageKHR()` can query the same image again and get the ownership.

The following is the implementation code that demonstrates the rendering of the object in Vulkan:

```
void VulkanDrawable::render()
{
  VulkanDevice* deviceObj       = rendererObj->getDevice();
  VulkanSwapChain* swapChainObj = rendererObj->getSwapChain();
  uint32_t&currentColorImage    = swapChainObj->
             scPublicVars.currentColorBuffer;
  VkSwapchainKHR& swapChain     = swapChainObj->
             scPublicVars.swapChain;

  VkFence nullFence             = VK_NULL_HANDLE;
  // Get the index of the next available swapchain image:
  VkResult result = swapChainObj->fpAcquireNextImageKHR(
  deviceObj->device, swapChain,UINT64_MAX,
  presentCompleteSemaphore, VK_NULL_HANDLE,
  &currentColorImage);

  VkPipelineStageFlags submitPipelineStages =
  VK_PIPELINE_STAGE_COLOR_ATTACHMENT_OUTPUT_BIT;

  // Prepare the submit into control structure
  VkSubmitInfo submitInfo = {};
  submitInfo.sType= VK_STRUCTURE_TYPE_SUBMIT_INFO;
  submitInfo.pNext= NULL;
  submitInfo.waitSemaphoreCount = 1;
  submitInfo.pWaitSemaphores= &presentCompleteSemaphore;
  submitInfo.pWaitDstStageMask= &submitPipelineStages;
  submitInfo.commandBufferCount= (uint32_t)sizeof(&vecCmdDraw
  [currentColorImage]) / sizeof(VkCommandBuffer);
  submitInfo.pCommandBuffers   = &vecCmdDraw[currentColorImage];
  submitInfo.signalSemaphoreCount= 1;
  submitInfo.pSignalSemaphores   = &drawingCompleteSemaphore;
```

Drawing Objects

```
    // Queue the command buffer for execution
    CommandBufferMgr::submitCommandBuffer(deviceObj->queue,
    &cmdDraw[currentColorImage],&submitInfo);
    // Present the image in the window
    VkPresentInfoKHR present;
    present.sType = VK_STRUCTURE_TYPE_PRESENT_INFO_KHR;
    present.pNext = NULL;
    present.swapchainCount= 1;
    present.pSwapchains= &swapChain;
    present.pImageIndices= &currentColorImage;
    present.pWaitSemaphores= &drawingCompleteSemaphore;
    present.waitSemaphoreCount= 1;
    present.pResults= NULL;
    // Queue the image for presentation,
    result = swapChainObj->fpQueuePresentKHR
    (deviceObj->queue, &present);
    assert(result == VK_SUCCESS);
}
```

The semaphore objects are created in the constructor of the `drawable` class and reused throughout the application as shown in the following.

```
VulkanDrawable::VulkanDrawable(VulkanRenderer* parent) {
    memset(&VertexBuffer, 0, sizeof(VertexBuffer));
    rendererObj = parent;

    // Prepare the semaphore create info data structure
    VkSemaphoreCreateInfo presentCompleteSemaphoreCreateInfo;
    presentCompleteSemaphoreCreateInfo.sType =
    VK_STRUCTURE_TYPE_SEMAPHORE_CREATE_INFO;
    presentCompleteSemaphoreCreateInfo.pNext = NULL;
    presentCompleteSemaphoreCreateInfo.flags = 0;
    VkSemaphoreCreateInfo drawingCompleteSemaphoreCreateInfo;
    drawingCompleteSemaphoreCreateInfo.sType =
    VK_STRUCTURE_TYPE_SEMAPHORE_CREATE_INFO;
    drawingCompleteSemaphoreCreateInfo.pNext = NULL;
    drawingCompleteSemaphoreCreateInfo.flags = 0;

    VulkanDevice* deviceObj = VulkanApplication::GetInstance()->
    deviceObj;

    vkCreateSemaphore(deviceObj->device,
    &presentCompleteSemaphoreCreateInfo, NULL,
    &presentCompleteSemaphore);

    vkCreateSemaphore(deviceObj->device,
    &drawingCompleteSemaphoreCreateInfo, NULL,
    &drawingCompleteSemaphore);
```

}

These semaphore objects can be destroyed using the user-defined `destroySynchronizationObjects()` function during the de-initialization process:

```
void VulkanDrawable::destroySynchronizationObjects()
{
   VulkanApplication* appObj = VulkanApplication::GetInstance();
   VulkanDevice* deviceObj = appObj->deviceObj;
   vkDestroySemaphore(deviceObj->device,
   presentCompleteSemaphore, NULL);
   vkDestroySemaphore(deviceObj->device,
   drawingCompleteSemaphore, NULL);
}
```

The following is the output of the program:

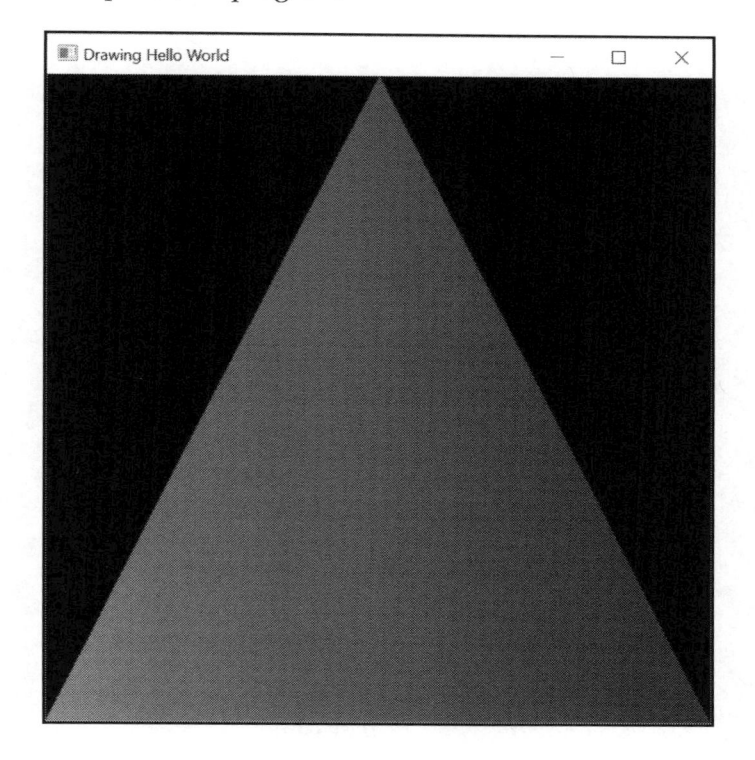

Drawing Objects

Rendering an indexed geometry

In this section, you will learn to use the `vkCmdDrawIndexed()` draw command. This command is used for drawing the index geometry. The `vkCmdDrawIndexed()` API is an index buffer's draw command. In an index buffer, each vertex is represented using an index number. This fashion of representing mesh data requires less memory and storage space to represent connected meshes when the mesh has shared vertices (such as enclosed shapes).

For example, a square geometry rendered using two triangles shares two common vertices as shown in the following example; as you can see, the first and third vertices are repeated:

```
static const VertexWithColor squareData[] =
{
  { -0.5f,  0.5f, 0.0f, 1.0f, 1.0f, 1.0f, 0.0f, 1.0 },
  {  0.5f,  0.5f, 0.0f, 1.0f, 1.0f, 0.0f, 0.0f, 1.0 },
  {  0.5f, -0.5f, 0.0f, 1.0f, 0.0f, 0.0f, 1.0f, 1.0 },
  { -0.5f, -0.5f, 0.0f, 1.0f, 0.0f, 1.0f, 0.0f, 1.0 },
};

uint16_t squareIndices[] = { 0,3,1, 3,2,1 }; // 6 indices
```

In this section, we will use the geometry data and indices to demonstrate the use of the `vkCmdDrawIndexed()` API. The following is the syntax:

```
void vkCmdDrawIndexed(
    VkCommandBuffer   commandBuffer,
    uint32_t          indexCount,
    uint32_t          instanceCount,
    uint32_t          firstIndex,
    int32_t           vertexOffset,
    uint32_t          firstInstance);
```

Let's take a look at the different fields used in this API and their respective descriptions:

Parameter	Description
`commandBuffer`	This field specifies the command buffer object (`VkCommandBuffer`) into which the recording is performed.
`indexCount`	This is the total count of the index elements in the index list of the buffer resources that are intended to be drawn.
`instanceCount`	This field indicates the total number of instances to be drawn using this command.
`firstIndex`	This field specifies the first index (into the indices) from where the indices are read.

`vertexOffset`	This field specifies an offset value that will be added into the vertex index to produce a resultant index. This computed index then is used to read the vertex from the vertex buffer.
`firstInstance`	This field specifies the very first instance ID into the instances to draw.

The following are the steps to render an indexed draw:

1. Using `squareData` and `squareIndices`, create a buffer resource (`VkBuffer`). Store `VkBuffer`'s handles in `VertexBuffer::buf` and `VertexIndex::idx`. For more information, please refer to the *Indexed Draw* example provided in this chapter.
2. Bind the vertex buffer using `vkCmdBindVertexBuffers()` and pass `VertexBuffer.buf` into it.
3. Similarly, the index buffer (`VertexIndex.idx`) is bound using the `vkCmdBindIndexBuffer()` API command.
4. Draw the object using `vkCmdDrawIndexed()`.

`vkCmdDrawIndexed()` is used in conjunction with the `vkCmdBindIndexBuffer()` API. Similar to `vkCmdBindVertexBuffers()`, which binds the vertex buffer, this command binds the index buffer. The following is the syntax of this API; for more information on the `vkCmdBindVertexBuffers()` API, please refer to the *Specifying the drawing object geometry information* section.

```
void vkCmdBindIndexBuffer(
    VkCommandBuffer         commandBuffer,
    VkBuffer                buffer,
    VkDeviceSize            offset,
    VkIndexType             indexType);
```

Let's take a look at the different fields used in this API and their respective descriptions:

Parameter	Description
`commandBuffer`	This specifies the command buffer object into which this command–`vkCmdBindIndexBuffer()`–will be recorded.
`buffer`	This indicates the handle of the index buffer (`VkBuffer`) that will be bound to this API.
`offset`	This is the starting offset specified in bytes in the index buffer that will be used for index buffer address calculation.

Drawing Objects

indexType	This field indicates whether the indices are 16-bits or 32-bits wide. This must be one of the `VkIndexType` types:
	`typedef enum VkIndexType {`
	`VK_INDEX_TYPE_UINT16 = 0,`
	`VK_INDEX_TYPE_UINT32 = 1,`
	`} VkIndexType;`

Similar to the `createVertexBuffer()` function, we have created a new function called `createIndexBuffer()`; it creates the index buffer and stores the index buffer handle in `VertexIndex.idx`. For a detailed implementation of this function, please refer to the accompanying source code. The implementation of `createIndexBuffer()` is very similar to `createVertexBuffer()`; for a detailed understanding on the implementation of this function, please refer to *Implementing the buffer resource–creating the vertex buffer for the geometry* in Chapter 7, *Buffer Resource, Render Pass, Framebuffer, and Shaders with SPIR-V*.

The following code demonstrates the rendering of the indexed geometry object:

```
// Local data structure in VulkanDrawable class
// for storing vertex buffer and index buffer metadata
struct {
   VkBuffer buf;
   VkDeviceMemory mem;
   VkDescriptorBufferInfo bufferInfo;
} VertexBuffer;

struct {
   VkBuffer idx;
   VkDeviceMemory mem;
   VkDescriptorBufferInfo bufferInfo;
} VertexIndex;

// Create the VkBuffer and store the handle in
// VertexBuffer.buf and VertexIndex.idx
. . . .
// Bind the vertex buffer
const VkDeviceSize offsets[1] = { 0 };
vkCmdBindVertexBuffers(*cmdDraw, 0, 1,&VertexBuffer.buf,
                                                offsets);

// Bind the Index buffer
vkCmdBindIndexBuffer(*cmdDraw, VertexIndex.idx,
               0, VK_INDEX_TYPE_UINT16);

// Draw the object
vkCmdDrawIndexed(*cmdDraw, 6, 1, 0, 0, 0);
```

The output of the preceding geometry data will be displayed as follows; for detailed code, please refer to the *Indexed Draw* example in this chapter:

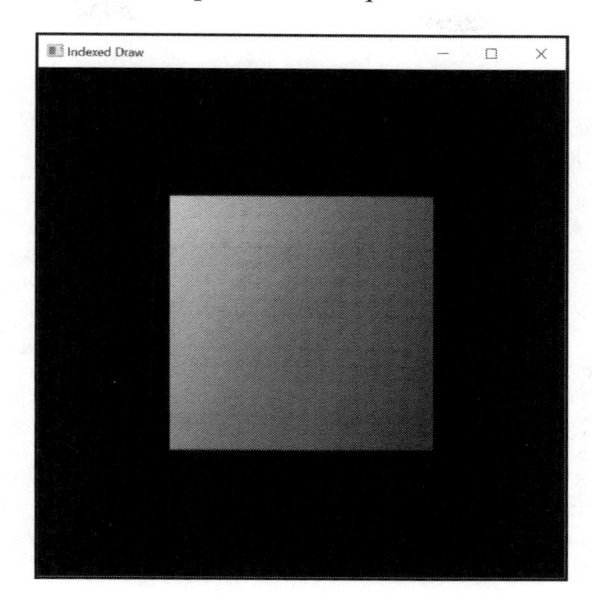

The `vkCmdDrawIndirect` and `vkCmdDrawIndexedIndirect` draw commands are very similar to `vkCmdDraw` and `vkCmdDrawIndexed`, except that the parameters here are read from the buffer memory. For more information on these APIs, please refer to the official Vulkan specification.

Understanding synchronization primitives in Vulkan

Synchronization is key to bringing order and discipline into asynchronous system. It not only improves resource utilization, it also benefits from parallelism by reducing CPU and GPU idle time.

Drawing Objects

Vulkan offers the following four types of synchronization primitive for concurrent execution:

- **Fences**: Offer synchronization between the host and device
- **Semaphores**: Synchronize between and within queues
- **Events**: Between queue submissions
- **Barriers**: Within a command buffer between commands

In this section, we will learn about synchronization primitives and understand their API specification. The drawing object example that we implemented in this chapter makes use of semaphores to synchronize swapchain image writing. In the next chapter, we will learn to draw textures and implement fence to synchronize the host and device.

Fences

When a host submits a command in a queue, it gets scheduled for device processing. Sometimes it may require to know the status of command execution on the GPU in order to control the execution of the next batch, to ensure that it never overlaps with the previous batch of commands, which may produce undefined results or a situation that causes resource access violation.

Fence provides synchronization between the host and the GPU; using this, an application instructs the host to wait until a certain submitted operation is completed. This way, the GPU can be prevented from piling up more operations into the command queues:

Creating the fence object: The fence object can be created using the vkCreateFence() API.

```
VkResult vkCreateFence(
    VkDevice                        device,
    const VkFenceCreateInfo*        pCreateInfo,
    const VkAllocationCallbacks*    pAllocator,
    VkFence*                        pFence);
```

Let's take a look at the different fields used in this API and their respective descriptions:

Parameter	Description
device	This is the logical device object, which will be used to create the fence object.
pCreateInfo	This is a pointer to an array of the VkFenceCreateInfo control structure.

pAllocator	This controls the host memory allocation. You can refer to *Host memory*, Chapter 5, *Command Buffer and Memory Management in Vulkan* for more information.
pFence	This is the handle of the created fence object.

The `vkCreateFence()` API takes `VkFenceCreateInfo` containing metadata, which is used to control the creation of the fence objects. Following is the syntax of this control structure:

```
typedef struct VkFenceCreateInfo {
    VkStructureType       sType;
    const void*           pNext;
    VkFenceCreateFlags    flags;
} VkFenceCreateInfo;
```

It has three fields: the first field `sType` indicates the type information of this structure, which must be `VK_STRUCTURE_TYPE_FENCE_CREATE_INFO`; the second field `pNext` is not in use and must be `NULL`; the last parameter is `VkFenceCreateFlagBits` (see the following code snippet), which indicates whether the created fence object will be in a signaled or nonsignaled state. The signal state is specified using `VK_FENCE_CREATE_SIGNALED_BIT`.

```
typedef enum VkFenceCreateFlagBits {
    VK_FENCE_CREATE_SIGNALED_BIT = 0x00000001,
} VkFenceCreateFlagBits;
```

Waiting on the fence object: Once a valid fence object is created, the host can inject this into a command and wait for it using the `vkWaitForFences()` API until it is not processed by the device. The device signals the fence object as soon as it processes the associated command, allowing the host to unblock the waiting state. Following is the API syntax:

```
VkResult vkWaitForFences(
    VkDevice              device,
    uint32_t              fenceCount,
    const VkFence*        pFences,
    VkBool32              waitAll,
    uint64_t              timeout);
```

Drawing Objects

The `vkWaitForFences` API takes the following parameters:

Parameters	Description
`device`	This is the logical device object (`VkDevice`) that will be used to destroy the fence object.
`fenceCount`	This is number of the fence object that needs to be destroyed.
`PFences`	This is an array of fence objects handles that needs to be destroyed. The array size must be equal to `fenceCount`.
`waitAll`	The block can be unblocked using this Boolean flag. When this flag value is: • **VK_TRUE**: It indicates that all the `pFences` must be signaled in order to successfully unblock the waiting. • **VK_FALSE**: At least one fence object in the `pFences` array must be signaled for successfully unblocking the wait state.
`timeOut`	This is the time-out period, specified (in nano seconds), which will be used to unblock the wait state if the fence object never got signaled. This field guarantees that the system never falls into an infinite blocking state that will bring the application to a halt.

Destroying the fence object: Once the fence is used and no longer required, it can be destroyed using the `vkDestroyFence()` API; this API takes three parameters–the first parameter `device` is the logical device that will be used to destroy the fence object, which is indicated by the second parameter called `fence`; the last parameter (`pAllocator`) manages host memory deallocation:

```
void vkDestroyFence(
    VkDevice                        device,
    VkFence                         fence,
    const VkAllocationCallbacks*    pAllocator);
```

Resetting the fence object: The application can also preserve the created fence object and reuse it by resetting them using `vkResetFences()`. This API takes three parameters as an input–the first parameter indicates the logical device to be used to reset the given fence objects. The number of fence objects that need to be reset is pointed by the second parameter called `fenceCount`. The last parameter `pFences` is a pointer of the array of fence objects that will be reset by this API. The following is the syntax of this API:

```
VkResult vkResetFences(
    VkDevice            device,
    uint32_t            fenceCount,
    const VkFence*      pFences);
```

Let's move to the next synchronization primitive: semaphores.

Semaphores

Semaphores give the flexibility to achieve synchronization at the queue level; they are used to synchronize one or more queues. A Semaphore has two states: *signaled* and *unsignaled*. Signaled semaphores are specified in the queue submission command `vkQueueSubmit()`; it blocks the rest of the batch until the semaphores are not unsignaled by the device. A created semaphore is visible across multiple queues. If two or more queue submission commands are waiting upon the same semaphore, then only one will receive the signaled state; others may continue to wait, ensuring atomicity.

Creating semaphore object: Semaphores are created using the `vkCreateSemaphore()` API; the following is the syntax of this API:

```
VkResult vkCreateSemaphore(
    VkDevice                         device,
    const VkSemaphoreCreateInfo*     pCreateInfo,
    const VkAllocationCallbacks*     pAllocator,
    VkSemaphore*                     pSemaphore);
```

The `vkCreateSemaphore` API takes the following parameters:

Parameter	Description
device	This is the logical device object, which will be used to create the semaphore object.
pCreateInfo	This is the pointer to an array of the `VkSemaphoreCreateInfo` control structure.
pAllocator	This controls host memory allocation. You can refer to *Host memory*, Chapter 5, *Command Buffer and Memory Management in Vulkan* for more information.
pSemaphore	This is the handle of the created semaphore object.

The `VkSemaphoreCreateInfo` type structure has three parameters–the first parameter `sType` indicates the type information of this control structure; the second parameter is `pNext`, which could be a valid pointer to an extension-specific structure or could be `NULL`. The last parameter is a flag value (`flags`), which is currently not being used and is reserved for future purposes. The following is the syntax of this structure:

```
typedef struct VkSemaphoreCreateInfo {
    VkStructureType          sType;
    const void*              pNext;
    VkSemaphoreCreateFlags   flags;
} VkSemaphoreCreateInfo;
```

Destroying a semaphore: The created semaphore is destroyed using `vkDestroySemaphore()` as declared in the following syntax. This API takes three parameters. The first parameter `device` is the logical device that will destroy the semaphore object specified in the second parameter (`semaphore`). The last parameter (`pAllocator`) manages host memory deallocation:

```
void vkDestroySemaphore(
    VkDevice                      device,
    VkSemaphore                   semaphore,
    const VkAllocationCallbacks*  pAllocator);
```

In this chapter, we used semaphores to ensure that a given swapchain image is only being used if it is not read by the presentation engine, in other words, when the presentation has finished reading the swapchain image and is ready to render it. For this, we created a semaphore object and passed it into `vkAcquireNextImageKHR()`; this API signals the semaphore when the image is ready to render. This signaled semaphore is next passed to `vkQueueSubmit()` using the `VkSubmitInfo` control structure; this ensures that drawing commands must only be drawn to the presentation image when it is not being used. The `vkQueueSubmit()` unsignals the semaphore, unblocking the next command (`vkQueuePresentKHR`) to be executed; this command renders the image to the output display.

Events

Events controls fine-grained synchronization and can exist in both signaled and unsignaled states. It allows synchronization of work within a single command buffer or sequence of command buffers submitted to a queue. Both the host and device can signal or reset the events. Similarly, both can wait on the event object; however, the device is only allowed to wait at some specific pipeline stage within the pipeline. You will learn more as we will proceed through the API specification:

Creating the event object: The event can be created using `vkCreateEvent()` API. This API accepts three parameters; the syntax is provided as follows:

```
VkResult vkCreateEvent(
    VkDevice                      device,
    const VkEventCreateInfo*      pCreateInfo,
    const VkAllocationCallbacks*  pAllocator,
    VkEvent*                      pEvent);
```

The `vkCreateEvent` API takes four parameters as described in the following table:

Parameter	Description
device	This is the logical device object, which will be used to create the event object.
pCreateInfo	Thhis is the pointer to an array of `VkEventCreateInfo` control structures.
pAllocator	This controls host memory allocation. You can refer to *Host memory*, Chapter 5, *Command Buffer and Memory Management in Vulkan* for more information.
pSemaphore	This is the handle of the created event object.

The `VkEventCreateInfo` structure has three parameters: the first parameter (`sType`) describes the type information of this create info data structure; it must be `VK_STRUCTURE_TYPE_EVENT_CREATE_INFO`. The second parameter is `pNext`; this could be a valid pointer to an extension-specific structure or could be `NULL`. The last parameter is flag value (`flags`), which is currently not being used and reserved for future purposes. Following is the syntax of this structure:

```
typedef struct VkEventCreateInfo {
    VkStructureType     sType;
    const void*         pNext;
    VkEventCreateFlags  flags;
} VkEventCreateInfo;
```

Destroying the event object: The created event is destroyed using `vkDestroyEvent()` when the event is no longer in use. This API takes three parameters—the first parameter `device` is the logical device that will destroy the event object specified by the second parameter (`semaphore`). The last parameter (`pAllocator`) manages host memory deallocation.

```
void vkDestroyEvent(
    VkDevice                     device,
    VkEvent                      event,
    const VkAllocationCallbacks* pAllocator);
```

Querying the event status: The event can be queried to check whether it is in the signaled or nonsignaled state. This is done using the `vkGetEventStatus()` API; the first parameter (`device`) of this API is the logical device (`VkDevice`) that owns the event object; the second parameter (`event`) is the event handle whose status is being queried. The following is the syntax of this API:

```
VkResult vkGetEventStatus(
    VkDevice    device,
    VkEvent     event);
```

This API returns `VK_EVENT_SET`, which indicates the event is signaled; for an unsignaled event, it returns `VK_EVENT_RESET`.

Setting and resetting events: Events can be set using `vkSetEvent()` and `vkResetEvent()`. Both APIs accept the same input parameters as described above for the `vkGetEventStatus()` API; for more information, please refer to `vkSetEvent` and `vkResetEvent` syntax:

vkSetEvent API	vkResetEvent API

`VkResult vkCmdSetEvent(`
`VkDevice device,`
`VkEvent  event);`
	`VkResult vkSetEvent(`
	`VkDevice device,`
	`VkEvent  event);`

Signaling and unsignaling an event from a device: An event can be updated to *set* or *reset* on the device using command buffers. The `vkCmdSetEvent()` and `vkCmdResetEvent()` APIs are used to *signal* and *unsignal* the events, respectively; following is the syntax of these APIs:

vkCmdSetEvent API	vkCmdResetEvent API

`VkResult vkCmdSetEvent(`
`VkCommandBuffer`
`commandBuffer,`
`VkEvent`
`event,`
`VkPipelineStageFlags`
`stageMask);`
	`VkResult vkCmdResetEvent(`
	`VkCommandBuffer`
	`commandBuffer,`
	`VkEvent`
	`event,`
	`VkPipelineStageFlags`
	`stageMask);`

Both APIs accept the following three parameters: the first parameter (`commandBuffer`) specifies the command buffer in which this command will be recorded. The second parameter (`event`) indicates the handle of the event object, which needs to be signaled or unsignaled. The last parameter (`stageMask`) is the `VkPipelineStageFlags` pipeline stage, indicating the point at which the event's state will be updated.

Waiting on event objects: One or more event objects can be waited upon to signal using the `vkCmdWaitEvents()` API. The following is the syntax of this API:

```
void vkCmdWaitEvents(
    VkCommandBuffer              commandBuffer,
    uint32_t                     eventCount,
    const VkEvent*               pEvents,
    VkPipelineStageFlags         srcStageMask,
    VkPipelineStageFlags         dstStageMask,
    uint32_t                     memoryBarrierCount,
    const VkMemoryBarrier*       pMemoryBarriers,
    uint32_t                     bufferMemoryBarrierCount,
    const VkBufferMemoryBarrier* pBufferMemoryBarriers,
    uint32_t                     imageMemoryBarrierCount,
    const VkImageMemoryBarrier*  pImageMemoryBarriers);
```

Drawing Objects

The fields and a description of each parameter follow:

Parameter	Description
`commandBuffer`	This is the command buffer object into which this command will be captured or recorded.
`eventCount`	This is the number of event objects to be waited upon.
`pEvents`	This is the array of the `VkEvent` objects; the size of the array must be equal to `eventCount`.
`srcStageMask`	This is the bitwise mask field that specifies the pipeline stages that will signal the event objects specified in the `pEvents` array.
`dstStageMask`	This is the bitwise mask field that specifies the pipeline stage at which the waiting should be performed.
`memoryBarrierCount`	This refers to the number of memory barriers.
`pMemoryBarriers`	This is the `VkBufferMemoryBarreir` object array that has the number of elements equal to `memoryBarrierCount`.
`bufferMemoryBarrierCount`	This refers to the number of buffer memory barriers.
`pBufferMemoryBarriers`	This refers to the `VkMemoryBarreir` object array that has the number of elements equal to `bufferMemoryBarrierCount`.
`imageMemoryBarrierCount`	This refers to the number of image type memory barriers.
`pImageMemoryBarriers`	This refers to the `VkImageMemoryBarrier` object array that has the number of elements equal to `imageMemoryBarrierCount`.

> Barrier have already been discussed and implemented in *Chapter 6, Allocating Image Resources and Building a Swapchain with WSI*; for more information, please refer to the *Image layout transition with memory barriers* section.

Resizing the display window

When a display window resizes, the Vulkan application is given the new window dimensions to re-paint the drawing images. On the Windows platform, the `WM_SIZE` message of the associated window's procedure can be used to indicate the change in the dimension size as shown in the following highlighted code. The new changes added to the `WndProc()` function are highlighted with bold; the new dimension size is updated to the `VulkanSwapChain` class using the `setSwapChainExtent()` function, which will be later used to recreate the new swapchain images with the indicated dimensions:

```
LRESULT CALLBACK VulkanRenderer::WndProc(HWND hWnd, UINT uMsg,
WPARAM wParam, LPARAM lParam)
{
  VulkanApplication* appObj = VulkanApplication::GetInstance();
  switch (uMsg)
 {
  case WM_CLOSE:
  PostQuitMessage(0);
  break;
  case WM_PAINT:
  // Many lines skipped please, refer to the source code
  case WM_SIZE:
  if (wParam != SIZE_MINIMIZED) {
  appObj->rendererObj->width = lParam & 0xffff;
  appObj->rendererObj->height = (lParam &
  0xffff0000) >> 16;
  appObj->rendererObj->getSwapChain()->
  setSwapChainExtent(appObj->rendererObj->
  width, appObj->rendererObj->height);
  appObj->resize()
 }
  break;

  default:
  break;
}
  return (DefWindowProc(hWnd, uMsg, wParam, lParam));
}
```

The `VulkanApplication` class is added with a new function called `resize()`; this function handles resize activities. The Vulkan application's resize function is called by the `VulkanRenderer::WndProc()` when a resize event happens.

Drawing Objects

The `resize()` function destroys created resources and recreates them again. The resource preparation status can be checked using the `isPrepared` flag in `VulkanApplication`; if this flag is false, it means resources are not prepared yet and resizing cannot be performed.

When the resources are recreated, the old swapchain images are destroyed and created again to match the new window size.

> A swapchain image must only be recreated when it is not being used by any pending command or presentation operation. This can be ensured by calling the `vkDeviceWaitIdle()` API; this API guarantees that there is no pending operation on this device. This API keeps the host waiting until the device become idle.

When the waiting in resize function finishes, it can go ahead and recreate the swapchain images; but before doing so we will also need to destroy and recreate the framebuffer, command pool, graphics pipeline, Render Pass, depth buffer image, image view, vertex buffer, and so on. The following is the implementation of the resize function showing this:

```
void VulkanApplication::resize()
{
    // If prepared then only proceed for
    if (!isPrepared) {
        return;
    }

    isResizing = true;

    vkDeviceWaitIdle(deviceObj->device);
    rendererObj->destroyFramebuffers();
    rendererObj->destroyCommandPool();
    rendererObj->destroyPipeline();
    rendererObj->getPipelineObject()->destroyPipelineCache();
    rendererObj->destroyRenderpass();
    rendererObj->getSwapChain()->destroySwapChain();
    rendererObj->destroyDrawableVertexBuffer();
    rendererObj->destroyDepthBuffer();
    rendererObj->initialize();
    prepare();

    isResizing = false;
}
```

The application must prevent any render operation when resizing is going on; for this purpose, the `isResizing` flag can be used to indicate the resizing status. The reinitialization is performed by calling the `VulkanRender'sinitialize()` function. The drawing commands are recorded in the Vulkan application's prepare function:

```
void VulkanRenderer::initialize()
{
    // We need command buffers, so create a command buffer pool
    createCommandPool();

    // Let's create the swap chain color images and depth image
    buildSwapChainAndDepthImage();

    // Build the vertex buffer
    createVertexBuffer();

    const bool includeDepth = true;
    // Create the render pass now..
    createRenderPass(includeDepth);

    // Use render pass and create frame buffer
    createFrameBuffer(includeDepth);

    // Create the vertex and fragment shader
    createShaders();

    // Manage the pipeline state objects
    createPipelineStateManagement();
}
void VulkanApplication::prepare()
{
    isPrepared = false;
    rendererObj->prepare();
    isPrepared = true;
}
```

Drawing Objects

The following screenshot shows the output of the resize window implementation:

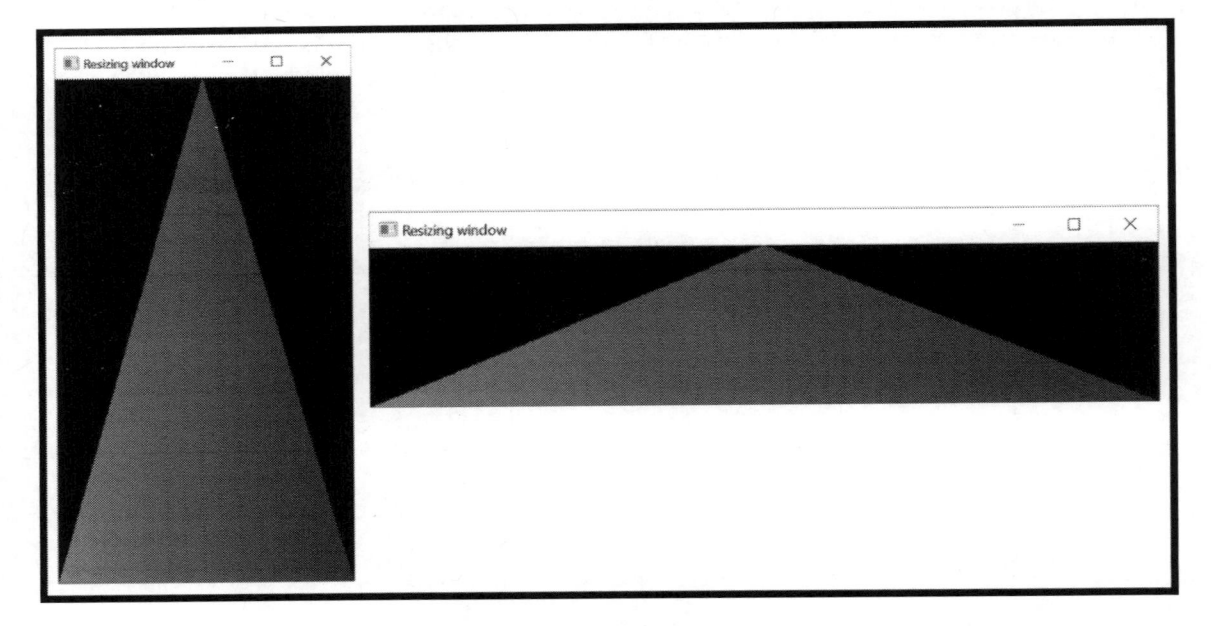

Summary

In this chapter, we rendered our first Hello World! program in Vulkan. Drawing it consists of two stages–*preparation and rendering* (execution). Preparation records the command buffers and the rendering executes them. The command buffers are recorded once and executed multiple times unless there is an explicit change in the pipeline state objects.

The preparation of the command buffer involves recording the Render Pass and graphics pipeline binding and drawing parameters, such as vertex buffers, viewport, scissor, and so on. Finally, the drawing API command is specified; we demonstrated both index- and nonindex-based drawing APIs using the sample application.

The recorded command buffer is executed in the rendering stage. The execution process acquires the swapchain image and submits the command buffer into the graphics queue. Painting is done on the acquired swapchain image. Once this is complete the image is sent to the presentation engine to be displayed on the output display. This chapter also demonstrated API commands for drawing indexed and non-indexed geometries. Towards the end of this chapter, we covered synchronization primitives in Vulkan and you learned how to perform synchronization in between the host and device, and queues and command buffers.

In the next chapter, we will learn about descriptors and the push constant, which allows the sharing of resource contents with the Shader program.

10
Descriptors and Push Constant

In the previous chapter, we rendered our first drawing object on the display output. In this chapter, we will take the previous implementation ahead and implement some 3D transformations on the rendered geometry with the help of **Uniforms**. Uniforms are read-only blocks of data accessible in the shader, and their value is constant for an entire draw call.

Uniforms are managed by descriptors and descriptor pools. A descriptor helps connect the resources with the shaders. But it may be expected to change frequently; therefore, the allocation is performed through a preallocated descriptor buffer called the **descriptor pool**.

In this chapter, we will also implement a push constant. A push constant allows you to update the constant data in the shader using an optimized high-speed path.

We will cover the following topics:

- Understanding the concept of descriptors
- How to implement Uniforms in Vulkan
- Push constant updates

Understanding the concept of descriptors

A descriptor consists of **descriptor set** objects. These objects contain storage for a set of descriptors. A descriptor set connects a given resource–such as a uniform buffer, sampled image, stored image, and so on–to the shader helping it read and interpret the incoming resource data through the layout bindings defined using the descriptor set layout. For example, resources such as image textures, sampler and buffers are bound to the shader using descriptors.

Descriptors and Push Constant

Descriptors are opaque objects and define a protocol to communicate with the shaders; behind the curtain, it provides a silent mechanism to associate the resource memory with the shaders with the help of location binding.

VulkanDescriptor – a user-defined descriptor class

In this chapter, we will introduce a new user class called `VulkanDescriptor` and keep our descriptor-related member variable and function here. This will be helpful in keeping the descriptor code separate from the rest of the implementation, providing a much cleaner and easier way to understand the descriptor functionality.

The following is the header declaration of the `VulkanDescriptor` class in `VulkanDescriptor.h` / `.cpp`. As we proceed through the various sections, we will discuss the purpose and implementation of declared functions and variables in this class in detail. Refer to the inline comments for a quick grasp:

```
// A user define descriptor class implementing Vulkan descriptors
class VulkanDescriptor
{
public:
    VulkanDescriptor();         // Constructor
    ~VulkanDescriptor();        // Destructor

    // Creates descriptor pool and allocate descriptor set from it
    void createDescriptor(bool useTexture);
    // Deletes the created descriptor set object
    void destroyDescriptor();

    // Defines the descriptor sets layout binding and
    // create descriptor layout
    virtual void createDescriptorLayout(bool useTexture) = 0;
    // Destroy the valid descriptor layout object
    void destroyDescriptorLayout();

    // Creates the descriptor pool that is used to
    // allocate descriptor sets
    virtual void createDescriptorPool(bool useTexture) = 0;

    // Deletes the descriptor pool
    void destroyDescriptorPool();

    // Create the descriptor set from the descriptor pool allocated
    // memory and update the descriptor set information into it.
```

```cpp
    virtual void createDescriptorSet(bool useTexture) = 0;
    void destroyDescriptorSet();

    // Creates the pipeline layout to inject into the pipeline
    virtual void createPipelineLayout() = 0;
    // Destroys the create pipelineLayout
    void destroyPipelineLayouts();
    public:
    // Pipeline layout object
    VkPipelineLayout pipelineLayout;

    // List of all the VkDescriptorSetLayouts
    std::vector<VkDescriptorSetLayout> descLayout;
    // Decriptor pool object that will be used
    // for allocating VkDescriptorSet object
    VkDescriptorPool descriptorPool;
    // List of all created VkDescriptorSet
    std::vector<VkDescriptorSet> descriptorSet;
    // Logical device used for creating the
    // descriptor pool and descriptor sets
    VulkanDevice* deviceObj;
};
```

Descriptor set layout

A descriptor set layout is a collection of zero or more descriptor bindings. It provides an interface to read the resource in the shader at the specified location. Each descriptor binding has a special type that indicates the kind of resource it is handling, the number of descriptors in that binding, the sampler descriptor arrays, and the respective shader stages to which it is associated with. This metadata information is specified in `VkDescriptorSetLayoutBinding`. Following is the image showing descriptor set layout which contains various resources layout binding in it where each resource is specified with a binding number uniquely identified in that descriptor layout:

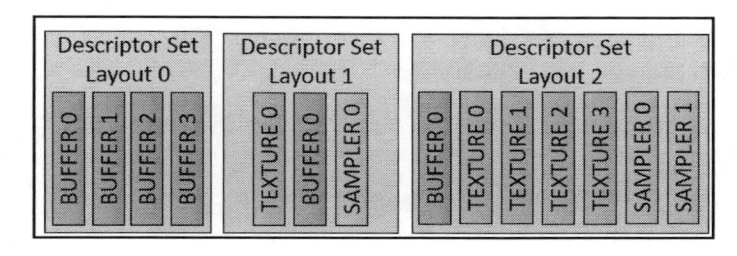

Descriptors and Push Constant

A descriptor set layout is created using the `vkCreateDescriptorSetLayout()` API. This API accepts the `VkDescriptorSetLayoutCreateInfo` control structure into which the preceding metadata information for zero or more descriptor sets is specified using the `VkDescriptorSetLayoutBinding` structure. The following is the syntax of this structure:

```
VkResult vkCreateDescriptorSetLayout(
    VkDevice                                device,
    const VkDescriptorSetLayoutCreateInfo*  pCreateInfo,
    const VkAllocationCallbacks*            pAllocator,
    VkDescriptorSetLayout*                  pSetLayout);
```

Here are the parameters defined in the `vkCreateDescriptorSetLayout()` API:

Parameters	Description
`device`	This field specifies the logical device (`VkDevice`) that is responsible for creating the descriptor set layout.
`pCreateInfo`	This field specifies the descriptor set layout metadata using the pointer to an object of the `VkDescriptorSetLayoutCreateInfo` structure.
`pAllocator`	This controls host memory deallocation. Refer to the *Host memory* section in Chapter 5, *Command Buffer and Memory Management in Vulkan*.
`pSetLayout`	The created descriptor set layout objects are returned in the form of `VkDescriptorSetLayout` handles.

Let's understand the `VkDescriptorSetLayoutCreateInfo` structure, which is given here:

```
typedef struct VkDescriptorSetLayoutCreateInfo {
    VkStructureType                        sType;
    const void*                            pNext;
    VkDescriptorSetLayoutCreateFlags       flags;
    uint32_t                               bindingCount;
    const VkDescriptorSetLayoutBinding*    pBindings;
} VkDescriptorSetLayoutCreateInfo;
```

The various fields of the `VkDescriptorSetLayoutCreateInfo` structure are defined in this table:

Parameters	Description
`sType`	This is the type information of this control structure. It must be specified as `VK_STRUCTURE_TYPE_DESCRIPTOR-_SET_LAYOUT_CREATE_INFO`.
`pNext`	This could be a valid pointer to an extension-specific structure or `NULL`.

`flags`	This field is of the `VkDescriptorSetLayoutCreateFlags` type and is presently not in use; it is reserved for future use.
`bindingCount`	This refers to the number of entries in the `pBindings` array.
`pBindings`	This is a pointer to the structure array of `VkDescriptorSetLayoutBinding`.

The following is the syntax of the `VkDescriptorSetLayoutBinding` structure:

```
typedef struct VkDescriptorSetLayoutBinding {
    uint32_t                binding;
    VkDescriptorType        descriptorType;
    uint32_t                descriptorCount;
    VkShaderStageFlags      stageFlags;
    const VkSampler*        pImmutableSamplers;
} VkDescriptorSetLayoutBinding;
```

The various fields of the `VkDescriptorSetLayoutBinding` structure are defined in the following table:

Parameters	Description
`binding`	This is the binding index that indicates the entry of this resource type, and this index must be equal to the binding number or index used in the corresponding shader stage.
`descriptorType`	This indicates the type of the descriptor being used for binding. The type is expressed using the `VkDescriptorType` enum.
`descriptorCount`	This indicates the number of descriptors in the shader as an array, and it refers to the shader that is contained in the binding.
`stageFlags`	This field specifies which shader stages can access the value for both the graphics and compute state. This shader stage is indicated by the bit field of `VkShaderStageFlagBits`. If the value is `VK_SHADER_STAGE_ALL`, then all the defined shader stages can access the resource via the specified `binding`.

Descriptors and Push Constant

`pImmutableSamplers`	This is a pointer to an array of sampler handles represented by the corresponding binding that will be consumed by the descriptor set layout. This field is used for initializing a set of immutable samplers if the `descriptorType` specified is either `VK_DESCRIPTOR_TYPE_SAMPLER` or `VK_DESCRIPTOR_TYPE_COMBINED_IMAGE_SAMPLER`. If `descriptorType` is not one of these descriptor types, then this field (`pImmutableSamplers`) is ignored. Once immutable samplers are bounded, they cannot be bounded into the set layout again. The sampler slots are dynamic when this field is `NULL`, and the sampler handles must be bound to the descriptor sets using this layout.

The following is the complete set of the `VkDescriptorType` enum signifying the various descriptor types. The enumeration name of each type is self-explanatory; each of them shows the type of resource it is associated with:

```
typedef enum VkDescriptorType {
            VK_DESCRIPTOR_TYPE_SAMPLER                    = 0,
            VK_DESCRIPTOR_TYPE_COMBINED_IMAGE_SAMPLER     = 1,
            VK_DESCRIPTOR_TYPE_SAMPLED_IMAGE              = 2,
            VK_DESCRIPTOR_TYPE_STORAGE_IMAGE              = 3,
            VK_DESCRIPTOR_TYPE_UNIFORM_TEXEL_BUFFER       = 4,
            VK_DESCRIPTOR_TYPE_STORAGE_TEXEL_BUFFER       = 5,
            VK_DESCRIPTOR_TYPE_UNIFORM_BUFFER             = 6,
            VK_DESCRIPTOR_TYPE_STORAGE_BUFFER             = 7,
            VK_DESCRIPTOR_TYPE_UNIFORM_BUFFER_DYNAMIC     = 8,
            VK_DESCRIPTOR_TYPE_STORAGE_BUFFER_DYNAMIC     = 9,
            VK_DESCRIPTOR_TYPE_INPUT_ATTACHMENT           = 10,
} VkDescriptorType;
```

Let's go ahead and implement the descriptor set in the next subsection.

Implementing the descriptor set layout

The descriptor layout is implemented in the `createDescriptorLayout()` function of the `VulkanDrawable` class. This function is a pure virtual function that is declared in the `VulkanDescriptor` class. The `VulkanDrawable` class inherits the `VulkanDescriptor` class. The following is the implementation of this:

```
void VulkanDrawable::createDescriptorLayout(bool useTexture)
{
```

```cpp
// Define the layout binding information for the
// descriptor set(before creating it), specify binding point,
// shader type(like vertex shader below), count etc.
VkDescriptorSetLayoutBinding layoutBindings[2];
layoutBindings[0].binding            = 0; // DESCRIPTOR_SET_BINDING_INDEX
layoutBindings[0].descriptorType =
                        VK_DESCRIPTOR_TYPE_UNIFORM_BUFFER;
layoutBindings[0].descriptorCount = 1;
layoutBindings[0].stageFlags = VK_SHADER_STAGE_VERTEX_BIT;
layoutBindings[0].pImmutableSamplers = NULL;

// If texture is being used then there exists a
// second binding in the fragment shader
if (useTexture)
{
    layoutBindings[1].binding        = 1;
    layoutBindings[1].descriptorType =
    VK_DESCRIPTOR_TYPE_COMBINED_IMAGE_SAMPLER;
    layoutBindings[1].descriptorCount = 1;
    layoutBindings[1].stageFlags =
      VK_SHADER_STAGE_FRAGMENT_BIT;
    layoutBindings[1].pImmutableSamplers     = NULL;
}

// Specify the layout bind into the VkDescriptorSetLayout-
// CreateInfo and use it to create a descriptor set layout
VkDescriptorSetLayoutCreateInfo descriptorLayout = {};
descriptorLayout.sType =
      VK_STRUCTURE_TYPE_DESCRIPTOR_SET_LAYOUT_CREATE_INFO;
descriptorLayout.pNext = NULL;
descriptorLayout.bindingCount = useTexture ? 2 : 1;
descriptorLayout.pBindings = layoutBindings;

VkResult   result;
// Allocate required number of descriptor layout objects and
// create them using vkCreateDescriptorSetLayout()
descLayout.resize(numberOfDescriptorSet);
result = vkCreateDescriptorSetLayout(deviceObj->device,
&descriptorLayout, NULL, descLayout.data());
assert(result == VK_SUCCESS);
}
```

Before you create the descriptor set object, the layout bindings need to be defined. There are two `VkDescriptorSetLayoutBinding` objects (an array) created in the preceding implementation.

Descriptors and Push Constant

The first layout binding, `layoutBindings[0]`, is used to bind the uniform block with the resource index specified in the shader. In the present case, the index of our uniform block in the vertex shader is 0, which is the same value that is specified in the `layoutBindings[0].binding` field. The other fields of the object indicate that the binding point is attached to the vertex shader stage (`stageFlags`), and the number of descriptors (`descriptorCount`) are attached as an array in the shader that is contained within the binding.

The second array object, `layoutBindings[1]`, indicates the layout binding for texture support in our geometry; however, this sample example only implements the uniform block to demonstrate a 3D transformation. In order to use the current implementation for texture support, the `useTexture` flag parameter of the `createDescriptorLayout()` function must be set to the boolean `true`. In the present example, although we are using two descriptor sets, only one is used, that is, `useTexture` is `false`. In the upcoming chapter, we will implement texture support.

Destroying the descriptor set layout

The descriptor layout can be destroyed using the `vkDestroyDescriptorSetLayout()` API. Here's the syntax for this:

```
void vkDestroyDescriptorSetLayout(
    VkDevice                     device,
    VkDescriptorSetLayout        descriptorSetLayout,
    const VkAllocationCallbacks* pAllocator);
```

The `vkDestroyDescriptorSetLayout()` API takes the following parameters:

Parameters	Description
device	This is a logical device that destroys the descriptor set layout.
descriptorSetLayout	This is the descriptor set layout object to be destroyed.
pAllocator	This controls host memory deallocation. Refer to the *Host memory* section in Chapter 5, *Command Buffer and Memory Management in Vulkan*.

Understanding pipeline layouts

Pipeline layouts allow a pipeline (graphics or compute) to access the descriptor sets. A pipeline layout object is comprised of descriptor set layouts and push constant ranges (refer to the *Push constant updates* section in this chapter), and it represents the complete set of resources that can be accessed by the underlying pipeline.

The pipeline layout object information needs to be provided in the `VkGraphicsPipelineCreateInfo` structure before the pipeline object is created using the `vkCreateGraphicsPipelines()` API. This information is set in the `VkGraphicsPipelineCreateInfo::layout` field. This is a compulsory field. If the application does not use descriptor sets, then you must create an empty descriptor layout and specify it in the pipeline layout to suffice the pipeline object (`VkPipeline`) creation process. For more information on the pipeline creation process, refer to the *Creating graphics pipeline* subsection in Chapter 8, *Pipelines and Pipeline State Management*.

The pipeline layout can contain zero or more descriptor sets in sequence, with each having a specific layout. This layout defines the interfaces between the shader stages and shader resources. The following image shows pipeline layout which comprises of multiple descriptor layouts contains various layout bindings for each resource:

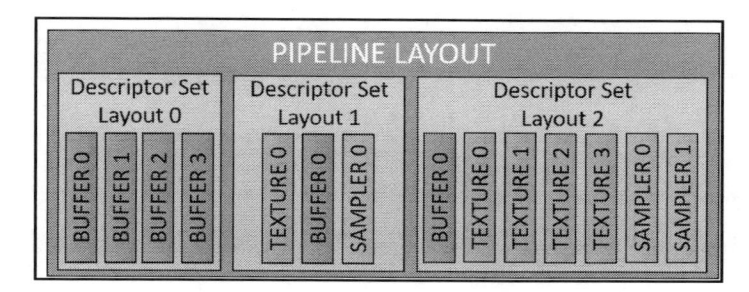

Creating a pipeline layout

A pipeline layout object can be created with the help of the `vkCreatePipelineLayout()` API. This API accepts `VkPipelineLayoutCreateInfo`, which contains the descriptor set's state information. This creates one pipeline layout. Let's take a look at the syntax of this API:

```
VkResult vkCreatePipelineLayout(
    VkDevice                                device,
    const VkPipelineLayoutCreateInfo*       pCreateInfo,
    const VkAllocationCallbacks*            pAllocator,
```

Descriptors and Push Constant

```
    VkPipelineLayout*                    pPipelineLayout);
```

The various fields of the `vkCreatePipelineLayout` structure are defined as follows:

Parameters	Description
`device`	This indicates the logical device (`VkDevice`) that is responsible for creating the pipeline layout.
`pCreateInfo`	This field is the metadata of the pipeline layout object specified using the pointer to the `VkPipelineLayoutCreateInfo` structure.
`pAllocator`	This controls host memory deallocation. Refer to the *Host memory* section in `Chapter 5`, *Command Buffer and Memory Management in Vulkan*.
`pPipelineLayout`	This returns the `VkPipelineLayout` object handle after the API is successfully executed.

Implementing the pipeline layout creation

The `VulkanDrawable` class implements the `createPipelineLayout()` interface from `VulkanDrawble`, which allows a drawable class to implement its own implementation based on the drawing object resource requirements.

First, `VkPipelineLayoutCreateInfo` is created (`pPipelineLayoutCreateInfo`) and specified with the descriptor layout objects (`descLayout`), which was created using the `vkCreateDescriptorSetLayout()` API. The descriptor set binding information is accessed with the pipeline layout within the pipeline (`VkPipeline`).

The created `pPipelineLayoutCreateInfo` is set into the `vkCreatePipelineLayout()` API to create the `pipelineLayout` object. During pipeline creation, this object will be passed to `VkGraphicsPipelineCreateInfo::layout` in order to create the graphics pipeline object (`VkPipeline`):

```
// createPipelineLayout is a virtual function from
// VulkanDescriptor and defined in the VulkanDrawable class.
// virtual void VulkanDescriptor::createPipelineLayout() = 0;
// Creates the pipeline layout to inject into the pipeline
void VulkanDrawable::createPipelineLayout()
{
    // Create the pipeline layout using descriptor layout.
    VkPipelineLayoutCreateInfo pPipelineLayoutCreateInfo = {};
    pPipelineLayoutCreateInfo.sType = VK_STRUCTURE_TYPE_PIPELINE-
                                            _LAYOUT_CREATE_INFO;
    pPipelineLayoutCreateInfo.pNext             = NULL;
```

```
        pPipelineLayoutCreateInfo.pushConstantRangeCount= 0;
        pPipelineLayoutCreateInfo.pPushConstantRanges   = NULL;
        pPipelineLayoutCreateInfo.setLayoutCount        =
                                        numberOfDescriptorSet;
        pPipelineLayoutCreateInfo.pSetLayouts   = descLayout.data();

        VkResult    result;
        result = vkCreatePipelineLayout(deviceObj->device,
        &pPipelineLayoutCreateInfo, NULL, &pipelineLayout);
        assert(result == VK_SUCCESS);
    }
```

Destroying the pipeline layout

The created pipeline layout can be destroyed using the vkDestroyPipelineLayout() API in Vulkan. The following is its description:

```
    void vkDestroyPipelineLayout(
        VkDevice                            device,
        VkPipelineLayout                    pipelineLayout,
        const VkAllocationCallbacks*        pAllocator);
```

The various fields of the vkDestroyPipelineLayout structure are defined here:

Parameters	Description
device	This is the VkDevice logical object used to destroy the pipeline layout object.
pipelineLayout	This indicates the pipeline layout object (VkPipelineLayout) that needs to be destroyed.
pAllocator	This controls host memory allocation. Refer to the *Host memory* section in Chapter 5, *Command Buffer and Memory Management in Vulkan*.

Let's use this API and implement it in the next section.

[371]

Implementing the pipeline layout destruction process

The `VulkanDescriptor` class provides a high-level function to destroy the created pipeline layout: the `destroyPipelineLayouts()` function. The following is the code implementation:

```
// Destroy the create pipeline layout object
void VulkanDescriptor::destroyPipelineLayouts()
{
    vkDestroyPipelineLayout(deviceObj->device, pipelineLayout, NULL);
}
```

Descriptor pool

In Vulkan, descriptor sets cannot be created directly; instead, these are first allocated from a special pool called a descriptor pool. A descriptor pool is responsible for allocating the descriptor set objects. In other words, it is a collection of descriptors from which the descriptor set is allocated.

> Descriptor pools are useful in efficient memory allocation of several objects of the descriptor set without requiring global synchronization.

Creating a descriptor pool

Creating a descriptor pool is simple; use the `vkCreateDescriptorPool` API. The following is the API specification, followed by the implementation of this API in our sample recipe:

```
VkResult vkCreateDescriptorPool(
    VkDevice                         device,
    const VkDescriptorPoolCreateInfo* pCreateInfo,
    const VkAllocationCallbacks*      pAllocator,
    VkDescriptorPool*                 pDescriptorPool);
```

The various fields of the `vkCreateDescriptorPool` structure are defined here:

Parameters	Description
`device`	This specifies the logical device (`VkDevice`) that is responsible for creating the descriptor pool.
`pCreateInfo`	This field is the metadata of the descriptor pool object, which is specified using a pointer to an object of the `VkDescriptorPoolCreateInfo` structure.
`pAllocator`	This controls host memory allocation. Refer to the *Host memory* section in Chapter 5, *Command Buffer and Memory Management in Vulkan*.
`pDescriptorPool`	This indicates the created descriptor pool object's handle of the type (`VkDescriptorPool`), which is a result of the execution of this API.

Implementing the creation of the descriptor pool

The `createDescriptorPool()` is a pure virtual function exposed by the `VulkanDescriptor` class. This function is implemented in the `VulkanDrawble` class, which is responsible for creating the descriptor pool in our Vulkan application sample. Let's understand the working of this function:

- First, the descriptor pool's size structure is defined indicating the number of pools that need to be created within the descriptor pool for allocating each type of descriptor set. There are two types of descriptor sets that are being used in the following implementation; thus, two `VkDescriptorPoolSize` objects are created. The first object indicates the descriptor pool that it needs to provide the allocation for the uniform buffer descriptor types. This pool will be used to allocate the descriptor set objects that bind to the uniform block resource types.
- The second object indicates the descriptor pool for texture samplers. We will implement the texture in the next chapter.
- These created objects (`descriptorTypePool`) are then specified in the descriptor pool's `CreateInfo` structure (`descriptorPoolCreateInfo`) to indicate the types of descriptor sets (with other state information as well) that are going to be supported by the created descriptor pool. Finally, the `descriptorTypePool` object is used by the `vkCreateDescriptorPool()` API to create the descriptor pool object `descriptorPool`.

Descriptors and Push Constant

The implementation of the descriptor pool is given here:

```
// Creates the descriptor pool, this function depends on -
// createDescriptorSetLayout()
void VulkanDrawable::createDescriptorPool(bool useTexture)
{
    VkResult   result;
    // Define the size of descriptor pool based on the
    // type of descriptor set being used.
    VkDescriptorPoolSize descriptorTypePool[2];

    // The first descriptor pool object is of type Uniform buffer
    descriptorTypePool[0].type = VK_DESCRIPTOR_TYPE_UNIFORM_BUFFER;
    descriptorTypePool[0].descriptorCount    = 1;

    // If texture is supported then define the second object with
    // descriptor type to be Image sampler
    if (useTexture){
            descriptorTypePool[1].type= VK_DESCRIPTOR_TYPE_-
                                            COMBINED_IMAGE_SAMPLER;
        descriptorTypePool[1].descriptorCount    = 1;
    }

    // Populate the descriptor pool state information
    // in the create info structure.
    VkDescriptorPoolCreateInfo descriptorPoolCreateInfo = {};
    descriptorPoolCreateInfo.sType = VK_STRUCTURE_TYPE_DESCRIPTOR_-
                            POOL_CREATE_INFO;
    descriptorPoolCreateInfo.pNext          = NULL;
    descriptorPoolCreateInfo.maxSets        = 1;
    descriptorPoolCreateInfo.poolSizeCount= useTexture ? 2 : 1;
    descriptorPoolCreateInfo.pPoolSizes = descriptorTypePool;

    // Create the descriptor pool using the descriptor
    // pool create info structure
    result = vkCreateDescriptorPool(deviceObj->device,
        &descriptorPoolCreateInfo, NULL, &descriptorPool);
    assert(result == VK_SUCCESS);
}
```

Destroying the descriptor pool

The descriptor pool can be destroyed using the `vkDestroyDescriptorPool()` API. This API accepts three parameters. The first parameter, `device`, specifies the logical device (`VkDevice`) that owns the descriptor pool and will be used to destroy `descriptorPool`. The second parameter, `descriptorPool`, is the descriptor pool object that needs to be destroyed using this API. The last parameter, `pAllocator`, controls host memory allocation. You can refer to the *Host memory* section in Chapter 5, *Command Buffer and Memory Management in Vulkan*, for more information:

```
void vkDestroyDescriptorPool(
    VkDevice                     device,
    VkDescriptorPool             descriptorPool,
    const VkAllocationCallbacks* pAllocator);
```

Implementing the destruction of the descriptor pool

In the present sample application, the `desctroyDescriptorPool()` function from `VulkanDescriptor` can be used to destroy the created descriptor pool object:

```
// Deletes the descriptor pool
void VulkanDescriptor::destroyDescriptorPool()
{
    vkDestroyDescriptorPool(deviceObj->device, descriptorPool, NULL);
}
```

Creating the descriptor set resources

Before the descriptor sets are created, it's compulsory to create the resources in order to associate or bound them with it. In this section, we will create a uniform buffer resource and later associate it with the descriptor set we will create in the following, *Creating the descriptor sets*, section.

All the descriptor-related resources are created in the `createDescriptorResources()` interface of the `VulkanDescriptor` class. Based on the requirements, this interface can be implemented in the derived class.

[375]

Descriptors and Push Constant

In the present example, this interface is implemented in the `VulkanDrawable` class, which creates a uniform buffer and stores a 4 x 4 transformation into it. For this, we need to create buffer type resources. Remember, there are two types of resources in Vulkan: buffers and images. We created the buffer resource in the *Understanding the buffer resource* section in `Chapter 7`, *Buffer resource, Render Pass, Framebuffer, and Shaders with SPIR-V*. In the same chapter, we created the vertex buffer (see the *Creating geometry with buffer resource* section). We will reuse our learning from this chapter and implement a uniform buffer to store the uniform block information.

The following code implements `createDescriptorResources()`, where it calls another function, `createUniformBuffer()`, which creates the uniform buffer resource:

```
// Create the Uniform resource inside. Create Descriptor set
// associated resources before creating the descriptor set
void VulkanDrawable::createDescriptorResources()
{
    createUniformBuffer();
}
```

The `createUniformBuffer()` function produces the transformation matrices information using the `glm` library helper functions. It computes the correct Model, View, and Project matrices as per the user specification and stores the result in the MVP matrix. MVP is stored in the host memory and needs to be transferred to the device memory using the buffer object (`VkBuffer`). The following are step-by-step instructions to create the buffer resource (`VkBuffer`) of MVP:

1. **Creating the buffer object**: Create a `VkBuffer` object (`UniformData.buffer`) using the `vkCreateBuffer()` API. This API intakes a `VkCreateBufferInfo` structure object (`bufInfo`) that specifies the important buffer metadata used to create the buffer object. For example, it indicates the usage type in `bufInfo.usage` as `VK_BUFFER_USAGE_UNIFORM_BUFFER_BIT` since MVP is treated as a uniform block resource in the vertex shader. The other important piece of information it needs is the size of the buffer; this will be required to hold the complete MVP buffer information. In the present case, it is equal to the size of a 4 x 4 transformation matrix. At this stage, when the buffer object is created (`UniformData.buffer`), no physical backing is associated with it. In order to allocate physical memory, proceed to the next steps.

2. **Allocating physical memory for the buffer resource**:
     - **Get the memory requirements**: Allocate the appropriate size of the memory required by the buffer resource. Query the essential memory by passing the `VkBuffer` object to the `vkGetBufferMemoryRequirements` API. This will return the required memory information in the `VkMemoryRequirements` type object (`memRqrmnt`).
     - **Determining the memory type**: Get the proper memory type from the available options and select the one that matches the user properties.
     - **Allocating device memory**: Allocate the physical memory (in `UniformData::memory` of the `VkDeviceMemory` type) for the buffer resource using the `vkAllocateMemory()` API.
     - **Mapping the device memory**: Map the physical device memory to the application's address space using the `vkMapMemory()` API. Upload the uniform buffer data to this address space. Invalidate the mapped buffer to make it visible to the host using `vkInvalidateMappedMemoryRanges()`. If the memory property is set with `VK_MEMORY_PROPERTY_HOST_COHERENT_BIT`, then the driver may take care of this; otherwise, for non-coherent mapped memory, `vkInvalidateMappedMemoryRanges()` needs to be called explicitly.
     - **Binding the allocated memory**: Bind the device memory (`UniformData::memory`) to the buffer object (`UniformData::buffer`) using the `vkBindBufferMemory()` API.

The following diagram provides an overview of the described process:

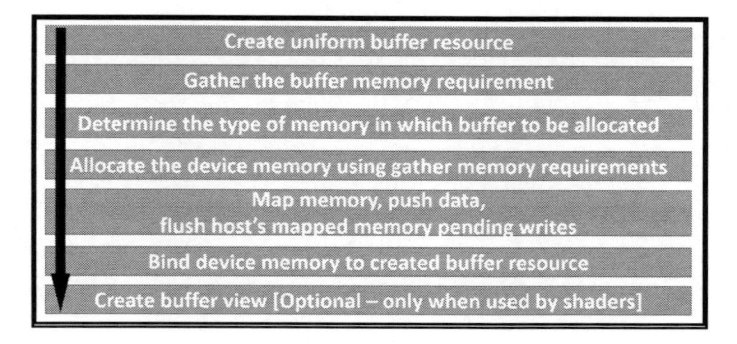

> Create uniform buffer resource
> Gather the buffer memory requirement
> Determine the type of memory in which buffer to be allocated
> Allocate the device memory using gather memory requirements
> Map memory, push data, flush host's mapped memory pending writes
> Bind device memory to created buffer resource
> Create buffer view [Optional – only when used by shaders]

Descriptors and Push Constant

Once the buffer resource is created, it stores the necessary information in the local data structure for housekeeping purposes:

```
class VulkanDrawable : public VulkanDescriptor
{
. . . .
    // Local data structure for uniform buffer house keeping
    struct {
        // Buffer resource object
        VkBuffer                    buffer;
        // Buffer resourece object's allocated device memory
        VkDeviceMemory              memory;

        // Buffer info that need to supplied into
        // write descriptor set (VkWriteDescriptorSet)
        VkDescriptorBufferInfo  bufferInfo;

        // Store the queried memory requirement
        // of the uniform buffer
        VkMemoryRequirements    memRqrmnt;

        // Metadata of memory mapped objects
        std::vector<VkMappedMemoryRange> mappedRange;
        // Host pointer containing the mapped device
        // address which is used to write data into.
        uint8_t*                    pData;
    } UniformData;

. . . .
};

void VulkanDrawable::createUniformBuffer()
{
    VkResult   result;
    bool   pass;
    Projection = glm::perspective(radians(45.f), 1.f, .1f, 100.f);
    View = glm::lookAt(
            glm::vec3(10, 3, 10),  // Camera in World Space
            glm::vec3(0, 0, 0),    // and looks at the origin
            glm::vec3(0, -1, 0) );// Head is up
    Model     = glm::mat4(1.0f);
    MVP   = Projection * View * Model;

    // Create buffer resource states using VkBufferCreateInfo
    VkBufferCreateInfo bufInfo = {};
    bufInfo.sType       = VK_STRUCTURE_TYPE_BUFFER_CREATE_INFO;
    bufInfo.pNext       = NULL;
    bufInfo.usage       = VK_BUFFER_USAGE_UNIFORM_BUFFER_BIT;
```

```cpp
bufInfo.size         = sizeof(MVP);
bufInfo.queueFamilyIndexCount = 0;
bufInfo.pQueueFamilyIndices  = NULL;
bufInfo.sharingMode  = VK_SHARING_MODE_EXCLUSIVE;
bufInfo.flags        = 0;

// Use create buffer info and create the buffer objects
result = vkCreateBuffer(deviceObj->device, &bufInfo, NULL,
        &UniformData.buffer);
assert(result == VK_SUCCESS);

// Get the buffer memory requirements
VkMemoryRequirements memRqrmnt;
vkGetBufferMemoryRequirements(deviceObj->device,
        UniformData.buffer, &memRqrmnt);

VkMemoryAllocateInfo memAllocInfo = {};
memAllocInfo.sType = VK_STRUCTURE_TYPE_MEMORY_ALLOCATE_INFO;
memAllocInfo.pNext                = NULL;
memAllocInfo.memoryTypeIndex      = 0;
memAllocInfo.allocationSize = memRqrmnt.size;

// Determine the type of memory required
// with the help of memory properties
pass = deviceObj->memoryTypeFromProperties
    (memRqrmnt.memoryTypeBits,
     VK_MEMORY_PROPERTY_HOST_VISIBLE_BIT,
     &memAllocInfo.memoryTypeIndex);
assert(pass);

// Allocate the memory for buffer objects
result = vkAllocateMemory(deviceObj->device, &memAllocInfo,
     NULL, &(UniformData.memory));
assert(result == VK_SUCCESS);

// Map the GPU memory on to local host
result = vkMapMemory(deviceObj->device, UniformData.memory,
0, memRqrmnt.size, 0, (void **)&UniformData.pData);
assert(result == VK_SUCCESS);

// Copy computed data in the mapped buffer
memcpy(UniformData.pData, &MVP, sizeof(MVP));

// We have only one Uniform buffer object to update
UniformData.mappedRange.resize(1);

// Populate the VkMappedMemoryRange data structure
UniformData.mappedRange[0].sType   =
```

```
                    VK_STRUCTURE_TYPE_MAPPED_MEMORY_RANGE;
    UniformData.mappedRange[0].memory   = UniformData.memory;
    UniformData.mappedRange[0].offset   = 0;
    UniformData.mappedRange[0].size     = sizeof(MVP);

    // Invalidate the range of mapped buffer in order
    // to make it visible to the host.
    vkInvalidateMappedMemoryRanges(deviceObj->device, 1,
            &UniformData.mappedRange[0]);

    // Bind the buffer device memory
    result = vkBindBufferMemory(deviceObj->device,
            UniformData.buffer, UniformData.memory, 0);
    assert(result == VK_SUCCESS);

    // Update the local data structure with uniform
    // buffer for house keeping
    UniformData.bufferInfo.buffer    = UniformData.buffer;
    UniformData.bufferInfo.offset    = 0;
    UniformData.bufferInfo.range     = sizeof(MVP);
    UniformData.memRqrmnt            = memRqrmnt;
}
```

Next, we will create the descriptor set and associate the created uniform buffer with it.

Creating the descriptor sets

The descriptor set creation process comprises two steps:

1. **Descriptor set allocation**: This allocates the descriptor set from the descriptor pool.
2. **Resource assignment**: Here, the descriptor set is associated with the created resource data.

Allocating the descriptor set object from the descriptor pool

The descriptor set is allocated from the descriptor pool using the `vkAllocateDescriptorSets()` API. This API intakes three parameters. The first parameter (`device`) specifies the logical device (of the type `VkDevice`) that owns the descriptor pool. The second parameter (`pAllocateInfo`) is a pointer to an object of the `VkDescriptorSetAllocateInfo` structure describing the various parameters that will be helpful in the allocation process of the descriptor pool. The last parameter (`pDescriptorSets`) is a pointer to an array of `VkDescriptorSet`; this will be filled by the API with the handles of each allocated descriptor set:

```
VkResult vkAllocateDescriptorSets(
    VkDevice                              device,
    const VkDescriptorSetAllocateInfo*    pAllocateInfo,
    VkDescriptorSet*                      pDescriptorSets);
```

Destroying the allocated descriptor set objects

The allocated descriptor set objects can be freed using the `vkFreeDescriptorSets()` API. This API accepts four parameters. The first parameter (`device`) is the logical device that owns the descriptor pool. The second device is the descriptor pool (`descriptorPool`) that was used to allocate the descriptor sets. The third parameter (`descriptorSetCount`) indicates the number of elements in the last parameter. The last parameter (`pDescriptorSets`) is the `VkDescriptorSet` object's array that needs to be freed:

```
VkResult vkFreeDescriptorSets(
    VkDevice                  device,
    VkDescriptorPool          descriptorPool,
    uint32_t                  descriptorSetCount,
    const VkDescriptorSet*    pDescriptorSets);
```

In this current sample implementation, the `vkFreeDescriptorSets()` API is exposed through the `destroyDescriptorSet()` helper function in the `VulkanDescriptor` class. The following is the implementation code:

```
void VulkanDescriptor::destroyDescriptorSet()
{
    vkFreeDescriptorSets(deviceObj->device, descriptorPool,
        numberOfDescriptorSet, &descriptorSet[0]);
}
```

Associating the resources with the descriptor sets

The descriptor sets can be associated with the resources information by updating them using the `vkUpdateDescriptorSets()` API. This API uses four parameters. The first parameter, `device`, is the logical device that will be used to update the descriptor sets. This logical device should be the one that owns the descriptor sets. The second parameter, `descriptorWriteCount`, specifies the element count in the `pDescriptorWrites` array (of the `VkCopyDescriptorSet` type). The third parameter, `pDescriptorWrites`, is a pointer to an array of `VkWriteDescriptorSet` in the `pDescriptorCopies` array. The last parameter, `pDescriptorCopies`, is a pointer to the array objects (the `VkCopyDescriptorSet` structures) describing the descriptor sets to copy between:

```
void vkUpdateDescriptorSets(
    VkDevice                    device,
    uint32_t                    descriptorWriteCount,
    const VkWriteDescriptorSet* pDescriptorWrites,
    uint32_t                    descriptorCopyCount,
    const VkCopyDescriptorSet*  pDescriptorCopies);
```

The update is an amalgamation of two operations, namely write and copy:

- **Write**: The allocated descriptor set is updated by filling an array of zero or more `VkWriteDescriptorSet` control structures with the resource information, such as buffer data, count, binding index, and more. The write operation is specified in the `vkUpdateDescriptorSets()` API. This API intakes the filled `VkWriteDescriptorSet` data structure.
- **Copy**: The copy operation uses the existing descriptor sets and copies their information to the destination descriptor set. The copy operation is specified by the `VkWriteDescriptorSet` control structure. There could be zero or more write operations possible.

> The write operations are executed first, followed by the copy operations. For each operation type (write or copy), zero or more operations are represented in the form of arrays, and within these arrays, the operations are performed in the order that they appear.

The following is the specification of `VkWriteDescriptorSet`:

```
typedef struct VkWriteDescriptorSet {
    VkStructureType    sType;
    const void*        pNext;
    VkDescriptorSet    dstSet;
    uint32_t           dstBinding;
    uint32_t           dstArrayElement;
```

```
            uint32_t                        descriptorCount;
            VkDescriptorType                descriptorType;
            const VkDescriptorImageInfo*    pImageInfo;
            const VkDescriptorBufferInfo*   pBufferInfo;
            const VkBufferView*             pTexelBufferView;
    } VkWriteDescriptorSet;
```

The various fields of the `VkWriteDescriptorSet` structure are defined as follows:

Parameters	Description
sType	This is the type information of this control structure. It must be specified as VK_STRUCTURE_TYPE_WRITE_DESCRIPTOR_SET.
pNext	This could be a valid pointer to an extension-specific structure or NULL.
dstSet	This is the destination descriptor set that will be updated.
dstBinding	This specifies the descriptor binding within the set. This should be the same as the binding index specified in the shader for a given shader stage.
dstArrayElement	This field indicates the starting element index in the array of descriptors within a single binding.
descriptorCount	This is the count of the descriptors to be updated in any of these: pImageInfo, pBufferInfo, or pTexelBufferView.
descriptorType	This field indicates the type of each participating descriptor (pImageInfo, pBufferInfo, or pTexelBufferView).
pImageInfo	This is an array of VkDescriptorImageInfo structures that represent the image resource. This field must be VK_NULL_HANDLE if not specified.
pBufferInfo	This is an array of VkDescriptorBufferInfo structures or it can be VK_NULL_HANDLE if not specified.
pTexelBufferView	This is an array containing VkBufferView handles, or it can be VK_NULL_HANDLE if not specified.

Let's take a look at the `VkCopyDescriptorSet` specification:

```
typedef struct VkCopyDescriptorSet {
    VkStructureType       sType;
    const void*           pNext;
    VkDescriptorSet       srcSet;
    uint32_t              srcBinding;
    uint32_t              srcArrayElement;
    VkDescriptorSet       dstSet;
    uint32_t              dstBinding;
    uint32_t              dstArrayElement;
    uint32_t              descriptorCount;
} VkCopyDescriptorSet;
```

The various fields of the `VkCopyDescriptorSet` structure are defined here:

Parameters	Description
`sType`	This is the type information of this control structure. It must be specified as `VK_STRUCTURE_TYPE_COPY_DESCRIPTOR_SET`.
`pNext`	This could be a valid pointer to an extension-specific structure or `NULL`.
`srcSet`	This specifies the source descriptor set that will be copied from.
`srcBinding`	This specifies the binding index within the source descriptor set.
`srcArrayElement`	This indicates the starting array element within the first updated binding.
`dstSet`	This specifies the destination descriptor set into which the source descriptor will be copied.
`dstBinding`	This specifies the binding index within the destination descriptor set.
`dstArrayElement`	This field indicates the starting index in the array of descriptors within a single binding.
`descriptorCount`	This refers to the total count of descriptors that will be copied from the source to the destination.

Implementing descriptor set creation

Descriptor sets are created in the `VulkanDrawable` class, which inherits the `createDescriptorSet()` interface from the `VulkanDescriptor` class and implements it.

First, the `VkDescriptorSetAllocateInfo` control structure (`dsAllocInfo`) is created and specified within the descriptor pool to allocate `descriptorSet` from the intended descriptor pool. The second important thing that needs to be specified is the descriptor layout information that we created and stored in the `descLayout` object. The descriptor layout provides an interface to read the resource in the shader.

The allocated descriptor sets are empty and do not hold any valid information. They are updated using the write or copy descriptor structures (`Vk<Write/Copy>DescriptorSet`). In this implementation, the write descriptor `write[0]` is specified with the uniform data buffer (`UniformData::bufferInfo`) along with other state information. This information includes the destination descriptor set object, `descriptorSet[0]`, into which this uniform buffer needs to be bound and the destination binding index to which it should be attached. The `dstBinding` must be equal to the index specified in the shader stage. The update operation is performed using `vkUpdateDescriptorSets()`, specifying the `write` descriptor into it:

```
// Creates the descriptor sets using descriptor pool.
// This function depends on the createDescriptorPool()
// and createUniformBuffer().
void VulkanDrawable::createDescriptorSet(bool useTexture)
{
    VulkanPipeline* pipelineObj = rendererObj->getPipelineObject();
    VkResult result;
    // Create the descriptor allocation structure and specify
    // the descriptor pool and descriptor layout
    VkDescriptorSetAllocateInfo dsAllocInfo[1];
    dsAllocInfo[0].sType            =
                VK_STRUCTURE_TYPE_DESCRIPTOR_SET_ALLOCATE_INFO;
    dsAllocInfo[0].pNext             = NULL;
    dsAllocInfo[0].descriptorPool    = descriptorPool;
    dsAllocInfo[0].descriptorSetCount = 1;
    dsAllocInfo[0].pSetLayouts       = descLayout.data();

    // Allocate the number of descriptor set needs to be produced
    descriptorSet.resize(1);

    // Allocate descriptor sets
    result = vkAllocateDescriptorSets(deviceObj->device,
                    dsAllocInfo, descriptorSet.data());
    assert(result == VK_SUCCESS);

    // Allocate two write descriptors for - 1. MVP and 2. Texture
    VkWriteDescriptorSet writes[2];
    memset(&writes, 0, sizeof(writes));
```

```
// Specify the uniform buffer related
// information into first write descriptor
writes[0]                  = {};
writes[0].sType            = VK_STRUCTURE_TYPE_WRITE_DESCRIPTOR_SET;
writes[0].pNext            = NULL;
writes[0].dstSet           = descriptorSet[0];
writes[0].descriptorCount  = 1;
writes[0].descriptorType   = VK_DESCRIPTOR_TYPE_UNIFORM_BUFFER;
writes[0].pBufferInfo      = &UniformData.bufferInfo;
writes[0].dstArrayElement  = 0;
writes[0].dstBinding       = 0;

// If texture is used then update the second
 // write descriptor structure. We will use this descriptor
// set in the next chapter where textures are used.
if (useTexture)
{
  // In this sample textures are not used
  writes[1]                  = {};
  writes[1].sType            = VK_STRUCTURE_TYPE_WRITE-
                               _DESCRIPTOR_SET;
  writes[1].dstSet           = descriptorSet[0];
  writes[1].dstBinding       = 1;
  writes[1].descriptorCount  = 1;
  writes[1].descriptorType   = VK_DESCRIPTOR_TYPE_-
                               COMBINED_IMAGE_SAMPLER;
  writes[1].pImageInfo       = NULL;
  writes[1].dstArrayElement  = 0;
}

// Update the uniform buffer into the allocated descriptor set
vkUpdateDescriptorSets(deviceObj->device,
        useTexture ? 2 : 1, writes, 0, NULL);
}
```

How to implement Uniforms in Vulkan?

In this section, we will understand the requirements and execution model for a Uniform implementation in Vulkan. We will also describe the step-by-step instructions to apply 3D transformations on the rendered object using Uniforms. Reuse the sample recipe from the previous chapter and follow the given instructions.

Prerequisites

Let's check out the requirements first.

3D Transformation: This implementation uses the `glm` mathematics library to achieve 3D transformation using the library's inbuilt transformation functions. GLM is a header-only C++ mathematics library for graphics software based on the GLSL specification. You can download this library from `http://glm.g-truc.net`. In order to use it, perform the following changes:

- **CMakeLists.txt**: Add GLM support by adding the following lines to the project's `CMakeLists.txt` file:

    ```
    # GLM SETUP
    set (EXTDIR "${CMAKE_SOURCE_DIR}/../../external")
    set (GLMINCLUDES "${EXTDIR}")
    get_filename_component(GLMINC_PREFIX "${GLMINCLUDES}" ABSOLUTE)
    if(NOT EXISTS ${GLMINC_PREFIX})
        message(FATAL_ERROR "Necessary glm headers do not exist: "
                ${GLMINC_PREFIX})
    endif()
    include_directories( ${GLMINC_PREFIX} )
    ```

- **Header files**: Include the header files for GLM in the `Headers.h` file:

    ```
    /*********** GLM HEADER FILES ***********/
    #define GLM_FORCE_RADIANS
    #include "glm/glm.hpp"
    #include <glm/gtc/matrix_transform.hpp>
    ```

Applying transformations: The transformations are executed just before the rendering happens. Introduce an `update()` function in the current design and call it just before the `render()` function is executed. Add `update()` to `VulkanRenderer` and `VulkanDrawable` and implement `main.cpp` as follows:

```
int main(int argc, char **argv)
{
    VulkanApplication* appObj = VulkanApplication::GetInstance();
    appObj->initialize();
    appObj->prepare();
    bool isWindowOpen = true;
    while (isWindowOpen) {
    // Add the update function here..
    appObj->update();
    isWindowOpen = appObj->render();
```

```
}
        appObj->deInitialize();
}
```

The descriptor class: The `VulkanDrawable` class inherits `VulkanDescriptor`, bringing all the descriptor-related helper functions and user variables together, yet keeping the code logic separate. At the same time, it allows different implementation-drawable classes to extend it as per their requirements:

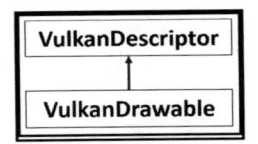

```
+------------------+
| VulkanDescriptor |
+------------------+
         ↑
+------------------+
|  VulkanDrawable  |
+------------------+
```

Execution model overview

This section will help us understand the execution model for Uniforms using the descriptor sets in Vulkan. The following are the step-by-step instructions:

1. **Initialization**: When an application is initialized, it calls the renderer's `initialize()` function. This function creates all the descriptors associated with each drawable object. The `VulkanDrawable` class is inherited from `VulkanDescriptor`, which contains the descriptor sets and the descriptor pool along with the related helper functions. The descriptor sets are allocated from the descriptor pool.
2. **Creating the descriptor layout**: Descriptor layouts define the descriptor bindings. This binding indicates the metadata about the descriptor, such as what kind of shader it is associated with, the type of the descriptor, the binding index in the shader, and the total number of descriptors of this type.
3. **The pipeline layout**: Create the pipeline layout; the descriptor set is specified in the pipeline object through pipeline layouts.
4. **Creating a uniform buffer for the transformation**: The transformation information is specified in a *4 x 4* transformation matrix. This is created (`createUniformBuffer()`) in a uniform buffer in the device memory that is used by the vertex shader to read the transformation information and apply it to the geometry vertices.

5. **Creating the descriptor pool**: Next, create a descriptor pool from which the descriptor sets will be allocated.
6. **Creating the descriptor set**: Allocate the descriptor set from the created descriptor pool (step 5) and associate the uniform buffer data (created in step 4) with it.
7. **Updating the transformation**: The transformation is updated in each frame where the uniform buffer GPU memory is mapped and updated with new transformation data contents.

Initialization

Initialization includes vertex and fragment shader implementation, the building of the uniform buffer resource, and the creation of the descriptor set from the descriptor pool. The descriptor set creation process includes building the descriptor and pipeline layout.

Shader implementation

The transformation is applied through a vertex shader using the uniform buffer as an input interface through the uniform block (bufferVals) with the layout binding index 1, as highlighted in bold in the following code.

The transformation is calculated by the product of the model view project matrix of bufferVals—mvp (layout binding = 0)—and the input vertices—pos (layout location = 0):

```
// Vertex shader
#version 450
layout (std140, binding = 0) uniform bufferVals {
mat4 mvp;
} myBufferVals;

layout (location = 0) in vec4 pos;
layout (location = 1) in vec4 inColor;
layout (location = 0) out vec4 outColor;
void main() {
 outColor = inColor;
 gl_Position = myBufferVals.mvp * pos;
 gl_Position.z = (gl_Position.z + gl_Position.w) / 2.0;
}
```

Descriptors and Push Constant

There is no change required in the fragment shader. The input color received at `location 0` (`color`) is used as the current fragment color specified by the output, `location 0` (`outColor`):

```
// Fragment shader
#version 450
layout (location = 0) in vec4 color;
layout (location = 0) out vec4 outColor;
void main() {
 outColor = color;
}
```

Creating descriptors

When the renderer is initialized (using the `initialize()` function), the descriptors are created in the helper function called `createDescriptors()`. This function first creates the descriptor layout for each drawable object by calling the `createDescriptorSetLayout()` function of `VulkanDrawable`. Next, the descriptor object is created inside the `createDescriptor()` function of `VulkanDrawable`. In this example, we are not programming textures; therefore, we send the parameter value as `Boolean false`:

```
// Create the descriptor sets
void VulkanRenderer::createDescriptors()
{
    for each (VulkanDrawable* drawableObj in drawableList)
    {
        // It is up to an application how it manages the
        // creation of descriptor. Descriptors can be cached
        // and reuse for all similar objects.
        drawableObj->createDescriptorSetLayout(false);

        // Create the descriptor set
        drawableObj->createDescriptor(false);
    }
}

void VulkanRenderer::initialize()
{
    . . . .
    // Create the vertex and fragment shader
    createShaders();

    // Create descriptor set layout
    createDescriptors();
```

```
        // Manage the pipeline state objects
        createPipelineStateManagement();
        . . . .
}
```

The `createDescriptorSetLayout()` function must be executed before you create the graphics pipeline layout. This ensures the descriptor layout is properly utilized while the pipeline layout is being created in the `VulkanDrawable::createPipelineLayout()` function. For more information on `createPipelineLayout()`, refer to the *Implementing the pipeline layout creation* subsection of the *Pipeline layouts* section in this chapter.

Descriptor set creation comprises of three steps–first, creating the uniform buffer; second, creating the descriptor pool; and finally, allocating the descriptor set and updating the descriptor set with the uniform buffer resource:

```
void VulkanDescriptor::createDescriptor(bool useTexture)
{
    // Create the uniform buffer resource
    createDescriptorResources();

    // Create the descriptor pool and
    // use it for descriptor set allocation
    createDescriptorPool(useTexture);

    // Create descriptor set with uniform buffer data in it
    createDescriptorSet(useTexture);
}
```

For more information on the creation of the uniform resource, refer to the *Creating the descriptor set resources* section in this chapter. In addition, you can refer to the *Creating the descriptor pool* and *Creating the descriptor sets* sections for a detailed understanding of descriptor pools and descriptor sets' creation.

Rendering

The created descriptor set needs to be specified in the drawing object. This is done when the command buffer of the drawing object is recorded (`VulkanDrawable::recordCommandBuffer()`).

Descriptors and Push Constant

The descriptor set is bound with the recorded command buffer inside `recordCommandBuffer()` using the `vkCmdBindDescriptorSets()` API. This API is called after the pipeline object is bound (`vkCmdBindPipeline()`) with the current command buffer and before you bind the vertex buffer (`vkCmdBindVertexBuffers()`) API:

```
void VulkanDrawable::recordCommandBuffer(int currentBuffer,
                                  VkCommandBuffer* cmdDraw)
{
    // Bound the command buffer with the graphics pipeline
    vkCmdBindPipeline(*cmdDraw, VK_PIPELINE_BIND_POINT_GRAPHICS,
                         *pipeline);
    // Bind the descriptor set into the command buffer
    vkCmdBindDescriptorSets(*cmdDraw, VK_PIPELINE_BIND_POINT_GRAPHICS,
    pipelineLayout, 0, 1, descriptorSet.data(), 0, NULL);

    const VkDeviceSize offsets[1] = { 0 };
    vkCmdBindVertexBuffers(*cmdDraw, 0, 1,
               &VertexBuffer.buf, offsets);
    . . . .
}
```

For more information on the `vkCmdBindDescriptorSets()` API specification, refer to the following subsection, *Binding the descriptor set*.

Binding the descriptor set

One or more created descriptor sets can be specified in the command buffer using `vkCmdBindDescriptorSets()`:

```
void vkCmdBindDescriptorSets(
    VkCommandBuffer            commandBuffer,
    VkPipelineBindPoint        pipelineBindPoint,
    VkPipelineLayout           layout,
    uint32_t                   firstSet,
    uint32_t                   descriptorSetCount,
    const VkDescriptorSet*     pDescriptorSets,
    uint32_t                   dynamicOffsetCount,
    const uint32_t*            pDynamicOffsets);
```

The various fields of the `vkCmdBindDescriptorSets` structure are defined as follows:

Parameters	Description
`commandBuffer`	This is the command buffer (`VkCommandBuffer`) to which the descriptor sets will be bound.
`pipelineBindPoint`	This field is a binding point to the pipeline of the type `VkPipelineBindPoint`, which indicates whether the descriptor will be used by the graphics pipeline or the compute pipeline. The respective binding points for the graphics and compute pipeline do not interfere with each other's work.
`Layouts`	This refers to the `VkPipelineLayout` object used to program the bindings.
`firstSet`	This indicates the index of the first descriptor set to be bound.
`descriptorSetCount`	This refers to the number of elements in the `pDescriptorSets` arrays.
`pDescriptorSets`	This is an array of handles for the `VkDescriptorSet` objects describing the descriptor sets to write to.
`dynamicOffsetCount`	This refers to the number of dynamic offsets in the `pDynamicOffsets` array.
`pDynamicOffsets`	This is a pointer to an array of `uint32_t` values specifying the dynamic offsets.

Update

Once the command buffer (bounded with the descriptor set) is submitted to the queue, it executes and renders the drawing object with the transformation specified in the uniform buffer. In order to update and render a continuous update transformation, the `update()` function can be used.

> Updating the descriptor set could be a performance-critical path; therefore, it is advisable to partition multiple descriptors based upon the frequency with which they are updated. It can be divided into the scene, model, and drawing levels, where the update frequency is low, medium, and high, respectively.

Updating the transformation

The transformation is updated in each frame inside the update() function of the drawable class (VulkanDrawable), which acquires the memory location of the uniform buffer and updates the transformation matrix with the new information. The uniform buffer memory location is not available directly because it is a resident of the GPU memory; therefore, the GPU memory is allocated by means of memory mapping, where a portion of the GPU memory is mapped to the CPU memory. Once the memory is updated with it, it is remapped to the GPU memory. The following code snippet implements the update() function:

```
void VulkanDrawable::update()
{
    VulkanDevice* deviceObj = rendererObj->getDevice();
    uint8_t *pData;
    glm::mat4 Projection = glm::perspective(glm::radians(45.0f), 1.0f,
                                    0.1f, 100.0f);
    glm::mat4 View = glm::lookAt(
        glm::vec3(0, 0, 5),     // Camera is in World Space
        glm::vec3(0, 0, 0),     // and looks at the origin
        glm::vec3(0, 1, 0));    // Head is up
    glm::mat4 Model = glm::mat4(1.0f);
    static float rot = 0;
    rot += .003;
    Model = glm::rotate(Model, rot, glm::vec3(0.0, 1.0, 0.0))
            * glm::rotate(Model, rot, glm::vec3(1.0, 1.0, 1.0));

    // Compute the ModelViewProjection transformation matrix
    glm::mat4 MVP = Projection * View * Model;

    // Map the GPU memory on to local host
    VkResult result = vkMapMemory(deviceObj->device, UniformData.
            memory, 0, UniformData.memRqrmnt.size, 0,
            (void **)&pData);
    assert(result == VK_SUCCESS);
    // The device memory we have kept mapped it,
    // invalidate the range of mapped buffer in order
    // to make it visible to the host.
    VkResult res = vkInvalidateMappedMemoryRanges(deviceObj->device,
                1, &UniformData.mappedRange[0]);
    assert(res == VK_SUCCESS);

    // Copy computed data in the mapped buffer
    memcpy(pData, &MVP, sizeof(MVP));

    // Flush the range of mapped buffer in order to
    // make it visible to the device. If the memory
```

```
        // is coherent (memory property must be
        // VK_MEMORY_PROPERTY_HOST_COHERENT_BIT) then the driver
        // may take care of this, otherwise for non-coherent
        // mapped memory vkFlushMappedMemoryRanges() needs
        // to be called explicitly to flush out the pending
        // writes on the host side
        res = vkFlushMappedMemoryRanges(deviceObj->device,
                  1, &UniformData.mappedRange[0]);
        assert(res == VK_SUCCESS);
    }
```

In the preceding implementation, once the uniform buffer is mapped, we do not unmap it until the application stops using the uniform buffer. In order to make the range of uniform buffer visible to the host, we invalidate the mapped range using `vkInvalidateMappedMemoryRanges()`. After the new data is updated in the mapped buffer, the host flushes out any pending writes using `vkFlushMappedMemoryRanges()` and makes the mapped memory visible to the device.

Finally, don't forget to unmap the mapped device memory when it is no longer needed using the `vkUnmapMemory()` API. In this present example, we unmap it before destroying the uniform buffer objects:

```
void VulkanDrawable::destroyUniformBuffer()
{
    vkUnmapMemory(deviceObj->device, UniformData.memory);
    vkDestroyBuffer(rendererObj->getDevice()->device,
        UniformData.buffer, NULL);
    vkFreeMemory(rendererObj->getDevice()->device,
        UniformData.memory, NULL);
}
```

Descriptors and Push Constant

The following is the output showing the revolving cube:

Push constant updates

Push constants are specially designed to update the shader constant data using the command buffer instead of updating the resources with the write or copy descriptors.

> Push constants offer a high-speed optimized path to update the constant data in the pipeline.

In this section, we will quickly implement an example to demonstrate a push constant. We will learn how push constants are used with command buffers to update the resource contents in the shader. This example defines two types of resources in the fragment shader—`constColor` and `mixerValue`—within the push constant uniform block `pushConstantsColorBlock`. The `constColor` resource contains an integer value that is used as a flag to render the rotating cube in a solid color (red, green, or blue). The `mixerValue` resource is a floating value that mixes with the cube color.

Defining the push constant resource in the shader

The push constant resource in the shader is defined using the `push_constant` keyword in a layout that indicates it is a push constant block. In the following code, we have modified the existing fragment shader and added two push constant variables, namely `constColor` and `mixerValue`. If the value of `constColor` is either 1, 2, or 3, then a solid geometry color (red, green, or blue) is rendered. Otherwise, the original color is mixed with `mixerValue`:

```
// Fragment shader
#version 450
layout (location = 0) in vec4 color;
layout (location = 0) out vec4 outColor;
layout(push_constant) uniform colorBlock {
    int constColor;
    float mixerValue;
} pushConstantsColorBlock;

vec4 red   = vec4(1.0, 0.0, 0.0, 1.0);
vec4 green = vec4(0.0, 1.0, 0.0, 1.0);
vec4 blue  = vec4(0.0, 0.0, 1.0, 1.0);

void main() {
    if (pushConstantsColorBlock.constColor == 1)
       outColor = red;
    else if (pushConstantsColorBlock.constColor == 2)
       outColor = green;
    else if (pushConstantsColorBlock.constColor == 3)
       outColor = blue;
    else
       outColor = color*pushConstantsColorBlock.mixerValue;
}
```

In the next section, we will update this shader push constant resource in the pipeline layout.

Updating the pipeline layout with the push constant

Update the pipeline layout indicating the push constant ranges. The push constant range is defined in a single pipeline layout using the `VkPushConstantRange` structure. The pipeline layout also needs to be informed how many push constants can be accessed by each stage of the pipeline.

Descriptors and Push Constant

The following is the syntax of this structure:

```
typedef struct VkPushConstantRange {
    VkShaderStageFlags      stageFlags;
    uint32_t                offset;
    uint32_t                size;
} VkPushConstantRange;
```

The various fields of the `VkPushConstantRange` structure are defined here:

Parameters	Description
`stageFlags`	This field indicates the shader stage to which this push constant range belongs. If `stageFlags` is not defined with the shader stage, then accessing the push constant resource member from that shader stage will produce an instance where undefined data would be read.
`offset`	This is the start offset of the push constant range specified in bytes and is a multiple of four.
`size`	This field is also specified in bytes and is a multiple of four, indicating the size of the push constant range.

Update `pushConstantRangeCount` of `VkPipelineLayoutCreateInfo` with the push constant range count and `pPushConstantRanges` with a pointer to an array of `VkPushConstantRange`:

```
void VulkanDrawable::createPipelineLayout()
{
    // Setup the push constant range
    const unsigned pushConstantRangeCount = 1;
    VkPushConstantRange pushConstantRanges[pushConstantRangeCount]={};
    pushConstantRanges[0].stageFlags    = VK_SHADER_STAGE_FRAGMENT_BIT;
    pushConstantRanges[0].offset        = 0;
    pushConstantRanges[0].size          = 8;

    // Create the pipeline layout with the help of descriptor layout.
    VkPipelineLayoutCreateInfo pPipelineLayoutCreateInfo = {};
    pPipelineLayoutCreateInfo.sType     =
                VK_STRUCTURE_TYPE_PIPELINE_LAYOUT_CREATE_INFO;
    pPipelineLayoutCreateInfo.pNext                     = NULL;
    pPipelineLayoutCreateInfo.pushConstantRangeCount =
                pushConstantRangeCount;
    pPipelineLayoutCreateInfo.pPushConstantRanges =
                pushConstantRanges;
    pPipelineLayoutCreateInfo.setLayoutCount    =
                (uint32_t)descLayout.size();
    pPipelineLayoutCreateInfo.pSetLayouts = descLayout.data();
```

```
    VkResult   result;
    result = vkCreatePipelineLayout(deviceObj->device,
            &pPipelineLayoutCreateInfo, NULL, &pipelineLayout);
    assert(result == VK_SUCCESS);
}
```

Updating the resource data

The resource data can be updated using the vkCmdPushConstants() API. In order to use this API, allocate a command buffer called cmdPushConstant, update the resource data with the appropriate values, and execute vkCmdPushConstants(). The following is the syntax of this API:

```
void vkCmdPushConstants(
    VkCommandBuffer        commandBuffer,
    VkPipelineLayout       layout,
    VkShaderStageFlags     stageFlags,
    uint32_t               offset,
    uint32_t               size,
    const void*            pValues);
```

The various fields of the vkCmdPushConstants structure are defined here:

Parameters	Description
commandBuffer	This is the command buffer object (VkCommandBuffer) that will be used to record the push constant update.
layout	This is VkPipelineLayout object that will be used to program the push constant updates.
stageFlag	This specifies the shader stage that will utilize the push constants in the updated range. The shader stage is indicated using a bitmask of VkShaderStageFlagBits.
offset	This starts the offset in bytes specifying the push constant range for the update.
size	This refers to the size (in bytes) of the push constant range to be updated.
pValues	This is an array containing the new push constant values.

The size of the push constant must never exceed the size specified in VkPhysicalDeviceProperties::limits::maxPushConstantsSize.

Descriptors and Push Constant

The following is the implementation of the push constants where the push constant is executed using the allocated command buffer `cmdPushConstant`. There are two push constant resource variables: `constColorRGBFlag` and `mixerValue`. These are set with the desired values and specified in the `vkCmdPushConstants()` API:

```
void VulkanRenderer::createPushConstants()
{
    // Allocate and start recording the push constant buffer.
    CommandBufferMgr::allocCommandBuffer(&deviceObj->device,
                        cmdPool, &cmdPushConstant);
    CommandBufferMgr::beginCommandBuffer(cmdPushConstant);

    enum ColorFlag {
        RED         = 1,
        GREEN       = 2,
        BLUE        = 3,
        MIXED_COLOR = 4,
    };

    float    mixerValue        = 0.3f;
    unsigned constColorRGBFlag = BLUE;

    // Create push constant data, this contain a constant
    // color flag and mixer value for non-const color
    unsigned pushConstants[2]  = {};
    pushConstants[0]           = constColorRGBFlag;
    memcpy(&pushConstants[1], &mixerValue, sizeof(float));

    // Check if number of push constants does
    // not exceed the allowed size
    int maxPushContantSize = getDevice()->gpuProps.
                        limits.maxPushConstantsSize;

    if (sizeof(pushConstants) > maxPushContantSize) {
        assert(0);
     printf("Push constant size is greater than expected,
            max allow size is %d", maxPushContantSize);
    }

    for each (VulkanDrawable* drawableObj in drawableList)
    {
        vkCmdPushConstants(cmdPushConstant,
          drawableObj->pipelineLayout,
          VK_SHADER_STAGE_FRAGMENT_BIT,
          0, sizeof(pushConstants), pushConstants);
    }
```

```
        CommandBufferMgr::endCommandBuffer(cmdPushConstant);
        CommandBufferMgr::submitCommandBuffer(deviceObj->queue,
            &cmdPushConstant);
}
```

The following is the output rendering the cube geometry with solid colors. In this example, `constColor` must be 1, 2, or 3 in order to produce the solid color:

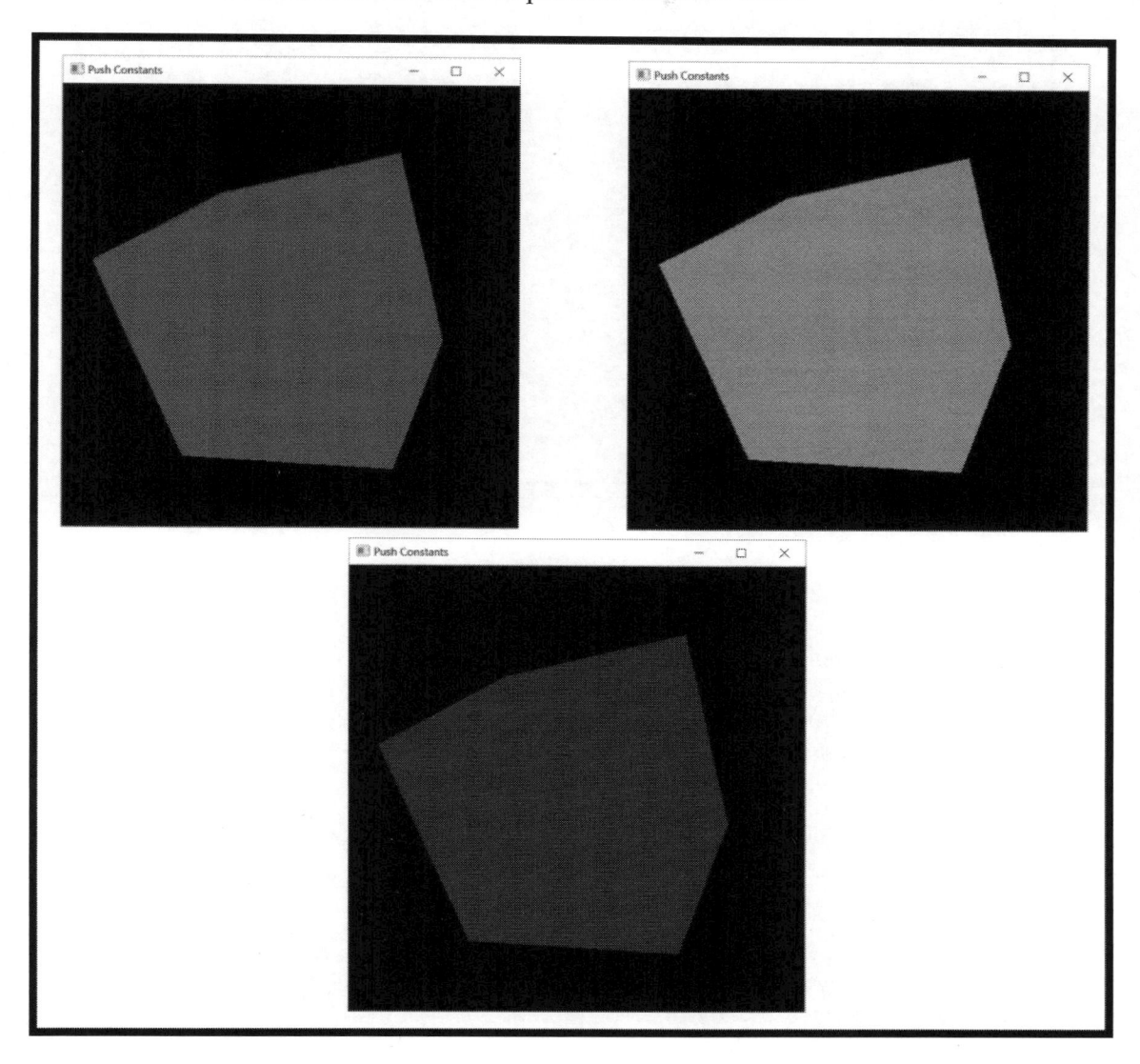

Descriptors and Push Constant

The following is the output of the original colored cube blended with the mixer value; for this output, `constColor` must not be 1, 2, or 3:

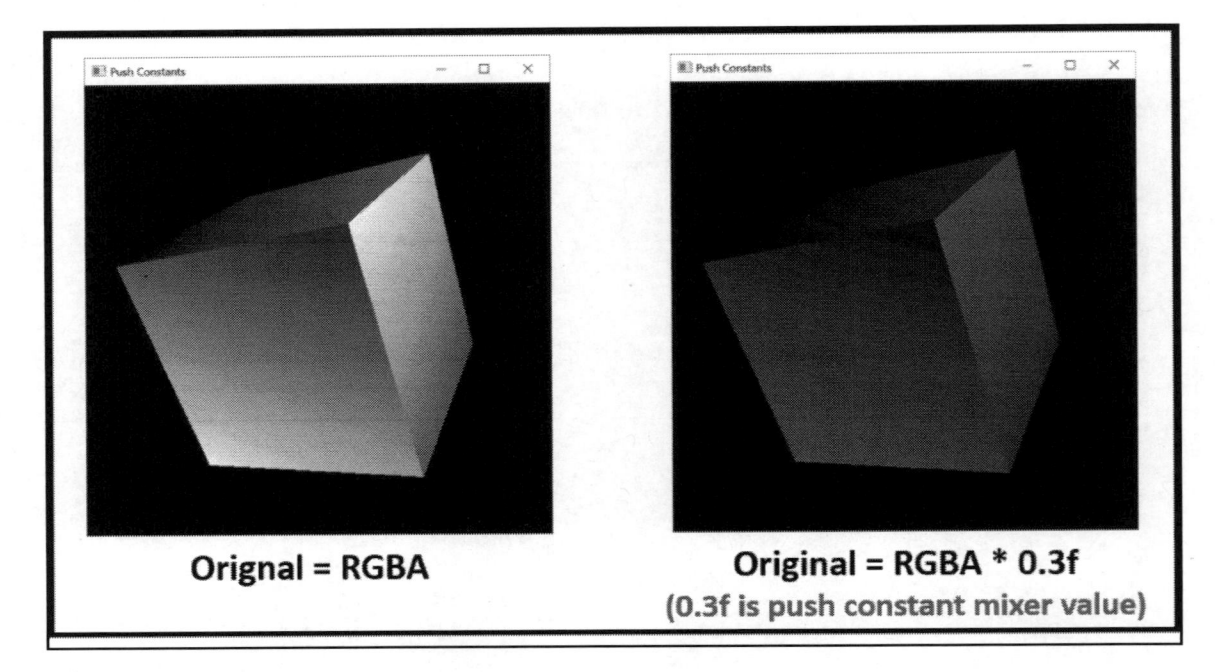

Orignal = RGBA

Original = RGBA * 0.3f
(0.3f is push constant mixer value)

Summary

In this chapter, we learned the concept of descriptor set and understood the implementation of Uniforms. We rendered a multicolor cube and added 3D transformation through uniform blocks. Uniforms are implemented using descriptor sets. We understood the role of the descriptor pool and used it to allocate the descriptor set objects.

We attached the descriptor sets to the graphics pipeline using the pipeline layouts; this allows a pipeline (graphics or compute) to access the descriptor sets. In addition, we also understood and implemented push constant updates, which is an optimized way to update the constant data using command buffers.

In the next chapter, we will play with textures. Textures are implemented in Vulkan through the image resource type. We will understand this resource type and also demonstrate how to bring these textures on the rendered geometries.

11
Drawing Textures

In the previous chapter, we learned how to update the resource contents and read them at the shader stage using descriptors. We also covered push constant, which is an optimized way of updating the constant data at the shader stage using command buffers. In addition, by making use of descriptors, we added 3D transformations to our rendering primitives and also demonstrated an example to learn push constants.

In this chapter, we will learn and implement textures; we will wrap them around the geometry surfaces to bring realism to the scene. Textures are created using the Vulkan image resource; its data can be stored in either a linear or optimal layout. We will implement these two layouts–the latter layout uses staging. In staging, two different memory regions are used for the physical allocation process. The ideal memory placement for a resource may not be visible to the host. In this case, the application must first populate the resource in a host-visible staging buffer and then transfer it to the ideal location.

In this chapter, we will cover the following topics:

- Image resource – a quick recap
- Prerequisites for texture drawing
- Implementing the image resource with linear tiling
- Implementing the image resource with optimal tiling
- Copying data content between images and buffers
- Updating the descriptor set

Image resource – a quick recap

Images are continuous array of bytes stored in 1D, 2D, or 3D form. Unlike the buffer resource, an image is a formatted piece of information stored in the memory.

The image resource in Vulkan is represented by the `VkImage` object and created using the `vkCreateImage` API. The creation of this object does not back with the actual image contents, yet. This has to be done separately, where device memory is allocated and the image contents are stored into it. This memory is then bound to the created object.

In order to utilize the created images' objects at the shader stage, they must be converted into the image view–`VkImageView`. Before you convert an image into an image view, it has to be made compatible with the underlying implementation using image layouts.

The image is converted into the implementation-dependent layouts using `VkImageLayout`. For a given image resource, multiple image layouts can be created and used across. Different layouts might expose different performance characteristics, as they are very dedicated to the `usage` type. Indicating a correct usage lets the driver choose a specific memory location or portion suitable to offer optimal performance.

If you like to get a detailed introduction of image resources, refer to the very first section, namely *Getting started with image resources* in Chapter 6, *Allocating Image Resources and Building a Swapchain with WSI*. In the same chapter, you can refer to the *Understanding image resource* section for detailed information on images, image views, and image layouts.

Creating an image resource is simple. It consists of the following steps:

1. **Image object creation**: First, the `VkImage` object is created. This object does not contain the image data, but it holds various important object states of the image resource, such as the format, dimension, image type, image's `usage` type, tiling fashion, and more. A given image can have multiple sub image resources, such as mipmaps. Following are the steps to create an image object:
    1. **Tiling**: There are two ways in which image tiling can be specified: linear and optimal. In the linear layout, the image data is mapped to contiguous memory on the device, arranged in a linear fashion. However, in an optimal layout, the image is stored in the form of tiles, and the texels inside each tile may be arranged in either a linear or some proprietary format to offer optimal performance. For a detailed view of linear and optimal layouts, refer to the *Introduction to tiling* section in Chapter 6, *Allocating Image Resources and Building a Swapchain with WSI*.
    2. **Allocating and assigning image data**: Read the image contents and

allocate the required memory to the image resource. Fill the allocated device memory with the image channel contents.
3. **Setting the correct layout**: Create an implementation-compatible image layout. A single image and its sub resource can be specified with multiple layouts.
2. **Image sampler**: Create samplers (`VkSampler`) to control texture filtering.
3. **Image view creation**: An image resource can only be accessed in the shader in the form of an image view (`VkImageView`).

Prerequisites for texture drawing

Implementing textures is easy and requires only a few steps. Let's have a quick overview of this first, then we will take a deep dive into it:

1. **Texture coordinates**: Textures are glued to the geometry surfaces using texture coordinates. For each vertex, there is a corresponding texture coordinate attached. In our implementation, we specified the vertices and texture coordinates in an interleaved form.
2. **The shader stage**: The vertex and fragment shader are modified to bound the texture resources. The shader stage allows the fragment shader to access the texture resource and paint the fragments. Textures are shared in the form of a sampler at the shader stage.
3. **Loading the image files**: Parse the image files and load the raw image data into the local data structure. This will be helpful in producing Vulkan image resources and sharing them at the shader stage.
4. **Local image data structure**: The `TextureData` local data structure stores all the image-specific attributes.

Specifying the texture coordinates

The geometry coordinates (x, y, z, w) are interleaved with texture coordinates (u, v) in the `VertexWithUV` structure defined in `MeshData.h`:

```
struct VertexWithUV
{
    float x, y, z, w;    // Vertex Position
    float u, v;          // Texture format U,V
};
```

Drawing Textures

In this present sample, we will render a cube drawn with textured faces. The following code shows one of the cube faces with four vertex positions followed by two texture coordinates. Refer to `MeshData.h` for the complete code:

```
static const VertexWithUV geometryData[] = {
   { -1.0f,-1.0f,-1.0f, 1.0f, 0.0f, 1.0f },   // -X side
   { -1.0f,-1.0f, 1.0f, 1.0f, 1.0f, 1.0f },
   { -1.0f, 1.0f, 1.0f, 1.0f, 1.0f, 0.0f },
   { -1.0f, 1.0f, 1.0f, 1.0f, 1.0f, 0.0f },
   { -1.0f, 1.0f,-1.0f, 1.0f, 0.0f, 0.0f },
   { -1.0f,-1.0f,-1.0f, 1.0f, 0.0f, 1.0f },
. . . .
// Similar, specify +X, -Y, +Y, -Z, +Z faces
}
```

Updating the shader program

In addition to the vertex coordinates, now our vertex shader will also take the texture coordinates under consideration. The input texture coordinates are received at the layout location 1 in the `inUV` attribute. These coordinates are then passed on to the fragment shading stage and received in `outUV`. The following code shows the modification in the existing vertex shader in bold:

```
// Vertex Shader
#version 450
layout (std140, binding = 0) uniform bufferVals {
    mat4 mvp;
} myBufferVals;

layout (location = 0) in vec4 pos;
layout (location = 1) in vec2 inUV;
layout (location = 0) out vec2 outUV;

void main() {
   outUV           = inUV;
   gl_Position     = myBufferVals.mvp * pos;
   gl_Position.z = (gl_Position.z + gl_Position.w) / 2.0;
}
```

The following code implements the fragment shader where the sampled texture is received at the layout binding index 1. The received texture is used with the input texture coordinates to fetch the fragment colors:

```
// Fragment Shader
#version 450
layout(binding = 1) uniform sampler2D tex;
layout (location = 0) in vec2 uv;
layout (location = 0) out vec4 outColor;

void main() {
outColor = texture(tex, uv);
}
```

Loading the image files

The image files are loaded in our sample application using the GLI library. **OpenGL Image (GLI)** is a header-only C++ image library that supports the loading of KTX and DDS image files for a graphics software application. It provides various features such as texture loading and creation, texture compression, accessing of the texture texels, sample textures, convert textures, mipmaps, and more.

You can download this library from http://gli.g-truc.net/0.8.1/index.html. In order to use this library, perform the following changes:

- **CMakeLists.txt**: Add GLI support by adding the following lines to the project's CMakeLists.txt file:

    ```
    # GLI SETUP
    set (EXTDIR "${CMAKE_SOURCE_DIR}/../../external/gli")
    set (GLIINCLUDES "${EXTDIR}")
    get_filename_component(GLIINC_PREFIX "${GLIINCLUDES}" ABSOLUTE)
    if(NOT EXISTS ${GLIINC_PREFIX})
        message(FATAL_ERROR "Necessary gli headers do not exist:
        " ${GLIINC_PREFIX})
    endif()
    include_directories( ${GLIINC_PREFIX} )
    ```

- **Header files**: This includes the header files for GLI in the Headers.h file:

    ```
    /*********** GLI HEADER FILES ***********/
    #include <gli/gli.hpp>
    ```

Using the GLI library

The following code is the minimal usage of the GLI library in our application. This code demonstrates image loading, the querying of a dimension, mipmap levels, and the retrieval of image data:

```
// Load the image
const char* filename = "../VulkanEssentials.ktx";
gli::texture2D image2D(gli::load(filename));
assert(!image2D.empty());

// Get the image dimensions at ith sub-resource
uint32_t textureWidth    = image2D[i].dimensions().x;
uint32_t textureHeight   = image2D[i].dimensions().y;

// Get number of mip-map levels
uint32_t mipMapLevels    = image2D.levels();

// Retrieve the raw image data
void* rawData            = image2D.data();
```

Local image data structure

The `wrapper.h` contains a user-defined `TextureData` structure to hold the image attributes and various pieces of image-specific information in the application. The following is the syntax and description of each field:

```
struct TextureData{
    VkSampler                sampler;
    VkImage                  image;
    VkImageLayout            imageLayout;
    VkMemoryAllocateInfo     memoryAlloc;
    VkDeviceMemory           mem;
    VkImageView              view;
    uint32_t                 mipMapLevels;
    uint32_t                 layerCount;
    uint32_t                 textureWidth, textureHeight;
    VkDescriptorImageInfo    descsImgInfo;
};
```

Chapter 11

The following table describes the various fields of the user-defined structure, `TextureData`:

Parameters	Description
`sampler`	This is the `VkSampler` object associated with the image object.
`image`	This is the `VkImage` object.
`imageLayout`	This contains specific implementation-dependent layout information of the image resource object.
`memoryAlloc`	This stores the memory allocation information bound with associated image object (`VkImage`).
`mem`	This refers to the physical device memory allocated for this image resource.
`view`	This is the `ImageView` object of `image`.
`mipMapLevels`	This refers to the number of mipmap levels in the image resource.
`layerCount`	This refers to the number of layer count in the image resource.
`textureWidth` `textureHeight`	These are the dimensions of the image resource.
`descsImgInfo`	This is the descriptor image information that contains the image view and sample information with proper image layout `usage` type.

In the next section, we will start implementing our image resource and see it in action.

Implementing the image resource with linear tiling

In this section, we will implement the image resource with linear tiling and display a textured image on the faces of our rendering cube that we implemented in the last chapter.

As we learned in the *Introduction to tiling* section in `Chapter 6`, *Allocating Image Resources and Building a Swapchain with WSI*, there are two types of image tiling–linear and optimal:

- **Linear tiling**: In this type of tiling arrangement, the image texels are laid out in a row-by-row manner (row-major order), which might require some padding to match the row pitch. A row pitch defines the width of the row; as a result, if the laid out texel row is smaller than the row pitch, then padding is needed. The `VkImageCreateInfo` indicates the linear tiling through the `tiling` field (of the type `VkImageTiling`). This field must be specified

Drawing Textures

　　　　as `VK_IMAGE_TILING_LINEAR`.
- **Optimal tiling**: As the name suggests, the image texels are laid out in an implementation-specific way meant for offering better performance by optimal memory access. Here, the `tiling` field must be specified as `VK_IMAGE_TILING_OPTIMAL`.

Linear image tiling is implemented in the `createTextureLinear()` function inside the `VulkanRenderer` class. This function takes four parameters. The first parameter (`filename`) specifies which image file to load. The second parameter is a `TextureData` data structure into which the created image and properties should be stored. The third parameter, `imageUsageFlags`, indicates the hints of the image resource specifying the purpose for which it will be used. The last parameter, `format`, specifies the image format into which the image object must be created. Here's the syntax of this:

```
void VulkanRenderer::createTextureLinear(const char* filename, TextureData
*texture, VkImageUsageFlags imageUsageFlags, VkFormat format);
```

Let's understand and implement these functions step-by-step.

Loading the image file

Use the GLI library and load the image file:

```
// Load the image
gli::texture2D image2D(gli::load(filename)); assert(!image2D.empty());

// Get the image dimensions
texture->textureWidth       = uint32_t(image2D[0].dimensions().x);
texture->textureHeight      = uint32_t(image2D[0].dimensions().y);

// Get number of mip-map levels
texture->mipMapLevels       = uint32_t(image2D.levels());
```

Creating the image object

Create the image object (`VkImage`) using the `vkCreateImage` API. The `vkCreateImage()` API uses `VkImageCreateInfo`. This structure specifies the image resource metadata. The `usage` field of `VkImageCreateInfo` must be passed with the `VK_IMAGE_USAGE_SAMPLED_BIT` bitwise flag since the textures will be consumed at the shader stage in the form of samplers:

```
// Create image resource states using VkImageCreateInfo
VkImageCreateInfo imageCreateInfo       = {};
imageCreateInfo.sType                   = VK_STRUCTURE_TYPE_IMAGE_CREATE_INFO;
imageCreateInfo.pNext                   = NULL;
imageCreateInfo.imageType               = VK_IMAGE_TYPE_2D;
imageCreateInfo.format                  = format;
imageCreateInfo.extent.width            = image2D[0].dimensions().x;
imageCreateInfo.extent.height           = image2D[0].dimensions().y;
imageCreateInfo.extent.depth            = 1;
imageCreateInfo.mipLevels               = texture->mipMapLevels;
imageCreateInfo.arrayLayers             = 1;
imageCreateInfo.samples                 = VK_SAMPLE_COUNT_1_BIT;
imageCreateInfo.queueFamilyIndexCount   = 0;
imageCreateInfo.pQueueFamilyIndices     = NULL;
imageCreateInfo.sharingMode             = VK_SHARING_MODE_EXCLUSIVE;
imageCreateInfo.usage                   = imageUsageFlags;
imageCreateInfo.flags                   = 0;
imageCreateInfo.initialLayout           = VK_IMAGE_LAYOUT_PREINITIALIZED,
imageCreateInfo.tiling                  = VK_IMAGE_TILING_LINEAR;

// Use create image info and create the image objects
vkCreateImage(deviceObj->device, &imageCreateInfo, NULL, &texture->image);
```

The usage bit field of the create info structure specifies how the image resource will be used, for instance, the color image type for presentation, depth image type for depth testing, source and destination image type for transfer commands, and more. This information, provided in advance, is helpful in optimal resource management.

The image's usage flag of the VkImageCreateInfo control structure is described using the VkImageUsageFlagBits enum flag. The following is the syntax and description of each type:

```
typedef enum VkImageUsageFlagBits {
        VK_IMAGE_USAGE_TRANSFER_SRC_BIT              = 0x00000001,
        VK_IMAGE_USAGE_TRANSFER_DST_BIT              = 0x00000002,
        VK_IMAGE_USAGE_SAMPLED_BIT                   = 0x00000004,
        VK_IMAGE_USAGE_STORAGE_BIT                   = 0x00000008,
        VK_IMAGE_USAGE_COLOR_ATTACHMENT_BIT          = 0x00000010,
        VK_IMAGE_USAGE_DEPTH_STENCIL_ATTACHMENT_BIT  = 0x00000020,
        VK_IMAGE_USAGE_TRANSIENT_ATTACHMENT_BIT      = 0x00000040,
        VK_IMAGE_USAGE_INPUT_ATTACHMENT_BIT          = 0x00000080,
} VkImageUsageFlagBits;
```

Drawing Textures

Let's look at these bitwise fields in detail to understand what they mean:

Enum type	Description
VK_IMAGE_USAGE_TRANSFER_SRC_BIT	With this, the image is used by the transfer command's (copy command) source.
VK_IMAGE_USAGE_TRANSFER_DST_BIT	With this, the image is used by the transfer command's (copy command) destination.
VK_IMAGE_USAGE_SAMPLED_BIT	This image type is used as a sampler at the shading stage through the image view type, where the associated descriptor set slot (VkDescriptorSet) type could be either VK_DESCRIPTOR_TYPE_SAMPLED_IMAGE or VK_DESCRIPTOR_TYPE_COMBINED_IMAGE_SAMPLER. The sampled image in the shader is used for address calculations, controlling the filtering behavior, and other attributes.
VK_IMAGE_USAGE_STORAGE_BIT	Use this image type for load, store, and atomic operations on the image memory. The image view is associated with a descriptor-type slot of the type VK_DESCRIPTOR_TYPE_STORAGE_IMAGE.
VK_IMAGE_USAGE_COLOR_ATTACHMENT_BIT	The image view created from this type of image resource is appropriate for either the color attachment or the resolve attachment associated with the framebuffer object (VkFrameBuffer).
VK_IMAGE_USAGE_DEPTH_STENCIL_ATTACHMENT_BIT	The image view created from this type of image resource is appropriate for either the depth/stencil attachment or the resolve attachment associated with the framebuffer object (VkFrameBuffer).
VK_IMAGE_USAGE_TRANSIENT_ATTACHMENT_BIT	The image type represented by this flag is allocated lazily. The memory type for this must be specified as VK_MEMORY_PROPERTY_LAZILY_ALLOCATED_BIT. Note that if this flag is specified, then VK_IMAGE_USAGE_COLOR_ATTACHMENT_BIT, VK_IMAGE_USAGE_DEPTH_STENCIL_ATTACHMENT_BIT, and VK_IMAGE_USAGE_INPUT_ATTACHMENT_BIT must not be used.
VK_IMAGE_USAGE_INPUT_ATTACHMENT_BIT	The image view created from this type of image resource is appropriate for the input attachment at the shader stage and in the framebuffer. The image view must be associated with the descriptor set slot (VkDescriptorSet) of the type VK_DESCRIPTOR_TYPE_INPUT_ATTACHMENT.

> The memory allocated with the `VK_MEMORY_PROPERTY_LAZILY_ALLOCATED_BIT` bit flag is not allocated upfront as per the requested size, but it may be allocated in a monotonic fashion where memory gradually increases as per application demand.

The `flag` field in the `VkImageCreateInfo` enum hints the underlying application how it manages various image resources, such as memory, format, and attributes, using the `VkImageCreateFlagBits` enum. The following is the syntax and description of each type:

```
typedef enum VkImageCreateFlagBits {
    VK_IMAGE_CREATE_SPARSE_BINDING_BIT      = 0x00000001,
    VK_IMAGE_CREATE_SPARSE_RESIDENCY_BIT    = 0x00000002,
    VK_IMAGE_CREATE_SPARSE_ALIASED_BIT      = 0x00000004,
    VK_IMAGE_CREATE_MUTABLE_FORMAT_BIT      = 0x00000008,
    VK_IMAGE_CREATE_CUBE_COMPATIBLE_BIT     = 0x00000010,
    VK_IMAGE_CREATE_FLAG_BITS_MAX_ENUM      = 0x7FFFFFFF
} VkImageCreateFlagBits;
typedef VkFlags VkImageCreateFlags;
```

Let's understand the flag definitions:

Flags	Description
VK_IMAGE_CREATE_SPARSE_BINDING_BIT	Here, the image is fully stored using sparse memory binding.
VK_IMAGE_CREATE_SPARSE_RESIDENCY_BIT	Here, the image can be stored partially using sparse memory binding. In order to use this field, the image must have the `VK_IMAGE_CREATE_SPARSE_BINDING_BIT` flag.
VK_IMAGE_CREATE_SPARSE_ALIASED_BIT	In this type of flag, the image is stored into sparse memory, and it also can hold multiple portions of the same image in the same memory regions. The image must be created using the `VK_IMAGE_CREATE_SPARSE_BINDING_BIT` flag.
VK_IMAGE_CREATE_MUTABLE_FORMAT_BIT	This allows the image view's format to differ from the image's format.

Drawing Textures

VK_IMAGE_CREATE_CUBE_COMPATIBLE_BIT	This flag indicates that the VkImageView of the type VK_IMAGE_VIEW_TYPE_CUBE or VK_IMAGE_VIEW_TYPE_CUBE_ARRAY can be created from the image (VkImage) object.

Memory allocation and binding

The created image object does not have any device memory backing. In this step, we will allocate the physical device memory and bind it with the created texture->image. For more information on memory allocation and the binding process, refer to the *Memory allocation and binding image resources* section in Chapter 6, *Allocating Image Resources and Building a Swapchain with WSI*:

```
// Get the buffer memory requirements
VkMemoryRequirements memoryRequirements;
vkGetImageMemoryRequirements(deviceObj->device, texture->image,
                             &memoryRequirements);

// Create memory allocation metadata information
VkMemoryAllocateInfo& memAlloc   = texture->memoryAlloc;
memAlloc.sType = VK_STRUCTURE_TYPE_MEMORY_ALLOCATE_INFO;
memAlloc.pNext           = NULL;
memAlloc.allocationSize  = memoryRequirements.size;
memAlloc.memoryTypeIndex = 0;


// Determine the type of memory required
// with the help of memory properties
deviceObj->memoryTypeFromProperties
        (memoryRequirements.memoryTypeBits,
         VK_MEMORY_PROPERTY_HOST_VISIBLE_BIT,
         &texture->memoryAlloc.memoryTypeIndex);

// Allocate the memory for buffer objects
vkAllocateMemory(deviceObj->device,
         &texture->memoryAlloc, NULL, &(texture->mem));

// Bind the image device memory
vkBindImageMemory(deviceObj->device, texture->image,
                                    texture->mem, 0);
```

Populating the allocated device memory

Push the image data on the GPU using the mapping (`vkMapMemory`) and unmapping (`vkUnmapMemory`) function. First, query the resource layout information with the `vkGetImageSubresourceLayout()` API. The layout information provides the `rowPitch` information that is utilized to store the image data in a row-by-row fashion:

```
VkImageSubresource subresource    = {};
subresource.aspectMask            = VK_IMAGE_ASPECT_COLOR_BIT;
subresource.mipLevel              = 0;
subresource.arrayLayer            = 0;

VkSubresourceLayout layout;
uint8_t *data;

vkGetImageSubresourceLayout(deviceObj->device,
            texture->image, &subresource, &layout);

// Map the GPU memory on to local host
error = vkMapMemory(deviceObj->device, texture->mem, 0, texture
   ->memoryAlloc.allocationSize, 0, (void**)&data);
assert(!error);

// Load image texture data in the mapped buffer
uint8_t* dataTemp = (uint8_t*)image2D.data();
for (int y = 0; y < image2D[0].dimensions().y; y++)
{
            size_t imageSize = image2D[0].dimensions().y * 4;
    memcpy(data, dataTemp, imageSize);
    dataTemp += imageSize;


    // Advance row-by-row pitch information
    data += layout.rowPitch;
}

// UnMap the host memory to push changes into the device memory
vkUnmapMemory(deviceObj->device, texture->mem);
```

Creating the command buffer object

The image resource objects are created using the command buffer object, `cmdTexture`, defined in the `VulkanRenderer` class:

```
// Command buffer allocation and recording begins
CommandBufferMgr::allocCommandBuffer(&deviceObj->device,
                            cmdPool, &cmdTexture);
CommandBufferMgr::beginCommandBuffer(cmdTexture);
```

Setting the image layout

Set the image layout (`VkImageLayout`) with the `setImageLayout()` function. For more information on this function, refer to the *Set the image layout with memory barriers* section in Chapter 6, *Allocating Image Resources and Building a Swapchain with WSI*:

```
VkImageSubresourceRange subresourceRange = {};
subresourceRange.aspectMask     = VK_IMAGE_ASPECT_COLOR_BIT;
subresourceRange.baseMipLevel   = 0;
subresourceRange.levelCount     = texture->mipMapLevels;
subresourceRange.layerCount     = 1;

texture->imageLayout = VK_IMAGE_LAYOUT_SHADER_READ_ONLY_OPTIMAL;

setImageLayout(texture->image, VK_IMAGE_ASPECT_COLOR_BIT,
    VK_IMAGE_LAYOUT_PREINITIALIZED, texture->imageLayout,
    VK_ACCESS_HOST_WRITE_BIT, subresourceRange, cmdTexture);
```

Submitting the command buffer

End the command buffer recording and submit the command buffer to the graphics queue. Also, create a fence that ensures the command buffer execution is completed. If the fence is signaled, it means the image object is successfully created with the specified image layout. Fences are used to synchronize the host and device operations.

In the following implementation, we create a fence object (`fenceCI`) on the host and submit it to the queue using the queue submission command (`vkQueueSubmit`). This fence will ensure that the first half of the memory operations is guaranteed to be executed before any further commands are executed. The guarantee is provided by the fence object, which is signaled by the device when the image layout is successfully created. The host must wait to execute any other operation until the fence is signaled.

Chapter 11

> For more information on fences, refer to the *Understanding synchronization primitives in Vulkan* section in `Chapter 9`, *Drawing Objects*.

The following code snippet shows two things, first, the command buffer recording is completed and ready to be submitted in the graphics queue. Second, we created the `fence` object and wait upon it on the host side to let the GPU finish operations on the submitted command buffer containing the texture processing request:

```
// Stop command buffer recording
CommandBufferMgr::endCommandBuffer(cmdTexture);

// Create a fence to make sure that the
// copies have finished before continuing
VkFence fence;
VkFenceCreateInfo fenceCI= {};
fenceCI.sType        = VK_STRUCTURE_TYPE_FENCE_CREATE_INFO;
fenceCI.flags        = 0;

vkCreateFence(deviceObj->device, &fenceCI, nullptr, &fence);

VkSubmitInfo submitInfo       = {};
submitInfo.sType              = VK_STRUCTURE_TYPE_SUBMIT_INFO;
submitInfo.pNext              = NULL;
submitInfo.commandBufferCount = 1;
submitInfo.pCommandBuffers    = &cmdTexture;

CommandBufferMgr::submitCommandBuffer(deviceObj->queue,
              &cmdTexture, &submitInfo, fence);

// Wait for maximum 10 seconds, if fence is not signaled
vkWaitForFences(deviceObj->device, 1, &fence,
                VK_TRUE, 10000000000);
vkDestroyFence(deviceObj->device, fence, nullptr);
```

Creating an image sampler

A sampler is an object that contains a set of algorithms that controls the appearance of formatted image data by controlling various parameters. These parameters control image transformation, minification and magnification filtering, mipmapping, and wrapping, and produces the final sample array of image texels.

[417]

Drawing Textures

In Vulkan, image samplers are created using the `vkCreateSampler()` API. This API accepts four parameters as shown in the following API syntax. The first parameter `device` is the logical device that is responsible for creating the sampler object. The second parameter is the image attribute controller structure of type `VkSamplerCreateInfo`; we will discuss this next. The third parameter (`pAllocator`) controls the host memory allocation; this API creates and returns the sampler object in the last parameter called `pSampler`:

```
VKAPI_ATTR VkResult VKAPI_CALL vkCreateSampler(
    VkDevice                            device,
    const VkSamplerCreateInfo*          pCreateInfo,
    const VkAllocationCallbacks*        pAllocator,
    VkSampler*                          pSampler);
```

These various relevant image attribute controller parameters are passed into the aforementioned API using the `VkSamplerCreateInfo` structure; the following is the syntax of this API:

```
typedef struct VkSamplerCreateInfo {
    VkStructureType         sType;
    const void*             pNext;
    VkSamplerCreateFlags    flags;
    VkFilter                magFilter;
    VkFilter                minFilter;
    VkSamplerMipmapMode     mipmapMode;
    VkSamplerAddressMode    addressModeU;
    VkSamplerAddressMode    addressModeV;
    VkSamplerAddressMode    addressModeW;
    float                   mipLodBias;
    VkBool32                anisotropyEnable;
    float                   maxAnisotropy;
    VkBool32                compareEnable;
    VkCompareOp             compareOp;
    float                   minLod;
    float                   maxLod;
    VkBorderColor           borderColor;
    VkBool32                unnormalizedCoordinates;
} VkSamplerCreateInfo;
```

Let's take a look at each and every field in the following table:

Parameter	Description
sType	This is the type information of this control structure. It must be specified as VK_STRUCTURE_TYPE_SAMPLER_CREATE_INFO.
pNext	This could be a valid pointer to an extension-specific structure or could be NULL.
flags	This future reserved field is not in use at present.
magFilter	This field corresponds to the magnification filter. It is of type VkFilter enum and can take VK_FILTER_NEAREST and VK_FILTER_LINEAR values as an input. We will discuss these filtering options and see their effects later in this section.
minFilter	This field corresponds with the minification filter.
mipmapMode	This field is used to specify the mipmapping filtering modes and accepts enum values of type VkSamplerMipmapMode, as follows: typedef enum VkSamplerMipmapMode { VK_SAMPLER_MIPMAP_MODE_NEAREST = 0, VK_SAMPLER_MIPMAP_MODE_LINEAR = 1, } VkSamplerMipmapMode;
addressModeU	This field controls image wrapping along the U coordinate, when the image texel coordinates are beyond the [0 .. 1] range.
addressModeV	This field controls image wrapping along the V coordinate when the image texel coordinates are beyond the [0 .. 1] range.
addressModeW	This field controls image wrapping along the W coordinate when the image texel coordinates are beyond the [0 .. 1] range.
mipLodBias	This is a floating bias value that is added to the mipmap **level of detail** (**LOD**) calculation.
anisotropyEnable	This Boolean field indicates whether anisotropic filtering is enabled (VK_TRUE) or disabled (VK_FALSE).
maxAnisotropy	This is the maximum anisotropic filtering value used for clamping purposes.
compareEnable	This Boolean field indicates whether to compare against the reference value while filtering lookups.

Drawing Textures

`compareOp`	The fetched texel data can be compared using the comparison function specified in this field before performing the desired filtering.
`minLod`	This indicates the minimum clamping value to be used for the computed LOD.
`maxLod`	This indicates the Maximum clamping value to be used for the computed LOD.

`borderColor`	This is the predefined color that is used to replace an existing texel with the specified border color. The border color is specified using `VkBorderColor`, as follows:
	`typedef enum VkBorderColor {`
	`VK_BORDER_COLOR_FLOAT_TRANSPARENT_BLACK = 0,`
	`VK_BORDER_COLOR_INT_TRANSPARENT_BLACK   = 1,`
	`VK_BORDER_COLOR_FLOAT_OPAQUE_BLACK      = 2,`
	`VK_BORDER_COLOR_INT_OPAQUE_BLACK        = 3,`
	`VK_BORDER_COLOR_FLOAT_OPAQUE_WHITE      = 4,`
	`VK_BORDER_COLOR_INT_OPAQUE_WHITE        = 5, }`
	`VkBorderColor;`

`unnormalizedCoordinates`	This Boolean field indicates whether to use unnormalized texel coordinates (`VK_TRUE`) or normalized texel coordinates (`VK_FALSE`) for texel lookup.

Filtering

Texture filtering controls the appearance of the texture quality when texture is scaled-in or scaled-out. At a correct depth, one texel may corresponds with exactly one pixel onscreen. However, mapping a smaller texture on a bigger geometry may cause the texture to appear stretched. This is called magnification; in other words, the image size is smaller than the geometry size onto which it needs to be mapped. On the other hand, when the geometry shape is smaller than the image size, many texels share a few pixels, resulting in the image shrinking. This is called minification.

Magnification and minification image effects can be controlled using filtering modes; Vulkan uses the `VkFilter` enum. This enum has the following two fields:

- `VK_FILTER_NEAREST`: The sample uses the texel closest to the specified texture coordinates.
- `VK_FILTER_LINEAR`: This uses the weighted average of the four surrounding pixels closest to the computing texture coordinates.

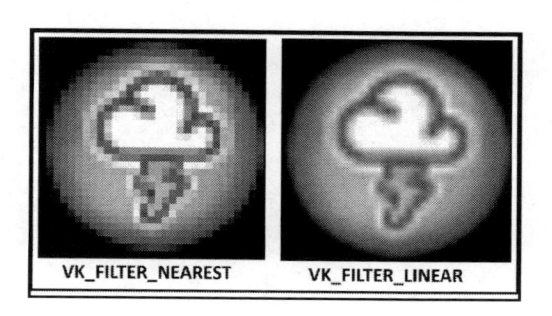

The filtering modes are specified in the `magFilter` and `minFilter` of `VkSamplerCreateInfo`.

Wrapping modes

Vulkan supports sample addressing modes through `VkSamplerAddressMode` along the U, V, and W texture coordinates when the range of texture mapping is greater than 1.0; Vulkan sampling allows the following types of wrapping address mode:

1. `VK_SAMPLER_ADDRESS_MODE_REPEAT`: This produces repeating patterns.
2. `VK_SAMPLER_ADDRESS_MODE_MIRRORED_REPEAT`: This produces a repeating pattern with adjacent texels mirrored.
3. `VK_SAMPLER_ADDRESS_MODE_CLAMP_TO_EDGE`: This repeats the border texels until edges are reached; refer to the following screenshot for more information.
4. `VK_SAMPLER_ADDRESS_MODE_CLAMP_TO_BORDER`: The texels beyond the border are clamped.

Drawing Textures

In the following screenshot, we used texture coordinates range greater than [0 .. 1] and demonstrated the use of wrapping modes:

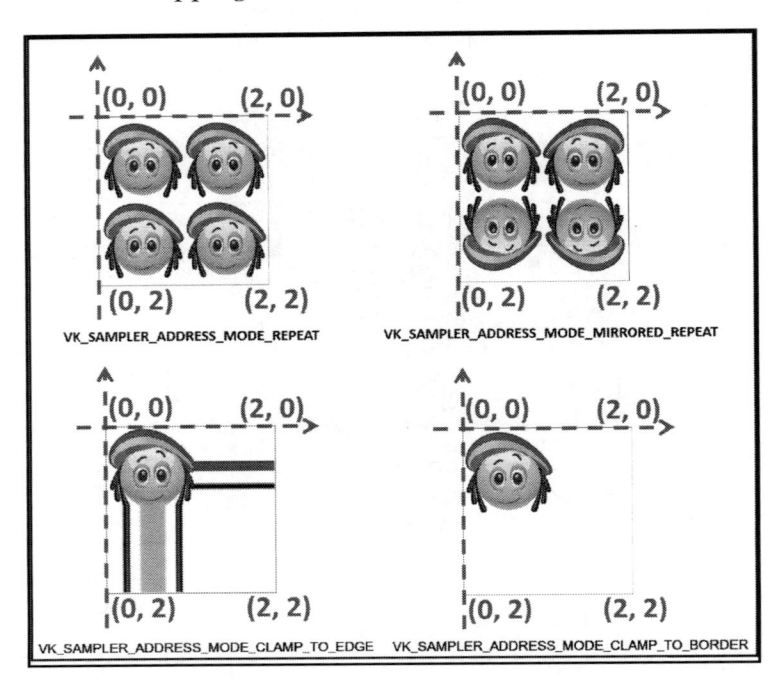

Addressing modes are specified in `VkSamplerCreateInfo` using the `addressModeU`, `addressModeV`, and `addressModeW` fields.

The following is the code implement sampler in the Vulkan API:

```
// Specify a particular kind of texture using samplers
VkSamplerCreateInfo samplerCI = {};
samplerCI.sType            = VK_STRUCTURE_TYPE_SAMPLER_CREATE_INFO;
samplerCI.pNext            = NULL;
samplerCI.magFilter        = VK_FILTER_LINEAR;
samplerCI.minFilter        = VK_FILTER_LINEAR;
samplerCI.mipmapMode       = VK_SAMPLER_MIPMAP_MODE_NEAREST;
samplerCI.addressModeU     = VK_SAMPLER_ADDRESS_MODE_CLAMP_TO_EDGE;
samplerCI.addressModeV     = VK_SAMPLER_ADDRESS_MODE_CLAMP_TO_EDGE;
samplerCI.addressModeW     = VK_SAMPLER_ADDRESS_MODE_CLAMP_TO_EDGE;
samplerCI.mipLodBias       = 0.0f;

if (deviceObj->deviceFeatures.samplerAnisotropy == VK_TRUE)
{
    samplerCI.anisotropyEnable    = VK_TRUE;
```

```
        samplerCI.maxAnisotropy        = 8;
}
else
{
    samplerCI.anisotropyEnable     = VK_FALSE;
    samplerCI.maxAnisotropy        = 1;
}

samplerCI.compareOp                = VK_COMPARE_OP_NEVER;
samplerCI.minLod                   = 0.0f;
samplerCI.maxLod                   = 0.0f;
samplerCI.borderColor              = VK_BORDER_COLOR_FLOAT
                                     _OPAQUE_WHITE;
samplerCI.unnormalizedCoordinates  = VK_FALSE;

// Create the sampler
error = vkCreateSampler(deviceObj->device, &samplerCI,
                        NULL, &texture->sampler);
assert(!error);

// Specify the sampler in the texture's descsImgInfo
texture->descsImgInfo.sampler = texture->sampler;
```

If isotropic filtering is used, then the device must enable the `samplerAnisotropy` feature. This feature can be enabled when the logical device is created (`VkDevice`), if the physical device is capable of supporting it.

The `vkGetPhysicalDeviceFeatures()` API queries the features of the physical device; this API accepts two parameters. The first parameter (`physicalDevice`) indicates the physical device handle. The second parameter (`pFeatures`) is the `VkPhysicalDeviceFeatures` control structure; it contains the predefined feature list that will be checked again to test whether it is supported or not:

```
void vkGetPhysicalDeviceFeatures(
    VkPhysicalDevice              physicalDevice,
    VkPhysicalDeviceFeatures*     pFeatures);
```

Once the `vkGetPhysicalDeviceFeatures()` API is called, it stores a Boolean value for each feature, indicating whether it is supported or not. The Boolean `VK_TRUE` indicates that the feature is supported; the Boolean `VK_FALSE` means the feature is not supported by the physical device.

Drawing Textures

If `VkPhysicalDeviceFeatures::samplerAnisotropy` is supported by your physical device, then enable it while creating the logical device. This can be done by creating a new object of `VkPhysicalDeviceFeatures` and setting `samplerAnisotropy` to `VK_TRUE` if `samplerAnisotropy` is supported, as shown in the following code:

```
VkResult VulkanDevice::createDevice(std::vector<const char *>& layers,
std::vector<const char *>& extensions)
{
    // Many lines skipped please refer to source code.
    VkPhysicalDeviceFeatures getEnabledFeatures;
    vkGetPhysicalDeviceFeatures(*gpu, &getEnabledFeatures);

    VkPhysicalDeviceFeatures setEnabledFeatures = { VK_FALSE };
    setEnabledFeatures.samplerAnisotropy =
              getEnabledFeatures.samplerAnisotropy;

    VkDeviceCreateInfo deviceInfo = {};
    deviceInfo.sType                    = VK_STRUCTURE_TYPE_DEVICE
                                          _CREATE_INFO;
    deviceInfo.pNext                    = NULL;
    deviceInfo.queueCreateInfoCount     = 1;
    deviceInfo.pQueueCreateInfos        = &queueInfo;
    deviceInfo.enabledLayerCount        = 0;
    deviceInfo.ppEnabledLayerNames      = NULL;
    deviceInfo.enabledExtensionCount    = (uint32_t) extensions.size();
    deviceInfo.ppEnabledExtensionNames  = extensions.size() ?
                                          extensions.data() : NULL;
    deviceInfo.pEnabledFeatures         = &setEnabledFeatures;

    result = vkCreateDevice(*gpu, &deviceInfo, NULL, &device);
    assert(result == VK_SUCCESS);

    return result;
}
```

Creating the image view

Create the image view and store it in the local `TextureData` object's `texture`. The `flag` field must be `VK_IMAGE_VIEW_TYPE_2D`:

```
// Specify the attribute used in create the image view
VkImageViewCreateInfo viewCI = {};
viewCI.sType    = VK_STRUCTURE_TYPE_IMAGE_VIEW_CREATE_INFO;
viewCI.pNext    = NULL;
viewCI.viewType    = VK_IMAGE_VIEW_TYPE_2D;
```

```
viewCI.format      = format;
viewCI.components.r = VK_COMPONENT_SWIZZLE_R;
viewCI.components.g = VK_COMPONENT_SWIZZLE_G;
viewCI.components.b = VK_COMPONENT_SWIZZLE_B;
viewCI.components.a = VK_COMPONENT_SWIZZLE_A;
viewCI.subresourceRange = subresourceRange;
viewCI.flags       = 0;
viewCI.image       = texture->image;

// Create the image view
error = vkCreateImageView(deviceObj->device, &viewCI,
                          NULL, &texture->view);
assert(!error);
```

The `flag` field indicates the type of the image view (`VkImageViewType`) that is going to be created. These types are provided as follows, which are self-descriptive:

```
typedef enum {
           VK_IMAGE_VIEW_TYPE_1D          = 0,
           VK_IMAGE_VIEW_TYPE_2D          = 1,
           VK_IMAGE_VIEW_TYPE_3D          = 2,
           VK_IMAGE_VIEW_TYPE_CUBE        = 3,
           VK_IMAGE_VIEW_TYPE_1D_ARRAY    = 4,
           VK_IMAGE_VIEW_TYPE_2D_ARRAY    = 5,
           VK_IMAGE_VIEW_TYPE_CUBE_ARRAY  = 6,
} VkImageViewType;
```

Implementing the image resource with optimal tiling

Optimal tiling is implemented through the staging buffer. First, a buffer resource object is created and stored with the raw image data contents. Next, the buffer resource data contents are copied to a newly created image object using the buffer-to-image copy command. The buffer-to-image copy command (`vkCmdCopyBufferToImage`) copies the buffer memory contents to the image memory.

Drawing Textures

In this section, we will implement the image resources using optimal tiling. In order to create an image resource with optimal tiling our user defined function `VulkanRenderer::createTextureOptimal()` can be used. This function takes parameters in the same way as the `createTextureLinear()` function:

```
void VulkanRenderer::createTextureOptimal(const char* filename, TextureData
*texture, VkImageUsageFlags imageUsageFlags, VkFormat format);
```

Let's understand and implement these functions step by step.

Loading the image file

Load the image file and retrieve its dimensions and the mipmap-level information:

```
// Load the image
gli::texture2D image2D(gli::load(filename)); assert(!image2D.empty());

// Get the image dimensions
texture->textureWidth    = uint32_t(image2D[0].dimensions().x);
texture->textureHeight   = uint32_t(image2D[0].dimensions().y);

// Get number of mip-map levels
texture->mipMapLevels    = uint32_t(image2D.levels());
```

Buffer object memory allocation and binding

The created image object does not have any device memory backing. In this step, we will allocate the physical device memory and bind it with the created `texture->image`. For more information on memory allocation and the binding process, refer to the *Memory allocation and binding image resources* section in `Chapter 6`, *Allocating Image Resources and Building a Swapchain with WSI*:

```
// Create a staging buffer resource states using.
// Indicate it be the source of the transfer command.
// .usage       = VK_BUFFER_USAGE_TRANSFER_SRC_BIT
VkBufferCreateInfo bufferCreateInfo = {};
bufferCreateInfo.sType              = VK_STRUCTURE_TYPE_BUFFER_CREATE_INFO;
bufferCreateInfo.size               = image2D.size();
bufferCreateInfo.usage              = VK_BUFFER_USAGE_TRANSFER_SRC_BIT;
bufferCreateInfo.sharingMode        = VK_SHARING_MODE_EXCLUSIVE;

// Get the buffer memory requirements for the staging buffer
VkMemoryRequirements memRqrmnt;
VkDeviceMemory devMemory;
```

```
vkGetBufferMemoryRequirements(deviceObj->device, buffer,
                        &memRqrmnt);

VkMemoryAllocateInfo memAllocInfo      = {};
memAllocInfo.sType                     = VK_STRUCTURE_TYPE_MEMORY_ALLOCATE_INFO;
memAllocInfo.pNext                     = NULL;
memAllocInfo.allocationSize            = 0;
memAllocInfo.memoryTypeIndex           = 0;
memAllocInfo.allocationSize            = memRqrmnt.size;

// Determine the type of memory required for
// the host-visible buffer
deviceObj->memoryTypeFromProperties(memRqrmnt.memoryTypeBits,
            VK_MEMORY_PROPERTY_HOST_VISIBLE_BIT |
            VK_MEMORY_PROPERTY_HOST_COHERENT_BIT,
            &memAllocInfo.memoryTypeIndex);
// Allocate the memory for host-visible buffer objects -
error = vkAllocateMemory(deviceObj->device, &memAllocInfo,
                        nullptr, &devMemory);
assert(!error);

// Bind the host-visible buffer with allocated device memory -
error=vkBindBufferMemory(deviceObj->device,buffer,devMemory,0);
assert(!error);
```

Populating the allocated device memory

Use `vkMapMemory()` and populate the raw contents of the loaded image into the buffer object's device memory. Once mapped, use `vkUnmapMemory()` to complete the process of uploading data from the host to the device memory:

```
// Populate the raw image data into the device memory
uint8_t *data;
error = vkMapMemory(deviceObj->device, devMemory, 0,
                    memRqrmnt.size, 0, (void **)&data);
assert(!error);

memcpy(data, image2D.data(), image2D.size());
vkUnmapMemory(deviceObj->device, devMemory);
```

Drawing Textures

Creating the image object

The image's create info object (`VkImageCreateInfo`) must be created using tiling (`.tiling`) options as optimal tiling (`VK_IMAGE_TILING_OPTIMAL`). In addition, the image's `usage` flag must be set with `VK_IMAGE_USAGE_TRANSFER_DST_BIT`, making it a destination for the copy commands to transfer data contents to `texture->image` from the `buffer` object:

```
// Create image info with optimal tiling
// support (.tiling = VK_IMAGE_TILING_OPTIMAL)
VkImageCreateInfo imageCreateInfo   = {};
imageCreateInfo.sType               = VK_STRUCTURE_TYPE_IMAGE_CREATE_INFO;
imageCreateInfo.pNext               = NULL;
imageCreateInfo.imageType           = VK_IMAGE_TYPE_2D;
imageCreateInfo.format              = format;
imageCreateInfo.mipLevels           = texture->mipMapLevels;
imageCreateInfo.arrayLayers         = 1;
imageCreateInfo.samples             = VK_SAMPLE_COUNT_1_BIT;
imageCreateInfo.tiling              = VK_IMAGE_TILING_OPTIMAL;
imageCreateInfo.sharingMode         = VK_SHARING_MODE_EXCLUSIVE;
imageCreateInfo.initialLayout       = VK_IMAGE_LAYOUT_UNDEFINED;
imageCreateInfo.extent              = { texture->textureWidth,
                                        texture->textureHeight, 1 };
imageCreateInfo.usage               = imageUsageFlags;

// Set image object with VK_IMAGE_USAGE_TRANSFER_DST_BIT if
// not set already. This allows to copy the source VkBuffer
// object (with VK_IMAGE_USAGE_TRANSFER_DST_BIT) contents
// into this image object memory(destination).
if (!(imageCreateInfo.usage & VK_IMAGE_USAGE_TRANSFER_DST_BIT)){
    imageCreateInfo.usage |= VK_IMAGE_USAGE_TRANSFER_DST_BIT;
}

error = vkCreateImage(deviceObj->device, &imageCreateInfo,
                      nullptr, &texture->image);
assert(!error);
```

Image object memory allocation and binding

Allocate the physical memory backing and bind it with the created `texture->image`. For more information on memory allocation and the binding process, refer to the *Memory allocation and binding image resources* section in Chapter 6, *Allocating Image Resources and Building a Swapchain with WSI*:

```
// Get the image memory requirements
```

```
vkGetImageMemoryRequirements(deviceObj->device, texture->image,
                                    &memRqrmnt);

// Set the allocation size equal to the buffer allocation
memAllocInfo.allocationSize = memRqrmnt.size;

// Determine the type of memory required with the help of memory properties
deviceObj->memoryTypeFromProperties(memRqrmnt.memoryTypeBits,
    VK_MEMORY_PROPERTY_DEVICE_LOCAL_BIT,
    &memAllocInfo.memoryTypeIndex);

// Allocate the physical memory on the GPU
error = vkAllocateMemory(deviceObj->device, &memAllocInfo,
                               nullptr, &texture->mem);
assert(!error);

// Bound the physical memory with the created image object
error = vkBindImageMemory(deviceObj->device, texture->image,
                               texture->mem, 0);
assert(!error);
```

Creating a command buffer object

The image resource objects are created using the command buffer object, `cmdTexture`, defined in the `VulkanRenderer` class. Allocate the command buffer to set the image layout and start recording the command buffer:

```
// Command buffer allocation and recording begins
CommandBufferMgr::allocCommandBuffer(&deviceObj->device,
                                cmdPool, &cmdTexture);
CommandBufferMgr::beginCommandBuffer(cmdTexture);
```

Setting the image layout

Set the image layout (`VkImageLayout`) to be `VK_IMAGE_LAYOUT_TRANSFER_DST_OPTIMAL` since the data contents will be copied from the staging buffer object (source) to the image object (destination). For more information on the `setImageLayout()` function, refer to the *Set the image layout with memory barriers* section in Chapter 6, *Allocating Image Resources and Building a Swapchain with WSI*:

```
VkImageSubresourceRange subresourceRange = {};
subresourceRange.aspectMask        = VK_IMAGE_ASPECT_COLOR_BIT;
subresourceRange.baseMipLevel      = 0;
subresourceRange.levelCount        = texture->mipMapLevels;
```

Drawing Textures

```
subresourceRange.layerCount      = 1;

// Set the image layout to be
// VK_IMAGE_LAYOUT_TRANSFER_DST_OPTIMAL
// since it is destination for copying buffer
// into image using vkCmdCopyBufferToImage -
setImageLayout(texture->image, VK_IMAGE_ASPECT_COLOR_BIT,
   VK_IMAGE_LAYOUT_UNDEFINED,VK_IMAGE_LAYOUT_TRANSFER_DST_OPTIMAL,
   (VkAccessFlagBits)0, subresourceRange, cmdTexture);
```

Buffer to image copy

Create buffer image copy regions for the image object and its subresource mipmaps. Use the copy command to transfer the buffer object's (`buffer`) device memory contents to the image object's (`texture->image`) memory contents:

```
// List contain buffer image copy for each mipLevel
std::vector<VkBufferImageCopy> bufferImgCopyList;

uint32_t bufferOffset = 0;
// Iterater through each mip level and set buffer image copy
for (uint32_t i = 0; i < texture->mipMapLevels; i++)
{
    VkBufferImageCopy bufImgCopyItem = {};
    bufImgCopyItem.imageSubresource.aspectMask =
               VK_IMAGE_ASPECT_COLOR_BIT;
    bufImgCopyItem.imageSubresource.mipLevel = i;
    bufImgCopyItem.imageSubresource.layerCount = 1;
    bufImgCopyItem.imageSubresource.baseArrayLayer = 0;
    bufImgCopyItem.imageExtent.width   =
               uint32_t(image2D[i].dimensions().x);
    bufImgCopyItem.imageExtent.height  =
               uint32_t(image2D[i].dimensions().y);
    bufImgCopyItem.imageExtent.depth   = 1;
    bufImgCopyItem.bufferOffset        = bufferOffset;

    bufferImgCopyList.push_back(bufImgCopyItem);

    // adjust buffer offset
    bufferOffset += uint32_t(image2D[i].size());
}

// Copy the staging buffer memory data containing the
// staged raw data(with mip levels) into the image object
vkCmdCopyBufferToImage(cmdTexture, buffer, texture->image,
```

```
                VK_IMAGE_LAYOUT_TRANSFER_DST_OPTIMAL,
                uint32_t(bufferImgCopyList.size()),
                bufferImgCopyList.data());
```

For more information on the copy commands, please refer to our next section, *Understanding the copy commands*.

Setting the optimal image layout

Set the image layout, indicating the new layout to be optimal tiling compatible. The underlying implementation uses this flag and chooses a suitable technique to lay out the image contents in an optimal manner:

```
// Advised to change the image layout to shader read
// after staged buffer copied into image memory
texture->imageLayout = VK_IMAGE_LAYOUT_SHADER_READ_ONLY_OPTIMAL;
setImageLayout(texture->image, VK_IMAGE_ASPECT_COLOR_BIT,
        VK_IMAGE_LAYOUT_TRANSFER_DST_OPTIMAL,
        texture->imageLayout,
        subresourceRange, cmdTexture);
```

> The layout of an image can be controlled at:
> a) Creation of the image resource by specifying the initial layout
> b) Specifying explicitly using memory barriers
> c) Or while using it in the Render Pass

Submitting the command buffer

Finalize the command buffer recording and submit it to the graphics queue:

```
// Submit command buffer containing copy
// and image layout commands
CommandBufferMgr::endCommandBuffer(cmdTexture);

// Create a fence object to ensure that the command
// buffer is executed, coping our staged raw data
//  from the buffers to image memory with
// respective image layout and attributes into consideration
VkFence fence;
VkFenceCreateInfo fenceCI    = {};
fenceCI.sType = VK_STRUCTURE_TYPE_FENCE_CREATE_INFO;
fenceCI.flags = 0;

error = vkCreateFence(deviceObj->device, &fenceCI, nullptr,
```

Drawing Textures

```
                                              &fence);
assert(!error);

VkSubmitInfo submitInfo = {};
submitInfo.sType = VK_STRUCTURE_TYPE_SUBMIT_INFO;
submitInfo.pNext = NULL;
submitInfo.commandBufferCount    = 1;
submitInfo.pCommandBuffers = &cmdTexture;

CommandBufferMgr::submitCommandBuffer(deviceObj->queue,
                &cmdTexture, &submitInfo, fence);

error = vkWaitForFences(deviceObj->device, 1, &fence, VK_TRUE,
                                     10000000000);
assert(!error);

vkDestroyFence(deviceObj->device, fence, nullptr);

// destroy the allocated resoureces
vkFreeMemory(deviceObj->device, devMemory, nullptr);
vkDestroyBuffer(deviceObj->device, buffer, nullptr);
```

Add a fence as a synchronization primitive to ensure the image layout is prepared successfully before it could utilize the image. Release the fence object once the fence is signaled. In case the fence fails to signal, then the wait command `vkWaitForFences()` waits for a maximum of 10 seconds to ensure the system never halts or goes into an infinite wait condition.

> For more information on fences, refer to the *Understanding synchronization primitives in Vulkan* section in `Chapter 9`, *Drawing Objects*.

Creating an image sampler

Create an image sampler with linear filtering for minification (`minFilter`) and magnification (`magFilter`) and also enable anisotropy filtering:

```
// Create sampler
VkSamplerCreateInfo samplerCI = {};
samplerCI.sType          = VK_STRUCTURE_TYPE_SAMPLER_CREATE_INFO;
samplerCI.pNext          = NULL;
samplerCI.magFilter      = VK_FILTER_LINEAR;
samplerCI.minFilter      = VK_FILTER_LINEAR;
samplerCI.mipmapMode     = VK_SAMPLER_MIPMAP_MODE_LINEAR;
```

```
samplerCI.addressModeU    = VK_SAMPLER_ADDRESS_MODE_CLAMP_TO_EDGE;
samplerCI.addressModeV    = VK_SAMPLER_ADDRESS_MODE_CLAMP_TO_EDGE;
samplerCI.addressModeW    = VK_SAMPLER_ADDRESS_MODE_CLAMP_TO_EDGE;
samplerCI.mipLodBias      = 0.0f;

if (deviceObj->deviceFeatures.samplerAnisotropy == VK_TRUE)
{
    samplerCI.anisotropyEnable    = VK_TRUE;
    samplerCI.maxAnisotropy       = 8;
}
else
{
    samplerCI.anisotropyEnable    = VK_FALSE;
    samplerCI.maxAnisotropy       = 1;
}

samplerCI.compareOp              = VK_COMPARE_OP_NEVER;
samplerCI.minLod                 = 0.0f;
samplerCI.maxLod                 = (float)texture->mipMapLevels;
samplerCI.borderColor = VK_BORDER_COLOR_FLOAT_OPAQUE_WHITE;
samplerCI.unnormalizedCoordinates = VK_FALSE;

error = vkCreateSampler(deviceObj->device, &samplerCI, nullptr,
                        &texture->sampler);
assert(!error);

// Specify the sampler in the texture's descsImgInfo
texture->descsImgInfo.sampler = texture->sampler;
```

Creating the image view

Create the image view and store it in the local `TextureData` object's `texture`:

```
// Create image view to allow shader to// access the texture information
VkImageViewCreateInfo viewCI = {};
viewCI.sType = VK_STRUCTURE_TYPE_IMAGE_VIEW_CREATE_INFO;
viewCI.pNext                       = NULL;
viewCI.image                       = VK_NULL_HANDLE;
viewCI.viewType                    = VK_IMAGE_VIEW_TYPE_2D;
viewCI.format                      = format;
viewCI.components.r                = VK_COMPONENT_SWIZZLE_R;
viewCI.components.g                = VK_COMPONENT_SWIZZLE_G;
viewCI.components.b                = VK_COMPONENT_SWIZZLE_B;
viewCI.components.a                = VK_COMPONENT_SWIZZLE_A;
viewCI.subresourceRange            = subresourceRange;
viewCI.subresourceRange.levelCount = texture->mipMapLevels;
```

Drawing Textures

```
// Optimal tiling supports mip map levels very well set it.
viewCI.image                              = texture->image;

error = vkCreateImageView(deviceObj->device, &viewCI, NULL,
                                &texture->view);
assert(!error);

// Fill descriptor image info that can be // used for setting up descriptor sets
texture->descsImgInfo.imageView = texture->view;
```

Copying data content between images and buffers

Copy commands are special transfer commands that transfer data contents from one memory region to another. These regions could be between buffers objects, image objects, and buffer-to-image and vice versa.

Depending upon the application need, you may need to copy data between buffers and images in various situations. There are four types of copy commands available to accomplish this job:

- `vkCmdCopyBuffer`: Data contents are copied from the source buffer to the destination buffer object's device memory
- `vkCmdCopyImage`: A specific portion of the source image object is copied to the destination image region
- `vkCmdCopyBufferToImage`: Buffer object data contents are copied to the image objects
- `vkCmdCopyImageToBuffer`: Image object data contents are copied to the buffer objects

In the optimal tiling implementation, we used `vkCmdCopyBufferToImage`. The following is the syntax:

```
void vkCmdCopyBufferToImage(
            VkCommandBuffer         commandBuffer,
            VkBuffer                srcBuffer,
            VkImage                 dstImage,
            VkImageLayout           dstImageLayout,
            uint32_t                regionCount,
            const VkBufferImageCopy* pRegions);
```

[434]

This API accepts six parameters, which are explained in the following table:

Parameters	Description
commandBuffer	The vkCmdCopyImageToBuffer command will be recorded in this command buffer object.
srcBuffer	This refers to the source buffer (VkBuffer) object from where the data contents will be copied.
dstImage	This refers to the destination image (VkImage) object into which a portion of the data contents will be copied.
dstImageLayout	This is the dstImage object's image layout object (VkImageLayout).
regionCount	This is the total count of the copy regions upon which the transfer of data contents will be performed.
pRegions	This field is a pointer to an array of VkBufferCopy holding the regions' specification that will undergo data transfer.

In the next section, we will update the descriptor set with the image object, which contains the image layouts and image views, and render the image object on the 3D cube.

Updating the descriptor set

Once the texture is prepared by linear or optimal tiling, it is just a matter of updating the descriptor set with the created image resource object. This is done in the implemented VulkanDrawable::createDescriptorSet() function. The input parameter useTexture must be true to support the texture. The following highlights a single-line change that is required in this function to support the texture.

When the useTexture parameter is true, the second VkWriteDescriptorSet element (with index 1) is populated with the texture information. Here are two things that are of utmost importance:

- **Setting the texture object**: The pImageInfo field of VkWriteDescriptorSet must be set with the texture object's (TextureData) descsImgInfo (of the type VkDescriptorImageInfo).

Drawing Textures

- **Layout binding**: This must be equal to the index number specified in the fragment shader. For instance, in the present example, the sampler is received at the layout binding 1, therefore, `writes[1].dstBinding= 1;`:

```
// Creates the descriptor sets using descriptor pool.
// This function depend on the createDescriptorPool()
// and createUniformBuffer().
  void VulkanDrawable::createDescriptorSet(bool useTexture)
{
VulkanPipeline* pipelineObj = rendererObj->getPipelineObject();
VkResult result;

// Create the descriptor allocation structure and specify
// the descriptor pool and descriptor layout
VkDescriptorSetAllocateInfo dsAllocInfo[1];
dsAllocInfo[0].sType     = VK_STRUCTURE_TYPE_DESCRIPTOR
_SET_ALLOCATE_INFO;
dsAllocInfo[0].pNext               = NULL;
dsAllocInfo[0].descriptorPool      = descriptorPool;
dsAllocInfo[0].descriptorSetCount  = 1;
dsAllocInfo[0].pSetLayouts         = descLayout.data();

// Allocate the number of descriptor set needs to be produced
descriptorSet.resize(1);

// Allocate descriptor sets
result = vkAllocateDescriptorSets(deviceObj->device,
              dsAllocInfo, descriptorSet.data());
assert(result == VK_SUCCESS);

// Allocate two write descriptors for - 1. MVP and 2. Texture
VkWriteDescriptorSet writes[2];
memset(&writes, 0, sizeof(writes));

// Specify the uniform buffer related
// information into first write descriptor
writes[0]          = {};
writes[0].sType    = VK_STRUCTURE_TYPE_WRITE_DESCRIPTOR_SET;
writes[0].pNext    = NULL;
writes[0].dstSet = descriptorSet[0];
writes[0].descriptorCount   = 1;
writes[0].descriptorType    = VK_DESCRIPTOR_TYPE_UNIFORM_BUFFER;
writes[0].pBufferInfo       = &UniformData.bufferInfo;
writes[0].dstArrayElement   = 0;
writes[0].dstBinding        = 0; // DESCRIPTOR_SET_BINDING_INDEX

// If texture is used then update the second
```

```
    // write descriptor structure
    if (useTexture)
    {
    writes[1]                  = {};
        writes[1].sType        = VK_STRUCTURE_TYPE_WRITE-
                                                    _DESCRIPTOR_SET;
        writes[1].dstSet          = descriptorSet[0];
        writes[1].dstBinding = 1;   writes[1].descriptorCount   = 1;
    writes[1].descriptorType   = VK_DESCRIPTOR_TYPE_
COMBINED_IMAGE_SAMPLER;
    writes[1].pImageInfo = &textures->descsImgInfo;
/
    }

    // Update the uniform buffer into the allocated descriptor set
    vkUpdateDescriptorSets(deviceObj->device,
            useTexture ? 2 : 1, writes, 0, NULL);
    }
```

For more information on this function and the creation of the descriptor set, refer to the *Creating the descriptor sets* section in `Chapter 10`, *Descriptors and Push Constant*.

The following is the output of the rendered texture:

Summary

This chapter implemented the image resources and rendered the texture on a 3D geometry object. It opened with a quick recap of the fundamentals of image resource and covered the basic concepts of image objects, image layouts, and image views.

We implemented texture rendering with linear and optimal tiling schemes. The former is simple to implement and is purely based on the image type resource. The latter scheme is implemented using staging, where both buffer and image resources are used; in this scheme, the image is first stored in the buffer object and transferred to the image object using copy commands.

Index

A

allocated memory
  binding 164
  binding, to image object 165
application flow
  initialization 208, 209
  output window, displaying 209
  summarizing 208

B

background color
  clearing 239, 240
  setting, in Render Pass instance 241
blending process
  about 296
  blending constants 297
  blending factors 297
  blending operations 297
  color blend states 297
buffer APIs 127
buffer resource object
  buffer, destroying 214
  creating 212, 213
buffer resource
  about 212
  buffer view, creating 214
  implementation, by creating vertex buffer 219
  type 212
  used, for creating geometry 216
buffer view
  about 43
  creating 214, 215
  destroying 215

C

characteristics, descriptor sets
  descriptor pool 26
  frequent change 26
  multithread scalability 26
CMake
  file, building 76
color blend states
  about 297
  implementing 299
colored background
  rendering 243, 244
command buffer functions
  using 139
command buffer initialization
  command buffer allocation 42
  command pool creation 42
command buffer, drawing
  descriptor 29
  drawing 29
  pipeline 29
  render pass 29
  scissor 29
  viewport 29
command buffers, types
  action 126
  state management 126
  synchronization 126
command buffers
  about 123
  allocating 130, 131
  allocation process, implementing 137
  allocation process, recording 138
  and queues 126
  command, types 126
  explicit synchronization 125, 126

freeing 132
order of execution 127
primary command buffer 124
queue submission 134
queue waiting 136
recording 133, 134
resetting 132
secondary command buffer 124
submitting, to queue 140
using 124
wrapper class, implementing 137
command pool
　about 127
　creating 128
　destroying 130
　resetting 129
command
　action 14
　set state 14
　synchronization 14
compute pipelines 277, 279, 280
control flow graph (CFG) 247
CreateWindowEx function
　reference 172

D

data content
　copying, between images and buffers 434, 435
debugging
　implementation, in Vulkan 112, 117, 118
depth image
　building 174
　creating 195
　depth buffer image object, creating 197, 198
　layout transition 201
　memory requirements, obtaining 199
　memory type, determining 199
　physical memory, allocating to 200
　physical memory, binding to 200
　tiling 195, 196, 197
　view, creating 207
depth stencil states
　implementing 304
depth test 302
descriptor pool

about 361, 372
creating 372
creation, implementing 373
destroying 375
destruction, implementing 375
descriptor set layout
　about 363, 364
　destroying 368
　implementing 366
descriptor set resources
　creating 375, 376, 378
descriptor set, updating
　about 435
　layout binding 436
　texture object, setting 435
descriptor set
　about 361
　allocated descriptor sets objects, destroying 381
　creating 380
　layout 363, 364
　object, allocating from descriptor pool 381
　resources, associating with 382, 384
　updating 435, 437
descriptors
　about 19, 361
　creation, implementing 384, 385
　pipeline layouts 369
　set resources, creating 375
device memory
　about 143, 145
　accessing, from host 148, 149
　allocating 146, 147
　freeing up 147
　memory heaps 144
　memory types 144
device
　and queue, implementing 105, 106, 107
display window
　resizing 355, 356, 357, 358
draw command
　about 328
　categories 328
　vkCmdDraw command 328, 329
drawing object, preparing
　command buffer object, implementing 324

draw command 328, 329
dynamic viewport, defining 324, 325
geometry information, specifying 323
pipeline object, binding 321
Render Pass commands, recording 316
scissoring 326, 327
drawing object, rendering
swapchain image, acquiring 333, 335
drawing object
preparation, implementing 330, 331
preparing 316
rendering 332
rendering, implementation 338, 341
drawing process
drawing object, preparing 314
drawing object, rendering 314
header declaration 315, 316
overview 314
dynamic states
about 282
implementing 283
dynamic viewport
defining 324, 325
dynamical control 324
implementation 325
statical control 324

E

enabled extensions, Vulcan instance
testing 89, 90, 91
enabled layers, Vulcan instance
testing 89, 90, 91
execution model, Uniforms
descriptor layout, creating 388
descriptor pool, creating 389
descriptor set, creating 389
descriptors, creating 390
implementation 389
initialization 388
pipeline layout 388
rendering 391, 392
shader implementation 389, 390
transformation, updating 389, 394
uniform buffer, creating 388
update() function 393

extensions
about 77
device-based 77
device-specific 36
instance-based 77
instance-specific 36
querying 78, 81

F

features, Vulcan
Direct access to GPU 12
Driver and Application layer 12
error checking and validation 13
explicit API 11
GPU hardware 13
memory controls 12
multithread scalability 11
precompiled intermediate shading language 11
predictable 12
reduced driver overhead 11
single API 12
framebuffer
implementing 237, 238, 239
used, for creating Render Pass 236

G

geometry
buffer creation overview 218
code flow 223
creating, with buffer resource 216
data, preparing 216
vertex buffer, creating 217, 219, 220, 221
GLSL shader compilation, into SPIR-V
about 248
offline compilation, with glslangValidator
executable 248
online compilation, with SPIR-V tool libraries 249
GLSL shader
implementing 250, 252, 253, 254
graphics pipeline shaders
vertex shaders 245
graphics pipeline
creating 271, 272
implementing 275, 276

[441]

H

Hello World!!! Vulkan application
  buffers, managing 42
  building 34
  command buffer initialization 42
  depth buffer, creating 46, 47
  descriptor layout 50
  device memory, allocating 48
  device memory, binding 48
  drawing images, connecting to Render Pass 52, 53
  images, managing 42
  pass attribute, defining 52
  pipeline layouts 50
  pipelines, creating 57
  presentation layer, displaying 64
  queue submission 63, 64
  Render Pass stage, executing 60
  shader compilation into SPIR-V 49
  swapchain, creating 44, 45
  synchronization 63, 64
  validation layer properties, initializing 35, 36, 38
  vertex, storing into GPU memory 54, 56
  working 65, 66
  WSI extension, querying 39, 40

I

image creation
  overview 153
image files
  GLI library, using 408
  loading 407
image resource implementation, with linear tiling
  about 410
  allocated device memory, populating 415
  command buffer object, creating 416
  command buffer, setting 416, 417
  image file, loading 410
  image layout, setting 416
  image object, creating 410, 412, 413
  image view, creating 424
  memory allocation 414
  memory binding 414
image resource implementation, with optimal tiling
  about 425
  allocated device memory, populating 427
  buffer image copy, creating 430
  buffer object memory allocation 426
  buffer object memory, binding 426
  command buffer object, creating 429
  command buffer, submitting 431
  image file, loading 426
  image layout, setting 429
  image object memory allocation 428
  image object memory, binding 428
  image object, creating 428
  image sampler, creating 432
  image view, creating 433
  optimal image layout, setting 431
image resource, creating
  image object, creating 404
  image sampler 405
  image view, creating 405
image resource
  about 155, 404
  implementing, with linear tiling 409
  implementing, with optimal tiling 410, 425
  starting with 152
image sampler
  creating 417
image
  and buffers, data content copying between 434
  created images, destroying 160
  creating 155, 159
  layouts 160
  view, creating 161, 162
  view, destroying 163
Implicit-Enabled layer 21
indexed geometry
  rendering 342
input assembly states
  about 286
  implementing 287
  primitive topologies 289
  primitive topologies, with adjacency 291, 292, 293
  primitive topologies, with no adjacency 290
intermediate representation (IR) 246

K

Khronos
  reference 10

L

layers
  about 70, 77
  querying 78, 81
loader 21, 70
logical device
  about 91, 96
  creating 97, 98
  host, waiting on 98
  losing 99
LunarG SDK
  Bin and Bin32 70
  config 70
  demo 71
  doc 71
  glslang 71
  Include 71
  installer source 71
  reference 20
  runtime 71
  SPIR-V tools 71
  starting with 70
LunarG
  reference 112
  validation layers 111

M

memory allocation extension functions
  reference 143
memory allocation
  about 163
  requirements, gathering 164
memory barriers
  about 201
  buffer 202
  global 202
  image 202
  image layout transition 203, 205
memory heap
  device local 24

host local 24
memory management
  about 141
  allocated memory 149
  device memory 143
  device memory, allocating 146
  host memory 141, 144, 145
memory
  allocating 49
  binding 49
  mapping 49
  requirements 48
model, Uniforms
  descriptor set, building 392, 393
multisample states
  about 305, 306
  implementing 307, 308

O

objects
  syntax, allocating 18
  syntax, creating 17
  syntax, destroying 17
  syntax, freeing 18
OpenGL Image (GLI)
  about 407
  reference 407
OpenGL Mathematics
  reference 387
OpenGL Shading Language (GLSL) 11, 246
order of execution, command buffer
  multiple queue submission 127
  single queue submission 127

P

physical device
  about 91
  enumerating 93, 94
  extensions, querying 94, 95
  memory properties, interrogating 96
  properties, obtaining 95, 96
physical memory
  allocating, on device 165
pipeline cache object (PCO)
  about 27, 264

[443]

   creating 267, 268
   implementing 271
pipeline caches
   data, retrieving from 269
   merging 268
pipeline layout
   about 28, 63, 264, 369
   creating 369
   creation, implementing 370
   destroying 371
   destruction process, implementing 372
pipeline objects
   about 27
   caching, between applications 267
   caching, between pipelines 266
   caching, with pipeline caching objects (PCO) 266
   compute pipeline 322
   graphics pipeline 322
pipeline shaders
   compute shaders 245
   fragment shaders 245
   geometry shaders 245
   GLSL shader, compiling into SPIR-V 248
   SPIR-V 246
   tessellation shaders 245
pipeline state objects (PSO)
   about 264, 271
   blending process 296
   color blend state 281
   depth test 302
   depth/stencil state 281
   dynamic state 281, 282
   input assembly state 281, 286
   multisample state 281, 305, 306
   rasterization state 281, 294
   stencil test 302
   vertex input state 281, 284
   viewport management 300
   viewport state 281
pipeline states 27
pipeline
   about 263, 264
   commands, recording 28
   compute pipeline 57
   compute pipelines 262

descriptor set 26
destroying 277
graphics 262
graphics pipeline 57
graphics pipeline, creating 59
implementing 308
Input Assembly 263
management 27, 28
queue submission 30
reference 262
setup 26
shaders with SPIR-V 27
states 57
using 262, 264
Vertex Shader 263
prerequisites, texture drawing
   image files, loading 405, 407
   local image data structure 405, 408, 409
   shader program, updating 406, 407
   shader stage 405
   texture coordinates 405
   texture coordinates, specifying 405
prerequisites, Uniforms implementation
   3D transformation 387
   transformations, applying 387
push constant
   pipeline layout, updating with 397, 398
   resource data, updating 399, 400, 402
   resource, defining in shader 397
   updates 396

Q

queue
   about 99, 100
   and devices, implementing 105
   and queue, implementing 106, 107
   creating 103, 104
   families 99
   families, querying 100, 101
   graphics queue handle, storing 102
   multiple queues 16
   single queue 16

R

rasterization states
  about 294
  implementing 296
Render Pass instance 225
Render Pass instance recording
  primary command buffer 317
  secondary command buffer 317
  secondary command buffer, uses 317, 319
  starting 316, 317
Render Pass stage execution
  about 61, 62
  drawing surface, acquiring 60
  structure, preparing 61
Render Pass
  about 225
  attachments 225
  commands, recording 316
  implementation 232, 320
  instance recording 316, 317
  instance recording, finishing 320
  next subpass, transitioning 319
  subpass 226, 227
  used, for creating framebuffer 236
  Vulkan APIs 227
resource management
  allocation and suballocations 24
  asynchronous transfer 25
  resource objects 24
  sparse memory 25
  staging buffers 25
resources
  buffer 43
responsibilities, loader
  drivers, locating 21
  injectable layers 21
  platform-independent 21

S

scissor parameters
  dynamic control 327
  implementation 327
  static control 326
shaders, with SPIR-V
  glslangValidator 27
  multiple entry points 27
  multiple inputs 27
  offline compilation 27
  Standard Portable Intermediate Language (SPIR-V) 11
states, pipeline
  color blend attachment state 58
  depth stencil 58
  dynamic 57
  multisample 58
  rasterization states 57
  vertex input 57
  viewport 58
static single assignment (SSA) 247
stencil states 303
swapchain
  about 166
  building 174
  color image views, creating 193, 194
  color images, retrieving 189, 192
  creating 44, 185
  graphics queue, with present support 182
  image formats, querying 184
  implementation flow 166
  implementation's class block diagram 169
  presentation mode 186
  presentation mode information, managing 187
  surface capabilities 185
  window management custom class 170
synchronization primitives
  barriers 346
  events 16, 346, 351, 353, 354
  fences 16, 346, 348, 349
  pipeline barriers 16
  semaphores 16, 346, 349, 350

T

tabular lookaside buffer (TLB) 196
technical jargon
  command 14
  command buffer 14
  memory type 13
  physical device and device 13
  queues 13

texture drawing
  prerequisites 405
texture filtering 420
texture, Vulkan
  image 152
  image layout 153
  image view 153

U

Uniforms implementation
  execution model overview 388
  prerequisites 387
Uniforms
  about 361
  implementing 386
user-defined classes
  headers.h 78
  main program 78
  VulkanDevice 78
  VulkanInstance 78
  VulkanLayerAndExtension 78

V

validation layers, LunarG 111, 112
vertex input states
  about 284
  implementing 285
Vertical Blanking Interval (VBI) 166
viewport management
  about 300
  viewport state 300
viewport state
  about 301
  implementing 302
Vulcan images
  using, as attachment 152
  using, as texture 152
Vulkan application
  about 18
  application 19
  driver 19
  LunarG SDK 20
  SPIR-V 19
  WSI 19
Vulkan installation

CMake, installing 34
Python installation 34
SDK, installing 34
Vulkan driver 34
Vulkan instance
  creating 83, 85
  extensions, enabling 87
  layers, enabling 87
Vulkan objects
  dispatchable handle 17
  non-dispatchable handles 17
Vulkan programming model
  hardware initialization 21
  pipeline setup 26
  using 20
  Window presentation surfaces 22
Vulkan
  about 9, 10, 303
  command syntax 17
  debugging 110, 111
  debugging, implementation 112, 117, 118
  drawing process 314
  error checking 18
  evolution 10
  execution model 14, 15
  fundamentals 14
  installing 34
  object lifetime 17
  object model 17
  pipeline state objects (PSO) 280
  queues 16
  reference 322
  shader, working with 245
  specification, reference 35
  synchronization primitives 16, 345
  Uniforms, implementing 386
  validation 18
  versus OpenGL 11
VulkanDescriptor 362
VulkanPipeline 265, 266
VulkanSwapChain
  about 175
  associating, with created window 180, 181, 182
  surface, creating 180, 181, 182
  swapchain extensions, querying 177, 178, 180

W

window management custom class
  about 170
  command pool, creating 174
  presentation window, creating 172, 173
  presentation window, rendering 175
  renderer, initializing 173
Window System Integration (WSI) 19, 22, 180
wrapper class
  implementing, for command buffer 137
wrapping modes
  types 421, 422, 424

Made in the USA
San Bernardino, CA
27 March 2018